INSIGHT GUIDES

Created and Directed by Hans Höfer

Hawkins
410-465-4341

Greece

Edited by Karen Van Dyck
Updated by John Chapple
Managing Editor: Roger Williams

Editorial Director: Brian Bell

W9-CBD-232

Houghton Mifflin

APA° PUBLICATIONS

ABOUT THIS BOOK

Höfer

Greece is one of those countries that we all know, or think we know. For centuries, travellers have covered its rocky mountains, ancient cities and myth-laden islands. The cradle of Western culture and Western democracy, it attracts those seeking the roots of modern civilization in what sometimes seems today an improbable environment. It is a land that is both hard and soft, with contrasts as sharp as its white-washed houses set against an intense blue sea.

As such, it is an ideal subject for the *Insight Guides* series, created in 1970 by **Hans Höfer**, founder of Apa Publications and still the company's driving force. Each of the 190 books encourages readers to celebrate the essence of a place rather than try to tailor it to their expectations and is edited in the belief that, without insight into people's character and culture, travel can narrow the mind, not broaden it.

To apply this formula to Greece, Apa appointed as project editor **Karen Van Dyck**, who had studied and travelled in the country for many years after completing her doctoral studies at Oxford University. From her many contacts in Greece, she assembled the team for this book, who now take their bow in alphabetical order.

Van Dyck

Katerina Anghelaki-Rooke had published seven collections of poems plus translations from English and Russian into Greek. She had taught modern Greek poetry at Harvard, the University of Utah and San Francisco State. She received the Greek State prize for poetry in 1986.

David Beatty worked as a researcher on documentaries before becoming a photographer travelling widely in Africa and Asia. His work has appeared in many publications, including *Insight Guide: Tunisia*.

John Chioles, a teacher at the University of Athens and at New York University, had his version of *Antigone* produced by Joseph Papp at the New York Shakespeare Festival.

Kay Cicellis, the author of *The Easy Way, Death of a Town* and *No Name in the Street*, also translated Stratis Tsirkas's *Drifting Cities*.

Cicellis

David Constantine, who taught German at Queen's College, Oxford, has published academic books on Hülderlin and on early travellers to Greece, as well as books of fiction and poetry.

Cowan

Jane Cowan, who studied sociocultural anthropology and ethnomusicology at Indiana University, returned to Greece for more than two years of fieldwork teaching and to do research for her doctoral dissertation on dance in a Macedonian town.

Sean Damer, a sociologist by training, has done stints as a waiter, trawlerman and mountain guide. His book *The White Mountains: Travels in Western Crete* took advantage of his mountaineering as well as his sociological skills.

Dragoumis

Markos Dragoumis, supervisor of the Melpo Merlier Centre for Greek Folk Music Studies and head of the Music Department at Athens College, studied Byzantine Music at Oxford. He also taught at the Athens Conservatory and lectured on folk music and *rembetika.*

Dimitri Gondicas, a lecturer in Modern Greek and assistant chairman of the Committee on Hellenic Studies at Princeton University, was an avid hiker, and has climbed most major mountains in Greece.

Kerin Hope, a former archaeologist, was Athens correspondent for several London newspapers, including the *Financial Times*.

Loomis

Nikos Kasdaglis was born on Kos and lived on Rhodes. He had published many well-loved novels and a collection of short stories.

Richard Kindersley, after going to Oxford in 1967 as a lecturer in Soviet Politics and Eurocommunism, was the editor of *In Search of Eurocommunism* and the author of *The First Russian Revisionists.*

Julia Loomis, although trained as a classicist, started the Modern Greek programme at Queen's College, CUNY. After being a Fulbright professor at the University of Thessaloniki, she became a freelance writer and travel agent.

Michèle Macrakis spent more than 10 years photographing Greece. She was awarded a Fulbright Fellowship to continue her work in Crete documenting the "works and days" of the grape growers.

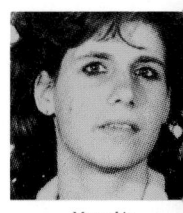

Macrakis

Peter Mackridge, a university lecturer in Modern Greek and a Fellow of St Cross College, an Oxford theological school, wrote *The Modern Greek Language,* published by Oxford University Press in 1985. He has travelled in Greece and Turkey transcribing disappearing dialects.

Mark Mazower, who read Classics and Philosophy at Oxford, was a research lecturer 20th-century Balkan History at Christ Church, Oxford.

Moe

Nelson Moe went to Greece to teach English for a year before embarking on his study of Southern Italy on a Watson fellowship. Although he now teaches English Literature at Naples University, his interest in Greece continues to entangle him in projects such as this guide, for which he was Assistant Project Editor.

David Ricks, after studying Classics at Oxford writing a doctoral thesis on Modern Greek literature, became a research fellow at the University of Birmingham. **Katy Ricks** studied English at Oxford, then taught English at a school in Birmingham.

Anastasia Rubis spent two semesters with College Year in Athens during her undergraduate years at Brown University, and later became advertising manager of the National Tourist Organization of Greece (NTOG).

Rushton

Lucy Rushton did research in northern Greece for her PhD thesis on religion and identity. Thanks to a post-doctoral grant from Oxford, she was able to continue her work in Greece.

Samantha Stenzel, a feature writer for *The Athenian* magazine, also taught at the Hellenic-American Union in Athens.

Stenzel

Haris Vlavianos studied Economics and Philosophy at Bristol University and Politics at Oxford. His PhD thesis covered the policy of the Greek Communist Party during the Civil War.

Amanda Weil worked at the Whitney Museum of Art after graduating from Harvard and later travel photography and her own studio work.

Fay Zika graduated from Oxford, and then earned a PhD in Philosophy at the Aristotelian University of Thessaloniki.

Sofka Zinovieff was born in London. She studied social anthropology at Cambridge University, combining work on her PhD with frequent fieldwork visits to Greece.

This latest edition of *Insight: Greece* has been thoroughly revised and updated by **John Chapple**, who has worked in Greece as a writer and editor since 1969. Assisting him in various parts of the country were **Jeffrey Carson**, **Diana Farr Louis** and **Nikos Stavroulakis**. Proofreading and indexing were completed by **Pam Barrett**.

CONTENTS

CONTENTS

TRAVEL TIPS

WELCOME TO GREECE

Whether you arrive in Greece by boat, train or plane, your first impression as you stretch your legs and climb down the stairs is sure to be of the sun. Glimmering on the water, reflecting off metal and glass, casting shadows, the Mediterranean sun is omnipresent. Like the flash of a hidden camera, the brilliant light catches you unaware and transfixes you.

From the minute you set foot in Greece, you are a part of the Greek landscape – blue sky above, white sand below, the Parthenon, olive groves, a collapsing mosque, a wine festival; whatever the scene, you are in the picture as well. There is a sense that, no matter how many holiday snapshots you may take, Greece will already have taken as many of you.

This country is not merely a holiday resort, ready to satisfy your every desire – it is a population of 10 million people working, eating, drinking, arguing and dancing, who will initiate you into the bustle of their everyday life, into the splendour of their mountains, their ancient temples and white pebbled shores and into the fellowship of their company. When an older woman offers you a sprig of basil, the traditional gesture of hospitality, she simultaneously introduces you into her world and enters yours.

This country is no escape from the everyday; it is an invitation to participate with all your senses – to dive in, smell it, hear it, feel it, taste it, consider it from another perspective, to roll the basil between your fingers, breathing in its fragrant greeting, and to exchange a smile with this generous woman who has invited you into her world. A Greek poet, Olga Broumas, remembered it this way in her collection *Beginning with O* (Yale University Press):

> *When the Greek sea*
> *was exceptionally calm*
> *the sun not so much a pinnacle*
> *as a perspiration of light, your brow and the sky*
> *meeting on the horizon, sometimes*
>
> *you'd dive*
> *from the float, the pier, the stone*
> *promontory, through water so startled*
> *it held the shape of your plunge...*

Just as Greece over the centuries has shaped Western civilisation, so it holds the shape of your plunge. Greece's history would be incomplete without you and all the other travellers who have come before you. Welcome to Greece. You are a part of the story that is about to be told.

Preceding pages: kitsch art in Athens; shop in Aegina; priest plus Raybans. Spreads: sailing into Kastellorizo at dawn; a rural retreat; windmills on Karpathos; the bell towers of the Monastery of St John the Theologian on Patmos. Left, passengers descending the gangway of an Aegean ferry.

CHANGE AND CONTINUITY

In Greece the classical past overwhelms you. The visitor's first glimpse of Pláka seems to dissolve the intervening centuries. In a country whose inhabitants proudly remind you of their ancient heritage, it is easy for the newcomer to assume that a simple thread of continuity runs from the ancient world to modern Athens.

But closer acquaintance throws up new historical and linguistic surprises: a crumbling 15th-century house in Pláka offering a reminder of Ottoman Athens, communities to the south of the city where the old people, refugees from Asia Minor, still speak Turkish; and suburbs to the north where you can hear Albanian. Or further afield, the roadside tents of a group of nomadic Sarakatsanáoi shepherds, a Roman Catholic church on a Cycladic island, or a Jewish cemetery in Ioannina.

Migrations and invasions: The history of Greece is the story of endless movements of people: invasions, migrations, depopulation, resettlement. Sometimes, the invasions were brief, as was the case with the Arab attacks from the sea in the 8th to 10th centuries. At other times they were gradual, bringing new settlers, such as the Dorian tribes three millennia ago, or more recently the Slavs, both entering Greece through Epirus and then moving down the west of the country into the Peloponnese (Pelopónnisos).

The other side of the coin was depopulation. In the face of invasion whole populations would leave their towns and villages. The Slav invasions wiped out urban life in southern Greece. Similarly, pirate raids led to the wholesale evacuation of Aegina in AD 896 and the abandonment of Sámos late in the 15th century. Even later, in 1821, the inhabitants of Chíos fled from Turkish savagery to Syros.

Depopulation was often a major economic headache: the strain of maintaining Alexander's empire weakened Macedonia for generations. Byzantine and Ottoman rulers both tried to improve matters by mass transfers of settlers. Alternatively they welcomed newcomers, like the Albanians, who were admitted to the Peloponnese in 1338 on condition they fought for the local ruler and cultivated the land he gave them.

Albanian tribes were often ready to move; their livelihood involved shifting their sheep between mountain pastures in the summer and lowland grazing in winter. Such communities covered vast distances each year. Two other nomadic groups, the Vlachs and the Sarakatsanáoi, also moved into Greece in large numbers. The Vlachs in particular pros-

pered during the 18th century, and produced a number of Greece's most famous poets and politicians.

In more recent times these large movements of population have continued. At the turn of the century there was an enormous wave of emigration from the Peloponnese to the United States caused by over-population and economic distress. And in 1923 a compulsory exchange agreed between Greece and Turkey led to the departure of half a million Muslims from Greece and the arrival of well over 1 million Orthodox Greeks from Asia Minor.

Continuities in daily life: In the long run

Left, a Syros kiosk owner with a picture of himself as a boy. **Right**, the picture in close-up.

people change, the endless cycle of invasion and assimilation introduces new inhabitants with new customs. But equally in the long run, daily life may change very little, especially in the Mediterranean. Take security, for example: for most of recorded history social life in Greece has been precarious and insecure. Only our own times provide an exception to this rule.

The pirates who lurked in coves in the Máni in the 18th century – taking prisoners everywhere, as a French traveller reported, "selling the Christians to the Turks and the Turks to the Christians" – were merely following in the steps of their Homeric predecessors who had infested just the same area.

there was also the perennial problem of highway robbery.

An English traveller in the 17th century noted that "in order to insure the safety of Travellers, drummers are appointed in dangerous passages; and in Macedonia, in a narrow passe, I saw an old Man beating a drum upon the ridge of a Hill; whereby we had noticed that the passage was clear and free from theeves." In those short periods when an effective central authority held sway, it generally had such limited resources that it could do little to enforce the law. At the end of the last century the Ottoman authorities refused to permit trains to run through Macedonia at night since they could not guard

When no naval power was strong enough to control their activities, the pirates operated on a large scale. The Genoese were obliged to move the inhabitants of Sámos *en masse* to Chíos when pirate raids made life impossible for them. And in the 8th century, Arab raiders from North Africa left Páros such a wilderness that hunters used to sail over from Euboea (Évia) after the deer and wild goats which had become plentiful on the island.

Highway robbery: Life on the mainland was no easier. Pirate bands were likely to raid villages inshore, particularly in daylight when the menfolk of the village would be away working in the fields. For travellers by land,

them against armed attack. The Germans faced a similar problem when they occupied Greece in World War II.

Local communities were left to their own devices. The cheapest security device, if not the most convenient, was a pack of dogs. More solid was a good set of walls and a defensible location. Travelling around Greece today, the visitor still notices how many towns and villages lie off the main road in foothills. Coastal settlements were often set on high ground at some distance from the shore, for better protection.

Though life was insecure, frightening and violent, it embraced rigidly-observed codes of courtesy and honour. Today the blend is difficult to recapture, except in the Máni, and on Crete, where blood feuds still thrive. Vendettas, for example, which were common in parts of Greece, were conducted according to strict rules which changed little over the centuries. In 18th-century Epirus, as in Homeric Greece, an intended victim was immune from attack while he was farming, but was fair game the moment he picked up his weapon.

Pirates, too, observed rigid codes. When a European aristocrat was ransomed by his friends in the early 19th century his captors were hospitality itself: "Baron Stackelberg was then shaved by one of the gang, a cere-

Greece was told, "in your petty Kingdoms and States men are tryed and convicted, but our great Empire cannot be so maintained, and if the Sultan should now send for my head, I must be content to lay it down patiently, not asking wherefore… in this country we must have… patience even to the losse of our heads and patience after that."

Rulers might come and go, but to the poor such patience remained a necessity for centuries. Their very existence depended upon factors beyond their control. Even when their villages escaped the attention of armies, bandits or the tax-man, a poor harvest raised the spectre of starvation.

The past has never offered these people a

mony which they never omit on these occasions, and handed over to his friends. They were all pressed to stay and partake of a roasted lamb and an entertainment about to be prepared…. The robbers then wished them a good journey and expressed their hopes of capturing them again at some future time…."

No doubt such accounts are highly romanticised. Certainly, even if pirates kept to their word, statesmen and those in power often failed to keep theirs. A traveller in Ottoman

"Golden Age", but has always threatened starvation – for the hungry citizens of Athens in the harsh winter of 1941 right back to their exhausted ancestors at the end of the Peloponnesian wars, and back much further still. The account that follows describes the changing fortunes of dynasties and kingdoms. However, the history of a country involves more than a succession of names and dates. The essential backdrop is provided by the generations of nameless inhabitants whose lives involved those countless imperceptible changes which may escape our gaze but which provide the real origins of modern Greece.

Left, etching of Ermoúpolis on Sýros, built on a hill as protection against piracy. **Above**, the famous Dillesi brigands before and after capture.

The basis for the modern way of life in Greece was laid around 3000 BC, when settlers moved down from the northeast plains onto rockier land in the Peloponnese (Pelopónnissos) and the islands, and began to cultivate olives and vines, as well as the cereals they had originally grown. At about the same time a prosperous civilisation arose on Crete (Kríti) and spread its influence throughout the Aegean.

The Minoans, whose rituals have filtered down to us through the legend of Theseus and his labyrinthine struggle with the Minotaur, left proof of their architectural genius in the ruined palaces of Knossós and Festós. Daring sailors, they appear to have preferred commerce to agriculture. They established outposts in the Peloponnese and made contact with the Egyptians.

By 1500 BC their civilisation had reached its zenith. Yet barely a century later, for reasons which remain unexplained, most centres of their power were destroyed by fire and abandoned. The settlement on Thíra (Santoríni), at Akrotíri, was annihilated by a volcanic eruption. But the causes of the wider disintegration of Minoan control remain a mystery. Only Knossós continued to be inhabited as Cretan dominance in the Aegean came to an end.

Its place was taken by Mycenae (Mikínes) the bleak citadel in the Peloponnese. We do not know whether the rulers of Mycenae exerted direct power over the rest of the mainland. But in the *Iliad* Homer portrays their king, Agamemnon, as the most powerful figure in the Greek forces, and this suggests that Mycenae had achieved some sort of overall authority. In its heyday the Mycenaean world contained men rich enough to commission massive stone tombs and delicate gold work. Rulers were served by an array of palace administrators and scribes who controlled the economic life of the state, exacting tribute, collecting taxes and allocating rations of scarce metals.

The Dark Ages: In the 13th century BC this

civilisation, like the Cretan one before it, came to a violent end. Classical myth connects the end of the Mycenaean age with the arrival of the Dorian tribes.

In fact, there was no clear connection between the two events. Mycenaean power had broken down irreversibly by the time the Dorian settlers entered Greece. These invaders, like later ones, entered Greece from the northwest, down over the Píndos mountains into the Peloponnese. Probably they were nomads, which would explain their willingness to travel and account for their lower level of culture.

They also brought their own form of Greek. In areas where they settled heavily we find West Greek dialects, whilst Attica, the Aegean islands and the Ionian colonies continued to use East Greek forms. The hostility – at a later date – between Athens and Sparta (Spárti) was based in part on this division between Ionian and Dorian peoples.

The Dorian invasion coincided with the onset of the Dark Ages. Historical evidence for the period between the 11th and 8th centuries BC is patchy, but it is clear that civilised life suffered. The art of writing was forgotten. Trade dwindled and communities became isolated from one another. Building in stone seems to have been too great an effort for the small pastoral settlements that had replaced the centres of Mycenaean power. Homer's *Odyssey* is set in a simple society where even the rulers busy themselves with menial tasks; where wealth is measured in flocks and herds.

Writing revives: In the 8th century there were signs of revival: trade spread further afield. There were contacts with civilized peoples such as the Etruscans in the west, and the Phoenicians and Egyptians in the east. Artistic influence from the east was increasingly evident in metalwork and pottery. With the adoption of the Phoenician alphabet, writing revived amongst a much larger circle than before.

Another Greek concept which was borrowed from the Phoenicians was equally important; this was the notion of the *pólis* (city-state). In the Dark Ages small, isolated settlements were loosely grouped together

Preceding pages: 17th-century map of Ancient Greece. Left, sunrise at Cape Soúnion on the Áttica Peninsula, southwest of Athens.

into large kingdoms. This system survived in western and northern Greece into classical times when Thucydides described how "the Aetolian nation, although numerous and warlike, yet dwell in unwalled villages scattered far apart."

Elsewhere, however, a network of small independent states grew up. These were initially based around clusters of villages rather than one large urban centre. With the population explosion of the 8th century, however, large conurbations evolved and expanded as surplus population moved from the country to the town. Land became more intensively cultivated and highly priced. In the Dark Ages the slump in population had caused

Thessaly, an *éthnos*. On the other hand, there were states with a more broadly based citizen body, such as Athens.

From kings to aristocrats: In general the kings mentioned in Homer must have surrendered power towards the end of the Dark Ages to an aristocratic form of rule. But the aristocracy too became entrenched in power and increasingly resistant to change. As commoners settled on land and amassed wealth, pressure grew for constitutional reform. Aristotle seems to have been right in tying the demand for such reform to changes in military techniques. He noted that "when states began to increase in size, and infantry forces acquired a greater degree of strength, more

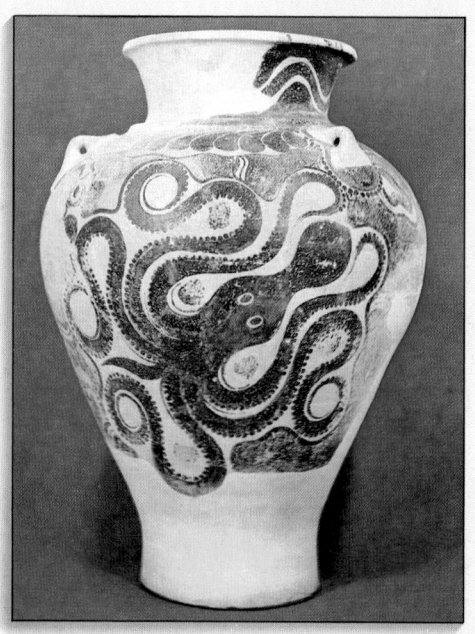

arable land to fall into disuse. Farmers turned from sowing cereals to stock-breeding; now the process was thrown into reverse. The available land could not support such a rapidly-growing population. There is a clear parallel with the Peloponnese in the 19th century, and in both cases the outcome was the same: emigration on a massive scale.

Together with the division between the new *pólis* and the older *éthnos* (kingdom), a further distinction cuts across the first one. On the one hand, there were states, generally in the Dorian-speaking parts of the country, with a serf population, permanently excluded from power, like Sparta, a major *pólis,* and

persons were admitted to the enjoyment of political rights." Just as the shift from monarchy to aristocracy had been reflected in the move from chariots to horseback fighting, so too the emphasis switched from cavalry to infantry; aristocracy lost ground to democratic pressure. Men would only fight in the new larger armies if the aristocrats granted them political rights.

Military power swung away from the traditional horse-breeding aristocracies of Chalkis, Eretria and Thessaly to new powers: Corinth (Kórinthos), Argos and, above all, Sparta, where the state was protected by a hoplite army whose core was a body of citizens who were trained as infantry soldiers from birth.

Often the demand for radical reform met with resistance. The lament of the poet Theogenis typified the aristocrats' response: "Those who previously did not know justice or laws, but wore goatskins on their sides, and had their pasture outside this city like deer, they have become respectable men; those who formerly were of high estate have now fallen low. Who can bear such a spectacle?" But other aristocrats, more far-sighted, often recognised the need for change. One such was Solon, elected in early 6th-century Athens to introduce sweeping constitutional changes. Realising that the city's strength

Greeks the word "tyrant" was not pejorative; it simply referred to a ruler who had usurped power instead of inheriting it. In the 6th century, tyrants seized power in a number of states. Usually they were dissident aristocrats, who gained the support of the lower classes with promises of radical change – promises which were often kept, as it was in the new ruler's interest to weaken the power of his peers. In the mid-7th century, for example, Kipselis of Corinth was supposed to have redistributed land belonging to fellow-aristocrats.

But it would be wrong to regard the tyrants as great innovators. They were symptoms of social change rather than causes of it. Con-

would depend upon the organisation of the citizen body, he opened up the Assembly to the poorest citizens and in other ways loosened the grip of the upper class. Inevitably these changes were attacked from both sides, as Solon himself complains in a number of his poems. However, they laid the foundations for the expansion of Athenian power in the next century.

Tyrants: Another symptom of these political tensions was tyranny. To the ancient

scious of their own vulnerability, they resorted to various propaganda expedients in order to stay in power. The most potent of these was the religious cult, and it is from the time of the tyrants that religion came directly to serve the purposes of the state. This ploy was seen at its most cynical in late 6th-century Athens where the tyrant Peisistrátos, making a second bid for power, tried to impress the inhabitants by entering the city on a chariot accompanied by a tall blonde dressed as the goddess Athéna.

Religion was not only important to the state as propaganda; it was also a major economic factor. While religious festivals

Left, vase painting of Theseus and the Minotaur, and an earlier octopus painting. **Above**, a real octopus in the Irakleíon fish market, Crete.

and games earned revenues, enormous in some cases, for the city which staged them, temples, sacrifices and other rituals were very costly. Apart from wars, temple building was probably the greatest drain on a community's resources. Thus the scale of its religious activities provided some measure of the wealth of a community.

The developing arts: Artistic developments too were pushed forward in the archaic period. Though it is the 5th century which received the most attention, the crucial innovations in pottery and sculpture had been made earlier.

Monumental sculpture in stone was at first derived from Egypt, but by the end of the 6th

at one point to have been paralleled by a process of political unification. People in different cities became aware of a common Hellenic culture. The historian Herodotus was a keen promoter of the idea of one Greece, and asserted that the Greeks are "a single race because of common blood, common customs, common language and common religion." The increasing prominence of interstate religious games and festivals spread this view.

But the sharpest spur to unity was a threat from outside: the rise of the Persian empire. Cyrus, halfway through the 6th century, had conquered the Greek cities on the Asia Minor coast, and Persian aspirations were fur-

century Greek sculptors had successfully broken away from the stiff poses favoured by the pioneers towards a much more expressive and naturalistic style. On vases black-figure painting gave way to red-figure in the second half of the 6th century and the greater flexibility of the technique began to open up new artistic possibilities. By the end of the 6th century the scale of public building and artistic projects in numerous city-states clearly reflected the resources which these communities had acquired over the previous three centuries.

Greeks and outsiders: The rise of an artistic culture shared across state boundaries seems

ther encouraged by his son Darius (521–486 BC) who conquered Thrace, subdued Macedonia and, after quashing an Ionian revolt in Asia Minor, sent a massive expeditionary force southwards into Greece. Athens appealed for help from Sparta, the strongest Greek city, but succeeded in defeating the Persians at Marathon before the Spartan forces arrived.

This victory did more than save Attica; it also confirmed Athens as the standard-bearer for the Greek military effort against the Persians. This explains why a frieze displaying the warriors killed at Marathon (situated just over 20 miles/23 km from Athens) was placed in a prominent and highly unusual position around the Parthenon in the 440s BC. Only then was Athens becoming a power to be reckoned with. The silver mines at Lávrion only began producing enough ore to finance a major shipbuilding programme from early in the 5th century. For two generations after that, Aegina remained superior to Athens as a trading force in the Saronic Gulf.

Athens and Sparta: Ten years after Marathon, when Darius's son Xerxes organised a second attack on Greece, the city-states rallied around Sparta. For while Athens had the largest navy, the Spartans controlled the Peloponnesian League, with its considerable combined land forces. Both the crucial naval

became obvious as Athens extended its control over the Aegean. It did so through the Confederation of Delos, formed in 478 BC with the professed aim of liberating the East Greeks and continuing the struggle against the Persians. In fact, a good deal of anti-Spartan sentiment underlay it. The alliance was primarily a naval one, which brought out a crucial distinction between it and the Spartans' alliance, the Peloponnesian League; for whereas the latter consisted of land forces, requiring minimal financing, the creation of a navy required long-term planning and central coordination. Gradually, the smaller allies found it difficult to equip their own ships for allied use, and turned

victory at Salamis in 480 BC and the military victory on land at Plataea the following year, were won under Spartan leadership.

But no sooner had the Persian menace been banished than the Greek alliance broke up. There was intense suspicion, especially between Sparta and Athens. Thucydides described how as soon as the Persians withdrew, the Athenians quickly rebuilt their city-walls for fear that the Spartans would try to stop them.

The development of a classical "cold war"

Left, the ancient stadium at Delphi. Above, a red-figure vase painting of dancing.

instead to sending money for the Athenians to use. Athens grew in strength as its allies became impoverished.

The Persian threat had receded long before peace was officially declared in 449 BC. By that time the Confederacy had become an Athenian empire whose resources were used to serve Athenian interests. Between 460 BC and 446 BC Athens fought a series of wars with her neighbours in an effort to assert her supremacy. Naval rivals such as Aegina were singled out for attack.

In 430 BC war erupted again when Corinth appealed to the Peloponnesian League for help against Athenian attack. This, the Second Peloponnesian War, dragged on for years since neither side was able to deal the death blow to the other. Athens lacked the infantry to mount an attack on Sparta, whilst the League fielded conventional hoplite forces, unprepared for siege warfare and unable to stop food supplies reaching the city by sea. The war was conducted for the most part in the countryside around Athens on a seasonal basis.

The Peace of Nikias in 421 BC gave both sides a breathing space, but lasted only six years. Only when the Spartans got financial support from the Persians and managed to inflict a catastrophic defeat on the Athenian navy was Athens forced to surrender.

military strength of Athens, for example, could never keep pace with its imperial commitments. This explains the permanent cycle of conquest and revolt. The Spartans had the additional headache of a large serf population, the helots, often prone to revolt in their own province.

The first half of the 4th century continues the pattern. On the one hand, there were long wars between cities; on the other, evidence of prolonged economic difficulties as Corinth fell into irreversible decline and Athens struggled to recapture its previous prominence. This it failed to do. Spartan power remained supreme until 371 BC when Thebes defeated the Spartan army at Leuctra.

Civic breakdown: Literature and art both flourished even during these incessant periods of fighting, but economic activity did not. In a world where each tiny *pólis* was determined to safeguard its independence at any cost, war was endemic. Such a world carried the seeds of its own destruction.

The paradox was that city-states with imperial pretensions chose not to take the steps that might have brought success. Unlike Rome, Greek city-states did not extend citizenship to their subject territories. The Emperor Claudius rightly observed that the Greek states failed as imperial powers because they "treated their subjects as foreigners." The

The city-state system was gradually falling apart. The old form of citizen army was superseded by a more professional force, relying on trained mercenaries. Aristotle noted that "when the Spartans were alone in their strenuous military discipline they were superior to everybody, but now they are beaten by everybody; the reason is that in former times they trained and others did not." Now things had changed.

The spread of mercenaries, in fact, reflects the economic problems of the 4th century. Mercenary service, like emigration or piracy, was a demographic safety-valve, and whereas in archaic Greece mercenaries had only come from a few backward areas, in the 4th century they were increasingly drawn from the major cities as well. This points to economic difficulties over an increasingly wide area.

As in earlier times, military changes linked up with political ones. The decline of the citizen armies coincided with a trend away from democracy in favour of more autocratic government. Power shifted from the city-states towards Thessaly, an *éthnos* state, and later still, towards Macedonia, another old-fashioned kingdom.

Both regions had the advantage over Attica in that they were fertile and not short of land. More rural than the city-states to their

south, they managed to avoid the domestic political turmoil that periodically erupted in the latter. The military successes of the Thessalian tyrant, Jason of Pherae, in the early 4th century, indicated the growing confidence of these newcomers.

A little later Philip of Macedonia moved southwards, secured the vital Thermopylae (Thermopýles) Pass, and after gaining control of Thessaly, defeated an alliance of

Left, scene from a mosaic floor in a Roman house: a man from Kos welcomes the healer Asclepius while Hippocrates sits thinking on the steps. <u>Above</u>, an "early owl" Attic drachma.

Thebes and Athens at Chaironeia in 338 BC. Banded together in the League of Corinth, the Greek city-states were compelled to recognise a new centre of power, Macedonia.

Alexander's Greece: In the *Republic,* Socrates asserts: "we shall speak of war when Greeks fight with barbarians, whom we may call their natural enemies. But Greeks are by nature friends of Greeks, and when they fight, it means that Hellas is afflicted by dissension which ought to be called civil strife."

This passage reflects three sentiments that were becoming widespread in the 4th century: first, that the Greeks were all of one race; second, that warfare between city-states was undesirable; third, that it was natural for the Greeks to fight their enemies in the east. It is ironic that a successful concerted effort against the Persians was only made under the leadership of Macedonia, traditionally a border power in the Greek world.

The rapid growth of Alexander the Great's Asian empire drastically altered the boundaries of the Greek world. The city-states of mainland Greece no longer occupied centre stage. The mainland was drained of manpower as soldiers, settlers and administrators moved eastwards to consolidate Greek rule. At the same time, the intellectual and religious world of the Greeks was opened up to new influences.

The Greek-speaking world was not only expanding, it was also coming together: "common" Greek replaced local dialects in most areas. In 3rd-century Macedonia, for example, local culture was "hellenised", and the native gods were replaced by Olympian deities.

For the first time coins became widely used in trade – something which had been impossible so long as each city had its own currency. Now the Attic drachma became acceptable in an area ranging from Athens to the Black Sea, from Cappadocia to Italy.

But there were limits to this process, for although the city-states gave up their political freedom, they clung to self-determination in other spheres. Local taxation and customs duties offer examples of this passion for independence. Likewise the calendar: in Athens the year began in July, in Sparta in October, on Delos in January.

Philosophers were debating ideas of communal loyalties which transcended the old civic boundaries. Perhaps this reflected the way in which these boundaries were being absorbed within larger units like the Hellenistic kingdoms, the Greek federal leagues and, eventually, the Roman Empire.

Whatever the cause, the most influential philosophical school, Stoicism, emphasised the concept of universal brotherhood and talked of a world state ruled by one supreme power. Elements of such ideas could be found in earlier Greek thought, but in its moral fervour, Stoicism was very much a product of the Hellenistic age, and it brought Greek philosophy closer to Jewish and Babylonian religious doctrines.

Roman expansion: The expansion of Macedonia curtailed the political autonomy of the city-states. The process was gradual but nonetheless inexorable. In the 3rd century they formed federations, and tried to exploit disputes between the generals who had inherited Alexander's empire. The policy had only limited success, mainly because of the paltry military resources available to the Greek leagues.

Early in the 2nd century, disputes among the city-states brought about Roman intervention for the first time in Greek history. Within 20 years Rome had defeated first Macedonia, and then the Achaean League which had organised a desperate Greek resistance to Roman rule. The Roman consul Memmius marked his victory by devastating Corinth, killing the entire male population, and selling its women and children into slavery. As a deterrent to further resistance this was brutal but effective. Conservative factions were confirmed in power in the cities and Greece became a Roman protectorate. In 27 BC, when the Roman Empire was proclaimed, the protectorate became the province of Achaea.

Greece – a Roman backwater: Among the educated classes it became commonplace to lament the decay of Greek civilisation. Seneca, in the 1st century, wrote: "Do you not see how in Achaea the foundations of the most famous cities have already crumbled to nothing, so that no trace is left to show that they ever existed?" But this is misleading. True, Greece was no longer the centre of the civilised world. Athens and Corinth could not rival Alexandria or Antioch, let alone Rome. The main routes to the east went overland through Macedonia, by sea to Egypt.

Thus Greece was a commercial backwater. But its decline was only relative: along the coast, cities flourished. The *pólis* remained much as it had been in Hellenistic times and the Roman authorities permitted a degree of political self-rule. Philhellene emperors like Hadrian even encouraged groups of cities to federate in an effort to encourage a panhellenic spirit.

But the *pólis* was no longer a political force. Hellenistic rulers had feared the Greek cities' power; the Roman, and later the Byzantine emperors feared their weakness and did what they could to keep them alive. After all, the cities were vital administrative cogs in the imperial machine. If they failed, the machine would not function.

They continued to provide a social ideal for educated Greeks. Pausanias wrote of a town in central Greece "if one may call it a *pólis*, when it has no government offices and no gymnasium; they have no theatre, no market, no piped water supply, but live in hovels, rather like the huts up in the mountains, on the brink of a ravine…"

This was the age of the great benefactors, like Hadrian himself, and Herod Atticus, both of whom lavished fine buildings on Roman Athens. Since the poorer classes were permanently excluded from power, the rich were obliged to guarantee social stability by making donations – both for emergency items, like imports of food when a harvest failed, and for more long-term benefits such as public buildings and facilities.

Two centuries of relative tranquillity were shattered by the Gothic invasions in the 3rd century AD. The invasions were successfully repelled, but the shock led to a loss of confidence and economic deterioration. Civic building programmes continued on a much reduced scale. The wealthy classes became increasingly reluctant benefactors, and two centuries passed before imperial authorities and the church revived the demand for architectural skills.

By that time much had changed. The emperor Constantine had moved his capital from Rome to Constantinople. Christianity had been made the official religion of the empire. The transition from Rome to Byzantium had begun.

Right, a Coptic angel reminiscent of St George the dragon slayer – but here she's a woman.

35

A revealing incident occurred in the Byzantine capital, Constantinople, in AD 968. Legates from the Holy Roman Empire in the west brought a letter for Nicephorus, the Byzantine Emperor, in which Nicephorus was simply styled "Emperor of the Greeks" while the Holy Roman Emperor, Otto, was termed "august Emperor of the Romans." The Byzantine courtiers were scandalised. The audacity of it – to call the universal emperor of the Romans, the one and only Nicephorus, the great, the august, "emperor

of the Greeks" and to style a poor barbaric creature "emperor of the Romans"!

Behind this reaction lies the curious fusion of cultures which made up the Byzantine tradition. From the Hellenistic world came the belief in the superiority of the Greek world, the summary dismissal of outsiders as barbarians. From Rome came a strong sense of loyalty to empire and emperor. And in the fervour which marked their belief in the moral superiority of *their* empire – which they regarded not as the "Eastern Roman Empire" but as the only true empire – is the stamp of evangelical Christianity.

The inhabitants of this empire did not call themselves either Greeks or Byzantines: they were Romans, "Roméï". But the mark of a *Romaiós* was that he spoke Greek and followed the rite of the Orthodox Church. Thus the three elements intermingled.

The end of antiquity: The real break with antiquity came late in the 6th century when Greece was first attacked and then settled by Slavic-speaking tribes from the north. The invasions marked the end of the classical tradition in Greece, destroying urban civilisation and with it Roman and Christian culture. An 8th-century chronicler reported that the Slavs were "subject neither to the emperor of the Romans nor to anyone else." But the empire fought back. Christian missionaries converted the pagan Slavs in the Peloponnese, and taught them Greek. The language survived but the old urban culture did not. The disappearance of the city-states is shown by the way in which the word *pólis* came to refer exclusively to Constantinople as though there were no other cities. A small urban elite studied and wrote in ancient Greek but had little impact on the mass of the population; their books were probably not read by more than about 300 people at any one time. Ancient monuments were left untouched because peasants thought that they were inhabited by demons.

An archbishop, Michael Choniates, arrived in Athens from Constantinople in 1182 with a solid education and high hopes of discovering traces of Athens' former glory. He was disappointed. Not only was the inhabitants' knowledge of the classics lamentable, but they lived in such a primitive fashion. The unwalled *pólis* had become a medieval fortress, as at Mystrás near Sparta, a place of refuge for the outlying district.

The weaknesses of Byzantine rule: The Byzantine Empire lacked the resources to maintain tight control over its territories. It was beset on all sides by the Italian city-states, the Slav kingdoms to the north, the Persians and Turks in the east. The Greek provinces, being less vital than Anatolia, which supplied Constantinople with corn, were ceded more readily to other powers.

Byzantium's period of glory was short-lived, lasting from the mid-9th to mid-11th centuries. Its prosperity under a succession of Macedonian emperors ended in 1071 when a new enemy, Turkoman tribes of nomads from central Asia, cut its army to pieces at Manzikert in Anatolia. The threat from the west was soon felt too. A possible Norman invasion was feared in the 12th century when the Norman ruler, Roger of Sicily, invaded Greece and sacked Thebes and Corinth.

But this was only a foretaste of still worse misfortune. In 1204 Constantinople itself was sacked by the Crusader forces *en route* to the Holy Land for the Fourth Crusade. The empire was fragmented. Successor states arose in Epirus, Nicaea and Trebizond. Greece itself was divided into small king-

separate principality. Southern Greece and the islands remained under the control of the Crusaders' successors until in the 14th century the Paleologoi reestablished a Byzantine presence at Mystrás. This political confusion led to ethnically mixed populations.

Turkish mercenaries began to play a significant role. The Byzantine Empire, like the Roman, lacked the men to do its own fighting. Turkish forces were enlisted to act as a buffer against the Serbs and the Bulgars. Their successes alarmed the Greeks, and even occasional marriages between Ottoman princesses and Greek princes failed to negate the threat posed by this new power.

By 1400 the empire had shrunk to Con-

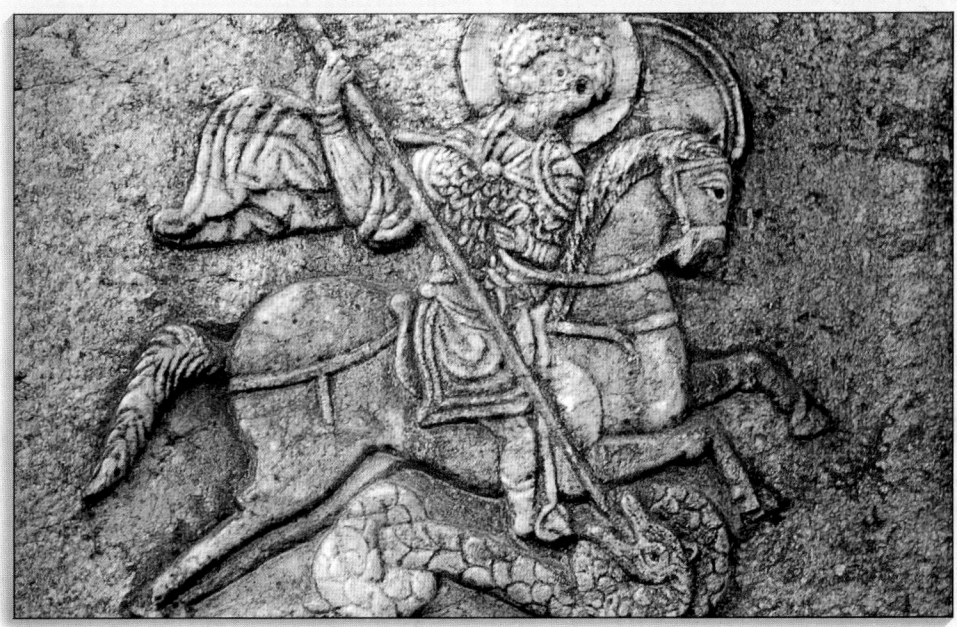

doms – the Duchy of Athens under the Burgundian de la Roche, the principality of Achaea under Villehardouin, islands to various Italian adventurers, crucial ports on the west coast retained by Venice.

Over the following 50 years Byzantium reemerged as Nikean rulers, the Paleológoi, fought back into mainland Greece and recaptured Constantinople. But there was considerable confusion in western Greece, which briefly came under Serbian control, and in Thessaly where the Vlachs established a

Left, an old ascetic. **Above**, carved in stone at Mystrá, St George slaying the dragon.

stantinople, Thessaloniki and the Peloponnese. In April 1453 Sultan Mehmet II besieged Constantinople and took the city within two months; eight years later the rest of the mainland had succumbed too. The Aegean islands held out longer – Tínos until 1715 – but mainland Greece was now part of the Ottoman Empire.

The fall of "The City" reverberated throughout Europe: with it had fallen the last descendants of the Roman Empire itself. Although in the West this seemed the inevitable result of Byzantine decline, to the Greeks it was a more traumatic moment. They had passed from freedom into slavery.

The Ottoman Turks who now controlled the Balkans were the latest in a stream of nomadic tribes who had moved westwards from central Asia. They were highly mobile, and their determination to pursue military conquests made up for their lack of numbers.

From Constantinople the sultan strove to maintain control of his far-flung empire with a minimum of expense. He avoided the creation of rivals with local power-bases by shifting regional governors from place to place, and by rewarding Muslim officers with estates which reverted to imperial control on their owners' death.

Special privileges: Religious tolerance was reflected in the "millet" system of government. The Turkish authorities recognised minority religions, and permitted each "millet", or religious community, a measure of self-government. The Greek Orthodox Church was granted special privileges and came to exert both religious and civil powers over Ottoman Greeks.

Under their new masters the Greeks lived in much the same way as they had done earlier. Their houses, like those of the Turks, tended to be miniature fortresses, built on two floors around a central courtyard. The restored merchant's house in Kastoriá gives a good idea of the effect. Most elements of contemporary Greek cuisine were common then – from the *resináto* wine so distasteful to foreign travellers to the strong coffee which Ali Pasha, the "Lion of Ioánnina", found helpful in poisoning his rival, the Pasha of Vallona.

But autonomy did not rule out oppression. When, from the 17th century onwards, central authority weakened, local magnates were free to burden the peasantry with their own impositions. Many revolts in the Ottoman Balkans, notably that in 1805 which revived the state of Serbia, involved appeals to the sultan for help against corrupt local landowners or bishops.

Powerful enemies continually threatened the Ottoman grip on the country. The Venetians, and later the French, were thorns in the Ottoman flesh. Within the empire the wild Albanians, the backbone of the Ottoman armies, often threatened to break loose

and establish claims of their own. The resulting conflicts left Greece much the weaker.

Thus in 1537 a Turkish army carried off half the population of Corfu after an attack on the Venetian colony there, leaving the island with barely one-sixth of the population it had had in antiquity. The Peloponnese suffered in a similar way, caught in a bloody tug-of-war between the same two rivals. It was ravaged by Albanian forces fighting for the Ottomans in 1715 and again in the 1770s. Further destruction came in the wake of the 1821 uprising. Greeks slaughtered Turks in Trípolis; the Turks uprooted the Greek inhabitants of Chíos. Finally Egyptian troops, under Ibrahim Ali, laid waste to most of the Peloponnese.

Deadly foes: Brigands and pirates provided a perpetual undercurrent of violence in daily life, while plagues often reduced populations more dramatically than wars and made entire regions – Thessaly was especially notorious – impassable to travellers.

When, during the 17th century, the Ottoman Empire ceased to expand, new problems appeared. In the hills and mountains, where the Ottoman grip had never been as firm as elsewhere, groups of brigands, known as *Kléphts*, were formed. They were bandits, equally prone to plunder a Greek village as a Muslim estate, but in peasant folklore they came to symbolise the spirit of Greek resistance to the Ottoman authorities.

Perhaps more important for the development of Greek nationalism was the growth of a Greek merchant community. Commercial links with Europe introduced wealthy Greeks to European lifestyles, but they also encountered European cultural and political ideas. Late in the 18th century two ideas in particular, philhellenism and nationalism, found a fertile ground among young educated Greeks.

The Turks had favoured certain groups of Greeks in the hope of heading off rebellious inclinations. Senior posts in the Ottoman administration were frequently filled by Greeks, and in Constantinople aristocratic families, who were known as the Phanariots, forged close links with the imperial court. The Orthodox Church benefited similarly from this policy. Consequently these two powerful groups in the Greek community were badly placed to head a revolt against Ottoman rule.

The French Revolution provided the political stimulus for revolt, but the ground had already been prepared by the spread of nationalist ideas among the Ottoman Empire's Christian inhabitants. In 1814 three Greek merchants in Odessa formed a secret organisation called "The Friendly Society" (*Filikí Etaireía*) devoted to "the betterment of the nation", which rapidly acquired a network of sympathisers throughout the Ottoman lands. A number of vain attempts to secure themselves powerful and decisive backing were finally rewarded when their

the Turks they turned on each other. Ironically, the belief that this was a national struggle was held with greatest conviction by the foreign philhellenes – Byron and others – who came to help the Greeks. These men were influential in getting Western public opinion behind the Greeks. Thus the major powers, initially unsympathetic to the Hellenic dream, came to put military and diplomatic pressure on the Turks to acknowledge Greek independence. The turning point came with the almost accidental destruction of the Ottoman fleet by an allied force at Navarino in 1827.

Count Ioánnis Kapodístrias, a Greek diplomat formerly in the service of the Rus-

members organised an uprising against Ottoman rule in 1821.

The struggle for Greek independence, which lasted from 1821 to 1832, was not a straightforward affair. Greek propaganda glossed over the difficulties of a nationalist struggle in a kaleidoscopic society. Fighting the Ottomans was a motley crew of *kléphts*, merchants, landowners, primates and Phanariots – all as keen to further their own interests as to advance the cause of Greek nationalism. When they were not fighting

Above, dinner at a house at Chríssa in 1801, painted by Dodwell, author of *Views of Greece*.

sian Tsar, was elected president by a National Assembly in the same year. He encouraged Greek forces to push north of the Peloponnese and was rewarded when the 1829 Conference of London fixed the new state's northern boundary on the Árta-Vólos line. But numerous Greeks were dissatisfied with his administration and suspected him of aiming at one-man rule.

In 1831 he was shot by two chieftains of Máni as he entered a church at Nauplion. While the major powers – Britain, France and Russia – tried to find a suitable candidate for the Greek throne, the country fell into a period of anarchy and civil war.

The new state had a difficult birth and a sickly infancy. It was desperately poor, overrun by armed bands of brigands, beset by quarrelling among various political factions. In 1834 a rebellion in the Máni resulted in government troops being defeated and sent home without their equipment. There were few good harbours or roads. Athens remained the squalid, provincial town that Byron had visited. Internally, conditions were worse than they had been under Ottoman rule.

Bavarian absolutism was partly to blame. Kapodístrias's death had confirmed the reluctance of Greeks to be ruled by Greeks. The crown of the new kingdom, which had been offered to various candidates, was eventually accepted by Otto, son of Ludwig I of Bavaria, who arrived at Nauplion in 1833 on a British man-of-war. Since he was under age, a succession of regents ruled. They ignored widespread calls for a constitution until in 1843 a brief, bloodless uprising in Athens forced Otto to dismiss his Bavarian advisers and accept the idea of constitutional rule and parliamentary government.

Despite a poor and backward economy, the 1844 and later the 1864 constitutions endowed the country with the trappings of an advanced democratic state. Politics reflected the country's strange situation. Rather than political parties representing different classes, factions grouped around individuals, valued as much for their powers of patronage as for their ideas. In the absence of class distinctions, other issues, generally of foreign policy, separated these factions. During Otto's reign, the three main parties were named for the foreign powers they supported: Britain, France and Russia.

The "Great Idea": The new kingdom contained less than one-third of the Greeks in the Near East. The prospect of "liberating" Ottoman Greeks, of creating a new Byzantium by recapturing Constantinople and avenging the humiliation of 1453 was the "Great Idea" which aroused enormous enthusiasm. This had roots embedded in the soil of a fervent nationalism. It was rarely a realistic policy since the Greek army was never on its own a match for the Ottomans; yet it survived repeated humiliations. After the defeats of

1897 and 1922 it continued to rear its head. King George I, who succeeded the ousted King Otto in 1863, was titled not only "King of Greece" but also "King of the Hellenes".

The most prominent populist of the late 19th century, Theodore Deliyiánnis, encouraged foolhardy expeditions to Thessaly and Crete. His more far-sighted rival, Harílaos Trikoúpis, realised that such a policy was unwise so long as Greece lacked the resources to sustain it. Greece was dependent on foreign loans, which gave its foreign

creditors the whiphand over any foreign policy initiatives. Only economic growth would reduce such dependence. Trikoúpis, therefore, set out to encourage economic activity. Roads were improved, the Corinth Canal built. Piraeus expanded to become one of the busiest ports in the Mediterranean.

But despite the appearance of a few textile and food factories, industrial activity remained minimal right up to World War I. Greece was a rural nation, a country of peasant small-holders. The lack of large estates ironed out social inequalities but it did mean most farmers remained miserably poor, too poor to adopt modern farming methods. The export of currants brought prosperity for a while, but a world slump in 1893 hit the entire economy. Greece became bankrupt and hunger drove many peasants to emigrate. By 1912 numerous villages throughout the country lived on remittances which were sent from the United States by young exiles.

Such domestic problems seemed to increase Greek enthusiasm for the Great Idea. Further territory had been acquired in 1881, without fighting, as a by-product of the Congress of Berlin. When troubles on Ottoman Crete in 1897 provoked a wave of sympathy on the mainland, Greek naval forces were sent to the island while the army marched northwards – only to be checked by the

Ottoman forces who pushed back down into Greece. This defeat was humiliating for the Greeks, but it proved only to delay the future enlargement of the kingdom.

On Crete and in Macedonia (Makedonía) Ottoman rule was crumbling. But the rise of the new Balkan nations – Serbia and Bulgaria – added a new complication to Greek

ambitions. Macedonia was a melting-pot of different racial groups (which is why the French call a fruit salad a *macédoine*).

Within Greece, political changes had often been forced through by military uprisings. This had happened in 1843 and 1862. In 1909 it occurred again. Junior army officers staged a revolt against the political establishment and invited a new politician with a radical reputation, Elefthérios Venizélos, to come over from Crete and form a government. A consummate diplomat and a man of great personal charm, Venizélos channelled the untapped energies of the Greek middle class into his own Liberal Party, which dominated Greek politics for the next 25 years.

A decade of wars: When the Balkan Wars erupted in 1912, Greece was strong enough to wrest southern Macedonia from the Ottoman forces and then to defend its gains, in alliance with Serbia, from a hostile Bulgaria. The full gains from the fighting included – in addition to Macedonia – Epirus, Crete and the east Aegean islands. Greece's area and population were doubled at a stroke.

There was barely time to consider what burdens the new territories would impose before the country was embroiled in World War I. Venizélos and King Constantine quarrelled over whether to bring Greece into the war. The prime minister wanted Greece to give the Entente active support, while Constantine insisted on keeping the country neutral. The quarrel raised vital issues: who had the final say over foreign policy – the king or parliament? The dispute reached the point of open civil war which ended in 1917 with Constantine being forced to leave the country and Greece entering the war.

Venizélos had hoped that the Entente powers would reward Greece for its support with new territories. Smyrna (Smýrni) and its rich hinterland in Asia Minor had been promised by the British to Greece during the war, and in 1919 Greek troops were invited to occupy the province and place it under Greek control. It began to look as though the Great Idea might at last be realised.

But in Greece in 1920 the Liberal Party was surprisingly voted out of power and succeeded by a royalist government. The fight against the Turks continued, however, invigorated by the myth that Constantine had been divinely named to lead the Greeks into Constantinople. Encouraged by the Allies,

Greek forces advanced inland from Smyrna against the Turkish Nationalists, led by a rebel general, Mustafa Kemal. Spirits were high, but the long march over hilly, waterless country weakened the Greeks and stretched their lines of communication. In September 1922, only 80 km (50 miles) from Ánkara, the Nationalists finally pushed them back. Retreat turned into rout. As Greek soldiers and civilians fled from the Turkish army, Smyrna was surrendered without a struggle.

The 1923 treaty, which finally ended the war between Greece and Turkey, fixed the boundaries between the countries which hold today (with the exception of the Dodecanese islands, at that time held by the Italians). In urban areas, often in squalid shanty towns outside the large cities, searching for poorly-paid jobs. With them they brought their music, and the Smyrna style of singing – a melancholy vocal line over violin and *bouzoúki* swept the Athenian cafés.

After the disaster of 1922, King Constantine was forced to leave Greece a second time, and a parliamentary republic was established. It lasted only 12 years, a succession of short-lived coalitions and minority governments, broken up by military dictatorships and abortive coups d'états. Governments regularly altered the electoral system to keep themselves in power. The only period of stability – Venizélos's years in power

10 SALONIQUE — Quartier Vardar, Groupe de Réfugiés - Vardar district, A groupe of Refugees

addition, a massive population transfer was agreed upon: half a million Muslim inhabitants of Greece moved to Turkey in exchange for over 1 million Orthodox Greeks. The Greek presence in Asia Minor, which had lasted for 2,000 years, was ended.

The interwar years: Buffeted and impoverished by 10 years of war, the nation now faced the huge problem of absorbing these indigent newcomers into an already crowded country. The economy benefited from the cheap labour, and it was in the interwar period that Greece began to industrialise. But the refugees also increased social tensions. Over half a million of them settled in from 1928 to 1932 – was terminated by the shock of the international economic depression. In 1933 the Liberals were succeeded by the royalist Populist Party, whose timid leaders only half-heartedly supported the republic. Apart from the constitutional issue, little separated the parties. Both ignored the signs of growing inequality and class conflict.

Lacking popular support, parliamentary government remained vulnerable to military pressure. In 1935 this led to the monarchy being restored. In 1936 the king dissolved parliament and offered the premiership to an extreme right-wing politician, Ioánnis Metaxas, a former senior army officer and a fervent royalist. Soon afterwards, Metaxas responded to a wave of strikes by declaring martial law. But the "First Peasant" (as Metaxas liked to be called) never succeeded in digging solid foundations for his longed-for Third Hellenic Civilisation.

World war and resistance: Metaxas had tried to steer a middle course in foreign policy between Britain and Germany. The latter's increasing dominance in the Balkans had to be set against Britain's naval strength in the Mediterranean. But Germany was not the only power with aggressive designs on the Balkans. In April 1939 Mussolini sent Italian troops into Albania and in 1940 he tried to emulate Hitler's record of conquest by crossing the Albanian border into Greece. Metaxas could no longer hope to keep Greece neutral. Receiving the Italian ambassador in his dressing-gown, he listened to a recital of trumped-up charges and responded to the fascist ultimatum with a curt "No!" Or so the story runs – a story commemorated every year on 28 October by "Ochi" (No) Day.

Fighting on their own in the mountains of Epirus, the Greek forces were remarkably successful and pushed the Makaronádes (Spaghetti Eaters) – as the Italians became known in later folksongs – back deep into Albania. But in the spring of 1941 Hitler sent German troops south to pacify the Balkans in preparation for his invasion of the Soviet Union.

Britain had sent reinforcements to support the Greeks, but the Germans managed to advance unchecked as far as Thessaloniki. German victory was swift. Their invasion of Greece began on 5 April; on 30 April they appointed General Tsokáloglu as a quisling prime minister.

Greece was occupied by German and Italian forces until late 1944. Their hold over the countryside was often tenuous, but it was firm in the towns, which suffered most from the shortage of food, notably in the terrible winter of 1941–42. It was also from the towns that the Germans deported and exterminated Greece's old and varied Jewish communities. King George and his official government had left the country in 1941 and passed the war under British protection. And when organised resistance did emerge

in the hills, most pre-war politicians remained in the towns or on the sidelines.

The earliest and most important group was known as the National Liberation Front (EAM in Greek). This was organised by the Communist Party, but rapidly attracted a broad base of support, including many Greeks for whom patriotism and anti-royalist feeling alone were sufficient motivating forces. Numerous other groups also sprang up. Drawing on the *klepht* tradition of mountain resistance these groups would make occasional forays down into the plains. Clashes between different groups were common.

The dominance of EAM meant that when the British began to establish contacts with

resistance groups in 1942, they found military considerations colliding with political ones. EAM, with over 1 million supporters, was well placed to pin down German troops. On the other hand, the British, suspecting that EAM intended to set up a communist state in Greece after the war, armed other groups as a counterweight. EAM, for its part, feared that Churchill wished to restore the monarchy without consulting the Greek people. This fear was amply justified. Churchill had little sympathy for the guerrillas, whom he described as "miserable banditti".

Into the Cold War: In autumn 1944, the German forces retreated, to be replaced by

Left, a group of refugees in Thessaloniki after the 1922 Asia Minor disaster. **Above**, British troops are greeted as they liberate Athens in 1944.

British troops. First Britain and then, after March 1947, the United States, believed themselves responsible for reintroducing civilian rule. The climate of suspicion made this almost impossible. Resistance forces mistrusted the Allies' intentions and refused to lay down their arms. The Allies feared the spectre of a communist rising and tried to find moderate politicians to whom they could hand over power. But these politicians relied on a heavily right-wing militia to keep order. It was in such circumstances that the king returned to Greece in September 1946 after a bitterly disputed plebiscite. Inflation was soaring, the black market flourished and violence spread rapidly through the country

of civil rights and the emergence of a powerful security service did not end in 1950. Again, politics were polarised: the old pre-war split between royalists and republicans gave way to one between Left and Right.

Greece looks West: Democracy had weathered the civil war – but only just. In the following decade a certain stability seemed to have been achieved, with only two prime ministers – both conservatives – in power between 1952 and 1963. Yet this stability was precarious, relying on a policy of outlawing the Communist Party and discouraging opposition to the regime. Anyone with a suspected left-wing past found life difficult.

Greece had joined NATO in 1951, and the

as old wartime scores were settled.

Greece, sliding into open civil strife, became a crucial stage in the rapidly evolving Cold War. The government survived on Allied loans and politicians became adept at exaggerating the communist threat in order to win further American support. In fact, the government forces had to abandon control of large parts of the countryside to the rebels.

Government forces, with American provisions and advice, defeated the rebel army in the mountains of northwest Greece in October 1949. But victory involved detaining suspected left-wing sympathisers and forcibly evacuating entire villages. The violation

pro-Western orientation of its foreign policy secured financial support from the United States. However, the relationship was not straightforward: when the Cyprus dispute flared up in 1954 Greece refused to take part in NATO manoeuvres. This foreshadowed the problems that later governments would have in defining Greece's role in Europe. The quarrel over Cyprus was resolved – for a time – when the island was created a republic in 1960. And Greek links with the West were strengthened by its entry into the Common Market as an Associate in 1962.

A troublesome "miracle": In the 1950s and 1960s, Greece, like Italy and Spain, experienced an "economic miracle" which transformed the country. Electric power became widespread, communications improved. As roads opened up new horizons, young Greeks went to meet them. Athens mushroomed outwards, a chaotic sprawl of concrete apartments, until it contained almost one-third of the country's entire population.

The old forms of political control which had operated best in small rural communities began to erode. A new urban middle class arose which regarded the conservative political elite as culturally backward, rooted in the rhetoric of the Cold War and lacking a vision of Greece as a modern state.

The 1961 elections saw the resurgence of

Shortly afterwards Karamanlís resigned and in elections Papandréou's Centre Union Party won power. This was the first centrist ruling party for over a decade. The way now seemed open for an extended period of centrist rule. But although conservative politicians were prepared to surrender power, right-wing groups in the military regarded the new government as a threat to their own interests.

When Papandréou demanded a reshuffle of senior army officers he found his own defence minister and the young king, Constantine II, opposed to him. The king tried clumsily to bring down the Centre Union Government, but when Papandréou agreed with the main conservative opposi-

the political centre, under the leadership of a former Liberal, George Papandréou. The contest was bitterly fought. When the results were announced in favour of Karamanlís, Papandréou alleged that police and rural gendarmes had been used to intimidate voters, and that the results were fraudulent.

Public disquiet at possible links between the ruling party and extreme right-wing violence increased in May 1963 when a left-wing deputy, George Lambrákis, was assassinated at a peace rally in Thessaloniki.

Left, women fought with the Resistance during the Civil War. Above, anti-dictatorship posters.

tion to hold elections in May 1967, Constantine was faced with the prospect of a further Centre Union victory. He held a series of meetings with senior army officers to make contingency plans for military intervention. But these plans were preempted when a group of junior army officers, working according to a NATO contingency plan, executed a swift *coup d'état* early on the morning of 21 April 1967. Martial law was proclaimed; political parties were dissolved. The Colonels were in power.

The Colonels: The junta was motivated by a mixture of self-interest and hazy nationalism. This combination was certainly not new;

on a number of occasions in the interwar period army officers had used the rhetoric of national salvation to head off a possible purge in which they feared they might lose their jobs. In their policies and attitudes, too, the Colonels drew on earlier traditions. With peasant or lower-middle-class backgrounds, they symbolised a provincial reaction to the new world of urban consumers brought about by the "miracle". Thus they stressed the need for a return to traditional morality and religion. They closed the frontiers to bearded, longhaired or mini-skirted foreigners – at least until the tourist trade was hit. They prevented Greeks from reading such subversive literature as Greco-Bulgarian dictionar-

lems of government. In the bloody aftermath of the November student sit-in at the Athens Polytechnic, Colonel Papadópoulos, the regime's figurehead, was deposed by army units and power switched to a more sinister figure, Dimítrios Ioannídes, commander of the military police.

In the end, it was the Cyprus problem which toppled the junta. A foolhardy Greek nationalist coup, supported from Athens, against the Cypriot president, Archbishop Makários, led the Turks to land troops in northern Cyprus. Ioannídes ordered Greek forces to retaliate, but mobilisation had been so chaotic that local commanders refused to obey his orders. On 24 July 1974 the former

ies. They wanted the country to "radiate civilisation in all directions" by establishing a "Greece of the Christian Greeks" which would make Greece once again "a pole of ideological and spiritual attraction." This was the old dream: an escape from the dilemmas of the modern world in a fantastic fusion of classical Athens and Byzantium.

The first signs of widespread discontent coincided with the economic downturn of 1973. The leaders of the protest were students, whose occupations of university buildings in March and November were brutally broken up. Increasingly the regime was proving incapable of dealing with ordinary prob-

premier, Karamanlís, returned from exile in Paris to Athens to supervise the restoration of parliamentary democracy.

A new start for democracy: The transition to democracy proceeded remarkably smoothly considering the enormous problems which Karamanlís faced. Aware of his own vulnerability, he moved slowly in dismissing collaborators of the regime. At elections held in November 1974, Karamanlís's New Democracy (*Néa Demokratía* or ND) party won an overwhelming victory, though many people seemed to have voted for Karamanlís simply as a guarantor of stability.

Karamanlís himself was well placed to

make any necessary political reforms, since a referendum the month after the elections produced a decisive vote for the abolition of the monarchy, which had been compromised by the king's actions before and during the junta. In its place Karamanlís created a presidency with sweeping powers. It was widely believed that in the event of a swing to the Left, Karamanlís would resign his parliamentary seat and become president.

Signs of such a swing were evident after the 1977 elections in which Andréas Papandréou's Panhellenic Socialist Movement (PASOK) made large gains. The younger Papandréou, George's son, represented a new, post-war generation – at home with the "miracle" and its fruits. With his background as a professor of economics in the US, he was well placed to lead a party of technocrats. At this time he still had a reputation as a radical and he vehemently attacked Karamanlís's policies, taking a more belligerent stand over relations with Turkey, and threatening that a PASOK government would take Greece out of both NATO and the EEC, subject to a referendum. The future was to show that Papandréou's promises were an unreliable guide to his actions in power. Yet support for PASOK was growing and in 1980 Karamanlís resigned as prime minister and was voted in as president by parliament.

After PASOK's victory in the October 1981 elections, based on a simple campaign slogan of *Allaghí* ("Change"), Papandréou took office and formed Greece's first ever socialist government. His significance lies not in his socialism, which existed in name only, but in his remarkable success in articulating the attitudes of his generation. In the 1960s he brilliantly blended the rhetoric of the Left with the social optimism of Kennedy's America. Twenty years later, and despite his recent loss to ND, the rhetoric still wins votes on the Left, but it is a middle-aged, middle-class Left seeking economic security, stability, a "better future" for their children.

The PASOK slogan, accompanied by images of a little girl symbolising a vague appeal to classless desires for peace and prosperity, won PASOK the 1985 general election, and even the scandals of the late 1980s failed to tarnish completely the wily Papandréou's image.

In 1989, in the wake of domestic and economic scandal, Papandréou finally succumbed at the polls, and ceded the position of power to Constantine Mitsotákis, leader of ND, and a Cretan. But he remained in the public eye, marrying his former air hostess mistress, Dímitra "Mimi" Liáni, 36 years his junior, while PASOK ministers were deeply implicated in high-level scandals. The fact that Papandréou was returned to power in 1993 speaks for the unwillingness of the Greek people to return to a right-wing government.

The break-up of Yugoslavia in 1991, and the baptism of Macedonian Yugoslavia as a new country calling itself Macedonia, caused outrage. Macedonia was the great empire of

Philip II from which the Hellenic world was born. It had also been a part of the Great Idea which had roused the country at the beginning of the century when southern Macedonia had been taken from the Ottomans. In 1994, Greece closed its borders with Macedonia.

Papandréou struggled on but finally ill health forced him to step down as prime minister in 1996, aged 76. He was succeeded by Kostas Simitis, but rumours persisted that before too long there would be another Papandréou as prime minister – none other than the glamorous Mimi, bare-breasted pictures of whom had appeared in magazines. Her denials, naturally, were taken as proof of her ambition.

A
JOURNEY
INTO
GREECE,
BY
George Wheler Esq;
In Company of
Dr SPON of LYONS.

𝕴𝖓 𝕾𝖎𝖗 𝕭𝖔𝖔𝖐𝖘.

CONTAINING

I. A Voyage from *Venice* to *Constantinople*.
II. An Account of *Constantinople* and the Adjacent Places.
III. A Voyage through the *Lesser Asia*.
IV. A Voyage from *Zant* through several Parts of *Greece* to *Athens*.
V. An Account of *Athens*.
VI. Several Journeys from *Athens*, into *Attica*, *Corinth*, *Bœotia*, &c.

With variety of Sculptures.

LONDON,
Printed for *William Cademan*, *Robert Kettlewell*, and *Awnsham Churchill*,
at the *Popes Head* in the *New-Exchange*, the *Hand* and *Scepter* in
Fleetstreet, and the *Black Swan* near *Amen-Corner*.
MDCLXXXII.

The Ancient Greeks had a strong sense of identity. From the Homeric age until at least the disintegration of Alexander's empire, Greeks were conscious of themselves as a people distinct from all others. These others they called barbarians. "Barbarous" first meant only that: non-Greek. The word was probably imitative of unintelligible foreign speech. It was in their common language and in their common culture that the Greeks, however various and widely distributed, knew themselves to be Greek.

According to myth, the goddess Athena chose the land of Greece for her favourite people because of its ideal location between the frozen north and the torrid south. Later civilisations, particularly northern ones, have endorsed that myth. The Greeks, it was thought, were Nature's favourites.

Brilliant glimpses: We have learned a few epithets from Homer, and discovered that they were exact and telling: windy Troy, sandy Pylos, Mycenae rich in gold. And in Pindar, Sophocles and Euripides there are brilliant glimpses of places within and around the limits of the Greek world: of Mount Tmolus and the golden Pactolus in the east, of Aetna in the west (where the Titans were confined), and of Kolonos, Thebes, Cithaeron and Delphi at the centre.

There were extraordinary travellers among the heroes of Greek myth and legend: Odysseus, who took 10 years getting home from Troy; Herakles, whose labours took him north into the land of the Hyperboreans and west to the Garden of the Hesperides; Jason, who sailed to Colchis on the Black Sea after the fleece.

The Greeks had a strongly mythical and religious sense of the places in their world; and this sense, or something like it in intensity, survived them and has inspired or coloured the vision of travellers in their country ever since. It should excite the traveller to know that places of terrific mythical resonance really exist. They are not beyond the zone, in a nebulous otherwhere but actually

within it, substantial and real. Hélicon, Parnassus (Parnassós), Olympus (Ólymbos) are real mountains and can be climbed – which affects the imagination very curiously: it is exciting but also almost seems an offence. The Acheron still flows and meets the Cocitus by the hilltop Nekromanteion of Persephone and Hades, just east of Párga. Párga was a fishing village and is now a holiday resort. It is one street wide, and on that one street you will have trouble buying anything as necessary as bread. But there are many

travel agencies, all offering the same thing: day trips by boat to the entrance to Hades.

The ancients sited many of their myths very precisely indeed. Citizens of Athens, Corinth or Thebes constantly saw with their own eyes places their divinities and heroes had operated in. Travel was difficult, but people *did* travel; they went about their ordinary business in a country the myths had illuminated. The everyday and the mythical seem to coexist very easily in Greece. Judging from the leaden tablets unearthed at Dodona, they were often very ordinary men and women who made their way to the sanctuary and oracle there. The questions they

Preceding pages: fresco from Knossós. **Left,** the title page of Wheler's illustrious account of his and Dr Spon's travels. **Above,** ancient gargoyle.

put to Zeus through his priests who, as Homer says, slept "on the ground with unwashed feet," were often very mundane ones: "Will it be all right to buy the small lake by the sanctuary of Demeter?" "Is it good and possible to sail for Syracuse at a later date?" "Shall I be successful in my craft if I migrate?" The answers were given in the rustling of the leaves of the sacred oak.

The mythical and religious sense of place coexisted, from quite early on, with a concern for topographical accuracy. Scholars and travellers in the 18th century made the important discovery that Homer had sited his story precisely. When Lady Montagu sailed through the Dardanelles it gave her great

pher Pausanias as their guides. The latter two particularly are frequently referred to at great length in the early modern travel literature of Greece. Quite simply, until the modern tradition itself became established, travellers in Greece seeking to locate places famous in antiquity *only* had ancient testimony to go on. Not only particular monuments – the Temple of Olympian Zeus in Athens, for example, or of Artemis at Ephesus – but even entire sanctuaries and cities of the very greatest importance (Delphi, Miletus, Sparta) had vanished if not from the face of the earth at least out of all local ken, and could only be located and identified by following ancient directions (converting *stádia* into miles, al-

pleasure, so she wrote to Pope, to check Homer's descriptions for herself and to find them exact. Others actually used the *Iliad* for their archaeological researches on the plain of Troy. Schliemann, in the 1870s, was only the most fanatical, credulous and fortunate of a long line. When travellers and critics called Homer a "truthful" poet, "a painter after Nature", they meant not just his depiction of human passions but also his eye (blind though it was) for the landscapes and topography of the real world.

Travellers were on firmer ground when they took the historian Herodotus, the geographer Strabo and the tourist-cum-topogra-

lowing for changes in the landscape) and searching hopefully for telling inscriptions.

The ancients themselves, then, were the best guides available to travellers when Greece in modern times began to be explored; and, not making any hard and fast distinction between poets on the one hand and topographers or historians on the other (Homer was thought to be accurate; Herodotus honours the myths and enhances the glamour of places), let us say that the texts worked in a dual way: they located the sites and aroused what Dr Johnson called "local emotion". The knowledge the travellers gained was, in varying proportions and intensity, both factual and imaginative. Most often, of course, the "local emotion" felt by a traveller at some important site in Greece would be very different from what we may suppose an Ancient Greek would have felt. The modern response is almost inevitably a sentimental one; its most characteristic colouring is nostalgia.

The "good old days": Nostalgia for Greece increased as the value of ancient Greek civilisation rose in the eyes of other nations. Early modern travellers came to Greece from countries – England, France, Italy – whose cultures were deeply indebted to the classical world, and naturally, in varying degrees, they brought that influence with them and it

They would quote Cicero's lament for the decline of Athens at the appropriate moment in their own accounts.

Classical influences: Once the tradition of travel in Greece was established, each new explorer could refer to and perhaps correct his predecessor's works on the spot; but he would not forget the ancient texts. The classical authors themselves continued to direct and influence travel in Greece in the 18th and 19th centuries, and perhaps they do so still. It was by the light and in the light of classical literature that the travellers saw the famous localities of Greece; and in Roman and Alexandrian works the moderns discovered the beginnings of their own nostalgia.

affected their responses.

It is worth noting that nostalgia for Greece, though not to the same degree, already existed in Roman and Alexandrian times. Both those ages were, in some respects, backward-looking to a civilisation which they thought superior to their own. European travellers of the 17th and 18th centuries found in Roman and Alexandrian sentiment towards Ancient Greece a precedent and an authority for what they more intensely felt themselves.

Left, a woodcut of Greece made in 1545. **Above**, statue of Odysseus, the Western world's archetypal traveller, found in a cave in southern Italy.

Serious exploration of Greece did not get underway until the late 17th century. There were many practical deterrents, not least the fact that nearly the whole of Greece, from the late 15th century onwards, was Ottoman territory. But also, and just as important, the cultural incentive was lacking still in those countries from which, later, the travellers would come. Medieval Christian Europeans, though they took a great deal of their learning from Plato and Aristotle, had no wish to visit Greece – unless as Crusaders or robber-knights to carve out feudal domains.

A confidently Christian culture had no reason to turn with any sentimental or nostalgic interest towards the land of Greece. Geography then was more figurative and symbolic than empirical; there was no impulse to map Greece or any other remote country accurately.

The *Mappa Mundi* (of about 1290) in England's Hereford Cathedral illustrates this very well. The world is disposed there almost entirely figuratively: Jerusalem at the centre; the River of Death all around the circumference. If you look on that map for information about the classical lands, you find some very strange shapes and locations. Greece itself has no general designation, unless the word *ICAYA* (Achaía) is meant as one. Famous ranges and rivers are hope-

existed. The trade-routes passed the city and Piraeus by; ships rounding the Peloponnese crossed to Smyrna through the islands. On the first modern maps Athens occurred as *Stines* – which is what the Franks heard when the Greeks said *stin Athéna* (in Athens) – and by that misnomer all connection with the ancient city was effectively severed.

In Holland and Germany in the 16th and 17th centuries scholars did write geographies of Greece, but bookish ones, entirely on the basis of classical texts. The author of one of them, Christoph Cellarius, was renowned for having taken only one short walk throughout the 14 years of his professorship in Halle. Such works prove the reverence

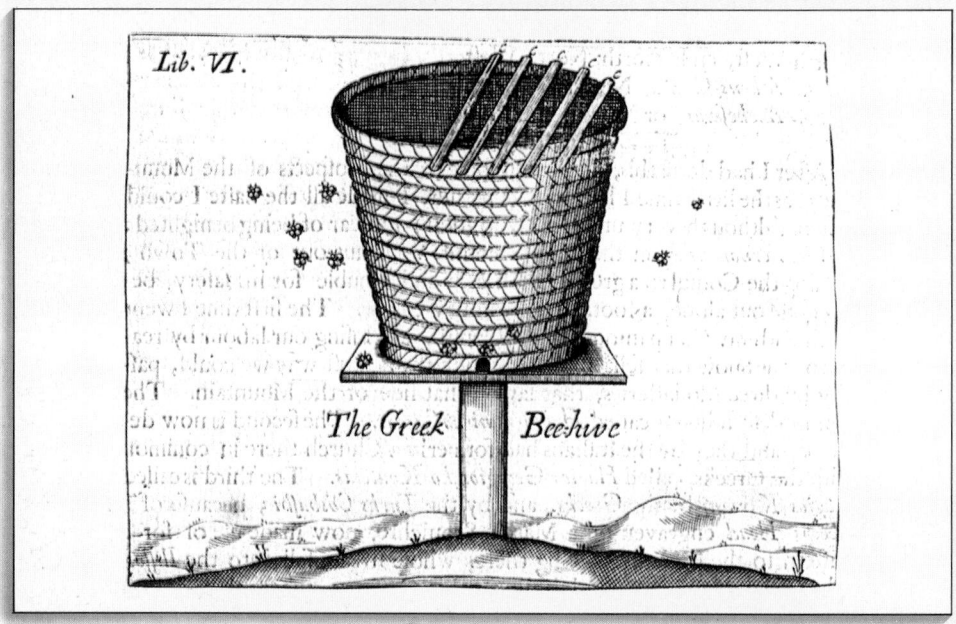

lessly misplaced, and there are some notable confusions: Athos appears as Atlas; Delphi as Delos. Thasos and Patmos have drifted north into the Black Sea. The Peloponnese is drawn as a rounded lump and labelled: *INSULA*. The Chersonese peninsula in Thrace has the shape which clever etymologists deduced for it from the name of its chief city Cardiá: the shape of a heart.

Two-and-a-half centuries later, even among the learned, the degree of knowledge was scarcely higher. Martin Crusius, for example, a German scholar writing in the 1550s, asked a correspondent in Greece whether it was true that Athens no longer

that Renaissance learning had for Greece, and at the same time an almost medieval indifference to empirical knowledge.

The shift that then took place is exemplified by Joseph Pitton de Tournefort who set off in 1700, funded by the King's Academy, to see for himself whether what the ancient geographers and botanists had written was true or false. It needed a cultural incentive to send travellers to Greece, and the Renaissance supplied that. But it also needed a shift in the manner of apprehending the world, a shift towards belief in the value of empirical enquiry. A lull in the wars between the Turks and Venetians, after the victory at Candia

(Irákleion) in 1669, made trade and travel easier. Travel for pleasure or scientific purposes was greatly facilitated when the trade routes and commercial contacts were secure.

The "Hellenic Ideal": Greece is not just any foreign country but the still surviving site of an excellent and – for the West – a supremely influential civilisation. True, there is more to Greece than its classical past; and having such a past, and having had so much outside passionate attention directed at it, has not always been an advantage. Greece, so far as the West is concerned, cannot be neutral ground. The first travellers, or those of them at least who set out deliberately to see Athens, Eleusis or Delos, were not impartial. Even the most reasonable and "scientific" among them had ideas and ideals in mind when they set out, which coloured their perceptions when they got there. Fortunately, the "Hellenic Ideal" is a many-faceted thing, and the company of travellers who might all be called Hellenists had very various interests and aspirations. We need not enumerate these. The point is that the earliest travellers *were* interested; they came with ideals and presuppositions, with a disposition to be affected each according to his bent.

These particular inclinations were contained within a more general attitude: admiration for the past. Modern Greeks have never had an easy time of it, being expected by Western Hellenists to live up to their glorious history. Admiration can all too easily lead to disappointment, which may turn hysterical and even vengeful.

Opening up: Greece was opened up to the West as scholarly and sentimental interest in its splendid past increased, and what was learned of Greece and brought back by the travellers further fuelled that interest. This is most apparent in the 18th century. Travel literature altogether was an important and popular genre. Within it, accounts of Greece had a wide circulation, often went through several editions, and were very quickly translated. Furthermore, booksellers, knowing the market, engaged hack writers to plagiarise and excerpt from the best available accounts and to compose compendium volumes out of them. *The Travels of the late Charles Thompson Esq.*, for example, was put together in this way (in 1744), and was very well received.

The best among the early books on Greece were written, naturally enough, by men who travelled there and who, back home again, related what they had learned. Spon, Tournefort, Wood, and Chandler were deliberate travellers who made their discoveries known to an interested public. Their undertakings were in that sense purposeful. But, especially at the beginning, much information about Greece and much assistance in the exploration of Greece was supplied by people who happened to be there on other business. Such figures occur *passim* in the pub-

lished accounts, and travellers were much indebted to them. They were, for example, Capuchin priests who, as residents of Athens, accommodated the first European travellers in their own religious house, showed them around the still visible monuments and supplied them surreptitiously with maps.

One of their number, *le père* Jacques Babin, based at Negropont (Euboea) but visiting Athens, wrote the very first modern account of the city, *Récit de l'état présent de la ville d'Athènes* (1674). This brief but curiously moving work (we witness in it a man opening his eyes to beautiful things around him; we hear the first accents of true admiration)

Left, 18th-century travellers' accounts detail local customs, dress and even bee husbandry. **Right**, watercolour of Naxos, 1795.

History: Travellers 57

was sent to Jacob Spon in Lyons. He edited it, and in so doing was inspired to make his own journey. An armchair traveller, Guillet de Saint-Georges, with whom Spon was later involved in controversy, got most of the material for his immensely successful *Athènes ancienne et nouvelle* (1675) from Capuchin priests in Pátras and Athens.

Some early travellers: All the early travellers were glad to make use of contacts on the spot and even to supplement their own accounts with eyewitness reports of places they were not able to visit themselves. Merchants were particularly useful in this respect, if they were intelligent observers and had some interest in classical things, since

he went. A Flemish painter in his party did drawings of the Parthenon frieze which, though crude, are of great value still, since they were done before the bombardment of 1687 in which much was damaged. When Spon and Wheler arrived in Greece they were entertained by Nointel, who gave them not only inspiration (he showed them the memorials of his own tour) but also protection and practical information.

The researches done and passed on by men who were in Greece in some professional capacity – diplomatic, commercial, religious – were important, but it was the travellers, particularly Spon and, later, Richard Chandler, who published them. An excep-

their business took them travelling. Consuls even more so, being in one place for a length of time. Consul Giraud, for example, who served first French and then British interests in Athens for some 30 years, offered hospitality to travellers and showed them around the sights. He also engaged in scholarly researches, which Spon made grateful use of. A most powerful figure at this time was the French Ambassador in Constantinople, the extravagant Marquis de Nointel. He considered it part of his diplomatic duty to travel through Greece, his domain, with a large entourage and much ostentation, collecting and recording curiosities and antiquities as

tion was Pierre-Augustin Guys of Marseilles, a most engaging man. He was a merchant who spent nearly all his working life in Greece and loved the land and its people and its classical past with passion. He was both a wealthy and a well-read man, a correspondent of Johann Winckelmann and a devoted admirer of his aesthetic works. Indeed, as he travelled throughout Greece, pursuing his commercial interests, he saw its landscapes, people, climate and customs with a vision as sympathetic and passionate as that of Winckelmann, who had never been there.

He was unusual in his day, for instead of dislocation and discrepancy he saw continuity, survival and connections wherever he went in Greece. By insisting on continuity, by refusing to think of the modern Greeks as hopelessly cut off from their heroic past, he contributed in a small way to that raising of expectations and of confidence by which, finally, the Turks were driven out.

Spon and Wheler were in Greece during 1675–76 and their explorations and their separate publications constituted the first coherent survey of the land in modern Europe. Spon especially wrote as a scholar and a Hellenist; Wheler followed him as well as he could. When he entered the church in 1685 he gave his souvenirs, the bits and pieces of marble he had brought back with

Turks, their masters, as barbarians who would deface as a matter of religious duty whatever statuary they came upon. Therefore, it was the perceived duty of civilized Western travellers to rescue precious relics.

The travellers recorded numerous instances of Greek neglect and Turkish maltreatment of ancient works – an architrave used in a cowshed here, a sculpted head used for target-practice there – and felt wholly justified in removing whatever they could.

Recording the visits: The first journeys to Greece were, in some cases, extensions of the Grand Tour beyond Italy. Spon, who perhaps always intended to go, made up a party with Wheler and two other English

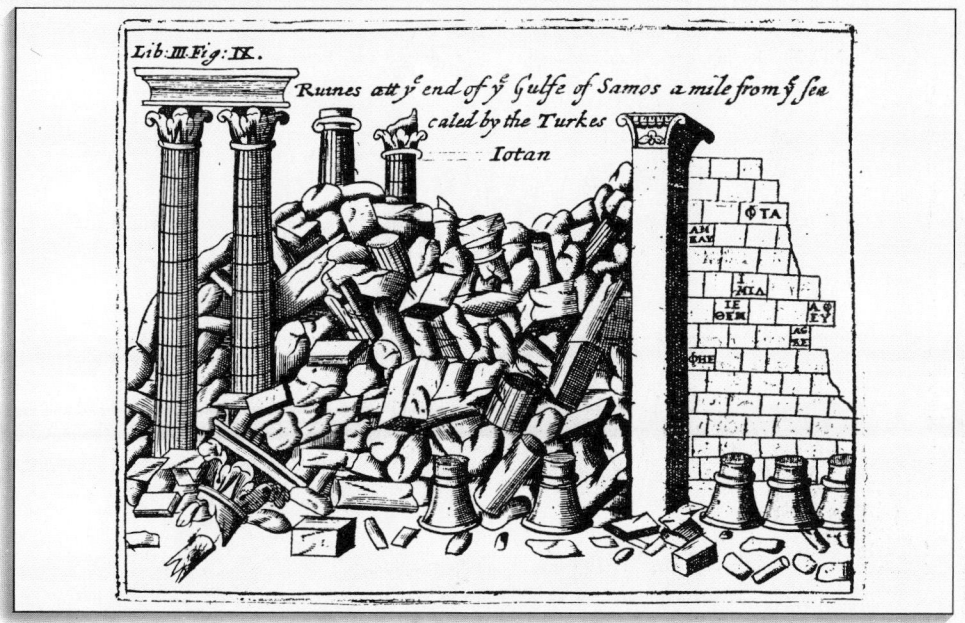

him, to Oxford's new Ashmolean Museum, which already housed the Arundel collection. Spon, for his part, had copied thousands of inscriptions. It is worth remembering that from the start journeys to Greece were undertaken with the intention of bringing things back – information, of course; copies of inscriptions; but also anything readily movable. The reasoning was simple: the Greeks were perceived as degenerate and the

Left, an engraving of a Turk and a Greek from Tournefort's *A Voyage into the Levant*, published in 1718. **Above**, early travellers seeking classical sites often found little more than piles of rubble.

gentlemen when they met in Rome. Wheler had been travelling through France with his Oxford tutor to complete his education. He had money; Spon had the scholarship and enthusiasm. They were an interesting combination at the outset of the tradition. Both professed Protestantism (Spon went into exile for it after his return), but Wheler, although he was the younger of the two, was much more hidebound and hectoring.

Quite simply, he preferred Restoration England to Greece, even to Periclean Athens, as the imagination of a Hellenist might reconstruct it. He was not a very open-minded man. We may recognise his type even today:

the man who travels to confirm his prejudices, and who is profoundly relieved to get home again unchanged.

Spon was the better traveller. True, he was disposed to feel in a certain way; but he was alive and awake on the spot to the places themselves. He was consequential in his passion for Greece. His travels, despite Wheler's assistance, impoverished him. When he went into exile he was penniless. He died in a pauper's hospital.

That first enterprise was a private one, largely undertaken on Wheler's funds. Tournefort in 1700 and the Abbé Fourmont in 1728 were sent and financed by the French Crown. For serious exploration some such

best of the early accounts. He gives the ancient and present state of places, what they produce and pay in taxes, how they are administered, how the people live, where the best harbours are. He exerts himself, climbs a high hill to have a good vantage-point, enquires diligently of the priest and village elders who might be able to inform him. Later accounts constantly refer to Tournefort as an authority and point of orientation.

Cultural expeditions: When the London Society of Dilettanti sent their expedition to Greece in 1764 it was with a more specific, more particularly Hellenist intention. Cultural demands had altered, and the society, founded in 1731 chiefly for convivial pur-

backing became increasingly necessary, and in France and England there were public bodies and a few wealthy private individuals who were willing to provide it. National pride was a factor certainly, but also a sense of social and cultural responsibility, and of *noblesse oblige*. The early exploration of Greece coincided with the opening of the first public museums and galleries. Tournefort, primarily a botanist, was a man of the broadest learning, an excellent traveller, wide-awake, good-humoured, resilient. He took in classical sites *en route* – not incidentally, but as part of a whole interest.

His book *Voyage du Levant* (1717) is the

poses, was by the middle of the century beginning seriously to respond to them. In 1751 they had taken up two energetic individuals, the architects James Stuart and Nicholas Revett, who had made their own way to Athens and were measuring and drawing the monuments there. The society financed the gradual publication of their work – as the *Antiquities of Athens* – and conclusively promoted the Greek style of architecture and furnishings by doing so. In 1764, directed by Robert Wood, they sent a party to Greece and Asia Minor specifically to locate and describe the ancient remains.

Chandler's account of the tour (in two

volumes, 1775 and 1776), may be set along-side Tournefort's as the century's best. Its appeal is rather different, just as the journey it describes was different in character and aims. Chandler knew what he had to look for, and what it was his duty to report. Though his tone is throughout reasonable, unenthusiastic, and his prose style deliberately plain, he was nevertheless writing in the service of a love and admiration of ancient Greece so assured in himself and in the society he represented as to need no special pleading.

By 1764, when Chandler and his party sailed, there was already a tradition of travel in Greece. In his two books he consolidated that tradition. To an extraordinary degree he

Travel practicalities: The tradition of Greek travel literature is a very rich one and this is only a cursory survey of it. Spon and Wheler, Tournefort, Chandler, being very distinctive figures, will have to serve a representative function. Their specifically detailed peregrinations give some sense of the real experience, of the practicalities of travel in Greece, in the years before it became an easy matter.

The starting point was very often Rome. The wish to go farther than Rome increased with the sense that the classical world was in fact more purely represented by Athens. Today this may seem self-evident, but the discovery of Greece, the recovery of Greece from concealment under Rome, took a long

worked as a compiler, editor and generous critic of other travellers and their accounts.

With Chandler's expedition the archaeological exploration of Greece was put on a professional footing. He consolidated the tradition to date, and his publications, together with others under the auspices of the society, established a firm scholarly basis for serious-minded successors in the next century to build on.

Left, in *Antiquities of Athens*, Stuart and Revett meticulously drafted reproductions of classical ruins such as the Pnyx in Athens. **Above**, colossal lion at the foot of Hymettus.

time. The Society of Dilettanti were themselves great movers in the process by which the status of Greece ascended at the cost of Rome. Rome was full of classical works – of noble buildings and, in galleries accessible to respectable travellers, of statuary. Most of the statues were Roman copies of Hellenistic copies of truly classical originals; but this was not known and could not be known, since the originals themselves had not yet been brought to light. When, finally, the Parthenon marbles were seen close up, connoisseurs used to the Apollo Belvedere suffered a severe shock. Travel to Greece, even though great works of art there (since few of the travellers were also excavators) were not often to be seen, was part of the process by which, very slowly, Greece, in the modern culture of western Europe, eventually triumphed over Rome.

In Rome, by the middle of the 18th century, travellers would meet with others who had come from Greece. Winckelmann, who, despite attractive offers, never made the journey himself, was in dealings with men who had been there and in his official capacity as Papal Antiquary he got to see shipments of finds as they arrived from Greece and Asia Minor for restoration and, alas, "completion" before going on to the markets of London and Paris. It was in Rome that Spon and

Wheler made up their party for Greece. A third member, Francis Vernon, had diplomatic contacts and was able to get them all a passage, from Venice, with the Italian ambassador. Such influence was of crucial importance. Spon and Wheler were fortunate in having Nointel's protection, and both travelled under French passports issued by him in Constantinople.

The Ottomans, who ruled Greece, were notoriously difficult to deal with. It happened that in the 1670s Nointel was in high favour with the Porte, and his English counterpart, Sir John Finch, was not. To travel at all, Westerners needed permission, written

permits issued by the sultan himself or by local aghas; but in remoter areas these might be valueless – in parts of the Peloponnese and Asia Minor the word from Constantinople was disregarded and, to make matters more difficult for travellers, local potentates were often in conflict with one another.

Misconceptions: Neither the Turks nor the Greeks had any understanding of what the travellers were about. If the travellers' interests were archaeological, they met with great incomprehension and mistrust. One energetic Turk, seeing a party inspecting the drums of a column, set to pulverising the marble with cannon balls in the belief that gold, at least, must be inside. Stuart and Revett, when they needed to erect ladders and scaffolding, met with objections from Turkish pashas who feared that from that height the Westerners would be able to spy into their harems.

It was also frequently the case that places the travellers wished to explore were of military importance to the Turks. The Acropolis of Athens was a Turkish citadel, the Parthenon was a store for powder and ammunition. It suffered accordingly when Morosini bombarded it. Drawing and measuring, which a traveller would naturally want to do, were extremely suspicious activities in Turkish eyes. Francis Vernon, examining the Theatre of Dionysios under the Acropolis, was fired on, and only escaped through the intervention of Consul Giraud. The Capuchin maps were drawn surreptitiously, which partly explains their inaccuracy, and circulated likewise.

In time the travellers produced their own maps. We know that Chandler in the Troad in 1764 had with him a map, done by a Frenchman, which Wood had with him in 1726. Their reliance on one another, and on the ancient authors, was very great. But how many books could they actually carry with them? Wood tells us that he and his companions took "a library, consisting chiefly of all the Greek historians and poets, some books of antiquities, and the best voyage writers." But they were perhaps unusually well-provided for, since James Dawkins, one of their party, was a very wealthy man. Spon and Wheler received the newly-published *Athènes ancienne et nouvelle* (by Guillet de Saint-Georges) just as they were sailing from Venice. They were able then to check its descriptions on the spot, and found them, in Vernon's phrase "wide from Truth".

A party would hire guides and interpreters and enquire locally, once they had established the area of their interest, whether any ruins were still apparent in it. The same employees would procure them food, and accommodation (often of a very wretched, flea-ridden kind). In many districts the travellers needed more than guides: they needed armed guards. Bocher, travelling alone, was murdered. James Stuart was two or three times set upon and robbed. The roads at the back of Smyrna were infested with bandits, and travellers there did well to join with caravans of merchants who had Janissaries riding with them.

These difficulties should be borne in mind when we evaluate the travellers' achievements. Chandler's party were deterred from climbing Parnassus by the menacing behaviour of some Albanian soldiery camped near them at the spring; they kept clear of Rhamnous because the local Turks there "bore a very bad character."

Other hardships: We should mention the sea's dangers, too. Spon and Wheler, crossing from Constantinople, were tossed to and fro for 37 days. Vernon was taken by pirates and stripped of all he possessed (he escaped with his life only to lose it a few months later in Persia, in a quarrel over a penknife). And had Chandler sailed home in the *Seahorse* as he intended, he and his party would very likely all have been drowned off Sicily when that ship went down.

Sir Giles Eastcourt, the fourth member of Spon's party, died on the road to Delphi near Náfpaktos. Wood's friend James Bouverie died at Magnesia on the Maeander. Plague was endemic still in many areas. It had a high season in the summer months. The Turks, with their fatalistic view of things, allowed it to carry them off in great numbers. The Franks were more circumspect and withdrew into isolation if they could. Chandler and his companions spent three months holed up in a village above Smyrna, the town itself being too dangerous to enter.

A certain piety entered the tradition. Earlier fates were remembered and commemorated. Tournefort got the whole story of

Vernon's death from the English Consul in Isfaham, and recounted it. Chandler searched for and found where Eastcourt and Vernon had scratched their names on the south wall of the Theseion (the names are still there and can still be read).

The journeys were often dangerous and – what with mosquitoes, heat, dirt and wolfish dogs – must almost always have been uncomfortable. Though some of the travellers were born adventurers, for others it was only an interlude, perhaps the only escapade of their lives, and they returned to Oxford common rooms and quiet country living with a few mementos and a fund of stories. They had many high moments to remember.

The "travel experience": Discovery was the essence of early travel in Greece. For those travellers seeking to identify, after a lapse of nearly 2,000 years, a particular site famous in antiquity, the satisfaction when they were successful must have been very great indeed. They weren't excavators; they didn't dig their way through to treasures like the Mask of Agamemnon or Helen's Gold: but, knowing their texts, they brought to such places as Marathon, Mystras or Delphi considerable reverence and a willingness to be moved. They were in a landscape such as they had not seen before. It was not only the botanists among them who were excited by

Left, detail of Skyros embroidery, probably 17th-century. **Right**, urban Cretan costume.

the flowers and shrubs, by their vivid colours and rich scents. Again and again they saw scenes that painters in the 18th and 19th centuries loved to depict: ruins among olive trees, broken columns on a headland against the sun, animals grazing in fields littered with marble. And their interest was not always antiquarian. Guys says rather pointedly of Spon that looking for ancient Greece he found only stones; Guys himself then, as a corrective, looked to the people and their present lives. True, he saw them through a veil of Homer and Theocritus, but perhaps our perceptions are always coloured. The first Western painters in Greece saw the landscape through a haze of Claude Lor-

for example, the gold of Mycenae, the palaces on Crete. Some sites have undergone marvellous resurrections. On Delos, at Delphi, Olympía and in Athens there is now infinitely more to be seen. Chandler discovered Olympía, Spon and Wheler Delphi, but having identified those sites they saw very little. When we see the richness of Delos nowadays we can scarcely believe that by the early 18th century it was thought nothing there merited a visit.

We have more knowledge nowadays, the museums are richer, the sites more extensive. On the other hand, it may not be easy in present-day Greece to get a sense of what early travel was like. Out of season, and out

raine. Our view is harsher now and more historical, but the 18th-century images are still appealing. Indeed, at times, in certain places, they are quite compelling.

Enormous changes, some of them irreparably damaging, have occurred in the experience of travel in Greece. Large areas are going to perdition as rapidly as money will permit. We may look even more to the past, in horror at what is being done in the present. Out of that past things have been brought to light – out of the earth, out of the sea, the like of which the early travellers never saw, though perhaps the poets of their day imagined them. The great bronzes in the National Museum,

of the way, is best: at Dion, for example, under Olympus, or at Gortyn in the centre of Crete (where the road runs through what was the ancient city). And of course when you least expect it there are places where a few yards of old walling, or the remains of old irrigation channels, or ledges and niches in a goatherd's cave, will suddenly bring the whole experience upon you with a rush.

In Turkey, in old Ionia, there are some potent reminders. Ephesus, for example, ends in a marsh. There you may see fallen pillars, broken architraves and beautiful carvings sinking among the bulrushes. The Temple of Artemis, one of the Seven Wonders of the ancient world, lies (what little is left of it) on swampy waste land, on a patch that serves as village green, football pitch, grazing ground and rubbish tip. The precinct falls away into a pond that looks malarial, and there blocks and drums of the temple, swarming with terrapins, emerge and sink according to the season. Selçuk was built out of the ruins of Ephesus. Dressed stones, portions of columns and many ornamented blocks bearing inscriptions were quarried from the public buildings and the temples of Ephesus for the castle walls, and even in the poorest houses, in some wretched slums, you may suddenly spot the glimmer of fractured marble. Your guesthouse in Selçuk might well have a

Pergamum something barbaric has been done, something at least as shocking as the things the early travellers were affronted by. The approach to the Sanctuary of Asclepeius, God of Healing, takes the visitor through barbed wire, past soldiers with submachine-guns. Photography of the famous view from the theatre is now forbidden because that famous view is now, largely, of a military camp. The Sacred Way, which used to link the Sanctuary with the Acropolis, is severed by wire now and blocked by a row of neatly parked tanks.

It is impossible not to feel empathy for those first explorers. Their interest was predominantly Hellenist. In what other spirit

Corinthian capital as a seat in the shade by the door. The Roman aqueduct still steps through the town and anyone so inclined to can copy the inscriptions embedded topsy-turvy in its pillars. Such details are the stuff on which the nostalgic imagination of the early travellers fed.

Téos, among thorns and holm-oaks, entirely deserted, is in that sense a classic site. The fields the peasants plough through are almost choked with shards. Priene on its hill looks across to Miletus over what was the sea, and what is now a dusty plain. And at

Above, Edward Lear's watercolour of Thessaloníki.

would they have gone? True, others were in the country for quite different purposes – commercial, diplomatic, military – but they are not the ones who wrote accounts. The documentation of early travel in Greece is very much coloured by the travellers' perception of that land as supremely important for their own and their national culture. It is doubtful that any traveller can be quite rid of that sense even today. There is something compelling about the old images still. Myths are as necessary as they ever were, and some myths are more productive than others. We all know what the worst ones are: in Greece, still, we can glimpse some of the best.

Imagine that you are a guest in a Greek family house on a Sunday afternoon. You have just finished an immense and leisurely dinner and though your head floats with a pleasantly sleepy *retsína* high, the weight in your stomach keeps you earthbound. Buoyant dinner repartee subsides as appetites are sated, and someone lazily flicks on the television. A low clarinet wails plaintively, and as the picture focuses, you perceive a dozen human forms clasping hands and gravely circling a green hilltop: women shapeless in weighty layers of embroidered frocks with wide bronze belts and men in white skirts and tights and pom-poms on their shoes. "Epirots," your hostess remarks off-handedly. "How do you drink your coffee?"

Our Greek Folk Songs is broadcast every Sunday afternoon on one of the state-run television stations. With the traditional Sunday afternoon dancing now mostly a picturesque memory, the broadcast makes a peculiarly appropriate substitute, but the "Epirotness" which these symbols evoke is oddly tamed. In the 1990s, regional consciousness verges on a sentimental *folklorismós*. It often seems a parlour game of regional trivia shorn of its divisive power: knowing that Kalymnians wrap *dolmádes* in cabbage – not vine – leaves, that potatoes in the "village salad" signal a Cycladic chef, that the novelist Kazantzákis hailed from Crete and the popular singer Kazantzídis, beloved of immigrants and workers, comes from Asia Minor.

But regionalism was in earlier days hardly a matter of songs and salads. Of neighbouring Italy in the early days of its nationhood, D'Azeglio remarked ruefully that "now that Italy had been created, it was necessary to invent the Italians." And was Greece so very different? The travel-writer Patrick Leigh Fermor once described the Greek world as "an inexhaustible Pandora's box of eccentricities," and doubtless an extreme topography has nurtured great variety in a relatively small land. Vlach-speaking shepherds in the Pindos mountains had little contact and little

enough in common with shipbuilders of Chíos or Jewish merchants of Ioánnina. Though not all communities were equally isolated by terrain they tended to be introverted socially. *Ksénos*, the "foreigner-stranger-guest", is in Greece an elastic designation, and brides marrying in from the next village forever remained "strangers" in their husbands' villages.

It was not just the land which came between them: but differences in language, culture, religion, education, class. At the

same time, that Koutsovlach shepherd was typically polyglot, speaking his own Romance language with his kin, Greek with the cheese-merchants, a smattering of Albanian and Slavic with the villagers he encountered on his treks with the sheep, and enough Turkish to outwit the odd Ottoman official. Under the tolerant Ottomans, a plethora of religious and ethnic communities thrived: Greek-speaking Orthodox, Slavic-speaking Orthodox, Romaniot and Sephardic Jews, Turkish farmers, gypsies, Franco-levantine Catholics in the Cyclades, Protestants converted by American missionaries in the Levant, Orthodox and Muslim Albanian

Preceding pages: orange seller, Piraéus; Cretans. Left, soldier on duty in Athens. Right, dolls in national costume can be found in some kiosks.

shepherds, Dönme, Masmin, Sephardic Jews who converted to Islam in the late 17th century, the list goes on. From this multiplicity, the inhabitants of a newly invented, formally secular nation-state of Greece were charged with inventing *themselves* anew.

The cultural homogeneity which undeniably exists today is as much a goal and a consequence as a precondition of this new nationalism. With one eye on the past and the other on the West, official policies of the Greek state have long worked to eradicate – or, at the very least, to trivialise – local variations in language, dialect and custom. Differences which seemed to threaten the integrity of the state – like the speaking of

groups coexist with stereotypes of regions and topographies. In a society fascinated with "appearances" the stereotype of a place becomes part of its reality, and to see the mountains, the plains and the islands as the Greeks do one must set out on the journey across their cultural terrain.

In the mountains: "The picturesque is found any time the ground is uneven." If there is any truth to the wicked verdict of the French critic Roland Barthes, Greece is a paradise of the picturesque. From the scrubby hills of central Greece to the soaring peaks and wide wooded vales of the majestic Pindos mountains, the land seems in continuous undulation, and even from the plains – a relative

Slavic – have been systematically suppressed. More insidious, the traditional refusal of both the state and private investors to develop the provinces economically has inflamed a ruinous pattern of poverty, massive emigration to Athens and abroad, and a frequent sense of cultural inferiority in those who have remained in the backwaters.

Even so, the monolithic vision of the official state, with its images of Pericles and Kolokotrónis, has always been quietly subverted from below. "The people" refuse to imagine themselves a lumpish mass, and remain stubbornly sure of essential differences amongst them. Stereotypes of ethnic

term, so little do they recall the great flats of Nebraska or Hungary – the mountains seldom disappear from view. Romantics who look for the truth in the land often claim that the irregularity of its surfaces has most forcefully shaped "the Greek character".

The settlement of Greeks in mountainous areas has not been stable or continuous and, for many groups, is "traditional" only if we don't look back too far. Of course, some settlements are of a Byzantine or Frankish vintage. And certain tribal groups of transhumant shepherds – Sarakatsanáoi, Karagoúnides, Koutsovláchoi, Arvanítovlachoi – who herd their sheep and goats on mountainsides in summer and move them to the plains in winter, have probably always wandered widely across the Balkan territories. Of these, all except the Sarakatsanáoi built permanent mountain villages where women, elders and young children kept home fires burning when the men descended each winter with the sheep. However, other sedentary mountain villages found their *raison d'être* in conditions of Ottoman life.

In island and coastal regions, many towns were (and many still are) situated not at the portside but high on the crest of the mountain, even – indeed, preferably – hidden from view altogether. This town plan was a response to the threat of pirates. In the late 16th all sides: from their Turkish landlord anxious for profits from maize and wheat sold to the west, from local bands of brigands who periodically helped themselves to the peasants' crops and livestock, from unruly Janissaries – the sultan's professional army extorting tributes for their "protection". By the 17th century, vast stretches of countryside began emptying, as peasants fled to the cities and upwards to the mountains.

Mountain settlements multiplied, interspersed among already established villages whose inhabitants made a living (sometimes a handsome living) not only by farming and shepherding, but as itinerant stone-masons and charcoal-burners, as wandering mer-

century when the Ottoman state began its long decline the time-honoured random piracy of the Aegean became systematic.

Pirates did not venture far inland, though, and in the first 100 years of Ottoman rule, when peasants enjoyed a level of justice and prosperity far above that of their counterparts in feudal serfdom in Europe, inaccessible mountain tops held fewer attractions. But as the centralised system – and the safeguards it had ensured – began to break down, Christian and Muslim peasants became increasingly vulnerable to exploitation from chants and muleteers and mountain guides to Turks and travellers, and as artisans and immigrant labourers to richer regions of the empire. Still required to pay the annual tithe to the sultan, newly settled peasants terraced the rocky mountainsides, wresting a meagre living from their flocks and gardens and small fruit orchards. Still vulnerable to extortion by brigand and Ottoman official alike, the community drew inward, socially and physically. In this setting developed the ethic and organisation of village life which has come to be regarded – by foreigners, but by Greeks, too – as classically Greek.

The "traditional" mountain village: Every

Left, Cretan shepherd. **Above**, two sisters.

Easter, Athens spits out its millions towards numberless villages, only to swallow them up again two weeks later, laden with baskets of olive oil, cheese, homemade bread. Every Athenian, every Thessalonikan speaks reverently of "his or her" village, usually, of course, a mountain village. The mountain village is never merely real but partakes of the archetype, the village poor in all but rocks. Ah, but so beautiful…

The mountain village typically comprises a cluster of houses, often with adjoining walls, circling a central church and a square. This physical arrangement reveals a moral geography, for the boundary between the "civilised" human space and an unsanctified

fragile. Tenuously bound by ties of religion and local patriotism, these families competed for scarce resources: for land, water, pasturage, and for that most ephemeral substance: honour.

Anthropologists, who have tended to study small villages, have conventionally identified "honour" and "shame" as key moral values in Greece. According to this moral code, a family could rarely be considered to have honour if its women were seen to be immodest. Since Orthodox teachings and native thought both agreed that woman was by nature sensual and seductive, social chaos was avoided by strictly segregating unrelated men and women, and defining various tasks

wilderness teeming with human and supernatural dangers is marked by a ring of tiny churches and shrines. United by Orthodoxy and a common way of life, villagers were nonetheless divided into separate households. The family, rather than the individual, was – and is – the central unit of Greek society, enormously interdependent economically, socially and emotionally, and whatever the harmony or tumult within its four walls, to the outside the "house" stood, and stands, united. Indeed, the unconditional loyalty to the family and the demand that each member must help further its collective interests made friendships outside the house inevitably

as "male" or "female". Segregation relaxed only during feast days and weddings.

Recent work suggests that the image of meek womenfolk in household purdah and domineering but protective men is both outdated and overly simplistic. Moreover, what acting "honourably" means varies from one Greek community to the next, and whether one is rich or poor, male or female. Today, to be *filótimos*, to "love honour", can mean something as vague as acting as a "good" person should, though this presupposes no small knowledge of what the community considers good. It differs from the Protestant idea of "conscience" in one crucial way: one must be *seen* to act honourably, for it is a judgement which only others – almost begrudgingly – bestow. In such conditions, reputation becomes all-important.

A Sarakatsanáoi feast: From the grounds of the monastery, thick with cherry and chestnut, to the encampment of Sarakatsanáoi it is less than an hour's walk. Yet the land itself never hints at any human presence in this high landscape, and it was on the barest trace of a path that we threaded our way along a mountainside choked with trees and brush one afternoon in August. Only Tassoúla, the daughter of a family which ran a restaurant for the visitors, could read its signs. She was engaged to a Sarakatsanáoi policeman who

yelping, and a laughing woman in a kerchief invited our little band of four to the campsite.

We stayed the afternoon, squeezed together all eight of us on a cot of branches, thick with woven blankets and sheep skin *flokátis*, fed on stodgy and slightly sweet cheese-pies warm from the oven, talking with the women and the young girls. Eléni, 15, was on holiday from secondary school in Lárissa, on the plains where she lived in the winter months with relations who had already left the difficult shepherding life. She loved the sheep and the mountains, she confessed, but she wanted to be a secretary.

Because it was a feast day – the Assumption of the Virgin Mary – the three Marias in

had taken her once to show her off to the distant kin camped in these mountains, and she plainly found them both quaint and exotic. "Sarakatsanáoi women," she insisted as we wended our way through the shadows, "they know nothing about sex. When they have their babies, they are still virgins!"

When we finally emerged from the canopy of trees, we could see a flat and treeless plateau, and upon it three huts constructed on branches, a mud-oven and a cooking fire. Tassoúla shouted a greeting, which set a dog

Gypsies, Greece's migrant farmers, stop for a midday picnic (left) and for the camera (above).

this encampment of 19 souls were celebrating, and by late afternoon, the central ground between the thatch houses filled with grimy children and many new adults. The old man, Eléni's grandfather, entered with a sheep's cape around his shoulder and a long carved shepherd's crook.

Three youths soon followed, dusty and smelling of sheep and Turkish tobacco. We discovered then the bittersweet twist to the celebration, for these three cousins were soon to be inducted into their army service. Amidst much giggling, the central ground became a dance floor, but as we had no music, we sang. The youths wrapped their arms across each other's shoulders, and in voices deepened with exaggerated bravado, started the simple tune, "I'll become a swallow, and fly to Arabia..."

The myth of the mountain man: The mythology of the mountains is emphatically masculine. Greeks are inclined to see in the mountain man an embodiment of alpine virtue. In his "craggy" face they discern a "harsh" pride, a "rugged" individualism, a moral "purity" as pristine as the mountain springs. For the ferocious clans of the Máni and Crete which always kept the Turks at bay, and the Souliot women who danced into the abyss rather than submit to the finally victorious Turks, they reserve their highest praise. In

honour and daring, and insist that their way of life upholds a Greek ideal degraded by morally slack, soft-palmed Athenian bureaucrats. And in the 1940s, during the German occupation, resistance fighters lived like *klephtic* heroes, in small wandering bands and attacked from the mountains. The great rebel leaders, the *kapetánoi,* absorbed that heroic aura and held control of a newly democratised, mountainous "Free Greece" long after the Germans were ousted. To many, the *kapetánoi* resuscitated a dream of a Greece liberated from foreign domination – not Turks this time, but Germans and British and Americans. The image lives, and the dream won't quite die.

the figure of the *klepht* they celebrate a more pugnacious heroism. Scholars protest that the *klepht* ("thief") was seldom more than a self-serving outlaw, preying on landlord and peasant alike, building a local empire in the time-honoured Balkan style, coercing the weak and awarding the spoils to his own minions. But in the national mythology, the *kléphts* became symbols of resistance to the "hated Turkish oppressor". If the myth glorifies a selfless *klephtic* patriotism, the Greeks do not fail to relish the cunning which turned patriotism to personal advantage.

On the slopes of Crete's Mount Ida shepherds steal each other's sheep to prove their

Of Vlachs and empty mountains: There is an underside to the myth of mountain man. The word *vláchos* – both the ethnic label of many of Greece's transhumant shepherds, and the simple occupational term for "shepherd" – holds a hint of scorn. It is the Greek equivalent of the term "hill-billy" and draws on the same imagery. Moreover, *vláchos* sounds almost like *vlákos*, "idiot", and though Greek ears keenly distinguish *chi* from *káppa,* the phonic resemblance is gleefully savoured. *Vlachs* – the lot of them – are the butt of countless jokes, which portray them as brawny but dull and silent.

This underside reveals less about ethnic

slurs than about a vaguely guilty disdain for a whole way of life. As people have gradually abandoned the mountains for Athens and Chicago and Vancouver, they have learned to reject that life, even to see that once "heroic" shepherd as uncouth, unlettered, slightly ridiculous.

On the lower slopes, some villages survive by combining small-scale shepherding and livestock raising with the growing of high-quality tobacco and cereals, and by cultivating orchards which thrive in the cooler climate: peaches, apples, pears, cherries, walnuts and chestnuts. If they happen to be beautiful – like old stone-built villages – and not too hard to find, they might attract tourists, and then sweaters and weavings and souvenir hand-carved shepherds' crooks may bring in needed income. All too many villages are hardly more than "old people's homes," with too few children to support a school (to say nothing of a doctor), where the only weddings are those of the children of urban migrants returning for a "traditional" celebration in their parents' beloved village, and where gypsy musicians complain that celebrations have become "cold" things. At the funerals – far outnumbering weddings – old women lament not only their dead kin but the empty houses of this high place, "forgotten by God".

On the plains: The plains – the *kámboi,* as Greeks call them – hold no hallowed place in the national mythology. Marshy and malarial, muggy in summer and muddy in winter, they have seldom inspired the poets, who find few metaphors in their flatness. So, absent among the rocks and mountains and sea and sun of tourist board posters, we are almost surprised that plains exist here. Redeemed at times by the curiosities of human architecture (the abundance of windmills on Crete's Lassíthi Plain) or by the surprise of mountains (Mount Parnassós rising from the Boeotian plains) the *kámboi* arouse our respectful interest, not our passions.

Yet the plains – flat, rolling, and if we stretch the term, sloping patches of plateau – have been among the most coveted of spaces in Greece. Certainly the Ottomans recognised their value. As their empire expanded in the 15th century, they awarded a parcel

(*timar*) of this most fertile of Greek land to each loyal warrior (*spahi*). In return for defending and managing (not owning) this land (since all land belonged to Allah, and was overseen by his earthly representative, the sultan), he was allowed to collect a set tithe from Muslim and Christian peasants who retained firm rights to cultivate it. It was a system designed to prevent a strong landed aristocracy (of the sort which wrought havoc in a deteriorating Byzantium) and as long as it worked, the peasants fared reasonably well. As it began to break down in the face of pressures from the West as well as from within the empire, peasants suffered.

Poorer peasants: From the l6th century on-

ward, the *timar* system gradually gave way to that of the infinitely more oppressive *chiflik*. The Ottomans had initially introduced the *chiflik* (a large tract of land under hereditary ownership) as a way of putting previously unused land under cultivation, but this relatively minor form of landholding gradually became dominant, coming to include former *timar* lands and expanding to the fertile plains areas of the Peloponnese, Thessaly, Macedonia and Thrace. These *chiflikia*, never recognised as legal by the Ottoman state, enriched the landlord but made the share-cropping peasant poorer and less secure, sometimes ending a harvest sea-

Left, today's youth, torn between tradition and modernity. **Right**, tradition on parade.

son with barely a third of what he and his family had produced.

Those who did not escape endured poverty and upheaval. Many such peasants joined in the early 19th-century independence struggles in the hope of acquiring a bit of the ousted Turks' lands. As it happened, some land fell into the hands of equally powerful Greek landlords, while other properties reverted to the state. Many families acquired small pieces by becoming squatters. In 1905 and 1910, the government's failure to redistribute *chiflikia* of the rich Thessalian plains, annexed to Greece in 1871, resulted in peasant revolts, bloodily repressed. Anxious to stave off a serious social revolution,

making a living on the plains has always been farming. Despite the richness of much of this land, most farmers have remained poor, especially in relation to their European counterparts. This is less a consequence of peasant fatalism, familism, and superstition than of a complex combination of factors, including historical patterns of land ownership, Greek state policies, patterns of economic interdependence between Greece and the West, and various commercial priorities and practices over which the farmer has had absolutely no control.

A chronic problem of Greek agriculture has always been too many farmers for the land to support. Small plots and inefficient

Venizélos in 1909 launched a programme of radical reform, including land reform; but this faltered in mid-course when Greece became embroiled in the Balkan Wars. The 1923 exchange of populations between Greece and Turkey in the aftermath of the Asia Minor catastrophe forced the government's hand, and thousands of the 1.5 million Greek speaking refugees were resettled in Macedonia and Thrace, on *chiflikia* and in houses and villages abandoned by the Turks. Major land reform was completed only when Metaxas, a bizarrely populist-fascist dictator, came to power in the 1930s.

A continuity of uncertainty: The major way of

farming methods made life on the land quite marginal, yet few alternatives outside of emigration to America existed in the 19th and early 20th century.

Historical conditions have also quite literally shaped agricultural lands. Large farmsteads are rare; rather, farmers have traditionally clustered their houses in a village and walked out daily (and today, ride out on donkeys or tractors) to scattered fields. Inheritance practices, though varying somewhat among localities, have generally ensured that a father's fields, and those his wife had brought as part of her dowry, would be divided equally among all his children, with daughters awarded their portion – or its equivalent in livestock, a house, or cash – as a dowry at marriage. Since fields varied in fertility, protection from wind and access to water, it has not been uncommon for even small parcels to be subdivided, and then re-subdivided, with each generation.

The system is not as mad as we might think. It is surprising to learn, accustomed as we are to thinking that only massive fields and mono-cropping make sense, that a handful of tiny plots, growing varied produce, may provide the farmer with real stability in areas where rain is unpredictable and soil fertility marginal. "A little bit of everything" can be better than a big crop that fails.

citrus groves to Naoússa's peach orchards and Thessaly's fields of cotton, estate owners search for extra hands at harvest time. Along with impoverished tourists and local day-labourers, gypsies figure importantly in this migrant labour force. Though wages are often low, such seasonal work allows them to preserve their independence. While their Romany-speaking compatriots (perhaps 100,000 or more live in Greece) survive as musicians or pedlars, these gypsies move across the land with the harvests, setting up roadside encampments of trucks and tents.

Like peasants everywhere, Greek farmers were – and are – vulnerable to all manner of disaster: drought and pestilence, crop fail-

Yet the land's progressive fragmentation has sometimes reached ludicrous proportions. Tales abound of single trees – an olive tree, say, or walnut tree – in which 15 households of second and third cousins own shares. Such a tree often goes unharvested: trying to gather all 15 representatives (some of whom have moved to Athens, others to Australia) to harvest together is a logistical nightmare.

The large agricultural estate – whether an Ottoman legacy or a more recent conglomeration – can be found, too. From Nauplion's

ures, fluctuations in the price of agricultural produce internationally and locally, the whims of changing governments. Indebtedness – to the grocer, as to the state-controlled Agricultural Bank (established in 1929) which they approach for loans – has been the rule. Farmers once dependent on the *chiflik* owner have become dependent on the state.

Indeed, one of the basic themes in farming life is the confrontation between the farmer and the state bureaucracy. Traditionally, the only place more crowded than the land was the civil service. When the state apparatus was being developed after 1830, politicians and lawyers with "pull" handed out endless

<u>Left</u> and <u>right</u>, Greek salads mix *féta*, olives and lots of the local baker's bread for dunking.

minor clerkships to constituents fleeing rural poverty. (By 1880, Greece had seven times as many civil servants per 10,000 as Britain.) Thus was created a bloated bureaucracy of barely literate peasants, mostly from the then-politically dominant Peloponnese. Even today, if you talk to plains farmers from the north (and since most such farmland is in Thessaly, Thrace and Macedonia their attitudes reveal a double antagonism: north versus south, farmer versus functionary), they are scornful of southerners who – until recently – seemed to occupy with all the self-importance they could muster the bulk of the clean and comfortable civil posts: as doctors, teachers, lawyers, policemen. Northerners

the piles of paper. Moreover, unless the farmer had some moral claim on him – as a relative, godparent or co-villager – the bored civil servant offered him only the most perfunctory assistance. Understandably daunted by this state of affairs, farmers turned to those they considered to have the clout (*méson*) to intervene at higher levels and push through their modest requests. The local politician, the ambitious lawyer, the doctor with connections, helped the less powerful, obliging them to return the favour (their votes or their custom) afterwards. Born of such conditions, patronage became endemic. Providing individualistic solutions to systemic problems (and obstructing the requests

are fond of saying that the poor but powerful southerners are parasitical on the north's wealth. "The civil service is a big cow," they explain, "and we Macedonians, we are the grass she eats and eats. When she is finished, the politicians milk her dry, and she is so happy, she drops a great load of dung on us!"

To farmers, the impersonal bureaucracy was just as arbitrary as any Ottoman official and infinitely less responsive. Its hierarchical character has meant that petty clerks refused to process even the most routine applications without the immediate superior's approval; while he, in turn, checked with *his* superior, and as requests climbed, so did

of the "uncooperative"), patronage thwarted collective action among farmers, at the same time as it ensured that they remained politically and socially docile. Yet resentment to the system grew as well, and it was in no small part PASOK's pledge to make war on *rousféti*, "string-pulling", that landed its election victory in 1981.

A Macedonian "coffee-bar-disco": In southern Macedonia, in the melodious-sounding region of Roumlouki, a refugee village of 800 sits on the crevice joining mountain to plain. Looking backwards, westwards, that is, you see only green mountain rising. Looking eastward – as all the houses do – to the sea, invisible yet present, you see an endless, hazy flatness. Once a *chiflik*, cultivated with tobacco, it is now covered with peach orchards and fields of wheat.

The village is described by one travel guide as "insignificant" – presumably it cannot compete with the spectacular ancient ruins found nearby. And although it is in summer deluged by busloads of tourists, in winter it supports only one young archaeologist and one bored archaeological guard. Oblivious to its fame the village carries on in its quite ordinary way. Like many in the area, it is ethnically mixed: half "indigenous Macedonians", wiry and taciturn with an accent both thick and abrupt; and half

their strange language "Turks." Though their children study and court and sometimes marry each other, those beyond middle-age stick mostly with their "own people," eyeing each other warily from across the coffee-house.

Amalía, namesake of Greece's first Bavarian queen, is 15, chubby, and wants to be an actress, and she is the only girl in the "Paradise," a bleak, chilly coffee-bar in the upstairs of a two-storey concrete cavern. She chatters gaily while her 17-year-old brother, Ioánnis, on whom she dotes, and who is now "chaperoning" her, slouches gloomily at the next table. Since it is winter, the young men aren't sitting on top of tractors or ladders wedged into peach trees, spraying fertilizer

"Póndoi", refugees from the Black Sea. Póndoi are a remarkable people: literate, progressive, solidaristic, they still write plays and TV serials in their distinctive dialect, while their rhythmically subtle, exhilarating dances are popular in the northern countryside. Yet they, along with the Chiots, remain the scapegoats of Greek national humour.

The village's Macedonians, though poorer, consider their indigenous status – *dópyi*, "of this place" – a source of irrefutable moral superiority, and view these interlopers with

Left, a happy farmer during harvest. **Above**, workers break for a mid-morning snack.

and pesticide: Instead they're sitting here, not playing cards, not arguing politics (like their fathers), just sitting, smoking, waiting for something to happen.

Amalía's mother, Stavroúla, grew up here, a child of Póndian refugees, but her father, Yiórgos, was born of refugee parents hailing from Bursa, who were resettled in 1923 in a village near Véria. Yiórgos's father was a cloth merchant before the 1912 catastrophe, and could never accustom himself to the farming life. Yiórgos, on the other hand, loved to make things grow, but with the devastations of the wars and the uncertainties of farming, he decided to leave the land in 1953, to work in a German plastics factory. When he came back in 1963, he married, and opened a small café in Véria. But, nostalgic for the "clean air" of the countryside, he made frequent visits to his wife's village, planting peach trees on land she'd inherited from her father, until he decided, in 1982, that they should move there permanently. They opened a small grill on the road at the bottom of town, which a stalwart but always exhausted Stavroúla manages. They began to build a "villa" on the plain. Still in mid-construction, it is a huge damp concrete mansion with marble floors and no toilet.

If it weren't for the "Paradise", Amalía would be miserable. The girls her age never her to marry a farmer; a bank teller would be nice, or some decent fellow with his own shop. Like the one with the record store who makes the pirated tape copies for the "Paradise Disco" where teenagers from the surrounding villages gather to primly sip beer and whisky, and smoke and watch each other. There, strobes throbbing, Madonna crooning in her little-girl voice, you'd never know you were on the edge of a Roumlouki plain, until the music shifts. An electric piano thumps out a fast 5/8 rhythm, and teenage stars of the local folk dance troupe, showing off the fancy improvisations they've been learning, lead a long line of pressed bodies through the taut, tiny movements of *tik*.

go there – their fathers are too strict, or they're cramming for university entrance exams, so they can escape this place – which just proves her theory that people here are "bad", that they have nothing to do but gossip! Sometimes, Amalía visits her aunt, whose house in the long empty spaces of winter is a gathering place for neighbourhood women, and one of them always reads the residue in her coffee-cup, for a laugh, telling her who she'll marry, while Amalía protests she's not interested in marriage.

She won't have to stay here forever. Her parents have already built her a flat in Véria – her "dowry" house. They don't really want

The changing face of the plains: On a drive through the towns and farming villages of the plains, one is struck by the amount of new house construction and farm machinery. Postwar economic aid helped rebuild the countryside. But the noticeable bourgeoisification of the wealthier farming villages has also depended on the surplus of farmers emigrating to Germany and Australia in the 1950s and 1960s, or to the oil rigs of Saudi Arabia in the 1970s. The village prospered from the money sent back to their families; at the same time, relatives and neighbours could rent or sharecrop the fields left behind.

It is one of modernisation's contradictions

that mechanised farming has frequently marginalised women, whose farming skills and labour are rendered obsolete. While women have by no means left the land completely, many find themselves imprisoned in a domesticity their mothers never knew. They remember the drudgery of farming in the pre-tractor era with little fondness, yet the oft heard remark that such a housewife "just sits" reminds them of their economic dependency on their husbands. It also betokens a loss of status and power, for men are sceptical when "the little housewives" (*nikokyroúles*) start talking *feminisimós*. "It's men who are oppressed," they protest. "We work so you can eat."

limited work opportunities that parents want an urban bridegroom for their daughter, and a professional job for their son. Here, women with no special skills may find jobs in light industry cutting or stitching in garment workshops, or stuffing sliced pears into cans. In a gesture which promotes – not just anticipates – this move, the "dowry" flat is now likely to be bought or built in Athens or Thessaloniki, or in one of the larger plains towns, like Sérres, Kateríni, Trípolis.

Some farming villages look more affluent, and some farmers are no doubt wealthier than before. Yet farming life is still perceived as dirty, exhausting and unpredictable, and the horizons of village life limited

High inflation and rising material aspirations mean that most families want the woman to bring in wages, but opportunities in farming villages are limited. A woman might earn a little extra by contracting with large garment companies to do piecework at her own sewing machine, a practice which alleviates the problem of finding childcare but denies her a secure income and most social security benefits. Other women work in family shops or small enterprises.

It is partly in response to the village's

by few jobs and a dearth of entertainment and cultural life. The farmers' children tend to marry out, and the migratory current still flows towards the cities. It remains to be seen whether decentralisation schemes – bringing small hospitals, day-care centres, adult education and greater administrative autonomy to the countryside – and the increasingly unlivable conditions of Athens, can turn the stream.

In the islands: When the foreigners began to descend on the islands, first in dribbles and then in droves, it was perhaps their worship of the sea which first amazed the island inhabitants. But tourists, who appear in the

Left, tobacco, grown in the northern plains, is prepared for drying. **Above**, tobacco leaves.

summertime, are to the sea only fair-weather friends, lured by its tranquil visage, azure and clear and benign. They lie dreamily on the sands, courting the sun for a golden-brown colour eschewed not so many years ago by the island aristocrats as the mark of a common labourer, in a state of public undress unimaginable to the sartorially puritanical natives.

If the tourist regards the island as a temporary escape and the sea as soothing and benevolent, the perspective of those who live, and who have lived for generations, on the islands, is rather different. In the early days of tourism, islanders seldom knew how to swim, and children who ventured too far

ritorial waters are born of the meeting of sea and mountain, for the isles are merely the crests of now submerged mountain ranges. About one-tenth of these are inhabited, some by only a few monks and goats. It is tempting to stretch the comparison, for the individuality of each island in its architecture, costume and dialect is striking, and would seem to suggest an isolation reminiscent of high mountain villages. Yet this individuality is not a simple matter of remoteness. On the contrary, there has always been frequent and intense contact among clusters of islands, and within each island group – the central Cyclades, the eastern Dodecanése, the northerly Sporades and the Ionian islands of the

into the waters were regularly snatched by shrieking mothers who had no reason to romanticise the sea. To them, the sea was no less treacherous for its beauty. "There are three things to fear in the world," goes an old proverb, "fire, woman, and the sea." Death by the sea is both a memory and an expectation to those who live, winter as in summer, at its edge. They know the winter squalls, the convulsions of rain and wind that erupt without warning and toss fishing *caïques* like so many toy boats in a bathtub. The sea gives life with its fish and its sponges, but also takes it back.

Geologically, the 1,425 isles in Greek ter-

western coast – songs are traded, wives are sometimes sought, house styles remain familiar. Rather, embedded in the houses and faces and words of each island is its own particular history of labour, ecology and foreign domination.

The pre-modern economy of sea-piracy and plunder, shipbuilding and manning vast merchant fleets, sponge-diving and trade made the islands until this century among the richest and most coveted territories in the Mediterranean world. The Ottomans held a much more tenuous and intermittent grip on the islands than on the mainland. European principalities, from the Hospitaler Knights of St John to the Venetians, the Genoese, the French and the British, sought through political control and trading privileges to exploit the strategic position and trade of particular islands.

Alhough the object of the European principalities was to extract wealth which passed as merchandise through the islands, some wealth stayed on the islands, concentrated in the hands of an indigenous elite. This local elite owned land (as in the Ionian Islands) or ships and shipyards, on islands spread from Hydra to Chíos and often cooperated with the Europeans on mutually profitable terms. At the turn of the century, many islands had a clear class hierarchy.

Tinos, between the islanders and a powerful monastery.

In many ways, the distinctiveness of each island is a legacy which is not always easily understood. The island economies of the present, for all except those blessed with fertile land and plenty of water, depend largely on the remittances of island migrants (and their pensions when they return home to retire) and on the development of tourism. The elegant mansions which rise along the hill encircling the Sími harbour bear mute witness to the incredible wealth of the sea traders and shipbuilders, and the renowned sponge-divers, but they are empty now, mausoleums, mute testimonies to a way of

On islands blessed with good soil and adequate water resources, some inhabitants lived then, as today, as farmers, and farmed very much as their compatriots did on the mainland. Grapes, melons, figs, tomatoes, oranges and lemons thrive in the arid summer heat of many islands, and beans and onions can be coaxed to grow as well. On luxuriant Corfu (Kérkyra), tenant farmers laboured on the estates of local aristocrats in a system not so different from Turkish *chiflikia*, while in the pre-independence Cyclades, the rocky hills were shared, as on

Left, octopus being cleaned and, **above**, drying.

life which collapsed when upstaged by a steamship economy. The wealthy pulled out their money and moved – to Athens, to Tarpon Springs, Florida, to Argentina. On the skeleton of this affluence a new prosperity is being built. For it is the stark and lovely grandeur of these abandoned houses and harbours which tourist agencies translate as "picturesque" and which draws the concrete-weary foreigners.

A Kalymnian close-up: If you happened to be on Kalymnos in November 1984, you would have seen the twisted wreck of a motor-scooter and a tractor, entwined in a grotesque metallic embrace, standing like a civic sculpture of some patriotic local hero on the central quay. The authorities put it there as an example, the crumpled outcome of yet another act of suicidal swagger. The death of two men and the crippling of a third resulted, or so a shocked and grieving town whispered to each other, when the severely short-sighted (and un-bespectacled) young driver of the motor-scooter decided on a very fast late-night ride. With his friend riding postilion he roared up a dark road in a braggadocio of speed and crashed headlong into a tractor coming from the other direction. It was a tragedy – but all too typical, for the rate of motorcycle deaths, of riders, passengers and unwary pedestrians, is horrifyingly high on

now, but there are other ways that Kalymnians show their *andrismós*, Greek "machismo." Becoming summer *kamákia* (see pages 110–112) is popular among the less imaginative, but this is not unique to Kalymnos and, anyway, tourism is not well developed here. Others show prowess with more dangerous feats. Throwing dynamite off the mountain tops announces, and honours, the Kalymnian who perishes tragically at sea; it is also thought the only seemly tribute to the old sponge-diver who disembarks the Athens steamer in a coffin. It is also thrown on a dare. Very much in the tradition of noise-makers everywhere in Greece, the crack of dynamite marks the beginning of Easter.

Kalymnos. Driving a motorcycle very fast is just a new manifestation of a very old code of male bravado.

The Kalymnians like to think of themselves as wild and fearless, rather like their own harsh mountains, and they scorn the soft life of the farmers of verdant Kos, who they sneeringly dub *kótes* (hens). But the tradition of swagger is almost certainly derived from the sponge-divers, who pushed themselves relentlessly in quest of wages and prestige, and profits for their captains, and who daily faced death (in the form of the "bends") in the deep waters.

The sponge industry is much diminished

Fewer men dive for sponges now, though many sign on with the merchant fleets for a few years in the island male's rite of passage, drinking and whoring and spending lavishly in the raucous pattern of sailor life, until they decide it is time to come home and get married. From the 1950s onwards, hundreds of men also left for periods of five to 25 years abroad, building highway bridges from Ohio to Florida or sweating in the factories, of Darwin, Australia, a city so full of Kalymnians the Australian-Greek taxi-drivers simply call it "Kalymnos". Sometimes these men married a Kalymnian bride and returned abroad with her to raise a family (re-emigrating to Kalymnos again a generation later). Just as often, though, men emigrated alone, or with a group of cousins and compatriots, leaving the daily management of the island to the women, as their fathers and grandfathers had done before.

The myth of the island woman: In the mythology of the land, the mountain man finds his apogee in the island woman. Mainland Greeks contrast their own heroic traditions of the "masculine" mountains with the "femininity" of the islanders. Island dances are soft and undulating, like the sea, and very quick, they insist, while theirs are upright, rigid and proud, like warriors dancing on mountain peaks. (They forget the low, quick, sweeping

cities of Smyrna and Constantinople. This style uses an ensemble of stringed instruments: a dolorous, hauntingly human-voiced violin; a *santoúri* – hammer dulcimer of the Orient – whose resonating strings create a waterfall of sound; and the long necked and deep throated voice of the Turkish *ud* (in Greek, the *úti*), or its smaller substitute, the strummed *laúto*. (The reedy island bagpipe, the *tsambúna*, goes unmentioned.)

Island songs, with an almost courtly and Venetian chivalry, celebrate love, courtship, beauty: from the Cretan verse-romance *erotókritos* whose verses still tunefully resound throughout the Aegean, to the improvised teasing couplets, the *pismatiká*,

zonarádhiko of the Thracian hills.)

The music, too, is "sweet." In this, they have given a sexual nuance to what is probably more accurately the difference between a refined urban sound and a raucous, rustic style. Never mind that the ubiquitous synthesiser has infiltrated the *nisiótika* of popular cassettes – it cannot destroy the lightness of that most popular and familiar genre of island music, a music developed in a network of wealthy Aegean port cities, including the sophisticated Greek-dominated Asia Minor

of the Cyclades and Dodecanése islands.

The "femininity" which mainlanders attribute to the islands is no doubt intertwined with their suspicion that women actually run things there. And indeed, the seasonal exodus of men as they followed the ships, the fish, the sponges or the factory job in Mannheim or Melbourne, has given many an island a strikingly female character. If tourism has enabled many men to return, the "feminine" quality is still perceptible in the way women dominate neighbourhood spaces. "A man is a visitor in his own house," Greeks say, and islanders with even more reason, as men are shooed out of the house every morn-

Left, transporting fish between the islands. **Above**, evidence of the angry sea, Ionian Islands.

ing so women can get on with their chores. Mainlanders slyly insinuate that island women not only dominate their men, but cuckold them. After all, they speculate, how do they manage while their husbands are away for months and years at sea? Tales of bored housewives and exhausted island-bound lovers proliferate even on the islands, although their veracity remains, of course, quite unverifiable.

Yet on some islands, the family of an unmarried girl guards her reputation against slander ("Better your eye come out than your name," the proverb warns) with a vehemence rarely found these days on the mainland. On Kalymnos, for instance, co-educa-

marital liaison of a lusty yet commendably fastidious housewife.

This last word translates badly. *Nikokyrá* (house-mistress), though an entirely ordinary title, holds no slur, and all the more so in the Aegean, for here, houses belong to women. If mainland brides used to move in with their mothers-in-law on many Aegean islands, the mother still gives her house to her oldest daughter when she marries, moving herself (and her husband) to smaller quarters: a tiny flat in the basement, a shed on the edge of the property, a rented room nearby. Second and third daughters, who once could expect little in the way of dowry, now almost always get a house as well.

tion in secondary schools was long resisted; it is only a few years since island teenagers first began to attend classes together, and some parents are sceptical that the camaraderie of these mixed student *parées* can really be innocent.

Consequently, an explicit moral and religious conservatism accommodates a tradition of feisty women with most peculiar results: the same community which, pleading local "custom," petitions the bishop to negotiate a Kalymnian exemption from Greek law, giving them permission to marry daughters off at 14 before they lose their hallowed chastity, amiably tolerates the 25-year extra-

Today, now married, that island daughter probably shares a room or two of this house with strangers. Like innumerable island houses, hers features a scrawled sign: "ROOMS. CHAMBRES. RAUME" and, summer after summer, countless blonde and sleek foreigners skip down her stairs on the way to the beach and struggle back up after a bout in the disco. They may pass in the hallway, but in many ways their worlds remain separate. She sells postcards in the family tourist shop, while her husband works in the construction crew of a new hotel. She watches *Dallas* as she crochets another doilie for her daughter's trousseau. She worries about her son becoming a *kamáki* and about her daughter passing her university examinations. "Tourism is good. It brings money," she hears everyone say – and she says it, too, but sometimes she wonders.

In the city: Viewed from the heights of Pendéli, which flanks the city to the east, Athens resembles – as the novelist John Fowles put it – a mass of dice scattered across the Attica plain. Block after block of more or less identical six-storey cement "multiple dwellings" (as they are known in Greek) do not make it the most beautiful urban centre in Europe. Moreover, the rapidity with which the city was thrown up effectively postponed questions of urban plan-

nonetheless scored for trying to make Athens more livable.

Of course, none of this ever stopped people from both visiting and enjoying the Greek capital. Beneath its horrific architectural visage Athens conceals a palpably human heart. Nowhere better than here does the ancient formulation "Man is the measure of all things" ring true. More than just a heart, Athens has soul and some districts, such as Athinás Street around the meat market or Plaka on a hot night, are downright funky.

What makes Athens attractive are its temperamental inhabitants. Clicking their worrybeads, making funny gestures with their hands, by turns provocatively rude or unex-

ning, zoning, and the siting of local parks to some later date. With over 4 million people living in the greater Athens area, Athens is today a concrete matter of fact.

Planners and politicians are attempting to make it more attractive by protecting those few houses still standing which possess any architectural merit and by converting certain side-streets into pedestrian walkways or turning the odd vacant lot into a playground for children. It may be a question of too little too late, but a good many political points are

Left, musicians serenade newly-weds. **Above**, a tourist portrait painter confers immortality.

pectedly friendly, arguing and laughing… it is enlivening to walk among these people. Athenians do not hesitate to show their feelings and it often seems that emotional states constitute a more powerful communicative device than words.

After a few days, visitors who expected to remain casual observers find themselves expressing long-forgotten feelings, exercising new facial muscles and vocal chords; unexpectedly at ease and unselfconscious. Aristotle described these as the effects of watching good drama and labelled them catharsis. In modern Athens catharsis is always on offer, only there is no strict demarcation between audience and actors and the drama never ends.

It should be kept in mind that Athens, as a sprawling urban metropolis, is a very recent, and unforeseen development. The city was suddenly transformed, increased by one quarter practically overnight, in 1923 with the influx of Greek refugees from Asia Minor. These newcomers were exceedingly poor, in many cases arriving from Turkey with just the clothes on their backs. At first they were settled in makeshift barracks around the city in areas such as Néa Ionía or Néa Smyrni, names which recall their land of origin. Thus the trend of urban expansion was founded and other characteristics such as inner city tomobiles are a prime cause of smog (the so-called *néfos*) which chokes the city during windless periods. This smog also mixes with atmospheric humidity to form an abrasive acid which has been dissolving stone monuments that have stood for millennia in the city. In recent years a restricted area has been drawn around the city centre in order to alleviate the problems of traffic and smog. On alternate days private cars with even and odd licence plate numbers are allowed to circulate within this exclusion zone. This is a great boon to taxi drivers but inevitably there aren't enough cabs to cope with the rush-hour demands. Be prepared to accept a jitney-like arrangement where other people

poverty, the dark underworld of petty criminals (*mánges*) and *rembétika* music came to form part of the capital's image.

Athens has mushroomed in the past 60 years, a period which saw the city's population soar from 453,000 to more than 4 million. That's a 883 percent increase over a stretch of time when the population of the country as a whole rose only by 93 percent. Clearly, there has also been a significant movement from the countryside into the city. All roads lead to Athens.

The sheer density of people makes for monumental traffic jams twice a day and four times when there is late shopping. Au-share stretches of the journey with you.

Urban attraction: While the disadvantages of the metropolis are all too apparent to the casual observer, the benefits which Athenians enjoy are perhaps less obvious. There are more doctors, medical specialists, and hospital beds here than in any other region of Greece. Educational opportunities are also superior. There are more schools, teachers and university places per capita in Athens than elsewhere. And when the studying is finished, there are jobs. Furthermore, Athenians are often more highly paid than workers in other parts of the country.

Greece as a whole may be underdeveloped

industrially, but 50 percent of the nation's industries (employing 10 or more people) are located in or around the capital; everything from chocolate factories and breweries to the massive dockyards and refineries sited along the coast at places such as Pérama, Skaramangá and Elefsína. The drive from Athens to Corinth is virtually a tour of Greece's industrial heartland.

Those who hold a high school diploma are eligible for a number of prestigious civil service positions which mean anything from working for the electricity company to serving as a government adviser. Such positions are desirable because salaries are inflation-indexed and hiked every year; best of all,

chic shepherd able to provide his family with goats' milk, cheese, meat and other basic needs. The image of the educated civil servant or professional has usurped earlier ideals, office workers do not dirty their hands or sully their clothes, and some civil servants will allow the fingernail on their little finger to grow extra long as evidence of their non-manual employment.

Education is thus consummately valued as it facilitates upward social mobility. In this striving for knowledge and in the fascination for foreign goods and ideas – for which the Greeks have a word, *ksenomanía* (see pages 131–132 in the Cultural ABCs section) – one may discern many symptoms of the "devel-

they are secure for life and include a pension scheme. This permanence and security are highly prized in a society which is emerging from a primarily agrarian mode of existence (until 1960 more than 50 percent of the population were living on the land).

Whereas in former times it was hoped that a son would work his father's fields and flocks, such a proposition is now scoffed at by young men in villages. Supreme admiration is no longer accorded the rugged, autar-

Left, ice cream and *loukoumádes*, hot puffs of butter soaked in honeyed syrup for sale in Athens. **Above**, cafés play an important role in Athens.

oping country" syndrome. People are engaged in the effort to secure white collar employment which they associate with an image of modernity and sophistication. Yet Greece has neither the industrial base nor the GNP to support such aspirations at present. In relation to the GNP there are twice as many students pursuing higher education in Greece as in the United States. Granted that most businesses originate in family enterprises, no real demand has arisen for managers at the executive level. Thus many of those who complete courses of higher education end up in positions which under-utilise their talents.

Some go to work as teachers in the private

tutorial schools (*frontistíria*) which one sees all around Athens. These institutions help students to cram for the state university entrance exams. Many talented students go abroad to study and, aware of how limited their opportunities for research or employment would be if they returned to Greece, they remain abroad. Who can blame them when, by some estimates, there are more lawyers in Athens than in all of France.

In the view of villagers, the move from the country to Athens is one which is likely to secure employment, relative financial prosperity, and prestige, though in which order it is not exactly clear. In any case it is not easy to move back to the village except for holi-

the navel of the Hellenic world. It is difficult to cut the cord.

East meets West: Athens is the primary point of entry into Greece. Around 2 million tourists, over half of all those arriving by air in Greece, land at Athens' Hellenikon Airport each year. In this and in other respects Athens is the main interface between Greece and the rest of the world. Here, villagers from outlying rural areas will probably encounter European and international culture for the first time. This is also the place where most Europeans will form a first impression of Greek culture.

It is said that approached from the East Athens is the first European city, and ap-

days or retirement because this would mean re-adapting to village life, which pales after a stretch of time in the city. Athens is the centre of Greek political, commercial and cultural life. More than 17 major newspapers are printed every day in the capital, accounting for 90 percent of national circulation. National government-sponsored, and most other Greek television also emanates from Athens, a fact apparent in the advertisement of products designed for the city dweller or in the promotions for Athenian stores, not to mention the weather reports, which concentrate on conditions in the capital. Living in this city, one feels oneself to be connected to

proached from the West, it is the first oriental city. This interplay of east and west may be put to use in making sense of the cityscape as well as the types of people living and interacting within it. On the Western pole, ideally speaking, is Sýntagma Square bounded by the offices of international airlines, deluxe hotels and the House of Parliament. Syntagma bears a smart Western look; Gucci, St Laurent and Chanel vie for the allegiance of the heart in this zone where English is the *lingua franca*. Visitors from rural Greece are totally awed when they stray into this area, and they feel slightly uncomfortable for there is nothing here to which they may readily relate. One man from a Cycladic island expressed alarm at not being able to tell who was Greek from who was not.

Less than a mile away is the opposite pole, Omónoia Square. Here one may savour a Greek coffee in some of the largest coffee houses (*kafeneía*) to be found anywhere in the country. (Try the "Alexander the Great" or the "Neon".) Women are served but one cannot help noticing that they form a distinct minority in these male domains. Omónoia is filled with hawkers and small merchants who peddle anything from wristwatches to rice pudding. At night, men appear wheeling large copper samovars with a warm drink called *tselépi*; a creamy, slightly gingery

choose a course so as to pass Athens' cathedral, the Mitrópolis, then proceed through a district of small shops selling cloth, jewellery, household and religious objects; that is, if he decided against dropping down to Athinás Street, which is itself practically a full-scale bazaar.

The more progressive Greek, the Hellene, would probably take a course so as to pass through Sýntagma and then proceed down Stadíou Street past numerous cinemas showing subtitled foreign films, department stores and neat shopping arcades. At one point there is a museum of folk art with a statue of Kolokotrónis, the hero of the Greek War of Independence, standing before it. For

concoction said to be the perfect antidote for an oncoming cold. Here, it is the tourist's turn to feel foreign.

Omónoia and Sýntagma are representative of two extremes of Athenian, one could even say Greek, identity. These two styles, the traditional and the modern, are to some degree apparent in every individual in what amounts to a cultural bi-polarity. As a hypothetical illustration, if a *Romaiós* (that is, a Greek of traditional leanings) needs to go from Plaka to Omónoia, he would possibly

Left, tourists are fair game in Athens's flea market. **Above**, kiosk and shopkeeper, Athens.

the Hellene, Greek traditionalism is a strange sign of backwardness and an embarrassing indication of Eastern influences. It belongs in museums.

In the different routes which they might choose, the imaginary Hellene and *Romaiós* confirm two very separate experiences of the capital – and life in general. This mixture of East and West may possibly account for the popularity of Greece as a holiday spot, and the attractiveness of Athens in particular. One explores and lives out romantic fantasies linked with the East, but in a constrained fashion. There is always the familiar, Western aspect of the city to fall back on.

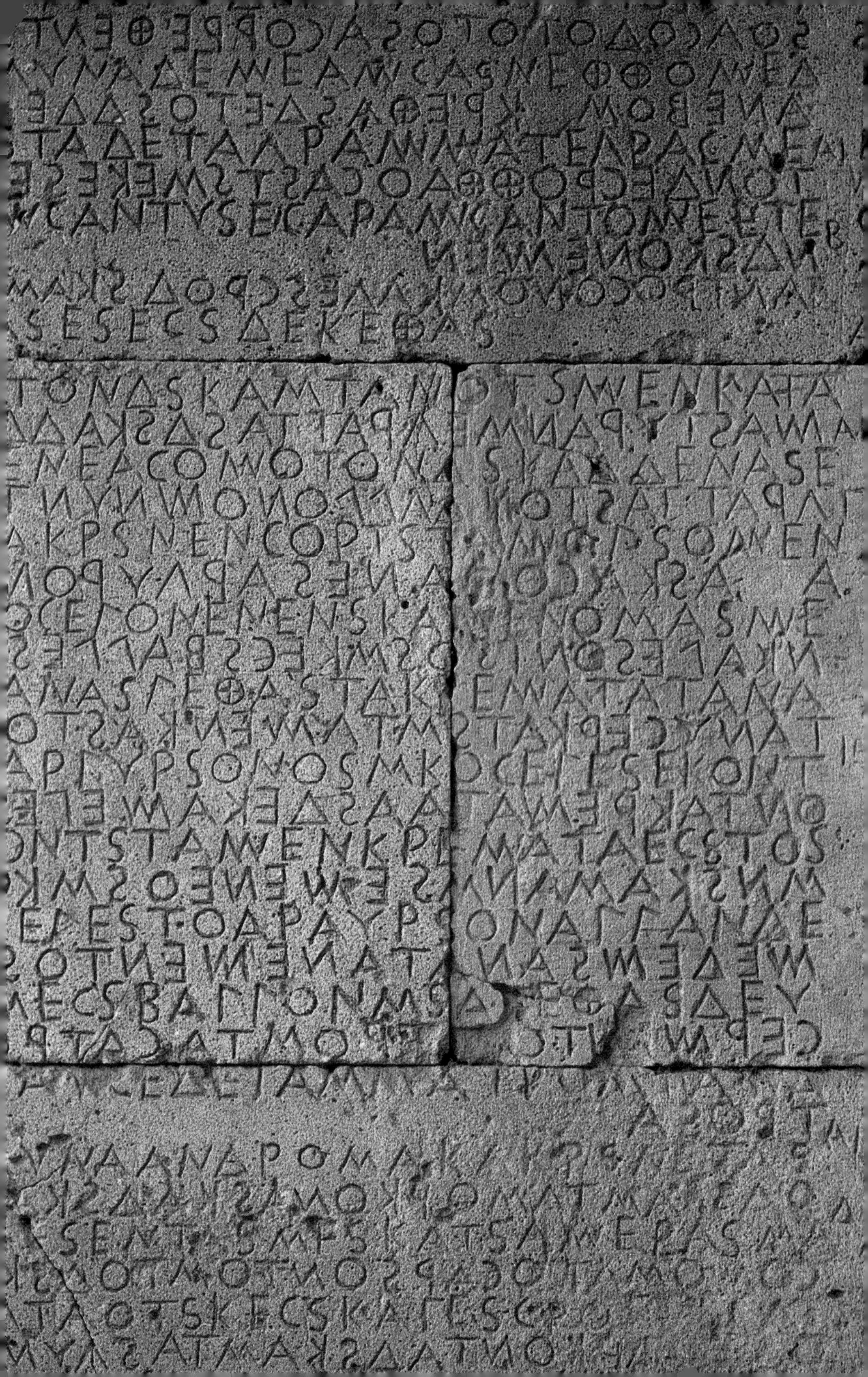

Newcomers to Greece are often baffled by the Greek alphabet. Even if they have trouble understanding other European languages they can at least read road signs and figure out which is the Ladies and the Gents. In Greece even international catch words like EXPRESS have a bizarre appearance. Perhaps as much as anything else it is the strange alphabet that makes foreigners throw up their hands and utter the ancient words of despair: "It's all Greek to me!"

The cultural ABCs that follow won't help anyone overcome their fear of Js, Fs, or Cs, but it may provide a key to another set of symbols that are equally strange. Greece is full of untranslatable concepts. What follows is an alphabet's worth of these indigenous phenomena. From E for Evil Eye to K for *Kamáki* to Z for Zorba, these entries introduce the newcomer to aspects of contemporary Greek culture which are not immediately obvious. Here readers will find out why no one bothers about birthdays (see Namedays), why kiosks dot every corner (see *Períptera*), why old women dress in black (see Women), and why Greeks are at odds over tourism (see *Xenomanía*).

Of course, this kaleidoscope of incongruous items is only one of many possible collections. The various writers who have contributed to this alphabet are not set on fixing Greece's cultural topography: on the contrary, each – whether linguist, anthropologist or journalist – is interested in tapping the shifting assumptions that go into making myths and shaping cultural identity. Sometimes humorous, sometimes serious, these entries map out another Greece, as important as the one already represented by geographical region in the following section. As a dictionary or as a set of social commentaries, use these pages as you please.

Preceding pages: girls during an Easter Epitáphios procession. **Left**, the law code of Gortyn on Crete must be read one line from left to right, the next line from right to left, and so on, "as a field is ploughed."

Acronyms

Even classicists who can bumble their way through the more conservative newspapers with their archaisms and purist forms would have a difficult time deciphering the strings of acronyms that appear in most articles today. Always used for the names of political parties (KKE, PASOK, ND, KODISO, EPEN, DIANA), acronyms now stand in for everything from social services (IKA, EES, ANAT, IKY, DEH) to soccer clubs (PAOK, AEK).

A contemporary Greek painter, commenting on the recent proliferation of acronyms, chided that soon the Greek novel would consist solely of abbreviations. It could be he was merely denigrating language as a lesser medium – we all know that, according to photographers, a picture is worth a thousand words – but even so he had a point: acronyms are the fast food of modern Greek discourse. Just as Americans have begun to wonder what McDonald's really means, so Greeks are beginning to wonder what acronyms are all about. Why have public announcements and newspaper articles started to resemble their ancient stone predecessors with their long lines of unpunctuated capitals?

Acronyms, like fast-food hamburgers, have an uncanny ability to camouflage what they contain. One soon forgets what an acronym really stands for and it suddenly acquires an association all its own, completely separate from its components. For example, the former prime minister Andréas Papandréou took advantage of this slippage and decided to use the same acronym for the Greek police force as the left-wing resistance fighters had used during Greece's civil war. ELAS now stands for both; so an acronym became a subtle way of legitimising a moment of left-wing history.

But subtleties aside, even if it would take a lifetime to decipher the politics of acronyms it doesn't take long to learn those that are most frequently used. And although Greek phrase books rarely mention them, you would be hard pressed to phone overseas if you didn't know that the public phones in every Greek town or city were housed in a building called OTE (pronounced "oté"). You might save yourself quite a bit of time if you knew that the Greek tourist organisation is called EOT (pronounced "eót"), and embarrassment if you knew that the great hordes shouting PAOK (pronounced "paök") in the streets of Thessaloníki on Sunday were not political activists but soccer fans.

Byzantine Church Music

An interview with Markos Dragoumis, of Athens College's music department

Q: *In most parts of Greece on Sundays and Namedays (see Namedays) radios are turned on full blast and towns resound with the nasal half- and less than half-tone dips of the Athens' Mitrópolis' cantors. Why does this chanting sound "Eastern" to a Westerner's ears?*
A: Traditional modern Greek music has many oriental features, as indeed had the music of the ancient Greeks: not only tones and semitones, but other smaller and larger intervals, oriental chromatic scales, a nasal quality in the voice and characteristic motifs decorated with grace-notes such as are particularly common in the East.

How did Byzantium give birth to two such different church musics as the Roman Catholic and the Greek Orthodox?
Were these two kinds of music really so different 1,000 years ago? Plenty of scholars doubt this. For example, this is what Igor Reznikoff believes: "At the end of the 19th century French Benedictines wanted to revive the Gregorian chant and created melodies based upon notes with identical time-value, often indeed beautiful, but which have no connection with the genuine ancient chant as we know it from manuscript sources on the one hand and from the tradition of model music on the other."

What does Orthodoxy have to say about music? Has it always been an integral part of the Greek church service? Has there ever been any instrumental accompaniment?
Music has been used in the Christian Church since Apostolic times, and is regarded by the Orthodox Church as an integral part of the liturgy, to be preserved by each generation as a holy relic and to be performed contritely,

humbly and with due decorum. Ancient ecclesiastical tradition, which is still maintained, holds that musical instruments are alien to the spirit of Orthodox worship, because their sounds are associated with worldly festivity. That is why Orthodox church music is purely vocal.

The history of Western music seems closely connected with the evolution of church music. Has there ever been any attempt in the Greek Church to compose new masses as in, for example, the Protestant and Catholic traditions?
A number of pieces of Greek church music have been written in a more modern style.

handed down by oral transmission. From then onwards, however, it was transmitted with the help of manuscripts, and later, since 1820, in books. But the pupil has to overcome a very considerable obstacle before he can be considered a good *psáltis* or cantor. He must learn to chant in the appropriate style, and in this no written music can help him, only his teacher.

Are there any women cantors? Do women play an active role in church music?
If a woman becomes a nun and has a good voice, then she may chant in her nunnery. Otherwise, it is not usual for her to chant. Nevertheless, a number of women in Byzan-

Theodorákis, for example, has composed a polyphonic Requiem for choir *a cappella*. These works could be performed in certain churches, but neither the congregations nor the clergy would ever wish to replace the traditional chant.

How has this music survived? Are cantors trained or are they just expected to pick it up from their elders?
The church music of the Byzantines, and of the Greeks in general, began to be written down around AD 950, and for that purpose a special system of notation was worked out. Thus, up to AD 950, religious music was

tine times did occupy themselves in writing hymns and setting them to music. An interesting study on this subject was written in the 1980s by Diane Touliatos-Banker, under the title of *Medieval Women Composers in Byzantium and the West*.

If visitors want to hear chanting at its best where should they go?
There are churches with good cantors and choirs in every Greek city, and also in Constantinople. In Athens, Insight Guides recommend the liturgy at Aghía Iríni (St Irene's), where Lykoúrgos Angelópoulos and his choir may be heard.

*C*offee

"Would you like a cup of coffee?" It's the classic come-on, from Syntagma to Sámos, for the homely brew of coffee has long been the drink of erotic encounters. Among Greeks themselves, offering coffee to a stranger is a gesture of hospitality and an excuse for light conversation. A chance invitation for coffee with an acquaintance and his or her *paréa* (circle of intimates) isn't easily refused. It's the perfect drink for "exploratory" sociability, for jokes and mild flirtation, and many a romance has

the Arabic original, *qahwah*, than the West's watery brew. Ground into a fine powder and boiled with water and varying amounts of sugar, *kafé* is served in tiny cups. You can order it sweet (*glykó*), very sweet and boiled (*varý glikó*), medium (*métrio*) and unsweetened (*skéto*) – and if those few teaspoonfuls don't satisfy your caffeine addiction, double (*dipló*). Connoisseurs know that what distinguishes the exquisite cup from the mediocre is a thick topping of froth (*kaïmáki*). Greeks used to call it "Turkish coffee" (*toúrkiko kafé*), until the 1974 war in Cyprus, when it was angrily crossed off menus across the land. Ask for Greek coffee (*ellinikó kafé*).

begun with shy glances over coffee cups.

Its place in more mundane social intercourse is just as prevalent. Greek men drink it in the ubiquitous *kafeneía*, housewives drink it at home with their neighbours. Working people drink it, too, but you won't find a coffee machine at their workplace. They "order out" from the local *kafeneía*, and on city streets, ducking in and out of office buildings, you can often see the white-aproned proprietor carrying an ingenious deep-dished tray crowded with coffee cups, the dish suspended, lantern-like, by three, bowed metal supports.

In name, as in quality, it's much closer to

Even the dregs have their uses. If you leave a trace of liquid so that the dregs can be swished around the cup, you can turn it over and let the wet residue run down the sides into the saucer. It leaves swirling patterns, and many a Greek woman can decipher symbols embedded in them to "predict" the future.

Most men wouldn't be caught dead "saying the cup" and, since the Church frowns on it, many women hesitate to admit to it. But in their houses, women trade cups and interpretations "for a laugh". Wedding rings and tall, dark, handsome men often seem to populate the cup.

*D*electables

"And I, hungry once more, gaze at the sweet biscuits." This yearning, expressed more than 2,000 years ago by a female character in one of Sophocles' lost plays, is still experienced in today's Greece, where sweets supply an important national need. The *zacharoplasteíon* (sweet-shop) is a mouth-watering sight, with mounds of crescent- and cone-shaped biscuits decorated with chocolate, almonds, sesame, apricots or coconut; with its giant baking-tins (*tapsiá*) crammed with diamond wedges of *baklavá* glossy with syrup and bulging with nuts; with its extravagant European-style *pástes* too.

No less tempting are the smells of rose- or orange-flower water, roasted almonds and cinnamon which drift from the kitchens often open to the street, where the curious may peer at the skills of the chef.

The *zacharoplasteíon* is more than a shop. One can often sit for some time, as in a café, eating a *kadaïfi* (finely shredded pastry stuffed with almonds and soaked in honey) or a *profiterol* (not the light French *choux* pastry but sponge softened with syrup and liqueur, covered with chocolate custard and cream), always served with a glass of iced water. In the northern cities – where the abundance of almonds and fruit and the large population from Asia Minor have fostered a sweet tooth among the inhabitants – sweet-shops are plentiful and often very smart. The city-dweller will eat a *baklavá* – or the even sweeter zeppelin-shaped *touloúmba* – in the early evening, after a siesta and before dinner.

At home deliciously fragrant sweet rusks, *koulourákia*, are dipped into tea or coffee at any time. On entering a home you are likely to be offered – refuse at your peril – a piece of preserved fruit in syrup, a *glykó tou koutalioú* (off the spoon), a cross between jam and crystallised fruit. All sorts of fruit and vegetables are preserved in this way; especially delicious are the green walnuts and little damsons of Thásos. The more adventurous will sample a jar of baby aubergines or marrows such as cram the stalls in Thessaloníki's street market. The humblest variety of the "spoon" family is the "submarine", a spoonful of vanilla (a vanilla-fla-

voured mastic cream) served in a glass of iced water which then makes a delicately perfumed drink.

The range of Greek confectionery is greater than some disappointed visitors suppose. Foreigners rarely meet with more than the ubiquitous stale *baklavá* or the oily *halvá* packaged in foil.

The best *baklavá* is to be found on Thásos, made unusually with walnuts and heavily spiced. Two variants of this oriental pastry found less often in shops are *galaktoboúreko*, milk pie (*fýllo* pastry filled with a thick egg custard flavoured with orange flower and cinnamon) and *reváni*, a Madeira-type sponge made with

semolina and soused with a cognac and orange syrup. (Be sure to try them when visiting Aegina.)

Halvá comes in many types. Smyrnan *halvá*, now hard to find in shops, is made in huge flat circles and is of a coarse, grainy texture and rich amber colour. Pharsalian *halvá*, to be found in Thessaly, is more gelatinous, closer to Turkish Delight (be sure to call it *loukoúmi*). Both are excellent when sprinkled with lemon and cinnamon. *Halvá* should be bought in the street market, sliced from huge loaves, spotted with pistachios and almonds or marbled with chocolate. Even more sybaritic is *karidó-*

plastos, a rich "paté" made from chocolate and walnuts. When surrounded by the proliferation of unknown delicacies, don't be overwhelmed. Ask for a bag of *amigdalotá* – almond macaroons of numerous shapes and flavours – and you can't go wrong.

*E*vil Eye

Greeks seldom call it the "evil eye" – just "the eye" (*to máti*). Perhaps the malevolence of "the eye" goes without saying. Belief in the existence of "the eye" is not confined to those from remote or provincial places. The

physical. Probably, the "evil eye" is about envy. It tends to appear in communities relatively undifferentiated by social class or wealth – "egalitarian" in a sense, but where resources are scarce and competition over them keen. In such places, the increments of "superiority" of one family over another are tiny, yet all-important.

Prestige or honour, variously, requires one to "stand out" from one's neighbours – but not too much, for that invites jealousy and bad will. Out of this paradox – the need to be better, the need to be the same – comes "the eye". It is a consequence of envy, but it is envy expressed surreptitiously, even unconsciously. This qualification is important.

jet set, the middle class as well as the proletariat, and not a few university-educated, swear that it exists. They insist that even doctors acknowledge its reality, just as the Church accepts the existence of demonic possession. Undoubtedly, the experience of "being eyed" is widespread, however much one might quarrel with the diagnosis of it.

Concepts of the "evil eye" abound in Mediterranean societies. Whether these different concepts are about the same thing is hotly contested by scholars of this region. But the debate itself underscores just how much the "evil eye" is a social affliction rather than anything particularly meta-

A Greek will rarely give "the eye" to someone intentionally. What we'd call "sorcery" – saying special words or doing special actions in order to make something happen to someone – falls into a rather different category, that of "magic" (*máyia*). "The eye", by contrast, is cast by accident.

The kind of person who casts "the eye" on you or yours is probably a neighbour or an acquaintance, someone with whom relations are – if not warm – at least cordial. It can happen inadvertently when something is praised, or even silently admired. This is why people take precautions by spitting delicately ("Phtoo! phtoo! phtoo!") on an infant they cuddle or admire, in order to forestall any ill effects.

The living beings and inanimate objects which are most vulnerable to "the eye" are those of unusual beauty, rarity or value. Tiny babies, appealing toddlers, pretty girls and twins are all at risk. Horses and cattle can be afflicted as well. When automobiles "die" for no apparent reason, people blame it on "the eye", and in certain parts of Macedonia you can find one tractor after another with an apotropaic string of blue beads hanging from its front fender.

On a parched islet in the Dodecanese, the water supply for one household is stored in whitewashed barrels on its rooftop; on each barrel has been painted, with unabashed simplicity, a large blue eyeball.

Certain people are said to be prone to casting the eye. Often, such an individual (sometimes called a *grousoúzis*) is quarrelsome, odd, or marginal in some way to the community. Blue-eyed persons (a trait Greeks associate with Turks) are especially hazardous. Wearing blue – blue beads or the little blue pupil encased in plastic – repels that danger. Many adults place one of these blue plastic eyes next to the cross they wear on a chain around their neck. And until recently all children had some sort of charm – a cross, an eye, an image of the Virgin and Child – pinned to their underclothes.

There is no way to know precisely who has cast "the eye". First, the effects are noticed, and only afterwards is a culprit surmised. All concerned pool their memories to reconstruct the recent past, straining to identify possible suspects with possible motivations. This response of suspicion reinforces belief in "the eye". It also reinforces its precipitating conditions: those of superficial cordiality and subterranean mistrust among unrelated families. Oddly enough, then, identifying the culprit is usually irrelevant to the cure's effectiveness.

Symptoms of affliction are fairly well-defined: in humans, they include sudden dizziness, headaches, a "weight" on the head or a tightening in the chest, a feeling of paralysis. Significantly, the head and chest are the sites of "breath" and "spirit". Animals show their affliction by bizarre behaviour or suddenly falling sick, while vehicles break down. When it happens, people know who to go to. It's often an old woman who is trusted and respected and who "knows about these things".

The cure has many variations, but this one is typical: the curer takes a glass of water and makes the sign of the cross over it three times. Then she repeats three times silently to herself a special, secret set of holy words, usually a short passage from the Bible, and simultaneously drops from her finger three droplets of olive oil into the glass. If the oil remains in globules, the person is not afflicted with "the eye". If it dissolves, this is both the proof and its cure. The curer may yawn and her eyes may fill with tears, while the afflicted person may feel a dramatic "lifting". The water is then dabbed on the forehead, belly, and two points on the chest – that is, at the points of the crucifix.

Often, it works. Why it works isn't clear, but the moral is: illness isn't about germs alone, it's also about social relations. If that fact has eluded the Western medical establishment, Greeks know it all too well.

Friends

American visitors in particular find it hard to put a name to it. "My gang" or "my buddies" sound embarrassingly corny. "My crowd"? Maybe, but most opt for the delicately vague "my friends". Yet these are seldom more than conglomerations of individuals, drifting together and then apart in a conspicuously mobile society. It's only in team sports, campus "Greek" societies and fringy cults that Americans experience that sense of a small tight-knit group that most of the world takes for granted.

Europeans seem more sociable. The English working classes have their "mates" from cradle to grave, but the French, with their *companie*, come closest to the Greek notion of *paréa*. For *paréa* combines both senses of the French word: of companionship, and of the group of friends itself.

"Do you have *paréa*?" means "Do you have company?" In Greece, without *paréa*, things aren't worth doing. Living alone, going off by yourself for a vacation, taking a lone stroll, these are not signs of independence but of desperation. This is a society whose language has no word for privacy. The closest translation is *monaxiá* (isolation), connoting deprivation, loneliness and loss. Who would choose such a state? Young women on their own are especially suspect: surely they're "looking" for something. Before mass tourism, big-hearted Greeks felt obliged to "adopt" lone tourists wandering their countryside, to "protect" the woman and befriend the fellow. Even today, "Do you have *paréa*?" is less a question than an offer: "I'll come along."

The "naturalness" of *paréa* for Greeks is fostered in their family experience. Traditional peasant houses had one main room for cooking, eating, working and sleeping, and even in new village houses and Athenian apartments, everything seems to hap-

pen in the living room-kitchen. With television droning in the background, the teenage girl pores over her school books while her father passionately argues politics with his brother-in-law, her brother shouts into the phone and her mother clangs pots and scolds the grandchildren.

People often say that the primary unit of Greek society is the family, not the individual, and this is manifested in a different sense of personal boundaries. Greek families are not a place for "respecting the other person's space". They are interactive – indeed, interfering. How else can they show they care? Greeks advise, criticise, make

sacrifices for and demand them from those they consider "their own". No laissez-faire here. If American individualism is about the lone cowboy, the Greek version is about the leader of the pack. "Twelve Greeks," they remark wryly, "13 captains."

Paréa partakes of both fixity and flux. "My *paréa*" can mean a fairly fixed group. For young Greeks, it's usually school friends. For those still childless, or far from home at university, the *paréa* becomes an alternative family which can last for years. Its members are always together, and think and talk about each other obsessively. They create a shared history. For their parents, especially if they've lived most of their lives in one place, the *paréa* combines long-time friends with relatives and new in-laws with their spouses, people with common interests and common responsibilities.

For the young and unattached, the *paréa* can be all-consuming. Its members meet for coffee before lunch, coffee after, a brandy at 4pm, and a meal in a *tavérna* at 10pm. Their political convictions probably don't diverge much (only kinship sometimes bridges political quarrels), yet over these cups of coffee, they debate the fine points of their differences incessantly. They also joke and tell stories, and in their fragmented state of twos and threes, take up their other favourite subject: relationships. Friendships, family relationships, the continuing saga of lovers – all are minutely examined and emotional intimacies are thus forged. Friends measure their closeness by the pain they've shared.

Like a family, such a *paréa* sometimes has a kind of incest taboo. Jokey flirtations are part of the *paréa*'s spice but, for serious affairs, members of the opposite sex are so familiar that they seem more like siblings. Lovers are brought to the *paréa* more than found within it. Except perhaps at marriage, people don't leave the *paréa* to form a "couple". "Dating" is alien to Greeks.

The *paréa* nurtures vehement loyalties, especially in the face of outsiders' criticisms. But such relentless intimacy can also be suffocating and breed a kind of bitchiness. *Paréa* life can verge on melodrama: imagined slights take on huge proportions. Sooner or later, there's a fight, or a cooling, and the membership changes.

Parées fluctuate over time but flux is also built into the notion itself. The *paréa* is always expandable – a Greek doesn't fuss about bringing along a new friend uninvited. He expects from the rest the implicit response, "your friend is our friend". They, in turn, don't fuss over this new person's "unique individuality" – the point is to make him part of the group. At the *tavérna*, chairs are always being added for friends who happen to come by. They cram chairs in until no more fit. Then everybody squeezes in, two broad bottoms sharing each lumpy, hard-backed chair. Comfort succumbs to sociability, but nobody complains.

For *paréa* life has its own etiquette. "Being together" is its object, not eating or drinking. In the *tavérna*, the *paréa* members

ble state (*kéfi*). For all they drink (usually less than it first seems) there are fewer alcoholics here than anywhere else in Europe.

They regard with distaste tourists who drink to stupefaction – especially women. Greeks may grudgingly respect a woman who can hold her liquor, but they are unforgiving when she can't. It's another proof of the immorality they already take for granted. So the double standard operates here with a vengeance, and in more puritanical locales, females ostentatiously spike their *retsína* with quantities of soda water or Coca-Cola.

As they've eaten collectively, so do they pay. Once, men always paid for women, splitting the bill among themselves. Things

submit these creaturely needs to a grander, collective ideal. Endless plates of food come to rest not at each individual's place but haphazardly on the table. Each wields his fork to spear a morsel, then rests it. Meals like this can last for hours. That is the point. The table must be brimming – stinginess Greeks find contemptible, but greediness in *paréa* is almost as bad. So, for all their exhortations to others to "Eat!" they can be surprisingly reluctant themselves.

The same goes for drinking. Greeks drink only with food, and never alone. The point is not to get drunk. Drinking is only a means of "opening up", to entering a pleasant, socia-

are more in flux these days. Men will pay for wives and girlfriends, but in university *parées* everyone is equally poor, regardless of sex, so all contribute. Guests, especially if they are foreigners, are a stickier matter.

Greeks are proud of their reputation for hospitality. And they would never let a foreigner pay his – and especially her – way without a fight. But they are sensitive about being taken advantage of. The best policy is always to plunk your money down with the rest – indeed, to show your willingness to pay with as much drama and determination as you can muster – and, if you find yourself overruled, to accept graciously.

*G*raffiti

In Procopius's day, Constantinople was brought to a standstill as fans of rival chariot teams, the Reds, Blues and Greens, rampaged through the streets. Nowadays the chariot-racing is gone, but its place in Greek life is filled by politics.

Come election time, Athens' streets are jammed solid with thousands of banners, flags and posters as supporters flood into Syntagma Square for the big rallies. Walls, bridges, the bare sides of apartment blocks become so many mottled configurations of slogans. Squads from the political parties' youth groups head out at night to whitewash opponents' slogans and paint up their own. Outside the towns, it's the same story.

Graffiti are essential to political success in Greece and they impose requirements of their own. Above all, colour. The choice is limited: white is out since it won't show up against whitewash; yellow likewise. Black is confined to the extreme Right. The conservative New Democracy has bagged blue, a light royal which conveniently echoes the national flag. The KKE, the communist party (now split into two) of course uses red.

One key to the success of the socialist party, PASOK, it's said, was its appropriation of the colour green: highly visible, suggesting close ties with the natural world, which helped to offset the party's radical reputation in the eyes of conservative farmers.

The other essential behind effective graffiti is the snappy slogan. Here's where the difference emerges between parties who know what they want and those who can't make up their minds. One word won the 1981 election for Andréas Papandréou: *allaghí* (change). This simple formula had already worked wonders four years earlier against a feeble array of alternatives such as New Democracy's own "It found Chaos: It created a State" which arguably might have been true but certainly fell flat, failing even to rhyme properly. The centre party's own motto, *allaghí me sigouriá* (change with security), was a laughable imitation of PASOK, a virtual admission of defeat.

PASOK's rise to power took place under the painted rays of a bright green sun, a symbol which did not have the disturbing effects that one might have expected. Defying the laws of nature seemed only to underline the party's potency.

This idea of a political rebirth, the dawning of a new era, was helped by the charisma of Andréas Papandréou himself. Charismatic political leaders recur in Greek affairs, but usually in the guise of elderly father figures, such as the Cretan Venizélos. The sons of such men tend to remain in their father's shadow.

But the case of the Papandréou dynasty is rather different; Andréas's father George achieved charismatic status late in life and was popularly known as "The Old Man". His son, referred to universally as "Andréas", managed to retain his charismatic mantle – an unprecedented feat in recent history and one which kept his opponents on the defensive.

*H*ospitality

Almost every guide to Greece opens its entry on "hospitality" with the story of Zeus, the disguised stranger-guest. And who are we to break tradition? In its ancient form – and still so, today – the word usually translated as "hospitality" was a bit of an oxymoron. *Philoksenía* is a compound word, combining *phílo*, "to love", and *xénos*, a word meaning – oddly – both "stranger" and "guest".

Zeus liked to travel incognito, the better to seduce lovely mortals. So, a trifle opportunistically perhaps, he decreed *philoksenía* not just an exalted virtue, but also an obligation. The *Xénos*, he said, should be treated in a princely fashion, because – who knows? – that stranger might really be a god in disguise, even Zeus himself.

Despite the onslaught of mass tourism, hospitality remains a virtue. Indeed, it is the very quality Greeks believe most distinguishes them from other peoples. They're positively competitive about it: every house insists its own hospitality is more genuine than the neighbour's, and "our" village is somehow always more hospitable than the one down the road. In some ways, the truth is in the declamation. But certain places achieve a national reputation. Cretans – never a folk for middling gestures – are thought to be as extreme in hospitality as they are in temper. Predictably, the label becomes self-fulfilling. Other locales (Chíos? The Máni?) fare less well in the eyes of their compatriots – but being an issue of local patriotism, well, it's all rather subjective, isn't it?

Hospitality isn't measured merely by its lavishness. It helps, of course. At weddings or namedays when guests are being fed, Greeks orchestrate an atmosphere of plenty – of copious quantities of meat, wine glasses constantly refilled, of a table choked with platters and bottles – so that all can enjoy themselves, and also, so that none can call them "cheap". Yet poverty is not an insurmountable barrier. Greeks quote little homi-

or drink twice, and only – after much coaxing – to relent the third time. It's quite a delicate game, and can be disastrous for the unsuspecting traveller. The Greek host thinks your refusals are just politeness, that by saying "no" you really mean "yes". There aren't any magic solutions. You can try to argue "diabetes" or "bad teeth" if you can't bear the sight of another dish of jellied fruit, but be prepared to accept something in the end so as not to insult your hosts.

Most travellers will have more superficial contacts with Greeks, but few will leave without being invited – at least once – into the house for coffee. Fortunately, rituals of hospitality have a fairly standardised form

lies about the poor having little but giving of it freely, and the old woman who brings a glass of fresh water, bread and a few olives to feed unexpected guests (since it's all she has) is thought almost saintly.

Hospitality creates a relationship, but it is not of equals. The host brings the guest into his own domain; then increases his prestige by giving. The guest, receiving, becomes obliged to the host. Once you know this, the common power struggle over food suddenly makes sense. The guest is obliged, ultimately, to receive but is at the same time ashamed to seem too eager. Proverbially, the guest was supposed to refuse an offer of food

(though this varies regionally). Their formality doesn't compromise their sincerity. And that very predictability can be a boon to the traveller. A few phrases, carefully memorised and strategically deployed, can put you on surer footing.

If you are invited for coffee, you will probably be led to the *salóni*, the formal living room, and left to wait while your hostess retires to the kitchen. She will return in a few minutes with a tray covered in a doily, with a tiny cup of coffee, a saucer of biscuits and a glass of water. Take the coffee first: raise it up slightly, and say *Stin iyiá sas*! ("To your health!"). When you've finished, raise the glass slightly, toasting your hostess, and drink the water. When you leave, you can say *Sas efharistó!* ("I thank you") or even better, *Chárika polí*. The latter is something you say when you've just been introduced ("I'm very pleased [to have met you]") but here, it can also mean "I've enjoyed myself." Hospitality, after all, is about both.

Icons

To be Greek is, in the case of 97 percent of the population, to be Greek Orthodox. True, many people demonstrate no interest in Or-

thodoxy. When asked what faith he belonged to, one young man pulled out his state identity card and said, "This card says I'm Orthodox. Personally, I don't really know."

Greek identity has always been strongly bound up with Orthodoxy. This includes the period of the Byzantine Empire when the populace viewed itself as dwelling in a world which had reached perfection and was a reflection of the Kingdom of Heaven. Later, after the Ottoman conquest of Constantinople (1453), the Greeks were administered as followers of the Orthodox faith, not as members of a particular national group. The Church was thus the main representative of

national identity until independence in 1832.

To those brought up in the largely Protestant if not wholly secular surroundings of northern Europe or North America, the religion of Greece appears threateningly mystical and obsessed with ritual. Any casual visitor to Greece could potentially pass the same verdict as the great Protestant theologian Harnack who wrote: "I do not expect to be contradicted if I answer that this official ecclesiasticism with its priests and its cult, with all its vessels, saints, vestments, pictures and amulets, with its ordinances of fasting and its festivals, has nothing to do with the religion of Christ."

Such a view is uncharitable in the extreme. The use of icons, for example, is one of the most frequently misunderstood aspects of Orthodoxy. These beautiful and highly stylized pictures are not objects of idolatrous worship, but this was precisely the indictment of the so-called iconoclasts in the 7th and 8th centuries. In an effort to purify the religion of this idolatry they proceeded to literally deface thousands of icons throughout Byzantium. Intact pre-9th-century icons are consequently very rare.

The use of icons was ultimately upheld by the Church with the understanding that they only symbolise the holy person depicted upon them. They are an instrument by means of which this holy person may be venerated. In no instance are they themselves objects of worship. This accounts for the absence of naturalism in their execution; the depiction of each personage is governed by strict conventions and approaches an ideal type.

Through the material icon we are directed beyond to a transcendental glory. As John of Damascus wrote, "I do not worship matter but I worship the Creator of matter, who for my sake became material and deigned to dwell in matter, who through matter effected my salvation. I will not cease from worshipping the matter through which my salvation has been effected."

The icons painted on the walls of churches are an early form of animation. They are a book explaining the Orthodox faith for those unable to read – a writing in images.

Icons are not only revered in church; virtually every house contains an icon stand (*iconostásis*) containing various icons deemed to have a particular importance for the family. They may represent certain saints for whom family members are named. Almost all personal names in Greece are shared in common with a saint and instead of birthdays, saints' days are celebrated (see Namedays). In times of need a person may beseech these saints for help.

Perhaps the single most widely revered icon in Greece is that of the Virgin Mary on the island of Tínos. It is said to have been painted by St Luke and to have special wonderworking power. Every year on 15 August, the celebration of the Assumption of the Virgin, thousands of pilgrims flock to the island to make requests of the Virgin or to leave devotions as repayment for miracles that have been performed. In one corner of the

way of life. Orthodox feasts mark public holidays and so touch everyone. Greeks may not all believe in it, but none can deny that it has exerted an influence over them.

Junta

At 2am on 21 April 1967, the people of Greece discovered that the army, in a swift, well-planned coup, had overthrown the government and in its place established a military regime. Using a NATO contingency plan developed for use in the event of a communist invasion from Greece's northern neigh-

monastery which houses the icon a pile of crutches left behind by those healed on the spot can be seen.

In Orthodoxy the miraculous and wondrous seem to be closer at hand than in other Christian traditions. When a miracle happens the people are not particularly surprised. In fact they expect them to happen. Stories abound regarding people who have been "illuminated" by one of the saints and are able to tell the future. Other traditions concern those who imprudently decided to work on the day of St Spyridon, or some other saint, and were smitten for not resting.

Orthodoxy is more than a religion. It is a

bours, and code-named "Prométheus", the conspirators justified their putsch on the grounds that they "were saving Greece from the precipice of communism".

Later that morning martial law was proclaimed. Various articles in the constitution guaranteeing human rights were suspended, military courts were established in Athens and Thessaloniki, political parties were dissolved and the right to strike abolished. Newspapers were submitted to strict censorship and were required to publish exactly what was supplied by the government, and all gatherings, indoors or outdoors, were forbidden.

Many thousands of people with a record of

left-wing political views or activity were arrested and sent into exile in bleak camps on remote islands. A large number of parliamentary leaders were taken into custody.

The new government ran true to form. Like other military dictatorships, its measures were alternately savage and ludicrous. Its leaders, the Colonels, were fanatical, if unintelligent, anti-communist salvationists who saw politics as a simple and fierce contest between good and evil. Like the pre-war dictator General Metaxás, they placed much emphasis on the need to discipline and reform the Greek character. They condemned long hair on men and mini-skirts on women and ordered both to go to church.

Even foreign tourists were subjected to some of these regulations, though the government was anxious not to frighten them away altogether. But like other "moralists", they did not escape making themselves ridiculous. For example, through the official propaganda machine they tried to humiliate the Nobel Prize-winning poet George Seféris for handing out a memorable statement of protest against the dictatorship; they deprived the film star Melína Mercoúri of her citizenship for criticising them; they banned the songs of Míkis Theodorákis, a leading composer, because he had been a left-wing deputy; and they censored the tragedies and comedies of the classical theatre.

After the coup, little was heard of the communist threat which was supposed to justify it, and the seizure of the papers of the left-wing party failed to produce any evidence in support. The coup was a simple seizure of power by a handful of military bigots. The regime resorted to torture and brutality on a big scale as a deliberate instrument of policy to maintain its grip on power.

The American government, under Richard Nixon, viewed these developments with no more than embarrassment and after a brief period of indecision gave the regime its accolade in the shape of arms supplies. Greece as a *place d'armes* for NATO seemed more important than Greece as a conforming member of the society of free and democratic nations which NATO was proclaimed to be.

The first blow in the downfall of the junta was initiated by students. In November 1973 a large number of them occupied the Athens Polytechnic and university buildings in Thessaloniki and Patras. When it became clear that they were attracting widespread sympathy, and when the Athens Polytechnic students began broadcasting appeals on a clandestine radio band for a worker-student alliance to overthrow the dictatorship, the regime sent in troops and tanks to crush them. The eviction of the students from the Polytechnic was carried out with extreme brutality, and at least 40 students and other sympathisers were killed, several hundreds wounded and thousands arrested. This ruthless demonstration of force in the centre of Athens turned the stomachs of most Greeks. The days of the dictatorship were numbered.

The regime collapsed eight months later, in July 1974, under the weight of its bungling in Cyprus; this led to a confrontation with Turkey and a military call-up for which the military rulers of the country had prepared with a farcical incompetence reminiscent of the equally empty militarism of an earlier Mediterranean dictator, Mussolini. The conservative leader Karamanlís, who had been living in exile in Paris, returned to Greece in the early hours of 24 July to oversee the dismantling of the dictatorship and the return to democratic rule. The brutal dictatorship ended as abruptly as it had begun.

Kamáki

Kamáki literally means a fishing trident, but now the word also refers to picking up or "hunting" foreign female tourists, and to the "hunter" himself. While picking up women is nothing new, the Greek *kamáki* knows that he is playing a well-defined game with its own rules, techniques and vocabulary. Another less romantic mythology has built up around this seasonal activity, fuelled by press and television coverage and, above all, by the exaggerated "fishing stories" of the perpetrators.

The development of *kamáki* has paralleled the increase in tourism in Greece over the past 30 years. In the 1960s young Greek women were extremely restricted in their movements, and were kept closely tied to the family. There was therefore little prospect for romance, sex, or even an evening out with a young woman for the comparatively independent young man. The arrival of women tourists, who were not only sexually liberated but were sometimes in search of "the four S's" (sun, sand, sea and sex), was an opportunity not to be missed. *Kamáki* started to be practised wherever foreign women were present, and not only by organised connoisseurs such as the members of the former "Octopus" club in Naúplion, but by any man who cared to try his luck. The "professionals", who roam certain highly touristic areas such as Syntagma Square in Athens, are said to make a living from their occupation, and they are certainly offensive to many women tourists. It could also be that their widely-publicised philosophy influences the way tourists view the potentially more genuine attentions of other Greek men.

ground, lay traps, and be ready to approach, or lay off until the time is ripe.

The intention is to make contact with the tourist without her realising that she is being picked up by a *kamáki*. One rather obvious *kamáki* ploy is to ask the woman the way to the Post Office, and if she does not know, explain the directions to her. The newer the arrival to Greece, the better, because she will not have become wise to the ways of Greek men. Women of different nationalities are said to require different techniques, and among the first questions the woman is asked is "Where are you from?"

There are various theories about which nationalities are easy, awkward, arrogant or

The aim of the pursuit is to have sex and, according to the *kamáki* rules, as soon as possible after meeting a tourist, and with as many women as possible. Competitive friends compare "scores" at the end of the summer season, and winter-time *kamáki* conversation dwells on the glory of summer-time conquests. It is obviously the chase and not the "kill" that provides the entertainment. Inexperienced men may get no further than asking dozens of foreign women for coffee, and being rejected.

Alternatively, the more sophisticated hunter realises that the initial approach is crucial, and that he has to survey the hunting-

beautiful, but all agree that if the respondent is Greek or Italian, there is little hope for success, and one should try elsewhere: Mediterranean women know the old tricks of their men too well to be duped.

If the tourist agrees to go for coffee, or whatever, she is unlikely to be seen as independent, but rather as naïve. Here lies the contradiction of the game: a *kamáki* does not like to view himself as the prey of a foreign female *kamáki*. A tourist who is evidently out to "catch" men in large numbers will probably be labelled a prostitute, as a Greek woman would be. The classic *kamáki* wants at least to appear to be in control; the kudos comes from luring unwilling or unknowing women into bed.

In general among Greeks, *kamáki* has a bad reputation. Most foreign women scoff at these men, and even former participants claim that the sport has lost its pioneering glamour, and become crude and vulgar. However, some see the *kamáki* as continuing the long tradition of hospitality in Greece. He can introduce or add to the delights of being abroad with sparkling sun and sea, exotic music and food, romance, and other elements of the ideal holiday. The foreign woman who understands the rules of *kamáki* can choose whether or not to play the game.

Language

Imagine a language which has two sets of unrelated words for basic concepts, such as "nose", "cheek", "shoe", "house", "door", "street", "moon", "red" and "white". Suppose, also, that, together with its own distinct grammar, one set is used in everyday life, while the other is obligatory in official parlance, in education, and newspapers.

That language is Modern Greek, or at least it was until 1974. For the first 150 years after Greece gained its independence from the Ottoman Empire in 1821, there were two versions of Greek, used in different situations, which overlapped in pronunciation and in many areas of vocabulary and grammar, but differed radically in others. This situation is not unique to Greece. The Arabs, for instance, also use different versions of Arabic in different circumstances.

The Greeks have traditionally revered the language of ancient Greek literature and the New Testament – almost as much as the Arabs have valued the language of the Koran. For centuries they have felt that their writings should depart as little as possible from the language of their illustrious ancestors and the language of their holy book.

Some acquaintance with the history of Greek language is essential for an understanding of Greek culture as a whole over the past 200 years, since the controversies over the language sum up the conflicting attitudes of the modern Greeks to their ancient compatriots. It has never been doubted in Greece that the present-day inhabitants of the country are the direct descendants of the ancient Greeks, who laid the foundations of European civilisation.

This assumption presented the Greeks who were preparing the way for independence in the 1820s with the problem of what national ideology to adopt in order both to unite the nation from within and to present a national image to the outside world. Within Greece itself – and among adherents to the Greek Orthodox faith in general – a bewildering variety of different languages was spoken and the Greek language itself was split into various dialects, some mutually incomprehensible. Nevertheless, Greek was the most commonly used and Greek (albeit Greek of more than one and a half millennia before) was the language of the Church. So Greek intellectuals of the early 19th century agreed that the best way to cement national unity and to secure assistance from the West in their national liberation struggle was to promote their links with Ancient Greece, to which Europeans and Americans had a romantic attachment. Their case was supported by the close connection between the ancient and modern Greek languages.

From here on, however, there was profound disagreement. Some intellectuals believed that the modern language was crude and barbaric (thanks to centuries of Turkish rule) and that the only way for the Greeks to prosper was a return to the pristine beauties of Ancient Greek. This would ensure the rebirth of ancient Greek culture, their belief being that anyone who learned to speak like Plato would also begin to think like Plato.

A related problem was that of what the modern Greeks should call themselves. From the early Christian era until the beginning of the 19th century almost all Greeks had called themselves "Romans" and their spoken language "Romaic", since they were conscious of belonging to the traditions of the Byzantine Empire, which was historically the continuation of the Roman Empire. They tended to reserve the words "Hellene" and "Hellenic" (i.e. Greek) for the pagan ancient Greeks and their language.

By insisting on calling themselves and their compatriots "Hellenes", some intellectuals were able to envisage the resurrection of the ancient Greek language along with its name. But at the same time, whereas everyone knows the difference between the Italians and the Romans, "Greek" is used indiscriminately to refer to the people and language of both ancient and modern Greece.

Others, realising the impracticality of persuading the Greeks to renounce their mother tongue, looked at the example of European nations such as the French, who had reached cultural eminence after abandoning Latin and cultivating their own language. These intellectuals argued that only through the use of the spoken language could the Greeks become sufficiently educated and enlightened to drag their country out of its economic and cultural morass. They urged their compatriots to follow the example of the ancient Greeks, who had used their mother

of being not too far removed either from any of the modern Greek dialects (thus avoiding giving an unfair advantage to the speakers of any one dialect) or from Ancient Greek. It would display both the underlying unity among the speakers of Greek of the present day and the profound identity (despite superficial differences) between the ancient and the modern Greeks. Korais's compromise language, which was neither fully ancient nor fully modern (and had never been spoken by anyone), was adopted by the fathers of the nation as the basis of the official language, later known as *katharévousa* (literally "the purifying language").

It is difficult for non-Greeks to imagine

tongue to reach the heights of civilisation.

Among those who opposed the imposition of a fully resurrected Ancient Greek was Adamántios Korais (1748–1833), a former merchant and physician living in Paris who became the leader of the intellectual movement preparing for Greece's independence. But although he constantly attacked the archaists, he was equally scathing about those who insisted on using the modern language as it was spoken by the common people. Instead he proposed a "cleansed" version of Modern Greek, corrected according to the rules of Ancient Greek grammar. This language would have the advantage

the almost magic power invested in the ancient written word in Greece. Throughout the 19th century Greek intellectuals, frustrated and disillusioned by the problems facing the Greek state (poverty, disunity, economic and political subjection to the West), seemed convinced that every aspect of modern Greece represented an inferior and tarnished version of some glorious ancient counterpart. The ancient language was looked upon, quite irrationally, as an instrument of absolute perfection; and – precisely because it was no longer spoken, but only written – it appeared to be timeless and eternal, exempt from the change and decay that affect all living bodies (including, of course, spoken language, which is constantly in a state of flux).

It is notoriously difficult to create a standardised language. Look at the differences between the varieties of English spoken within any one English-speaking country, let alone in different English-speaking countries. The Greek intellectual leaders created an added difficulty of trying to forge a standard that would contain material from two separate, albeit related, languages (Ancient and Modern Greek), each of which had never been standardised in itself but was split into widely diverging dialects.

So any user of *katharévousa* had to walk

an unsteady tightrope and avoid falling into either incomprehensibility or vulgarity. Those without laborious training in such verbal acrobatics (which meant the vast majority of the Greek population) could choose to ignore the official language altogether and thus exclude themselves from direct access to the law and the state apparatus. Alternatively, they could parrot-learn set formulas which they might not fully comprehend but which would in any case enable them to muddle through.

While the academics were busy deriding the popular language, the poets were writing in it and exhorting people to abandon their

prejudices against it. By the end of the 19th century almost all creative writers were using the "demotic" (spoken) language, so that *katharévousa* became solely the language of official parlance and no longer that of cultural life. Nevertheless the struggle continued: people were killed in riots involving adherents of the two opposing linguistic variants in 1901 and again in 1903, and the article of the Greek Constitution specifying *katharévousa* as the official language (inserted in 1911, in response to this violent polarisation) was not abolished until after the Colonels' dictatorship fell in 1974.

During the 20th century the language controversy has often tended to be identified with political divisions; *katharévousa* being promoted by the Right and demotic by the Left. It was partly because *katharévousa* had become tainted by its identification with the Colonels' regime that the more liberal (though still conservative) government of Karamanlís that immediately followed it was able to begin replacing *katharévousa* by demotic in all areas of public life.

But the Greeks haven't stopped arguing about their language; indeed, it is still a frequent topic of discussion among intellectuals and non-intellectuals alike. Beginning in 1981 Papandréou's socialist government continued the process of dismantling *katharévousa*, and the more laid-back style of its speeches and pronouncements offended many who have found it hard to accustom themselves to a casual use of language for official purposes. The government's abolition of many of the actually functionless diacritics used in writing Greek for 2,000 years (but not in the Classical period), which caused so much misery and embarrassment both to school-children and adults, has been widely criticised.

More justified is the criticism of the official policy on the teaching of Ancient Greek, which used to be a compulsory high-school subject but now cannot be studied at school before the age of 16. These moves are often seen as ploys to cut modern Greece off from its roots, depriving the nation of its firm basis in the past and making it easy prey for any foreign power that might wish to exert its cultural dominance.

The Greeks' desire to bridge the gap between their language and culture and those of the ancients has enormously enriched modern Greek life. However, the Greeks need not be ashamed (as generations of school-teachers tried to make them) of the language and culture that developed over the past millennium. Pride in their ancestors often gave the Greeks either an excessive sense of self-satisfaction or, conversely, a feeling of inferiority in relation to their glorious ancestors and their unsatisfactory contemporary condition. Others held the more constructive view that the Greeks should be proud of having kept the Greek language alive through successive periods of foreign domination. Having had their native language wrenched from their mouths in the first grades of school, the Greeks have now been given back their mother tongue.

The Greeks were probably the first people to win a war of national liberation against an alien imperial power; but the poet Dionysios Solomós warned in 1824, while this war was being waged, that the Greeks would not be free until they had rid themselves not only of their Turkish occupiers but also of the pedants who tried to teach them that they were something other than what they were. This second liberation did not come until 1974, a century and a half after the first.

Nevertheless, one positive consequence of the language controversy is a fondness shared by all Greeks – whether peasants, poets, neither, or both – for playing with the varieties of their language. Language isn't simply a means of expression, but an arena in which they can practise their creativity, display their wits, and generally have fun.

Movies

On sultry summer nights in Greece, most of the evening entertainment occurs outdoors, and movies are no exception. Few indoor cinemas are air-conditioned. Some are equipped with a rare innovation: the convertible roof remains closed during the screenings before sundown, then movable panels creakily slide apart to expose the audience to cool breezes and an occasional starry sky.

The rest of the indoor cinemas move to empty gravel-covered lots, alleys or rooftops where people are usually seated on sagging deck chairs. According to the union of outdoor cinema owners, a survey of tour-

ists named the open-air cinemas as the number two tourist attraction in Athens after the Acropolis.

The atmosphere is appropriately relaxed. Whole families attend and snack bars serve soft drinks, beer, crackers and crisps, but no fresh popcorn. A few operate as cinematic *ouzeriés* where one can sit at little tables and nibble on *mezéthes* (hors d'oeuvres) while sipping an *oúzo*. At drive-in movies, porn films are usually featured and carhops deliver orders of sandwiches, mini-pizzas and chilled bottles of wine to those adult viewers who are reticent about emerging from their vehicles.

Since many theatres are located in the

centre of the city, the volume is decreased during the late showing out of consideration for the neighbours. One has a choice of viewing a rather dim picture with adequate sound at the first screening, which starts before dark, or a clearly defined image with a faint soundtrack during the late showings. Fortunately for foreign viewers, Greeks, in contrast to the French or Italians, prefer subtitles to dubbing, so only original language versions are shown.

In any case, open-air cinemas are a relaxing, quaint form of entertainment. No new releases are shown during the summer. But there is a feast of films to choose from, including re-releases of the previous season and week-long festivals of older classics, plus the inevitable slapstick comedies.

Traditionally, domestic fare topped the popularity list but this has been reversed in recent years when foreign action adventures and romances have sold the most tickets. The heavy European influence in Greek cinema made many of the quality films too "arty" and slow-moving for general audiences who have grown used to a diet of fast-paced imports, or the crudely-made buffoonery of some Greek comedies.

Greeks often wander into a film in the middle and eat and talk throughout it. Yet, lest one think there is no serious audience, a few

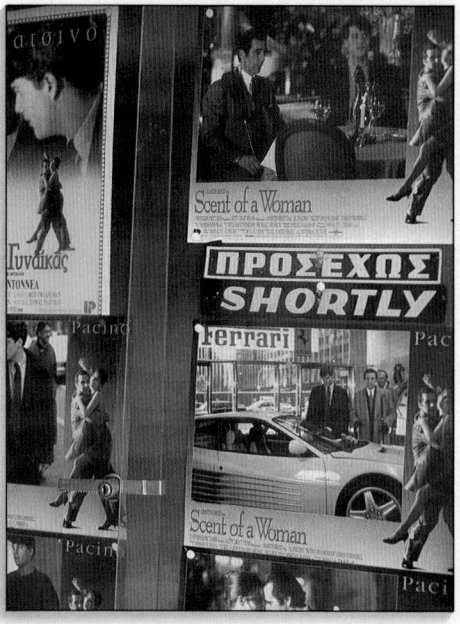

art houses in central Athens are doing a solid business by booking earnest European imports and a smattering of American independents. Meanwhile, the after-midnight movie trend has re-emerged in Athens in a few central cinemas which show "B" grade thrillers, science fiction and horror flicks.

Only a few Greek low-budget farcical comedies and a handful of quality films sold more than 100,000 tickets in recent seasons. The gulf between commercial movies and artistic ones has been great. However, the most popular domestic films of recent years managed to combine "Greekness" with well-developed scripts that have international appeal.

Namedays

"What's in a name?" asked Romeo. He should have asked a Greek! For here, all sorts of stories piggyback onto names, if you know how to read them. Place of origin, for instance: *Theodorákis* is clearly Cretan, for a name ending with *ákis* (meaning "little") bears the slyly ironic tag of this ferocious people. Any *Yánnoglou* is sure to have ties to "The City" (Constantinople), and the common suffix *poulos* (meaning "bird", or "child of") points back to the Peloponnese, as in the case of one clownish ex-dictator, Papadópoulos, "son of the priest".

Since 1983, women are obliged to keep their "maiden" name for life for legal matters. But before the revision of Family Law, a woman seldom imagined – unless she were rich or Melína Mercoúri – keeping her father's surname. In the possessive case, female surnames (single and married) are telling: Mrs Papadópoulos really reads "Papadópoulos's Mrs". In mainland Greece, a woman traditionally lost even her first name at marriage, and was known by the feminised form of her husband's: Yiórgos' wife became "Yiórgina". The symbolism persists. At weddings, girlfriends of the bride jokingly write their names on the sole of her shoe, and explain that she whose name is rubbed out first will marry first.

A Greek baby is not fully a person when it is born, but only when it is baptised and given a name. Baptism, a ritual more solemn than marriage, which initiates the child into the Orthodox community, is celebrated between 40 days and a year after birth. Until then, the child is called simply "Baby", and if (as was more common in past years of high infant mortality) it died before someone – anyone – could baptise it "in the air" by "making the cross" over it three times and uttering a name, it would not be buried in the church graveyard, and its soul was thought to linger in a nether-world between hell and paradise.

Greeks are amazed at how Westerners name their children, guided by little more than fashion and personal whim. They themselves follow strict rules: the first boy is named after the father's father, and the first girl after the father's mother (in mainland Greece) or the mother's mother (in most of the Aegean islands). Naming the son after the father, as Americans do, is thought extremely unlucky, even vaguely incestuous: a premature usurping of the father's name. But between grandparents and grandchildren, the inheritance is not fraught. The grandmother greets with delight the baptism of a child with her name. While it ritually acknowledges her individual mortality, it nonetheless assures family continuity: "The name will be heard."

Property, too, may be linked to names. On many islands, first-born Kalliópe inherits the house from her mother, Marína, who inherited it from her mother, Kalliópe, and so on in an infinite alternation of Kallíopes and

just to your own blood ancestors but to the entire Greek (or more accurately, Orthodox) community. Most Greek names refer to a saint or some holy quality, hence, "Sophía", the sacred wisdom. Birthday parties are for kids; the adult Greek has instead a "nameday", the day when the saint for whom he or she was named was "born into" the life hereafter, usually through a rather unpleasant martyrdom. This day is now celebrated by the Orthodox faithful. It's an ingenious system; everybody knows your nameday, sparing you the embarrassment of dropping hints to your friends when you want somebody to celebrate with. But there are a few new twists.

The one who celebrates "treats" the

Marínas. Likewise, the boy "with the name" will inherit his grandfather's fields, and he (and his wife) will be obliged to mourn for him when he dies.

Certain events can distort this ideal pattern. A man with many nephews bearing his father's name will yield to his father-in-law's desire for a namesake, or a woman trying to conceive may visit the miraculous icon of a particular saint and entreat its help by promising to give the child its name. These do not alter the Greeks' sense that names connect one to a long line of ancestors, perpetually reproducing itself.

If you are Greek, your name links you not

guests. The guest may bring sweets or flowers or a bottle of whisky, but the host provides the feast. On St Demétrios's Day, everyone with a friend or relative named Dimítris or Dímitra must "remember" him or her (and people often know many Dímitrises and Dímitras) by phoning or stopping by, and at the houses of all these Dímitrises and Dímitras, the evening is a jolly chaos of doorbells buzzing, phones ringing and a constant flow of guests slightly green with the evening's fifth peppermint liqueur, proffering formal good wishes, and absently munching roasted chickpeas.

Mortal namedays blend the formal and the

festive, but for the saint it's a more lavish affair. Every community has a saint (sometimes several) who specially protects it, and on that patron saint's feastday, the Orthodox community celebrates with a *paniyíri*. The word derives from ancient Greek, referring to a public assembly: all (*pan*) those gathered in the marketplace (*agora*). *Paniyíria* of pagan Greece honoured gods and goddesses in a manner which combined worship and pleasure, spiritual obligation and commercial interest.

Today's *paniyíri* involves the entire community. The saints are honoured with prayer and processions, followed by feasting and dance into the small hours. Crammed and haphazard on a dusty stretch of ground, often a good mile or two from the village, are parked a wild assortment of carts and caravans. At its edges, wizened old ladies and amputees sit cross-legged on shabby rags, beseeching believers, palms cupped for alms. Next to the van selling Sprite and cloying ice-cream bars is a horsecart spread with roasted chickpeas, peanuts, raisins and sunflower seeds. Wedged in between are tables covered with crocheted doilies and embroidered towels for sale to the girl preparing her trousseau, and next to that a table with religious trinkets. Amidst the crucifixes you can find tiny blue pupils cased in plastic, dangling alongside a silver cross, amulets against the "evil eye".

Baptismal names are public and fixed, but *paratsoúklia* celebrate the idiosyncrasies of individual lives. Nicknames of a sort, *paratsoúklia* are an insiders' code. Strangers and tax collectors aren't supposed to know them. Rude and ironic, they commemorate quirks of body and character: Manólis's brawny virility is wryly recalled in the feminised "Manóla", Yiórgos's philanderings in "Poúli" ("Birdie"), Theofánis's melancholy in "Katsoúfis" ("long-faced"). Men get *paratsoúklia* from their comrades, women hardly ever, except by way of men. The man who worked 20 years in America and returned to marry is dubbed "Amerikános", and his wife, "Amerikána", though she's never left Macedonia. Badges of individual peculiarity, they can get passed on to sons and grandsons, until (with the real surname erased from memory) the shaggy, secret *paratsoúkli* slips quietly into the bland respectability of an official surname.

*O*ral Tradition

Poetry matters in Greece, and this is due, in part, to the fact that for centuries it was sung, not read. Poetry has always been a kind of performance in Greece, a social event. Even today, contemporary poets can fill soccer stadiums with fans. Until the late 19th century Greek poetry had little in common with the solitary quill-pen traditions of other Western European cultures. This may be because oral poetry was a much more successful way of preserving Greek national identity during the many centuries that Greece was under foreign rule: writing could be censored but no despot could confiscate songs.

Even in this century oral transmission, because of its resistance to censorship, has been necessary. Yánnis Rítsos (born 1909), one of Greece's best-known poets, was sent to prison along with many other suspected communists during the civil war. There he continued to write his poems. He would bury them in bottles to keep them from the guards but the only way he could get them to his readers was with the help of freed prisoners who, before leaving, learned his poems by heart and smuggled them out.

The fall of Constantinople (or "The City" as Greeks commonly call it) paradoxically enough marked both the beginning of Turkish domination and of Modern Greek poetry. It is at this point that versions of folk songs still sung today were first recorded or referred to in literary texts. The stock formula "I come from The City", although obviously about the fall, is also found in modern folk songs, and the well-loved 16th-century Cretan romance *Erotókritos* incorporated many verses from folk songs, verses that are still familiar to Greeks. Since oral transmission is an inherently creative process, phrases are not expected to resemble their antecedents word for word; the old phrases serve merely as a structure on which to base new variations. While not all critics believe in a continuous poetic tradition dating back to Homer, most agree that a certain continuity can be traced from the 15th century.

Until the War of Independence in 1821 and the founding of the Greek State, song and poetry were inseparably linked, whether composed on paper or passed down orally from generation to generation. In fact writing and singing were often equated.

But with the emancipation from the Turks, national identity was no longer a clandestine matter. Oral transmission, formerly the *only* transmission possible, now was seen as unreliable. Writing – more fixed and more permanent – became the preferred means for spreading nationalist ideology. The folk song was a stepping stone for poets but not an adequate means of expression in itself. It wasn't reliable enough.

One of the first proponents of a National Greek Literature was the poet Dionysios Solomós (1798–1857) from the Ionian Islands. In a letter to a friend he expressed his

was all lyricism and nationalism. Over in Alexandria, Greece's greatest modern poet, Constantine Caváfy (1863–1933) was doing something totally different. His poetry emphasised the importance of writing over song, and seemed to suggest that the human intimacy associated with the oral tradition was no longer possible.

His historical frame was neither the glories of classical Greece nor the emancipation from the Turks but rather the slow decay of the pre-Christian and Christian eras. He invoked the pathos of deterioration, and repeatedly poetry was the only solace.

Written language had the power to construct something material out of what was

interest in klephtic folk songs but also stressed that the poet's task was different: "Klephtic poetry is fine and interesting as an ingenuous manifestation by the Klephts of their lives, thoughts and feelings. It does not have the same interest on our lips; the nation requires from us the treasure of our individual intelligence clothed in national forms."

Nationalist poets such as Solomós may have criticised the ingenuousness of the oral tradition but their poems always aspired to song – and indeed Solomós's *Hymn to Freedom* has become the Greek national anthem.

It would be too simple to suggest that Greek poetry in the 19th and 20th centuries

being lost. Writing for Caváfy was not just a more durable substitute for singing as it was for Solomós and Palamás but a radically different means of expression. The poem took the place of what was missing. It could even fill the geographical space left by the destruction of a city.

Continuing in the wake of Solomós and Palamás comes another nationalist poet, Angelos Sikelianós (1884–1951). But in Sikelianós's poetry "being Greek" has become less of the collective project it was in Palamás's poetry and more a matter of personal identity. The Delphic priestess with her wild, windswept words is the inspiration for the incantatory verse of this modern poet who lived in Delphi.

Very much a part of the established canon and probably best known of all the modern Greek poets are the two Nobel prize winners George Seféris (1900–71) and Odysséus Elýtis (born 1911). Although their poetry is not devoid of questions about the nature of writing, both these poets of the 1930s generation draw heavily on the oral tradition. Rather than comprising a Greek avant garde, they were just extremely adept at incorporating the techniques of other European modernisms. Seféris introduced Greece to the modernism of T.S. Eliot with its reliance on myth while Elytis imported the other extreme of modernism, French surrealism.

Perhaps it is telling that their poetry gained popularity by the oldest trick in the book, oral transmission, through the ingenious scores of the composer Míkis Theodorákis. As it was with the folk song, the bard in Seféris's and Elytis's poetry speaks for the community. Their poetry is meant to be read in the context of this longer oral tradition.

---

*P*eríptera

Although they may appear limited by their diminutive structures, kiosks are really multi-purpose powerhouses. Besides filling the obvious function of newsagent/sweetshop, they may double as mini-amusement parks (with children's rides), sporting goods stores (selling sleeping bags on occasion), ironmongers and locksmiths. For customers with problems, the proprietor may dispense psychiatric or medical advice.

Running a kiosk is like directing an orchestra – one eye on the telephone meter, one hand giving change and one ear tuned to the voice of a friend who has stopped around the back for a chat. How do kiosk owners cope?

The view from inside a kiosk, or *períptero* as it is called in Greek, is tight, complex and most resembles the cockpit of a DC-9. Down low are a series of tiny drawers in which are sequestered various sewing needles, thread, zippers, antibiotics and usually a supply of condoms; shelved up higher are sweets and the rainbow array of cigarettes, while still higher are assorted shampoos, washing powder and worry beads. Items of value, pocket calculators, watches and gold cigarette lighters are displayed in little show windows. In the centre sits the proprietor, jammed into two square feet of space yet firmly in control of the till, responding to the images as they appear on the screen – that small opening to the front where customers pronounce their orders.

It is not unusual for a *perípteras* to work shifts of 12 hours in conditions which vary from furnace-like in summer to chill and damp in winter (when most cramp their already tiny space with electric fires or some form of heating). Yet they remain a generally good-humoured lot, eager to oblige the lost foreigner with directions or even the recommendation of a good local *tavérna*.

The kiosks started as gifts from the government to wounded veterans of the Balkan War and World War I. Many will remark on the similarity between the architecture of kiosks and that of military guardposts such as those used by the honour guard in front of the Parliament Building on Sýntagma Square. In a symbolic way the *períptera* are also guard houses where old soldiers prolong their duty, emerging from the military into the commercial sector, watching over and serving the community.

In Greece people want to run their own business and the more than 3,000 *períptera* in Athens alone obviously make this a possibility. Kiosks are almost all family-run and one cannot help noticing the children or grandchildren of the proprietors stopping by for a sweet on the way home from school, or in summer the whole family sitting around a seafront *períptera* eating watermelon, which they may offer to share with customers. Kiosks have a personality and a charm which is part of Greek commerce generally; everything is personal. If a kiosk owner finds that you know a few words of Greek it may take a bit longer to conclude your purchase. They will want to know where you are from.

With only a quarter of the population of England, Greece has nearly the same number of retail shops. Partly this is the reflection of

mentality – the *períptero* mentality – the basis of which may be summed up in the slogan, "One family, one business".

Queueing

Americans call it "standing in line". Born of American straight dealing, it falls positively flat next to the elegant British verb, "to queue", from the Latin *cauda*, for "tail". American "lines" exude a democratic egalitarianism; British "queues" demonstrate fair play mixed with social distance. But both reveal a belief in rationality and order.

a society which subdivides itself sharply into family and kindred groups, each of which seeks to own a shop, a *magazí*. The idea of working for a stranger is odious; in fact, the word for "employee" in Greek literally means "someone beneath another". Consequently, instead of expanding and enlarging, businesses tend to remain relatively small in size while new businesses are opened to accommodate an expanding market. This swollen number of retail shops causes Greece to have the highest mark-up price in the European Union. Thus the profusion of kiosks throughout Greece is more than just a peculiarity or a coincidence; it is a part of a whole economic

The Greek version is something else altogether. Can you really call it a "queue"? Waiting at a bus stop in Akademías in central Athens, you can just make out a semblance of linearity among the bodies, if only because the metal rails installed for this purpose nudge them into orderliness. Once the bus appears, however, the pretence collapses and a chaos of anxiously pressing bodies pushes relentlessly through the doorway. Some Athenians say it's just life in a city bursting its seams – too many passengers squeezing into too few buses. That's indisputable. But you see the same anxious crowding on airport runways where, clutching a boarding pass with a guaranteed seat number, passengers trip all over one another to board the plane.

A different body language is no doubt part of the explanation. Greeks are comfortable with their bodies, and they touch each other constantly – in handshakes and kisses of greeting, in the loving pinch to a baby, in the slap on the arm to a comrade – in ways the colder northerners touch only their intimates. So you must interpret no hostility in the face of that old lady whose sharp finger jabs into your back and propels you forward on to the bus. But its blankness can be just as annoying: when you're a foreigner, with a different sense of your personal space, it's easy to feel you're being treated like just a bulky obstacle in the path of somebody else's seat.

This impersonality has a logic, though. It's the inverse of the much-vaunted "personalism" of the Greeks, but not its opposite. Greeks don't imagine they live in a rational universe where all things come to those who wait. There's no place here for the Anglo-Saxon concept of "fairness". For Greeks, the universe is arbitrary and unpredictable – and that goes for God, the Turks and the Greek bureaucracy. Life is a struggle. The goodies are few and the claimants many. You've got to push forward or you're lost.

For centuries, the little guys have survived through personal ties to the landowner, the grocer, the banker, and by making friends with more powerful men who had means (*méson*) enough to help, or who, in turn, had even more powerful friends. Perhaps these chains of influence linking the peasant farmer to the highest ranks in the centres of power are the nearest thing you get to an indigenous queue.

*R*embétika

An interview with Markos Dragoumis, of Athens College's music department

Q: *What is* rembétika*? The old* rembétika *composer Rovertákis said: "Rembétika songs were written for people who sing* rembétika *by people who sing* rembétika. *The* rembétis *is a man who had sorrow and threw it out." What political/historical environment originally brought about* rem-

bétika*? How is its early history linked to the 1922 Asia Minor disaster?*
A: The *rembétika* is the most original kind of song to have appeared in Greece over the past 100 years. A few examples of the type were already known throughout Greece by as early as 1930, and in the next 15 years these songs became more and more popular, without, however, managing to secure a following among the more well-to-do classes. They received their first recognition from respectable criticism in the 1950s.

Unfortunately we do not know either when or where or amongst whom they originated. Was it in 1850, in 1880, or in 1910? In Smyrna, on Syros, or in Piraéus? Among underworld characters living from hand to mouth by various petty illegalities on the margins of society, or among the deprived and impoverished urban dwellers? The destruction of Smyrna in 1922 certainly increased the production of *rembétika* and speeded up the processes that led to the development of their singular quality.

Do you think that in contrast to the rural folk song which is often a communal expression of a common sorrow or joy, these urban folk songs are an expression of a more alienated individual?
The words of the *rembétika* certainly express more specialised and individualised feelings than do the demotic or rural folk songs. They also differ to some extent from the demotic songs in their vocabulary and metrical structure, borrowing new elements from the lyrics of the light songs popular in the period between the wars, but using the phraseology in a different way, transforming it from the sugary and insipid into something serious and often tragic.

When and why did rembétika *come back into fashion? What made it possible for a larger audience to appreciate this music?*
Rembétika never completely lost its public. It is simply that in the 1960s this public was not to be found so much in the working-class districts of the towns, where most people had succumbed to the craze for light popular songs and "smooth" *rembétika*, but among the students and intellectuals.

These intellectuals initiated the rest of the middle class into the world of *rembétika*, which it had previously despised. Thus *rembétika* finally addressed itself to everyone, because it brought back a nostalgic and picturesque past, poverty-stricken perhaps, but in a way more carefree and certainly more genuine than the alienated present.

Do you think there's any use in comparing rembétika *with the American blues?*
The conditions that gave birth respectively to the *rembétika* and the blues are completely different, and the vast geographical distance separating Greece from the United States rules out any mutual influence. The occasional similarities one meets in the verses are entirely accidental.

most important rembétika *instruments, the* bouzoúki *and the* baglamá?
They are very ancient instruments, used by the Assyrians, the Egyptians and the ancient Greeks. The Greeks never ceased to use them, but from time to time simply modified them and changed their names. Thus the ancient *pandoúra* or *pandoúris*, the Byzantine *thamboúra* and the post-Byzantine *tamboúras* do not correspond exactly to the modern bouzoúki, but they certainly belong to the same family. It is not known when the word "bouzoúki" came into Greece from the Lebanon, but it is to be found in certain demotic songs.

What was the role of the rembétissa, *the woman who sang with these underworld characters?*
Woman, as mother, daughter, lover, is the central figure in the verses of the *rembétika*. But the title of *rembétissa* is appropriate only to the woman who follows the shiftless life of the *rembétis*. And she follows him because she has a good voice and wants to *be* someone. She in her turn inspires the men who surround her and, above all, liberates herself, becoming the original of the independent woman in Greek society.

Could you tell us something about the two

*S*hadow Puppets

Shadow puppet theatre, whose protagonist in the Greek version is Karaghiózis, was first recorded in Java, China and India, from where it spread to Turkey and then to Greece. Karaghiózis takes his name from his prominent black pupil or "karagöz" (black eye in Turkish). He is a short balding hunchback with a long arm that he uses to club others over the head. He is an uneducated Everyman dressed in rags and usually barefoot.

Yet Karaghiózis is comical rather than

pathetic. He is insatiably hungry, constantly preoccupied with finding food for himself and his family. He survives by his cunning and as need arises, impersonates prominent characters and professionals. These ruses provide only temporary solutions to his problems and eventually he is caught and often beaten and thrown in jail. Although he frequently moans *"Ach manoúla mou, ti épatha?"* ("Oh Mum, what's befallen me?"), he always reappears undaunted in the next episode.

The Karaghiózis stage has a screen of any fine white material stretched across a frame. The figures, which are designed by the player, are made of painted leather and syn-

The enraged Sultan had them hanged but later was remorseful and missed them. To console him, one of his subjects manipulated likenesses of the two dead men on a screen and Karaghiózis theatre was born.

The early plays were passed along orally and the puppeteers memorised them but added their own improvisations or created new scripts. Many players adapt classical plots to include comments on politics and to satirise local personalities and events.

Although the Karaghiózis player has assistants, he is still a one-man wonder with an endless array of intonations to suit all roles of both sexes. He is judged by his mastery of mimicry of regional dialects and speech de-

thetic material. They are flat, clean-cut silhouettes held against the screen by the operator and manipulated by horizontal rods with a hinge to facilitate change of direction. A light source from behind, originally oil lamps but now usually electric bulbs, shines through the transparent material of the figures to make them look like stained glass.

The most popular legend about the origin of Karaghiózis identifies him as a blacksmith in Turkey during the reign of Sultan Orhan (1326–59). While working on a mosque in Bursa, he and his friend, the mason Hadjiavat, had such humorous exchanges that all construction ceased as their co-workers listened.

fects such as stuttering. Energy and skill are needed to coordinate the actions of the figures with the speech. Besides all this, in many performances the player recites poetry, sings, and plays an instrument such as the guitar for the musical themes often associated with particular characters.

Above all, Karaghiózis is a theatre of laughter. At the most basic level, this is achieved through crude jokes and slapstick; Karaghiózis and his three mischievous children are chased by a foe, which results in furniture and bodies being catapulted through the air. More subtly, repetition is used in gesture, movement and speech to parody character types such as the pompous dandy Morfónios from the Ionian Islands. Disguise and concealment are common; Karaghiózis masquerades as a bride which shocks the hapless bridegroom as he lifts the veil. Oddity of physical appearance and behaviour is exaggerated.

Before World War II, Mollas, a famous puppet-master, commented: "A monster has come to us from America." He was referring to the cinema which had a technical sophistication that captured the general audience which had been attending the shadow theatre performances. With the emergence of television in Greece in the 1960s, the shadow plays which were once the entertainment highlight of many a neighbourhood, seemed to many old-fashioned and naïve.

Fewer than 10 older Karaghiózis players perform now in Greece with no young apprentices being recruited. Just one summer theatre and a weekly television programme are regularly devoted to shadow theatre. Yet this folk art has not lost its universal appeal. The cast of characters reflects the divergence of influences still evident in Greece today. Karaghiózis himself is the embodiment of the innate spirit of the Greek nation. He survives all adversity and starts every new adventure with renewed optimism and energy.

Theodorákis

Markos Dragoumis discusses the influence of the celebrated Greek composer Míkis Theodorákis, who was imprisoned from 1967 to 1970 for attempting to overthrow the regime.

Q: *What was happening in music during the 1967–74 military junta?*
A: Certain songs which in the ordinary way would have circulated freely went underground, while there was a general increase in the number of songs with hinted messages against the dictators; in fact, a kind of resistance activity and democratic communication went on through the medium of songs.

Why do you think Theodorákis and the ballad writers of the Néo Kyma (New Wave) had enough success in the 1960s to ensure Greece a popular music unchallenged by

disco and other Anglo-American imports?
The 1960s were a time of political unrest and saw the suppression of democratic institutions. Since the words "Greece" and "democracy" are inseparably linked, a tyrannical regime must always be foreign to Greece. In times of slavery all peoples go back to their roots, from which they derive the strength to survive as peoples. Nevertheless, this does not mean that the Greeks turned their backs on music from abroad during this period.

Could you describe some of the differences between the calculated compositions of Theodorákis, Hadjidákis and the other Greek composers who have studied abroad and the more spontaneous rembétika and folk music?
In certain of their songs (especially those written for the cinema), Theodorákis and Hadjidákis faithfully follow the spirit of the *rembétika*. But in their genuinely important songs they express themselves more personally, and in these one seldom finds striking similarities with the *rembétika*, even when these songs have a bouzoúki accompaniment. The public, of course, has its preferences, but it is not uncommon for the admirers of modern Greek "composer" songs to like *rembétika* too.

Even if Greek popular music is not at all like classical, rock, disco or punk, could you still say that it is more influenced by the West than by the East?
What is noteworthy in Theodorákis and Hadjidákis, as in quite a number of their successors, is how well they blend the frequently contradictory Western and Eastern (Greco-Byzantine) compositional processes. Which source influences them most? In this matter, surely each composer chooses his own path.

What is the extent of the collaboration that goes on between Greece's contemporary composers and poets?
I don't think we can talk about "collaboration" between composers and poets. The composers usually open anthologies of poetry and set those poems which they like, as they like; in fact, they often choose to set the work of poets who are no longer alive, such as Solomós, Kálvos, Sikelianós and Kavadías.

*U*nfinished Buildings

There are many jokes about Greek bureaucracy and endless red tape. It's a well-known fact that in the Greek civil service there are five people to every one job. Although this diminishes unemployment it has its side-effects as well: it often takes five times longer to do anything, whether it's going through customs, paying road tax, changing money or registering for school.

For many outsiders it is unfathomable that such simple tasks could take so long. But you have only to take into consideration such practices as *hartósima* (the tax stamps) to realise that efficiency is not one of the main objectives. By law you are required to affix these tax stamps to most official documents; but, for some reason, state offices rarely have their own stock. So in the middle of filing an application you must run down to the nearest kiosk (see *Períptera*) to buy some.

Then after climbing four flights of stairs or surviving the ancient elevator crammed with people and coffee trays (see Coffee) you arrive only to find that the coffee you so charitably balanced on your shoulder in the elevator on the way up was meant for the very civil servant who had been serving you and would therefore hold you up another half an hour. After his coffee break you find out that you also need three copies of one page and a photograph of yourself taken by a particular photographer on the other side of town... and so the story goes.

One of the main symptoms of this bureaucracy, or *graphiokratía* as the Greeks call it, is the multitude of unfinished buildings that dot the Greek cityscape. If paying road tax takes a day, just think how long a building project could take. It is impossible to foresee the many setbacks. Not only do the zoning laws change with every new government but cultural expectations shift as well. Fifteen years ago most parents felt it was their obligation to build their daughters houses as part of their dowry even if it was beyond their means. Now, though a young woman may receive an education rather than a house as dowry, many of these building projects persist, gaining a wall or floor every year. Whole floors and extensions and fences can go up illegally.

*V*endetta

Unlike brigandage, which was common throughout Greece, the vendetta tradition was found in only a few regions, where large families, a passionate sensitivity to personal honour and a love for fighting farmed an unholy trinity. Epirus was one such feud-ridden region, but the heartland of the Greek vendetta was the Máni. William Leake, visiting the Máni village of Vathiá in 1805, decided not to spend the night there after learning that a feud had been raging for the past 40 years, "in which time they reckon that about a hundred men have been killed".

Some observers, debunking the vendetta "myth", claimed that reports of casualties had been much exaggerated and that there was more shooting than bloodshed. But the 18th-century casebooks of Dr Papadákis, a Mániot surgeon with a flourishing practice, present a different picture of heads crushed by rocks, bullet-ridden limbs, stiletto and sword wounds commonplace.

But the turbulent Máni described by the doctor has subsided into a desolate silence. The main road built since the war transformed the old ways. Now the last signs of the vendetta visible to the traveller are the gaunt decaying stone towers in every village from which rival clans only a century ago attempted to exterminate one another.

*W*omen

In the traditional view, a woman without a house is as incomplete as a house without a woman. To a modern woman, a house may seem a paltry kingdom to inherit, especially if it is one box in a concrete block. But the link between the woman and the house has been a constant in Greece. Those wealthy merchants' houses of the 18th and 19th centuries which can still be seen in towns such as Kastoriá and Siátista were decorated inside with a painted profusion of flowers, fruit and friezes of wide rolling countryside. They were gilded cages for the women whose lives were passed within them.

A woman's relationship to her house, to its physical fabric, affects her whole life. In many areas of Greece (broadly speaking, the south and the islands) there has traditionally been the expectation that the family of a woman who is about to be married will provide a house as well as some furniture and other goods or property. The dowry has strongly affected women's marriage chances and in addition the balance of male and female children in families has been critical for economic success or failure. Sons have sacrificed their inheritance to dispose of their sisters, women have been driven to the brink of suicide as their market value plummets in a family crisis.

Attempts are now being made to limit the power of these expectations, and the dowry

routinely made available for the new couple. But in these cases it is still most likely to be the mother-in-law who will keep a supervisory eye on the household management and child-rearing practices of her son's wife.

Once a woman is established in her own house, she can exhibit her worth through the objects in it. As a visitor to a Greek house, you may be shown into the *salóni*, and the shutters may be thrown open in your honour so that every item in the room sucks up light like a sponge. The furniture gleams with a limpid varnish, the mirror-backed cabinet is filled with phalanxes of glasses of every category. There are glinting outposts of ornaments in every direction and, above, a

is technically illegal. In northerly areas the normal pattern is the reverse: it is the man's family which expects to provide a house, or house room, for each new couple. Traditionally, families extended as the sons married and brought their wives to the parental house where they were subject to the often tyrannical rule of the *petherá* (mother-in-law) who had no doubt suffered at the hands of her own *petherá* when she was the new bride. As families began to expect more comfort and privacy and, it is said, became less willing to have patience with each other, it became normal for only the latest married son to remain at home. Now new houses or flats are

formation of globes or crystal drops which defies both gravity and any creeping invasion of darkness at the room's edges.

The challenge to the housewife is clear; every speck of dust which is allowed to settle will be reflected back as two. But all is under her control. Her banner is raised victoriously on every side. Every item of furniture is dressed overall with a festive array of fabrics embroidered, crocheted, tasselled and trimmed. They are crisply ironed and draped just so, pressed so that their corners hang precisely at the midpoint of the table edges, or pushed into ripples by heavy vases.

The visitor who is left alone for a little

longer, while the *Kyría* goes to make coffee in her back kitchen, may begin to dwell upon the stitches, the accumulated moments of women's hours and days – subtly toned flowers in blues and reds and gold, with silky green leaves, intricately counted patterns of crosses, encrusted edges, and patient repetitions in the millions of tugged loops of a crocheted curtain.

Greek women's handiwork is no mere pastime. It is bound closely to the traditional sense of woman's role and destiny. A young girl learns to sew so that she will be marriageable. These skills symbolise, obscurely, all that she must be. The bride must show that she has the wherewithal to "dress" the

house, all the ornamental and comfortable fabrics which will line the nest of marriage. The usually impressive accumulation of fabrics and furnishings is brought to the new house with some ceremony – in the past on the backs of a string of well-laden mules, now more often in a truck which creeps through village or neighbourhood with the horn sounding and shouts of merriment issuing from the back.

Housework is, of course, a kind of display and in Greece the performance is almost always virtuoso. In both towns and villages many tasks are appropriately done in public view – hanging the washing, beating rugs.

airing bedclothes, taking food to the bakeries to be cooked, and shopping. A woman's work is manifested to the world.

Made in heaven: It would be difficult to exaggerate the importance given to marriage in Greece. The feeling that there is no more appropriate mode of living for an adult of either sex is prevalent, and it is widely assumed that monks and nuns who explicitly reject it must have been disappointed in love. The fact that marriage is essential for a complete life is symbolised by the ritual in which a young adult who dies unmarried must be dressed in wedding clothes and, in a poignant ceremony, is "married" in the coffin with a single wedding crown.

The pressure for women to marry is intense. They are given less time to do so than men; an unmarried woman in her late twenties is a matter for concern to her relatives whereas a man can retain his "freedom" (unmarried people are always described as "free") until 40 or so. Women who choose not to marry have to confront the stubborn belief that they are single not through their own choice but of necessity. Circumstances have proved too much for them, runs the typical interpretation, so that they have missed their chance of marriage.

Although childbearing is their fulfilment, Greek mothers often talk of the suffering involved in having children. They don't just mean the pains of childbirth, either. They expect to suffer anxiety on the child's behalf from its first breath until it is safely married. They share this suffering with the *Panaghía*, the Virgin Mary, who is the model of womanhood explicitly offered by Greek Orthodoxy, and whose sufferings on behalf of her son are remembered during the course of the Church's year. Women are "Eves", caught in the trammels of human sexuality and only redeem themselves by bearing a child, as the Virgin Mary did.

Motherhood means nurture. The mother gives substance to her child while she is pregnant and the process does not stop there. Mothers tend to feed their children with great anxiety (a reason sometimes given for preferring bottle-feeding is that "at least you can see what it has eaten"). Unfortunately many a Greek child is aware of this and exploits the mother's sensitivity on this matter. The degree of a mother's love for her family can be represented by the effort she puts into preparing food. If she produces boiled macaroni day after day she will be aware that she is skimping. The favourite dishes – *dolmáthes*, *pastítsio*, and *pítta,* for example – take hours to prepare and involve a number of different processes. A *hortópitta* even requires that the cook should wander the fields in search of the right kinds of greens.

While the ideal of motherhood is nurturing, ideally a mother should train her family to fast – that is, to control the types of food they eat at certain times in order to achieve religious purity. Fasting is regarded quite flexibly these days in many households, with the consequence that women often casually enquire what other families are eating – so that their

to be maintained for to make children fast more than is generally thought to be necessary is a denial of mother love.

A woman's care of the other members of the family extends to everyone in it but is concentrated especially on those who are most helpless, children and the dead. Care for the dead also, paradoxically, involves the preparation of food. But it is, in fact, a kind of reversal of the nurturing process. During life a person needs to build up the body for life and health. After death it becomes necessary to let the body "melt", unburdening the soul and purifying the person ready for ultimate resurrection. By giving food away to other families a woman helps the dead per-

standards are neither higher nor lower than the average. Strict fasting means abstention from meat, all animal products and oil. Special dishes are made with oil and vegetables as a kind of intermediary level of restraint. There are women, mostly old, whose faces light up as they say, during a fast period, "Not a drop of oil have I eaten, not a drop…", who take their gift of abstention to the Vespers every evening and appear to enjoy a peaceful detachment from physical needs. These women may be viewed with suspicion by the less devout and the irreligious, lest they start to use their piety as a ground for judging others. For families there is a balance of opposing values

son she is caring for to lose, symbolically, unwanted flesh.

On the five "Soul Saturdays" in the year black-clothed women can be seen in cemeteries all over Greece. They busy themselves with candles, or polishing the marble plaques around the graves; but most importantly, they take foil-wrapped bundles of food and, like children on a picnic, they swop with their neighbours – a piece of cake for a piece of *loukoúmi* (Turkish Delight) and the special kind of wheat porridge known as *kóllyva* for a long-ribbed biscuit. Such food is accepted with the words "May God forgive". It is an orgy of giving, each woman going away with a package as big as the one she brought. If for any reason a woman is unable to fulfil her duties towards the dead, she is quite likely to see the person in dreams. When she ceases to experience such dreams the dead person no longer needs her care.

Changed values: Today both old and new values coexist – the importance of being a wife and mother with the importance of being able to earn a good income. What has remained important has been the need for a woman to know that she has value. Where a woman's dowry has been external to herself she has been able to feel, once she is married, a solidity and security in relation to her husband. Where her value has been symbol-

ised by the trivia of household furnishing she has still had a means of display and self-presentation. Now more substantial, though less visible, qualities are being appreciated: education, competence, the quality of being a *drastíria*, a "woman of action". But these new values do not necessarily mean freedom, and certain visible indicators of a woman's character – the way she dances, what she drinks, whether she smokes – are still given weight. Most of all, a woman is still expected to be linked to a family.

This is the most shocking thing about foreign women in Greece. Women travelling in Greece are often a little unnerved by the separation of men's and women's worlds. Add to this the obvious attentions from men which foreign women attract in areas accustomed to tourism and the female traveller is left wondering how she is viewed by locals.

Because Greek fathers and brothers have traditionally been the guardians of female sexuality (the assumption being that individuals of either sex are not all that good at saying "no" on their own account), women who evidently have freedom of movement and economic independence are thought likely to be unconstrained in other ways. In this, they resemble men. Foreign women are often given small chances to be "pseudo-men", offered cigarettes or strong drink (offers which women from small villages would take as a joke or an insult but which Greek city women take in their stride) and even a seat in a *kafeneíon*. Acceptance of such "privileges" makes overt the foreign woman's peculiar position.

Women are likely to respond to the visiting anomaly with a barrage of questions: "*Mamá, babá, zoúneh?*" ("Mum, Dad, are they alive?"); "*Adélfia?*" ("Brothers and sisters?"); and, pointing to the ring finger of the right hand, "*Andras?*" ("Don't you have a husband?"). These are not routine polite enquiries but attempts to clarify what is, for them, the most important thing about a person – the link with family responsibilities.

The traveller can conduct herself as she wishes. She can allow herself to be placed in the sexually free category or emphasise that she's a nice family girl.

But, powerful as these stereotypes are, there is no need to be pushed into either. There is such a strong sense of "how *we* do things" that there is a corresponding streak of open-mindedness in most Greeks, who are ready to accept that in your country you do things differently.

This acceptance of other values is having to be exercised more and more within the Greek family, between generations. The family's sphere of interests was once visibly contained within its own four walls and its fields. Now it is interpenetrated by the world, by television, by education, by its members' movements throughout Greece and further afield. But it represents, still, the front line of contact with the real moral issues of human weakness, human needs and mortality. This is where women are effectively at work.

*X*enomania

As a small country, Greece has always had to contend with the *xénos*, the foreigner. Whether as invader or visitor, the *xénos* has had a big impact on the Greek conception of self. A *xénos* isn't simply a non-Greek, he or she might be a Greek from another town. In the past when a woman married a man from over the mountain she married a *xénos*. The songs sung at her wedding were often laments wishing her well in the "after-life". Departure for another village and departure for another world were equated. The *xénos* who carried

lems; in many ways Greece was not prepared for such a growth in tourism. A baker and his wife on Amorgós who can earn three times their salary by renting out rooms to foreigners in summer may not think too much about the aesthetics of the port or the influx of less traditional mores when they decide to add some guest rooms to the family house.

And although the wife may complain when her husband starts running after blonde Swedes or when her kids start demanding products she has never heard of like Coppertone tanning lotion, the causal relationship between a fast expanding tourist industry and her family's whims may not be deeply explored. And even if she does blame the

her off was viewed with as much suspicion as any foreigner. Even today in many places the Athenian is almost as much a *xénos* as the punk rocker on a package tour from England. But whereas 50 years ago xenophobia (*ksenofovía*) was predominant, today its flip side, *ksenomanía*, is by far more prevalent.

Tourism has been on the rise since the early 1960s. During the dictatorship (1967–74) foreigners were encouraged to buy property tax-free. By the end of the 1980s tourism was bringing in almost as much money as all other industries combined – from olive oil to scuba masks to large-scale machinery.

But xenomania is not without its prob-

tourists she depends on them for her family's livelihood. *Xénos* has clearly become a much more ambivalent term now that it pivots freely between "phobia" and "mania". One moment the tourist is the one to thank for the new road and the relatively high standard of living and the next the tourist is to blame for sex and drugs and rock and roll.

What is particularly interesting about Greek tourism is the way it attends to the foreigners' material needs but still obstinately refuses to accommodate their different pace of life. A trendy hotel on Hydra may serve all the right cocktails in its bar but the owner will refuse to get up before 10 am to fix breakfast.

According to him, no one who is anyone gets up that early. He hasn't thought that a trendy German may not have the same sleeping habits as a trendy Greek.

The speed with which Greece has become a vacation paradise means that until recently it was more equipped for backpackers than the clientèle of luxury liners. But this is changing as Greeks realise that they need to attract this latter group in order to profit from tourism. Tourists can look forward to more and more varied services – and also, perhaps, to a less manic reception, neither xenophobia nor xenomania but xenophilia.

Yoghurt

Most visitors to Greece rave about the yoghurt. Rich, thick and creamy in its commercial form or tart and slippery in the *spitikó* (home-made) version, it is a much more substantial food than the watery yoghurt you find in other countries. For this reason, the American habit of "drinking" a yoghurt for lunch is completely unfathomable to a Greek.

Yoghurt is neither a beverage nor a meal. It has its own peculiar culinary function. Like parentheses, it separates the meal from the rest of daily activities. It cleans the palate. Meals often start with a plate of *tsatzíki* (a delicious thick spread of yoghurt, cucumber and garlic) or finish with a bowl of yoghurt smothered in the region's honey and walnuts. Whether as a preface or a finale to a meal, the yoghurt's smooth consistency helps digestion.

In general, yoghurt is regarded as soothing. In fact, in Greece when the sea is calm they say it is "'like yoghurt". In recent years England has begun importing Greek yoghurt to sell to holidaymakers when they return to dreary Britain after two weeks of Mediterranean sun and sea. Once upon a time tourists brought back pockets full of pebbles and shards as mementos of their trip; now they can forego the fuss – a quick trip to the corner deli provides all the ingredients for real Greek *tsatzíki*. Although the commercial brands of yoghurt barely resemble their tangy, crusty *spitikó* counterpart, a good imagination can still conjure up the smell of thyme and oregano and the distant bells of sheep and goats scampering across a mountainside.

Zorba

Nobody has done more for the image of the earthy, passionate, impulsive Hellenic hedonist than Hollywood's ethnic chameleon, Anthony Quinn. Níkos Kazantzákis may have invented Zorba but only Quinn could have danced that lusty rogue of a peasant into the hearts of millions. Kudos must go, too, to director Elia Kazan, who captured in stark black-and-white the austerity (of the social mores no less than of mountains and architecture) of a highland Cretan village.

Though most foreigners know him as

"Zorba the Greek", the novel is titled *Aléxis Zorbás* – Kazantzákis would have found "the Greek" superfluous. In fact, it's clear that Zorba was a real person, hailing (some say) from a small town on the Macedonian peninsula of Chalcidice, whom the author met when Zorba came to work on Crete.

He may have been mortal once, but Zorba has acquired mythic qualities. He's a modern stereotype, perhaps, but with a long lineage. European elites long regarded peasants as "noble savages" close to home, and romantic literature and travellers' accounts abound with rustic peasants dancing their troubles away. In Greece, there's a special twist; the peasants' "wild" dances and "discordant" music get likened to ancient Dionysian revels.

Yet, however trivialised they have become, Zorba and his predecessors represent quite sober explorations of a very old philosophical problem in Greece: the power of passion and the limits of reason. This has also been a core issue of Orthodoxy, whose rational, worldly power always coexisted with the most mystical of theologies. This otherworldly faith flourished in the sensuous landscape of Kazantzákis's native Crete.

Kazantzákis was preoccupied with spiritual questions all his life. Though he eventually left the Orthodox Church, there is no

not just noble but wise. It's the scholar who needs to be taught by Zorba, the unlettered labourer who "knows himself".

It's somehow apt that for most of us today, Zorba is a celluloid, not a literary, figure. Words are not Zorba's *forte*. For all his pearls of earthy wisdom (laced with Quinn's exclamations in superbly accented Greek) Zorba knows the limits of words. When something profound happens – as when his daughter dies – Zorba must dance! Be it ecstasy or sorrow, Zorba seems to say, the body is better at translating the ineffable.

Zorba, Melína, Dionysios, the dancing Greek reincarnated under tourism in distorted guises to sell everything from package

doubt that his own personal conflicts over sex as well as his literary themes, come from early religious experiences. His novel about Zorba explores the problem of body and soul which always obsessed him. "The Boss" – who many say was really Kazantzákis himself – is an intellectual trapped in a world of words. He keeps himself from sin by repressing all feelings of desire for forbidden things. But he is totally unable to act. The Boss's paralysis finds its antithesis in Zorba, who confronts his desires – for food, for wine, for the charms of women – naturally, even defiantly. Kazantzákis may be forgiven his hint of Romanticism, for the rude peasant here is

holidays to tape cassettes, still express something about what it means to be Greek: about dramatic self-assertion before a sceptical public, about the pleasures and tensions of sociability, about passion and control.

If foreigners barely understand what dancing, feasting, even smashing plates, mean to Greeks, we nonetheless find the exuberance we see there irresistible. For in Zórba and the rest we discern a spontaneity and collective *bonhomie* lost in the anonymity of our own more industrialised societies. Greeks and foreigners alike keep Zorba alive, because Zorba is "good to think with" – not just about Greeks, but about ourselves.

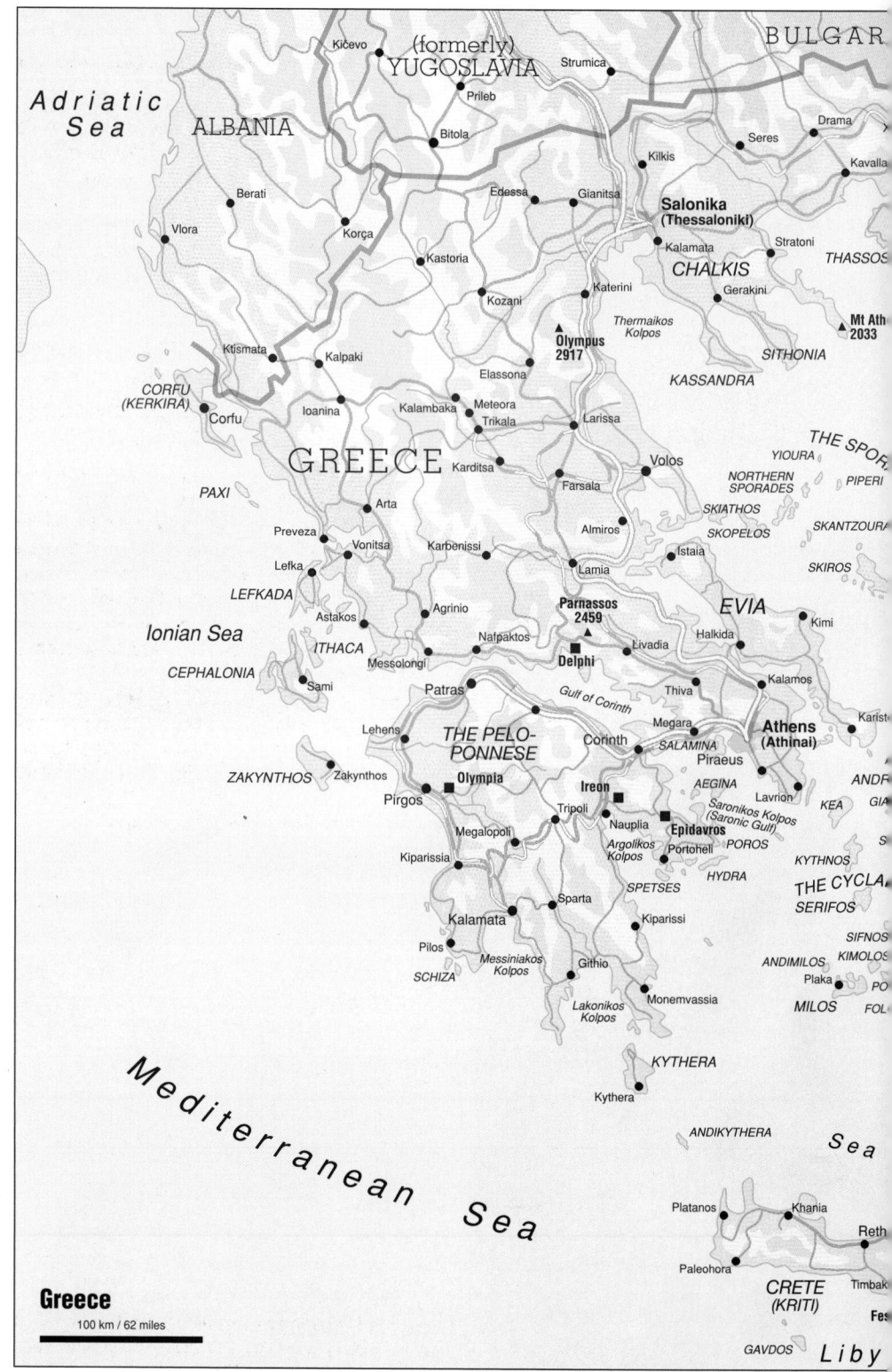

Greece

100 km / 62 miles

PLACES

"Marvellous things happen to one in Greece," wrote Henry Miller in *The Colossus of Maroussi*, "marvellous *good* things which can happen to one nowhere else on earth. Somehow, almost as if He were nodding, Greece still remains under the protection of the Creator. Men may go about their puny, ineffectual bedevilment, even in Greece, but God's magic is still at work and, no matter what the race of men may do or try to do, Greece is still a sacred precinct – and my belief is it will remain so until the end of time."

In this section, our writers will take you on 10 individual journeys, each author to the part of Greece he or she knows best. Starting in the northeastern corner near Turkey and Bulgaria and travelling in a zigzag fashion down to Crete, you'll find the history, geography and local culture of each area covered in detail.

The 10 sections have been loosely designed as two-week itineraries, but of course the longer you stay, the better. Perhaps, like Lord Byron, you will one day be able to declare: "It is the only place I ever was contented in."

Preceding pages: fishing boats moored off Kálymnos; the town of Kastráki in Thessaly; olive grove on Crete.

THE NORTHEAST

Thessaloniki stands about halfway between the Ionian Sea to the west and the Évros River to the east. It is the second largest city of Greece and is often referred to as co-capital with Athens. A line projected north of Thessaloniki reaches the tripartite border between the former Yugoslavia, Bulgaria and Greece. This line also divides the northwest of Greece, comprising Epirus and western Macedonia, from the northeast, which includes eastern Macedonia and Thrace.

The history of the northeast is dominated by the movement of tribes, races and nationalities across its territory. The local Macedonian and Thracian populations were subject to constant invasion and flux. On his way to fight Athens and Sparta, the Persian Xerxes marched countless troops across the north Aegean land route, while his fleet followed along the coast. It was from here that Alexander the Great set off to conquer the east, and here that the Romans established the Via Egnatia stretching from the Adriatic coast to the Hellespont (Dardanelles). Later, the disintegrating Byzantine Empire would face continuous incursions from the north due to Slavic expansion. And the Ottoman Turks, advancing from the east, would make a circle across the Balkans, conquering the Macedonian and Thracian lands before closing in on Constantinople.

The sea provided an important access to the northeast, despite the fact that the coast is tucked away at the northeastern-most corner of the Aegean. Odysseus, leaving Troy for his return journey to Ithaca, drifted to the land of the Kikones, the ancient site of Maronia. Southern Greek cities, especially Athens and Chalkis, began their colonisation of the Chalcidice (Chalkidike) peninsula via the sea as early as the 7th century BC. Later, when Thessaloniki became the second largest city of the Byzantine Empire, Venetians, Crusad-

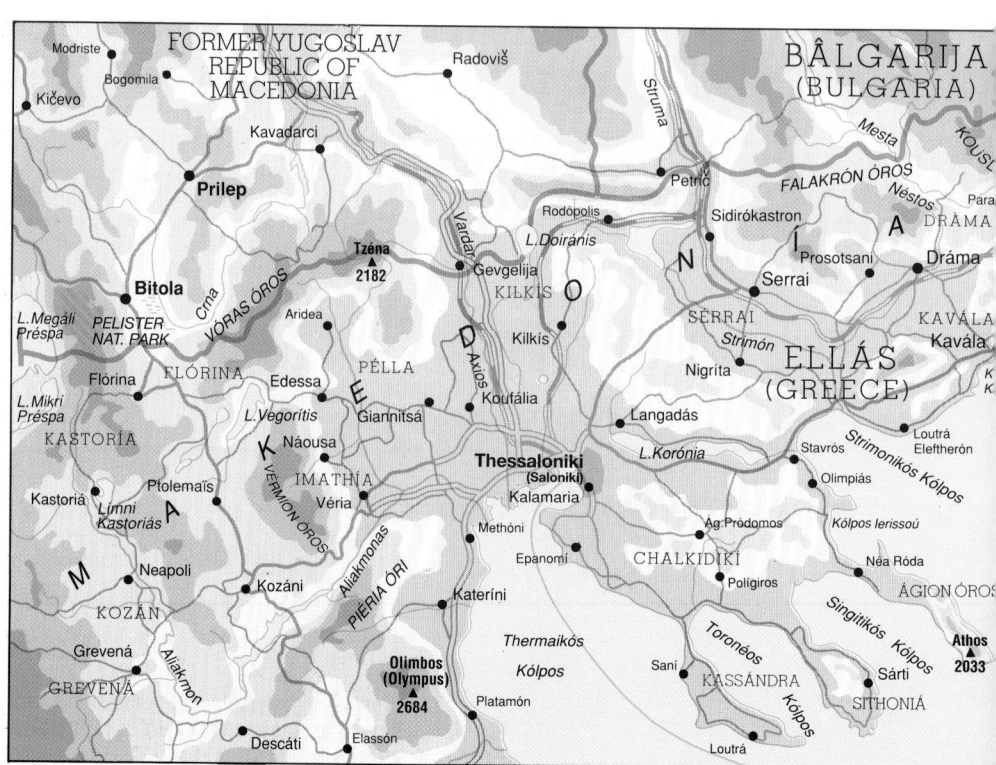

ers and other seafarers skirted the coast to and from Constantinople.

The northeast does not offer the traveller the magnificent large-scale archaeological sites and stunning temples of central and southern Greece. However, its proximity to other Balkan states and its rather late acquisition by Greece give it greater ethnic variety and more unspoiled natural beauty. Both these features are rapidly changing due to modernisation and integration into a more uniform national culture. The region's sites fall into two categories: either they are too bare to astound, or they are palimpsests where layers of civilisation can be read one after another. One of the best examples of the latter category is Thessaloniki itself.

Thessaloniki: To the visitor approaching it by sea, the modern city presents the solid facade of apartment blocks characteristic of many Mediterranean seaside cities. At the beginning of this century, the same view was marked by elegantly rising minarets, which were destroyed either by the Great Fire of

1917 (which turned nearly three quarters of the city to ashes), or by Greek nationalism retaliating for previous Turkish desecration of churches. Behind today's high-rise facade, encircled by the Roman and Byzantine walls, and scattered in the midst of main traffic arteries and pedestrian alleys, lies the city's historical wealth. Roman ruins, Byzantine churches, Turkish buildings and Jewish tombstones are hidden away behind the greenery of *plateíes* or the colourful houses of the old Áno Póli (upper town).

Thessaloniki was founded in 315 BC by the Macedonian king Kassander, who named it after his wife. It was not an important city during the rise of the Macedonian Empire in the 4th century BC. Today its **Archaeological Museum** houses Macedonian, Hellenistic and Roman finds from the whole region, including the notable Sindos and Vergina collections. The latter comprises the magnificent treasures of what are alleged to be Philip II's royal tombs.

Macedonian sites: Philippi, north of

The White Tower, Thessaloniki.

Kavála and founded by Philip II himself, has little that is Macedonian to show, for it developed in later Roman times. **Vergina**, on the way to Véroia, was the capital before Pella and remained the royal cemetery.

The tombs of Philip of Macedonia, discovered in 1977, are closed for further excavation. But there are other tombs and a half-standing palace situated in a pleasant landscape. **Díon**, at the foot of Mount Olympus (Ólymbos) farther south, was founded by Macedonian kings as a place of worship to the Olympian Zeus and, most likely, as a Macedonian show-case to the rest of Greece.

Pella, on the road to Edessa, is the most outstanding site. The rather small scale of its revealed grounds, and its location right by the side of the road, give it a humbleness which doesn't correspond to its past glory. Standing in the courtyard of the **House of the Lion Hunt**, surrounded by graceful Ionian columns and the exquisite floor mosaics that have survived (some on site, some in the local museum), one cannot help but sense that here stood the imperial court craeted by the masters of the Greek world in the 4th century BC. It was here that Philip of Macedonia planned the conquest of Greece. And here that his son, Alexander the Great, trained at arms and was taught by the philosopher Aristotle in preparation for a brilliant though short-lived career as conqueror of the east.

City tour: Thessaloniki gained renown as a Byzantine city. It has no Byzantine museum, but an interesting exhibition outlining the city's history is housed in the **White Tower** by the waterfront. This is the city's landmark. Built in the 15th century, it served as a prison under Ottoman rule. In 1826, it was the site of a massacre of mutinous Janissaries which earned it the name of "Bloody Tower". The memories of this event were brushed away with a coat of whitewash and a consequent change of name. Today this name is misleading, for the tower is no longer white. The steps going up in a spiral around the inner

A quiet moment on the Thessaloniki waterfront.

wall are flanked by small deep-set windows which frame partial views of the city and gulf. One can then assemble the different pieces into a single panorama from the battlements.

The Roman ruins are distributed along the two main avenues leading to the waterfront: the **Forum** and **Odeon Galerius Palace Complex** along Dimitríou Goúnari Street. Caesar Galerius built this complex at the beginning of the 4th century, when he chose Thessaloniki as his seat of residence. He was famous for his ruthless persecution of Christians, including the martyrdom of St Demétrios, patron saint of the city. The palace ruins are scattered in the midst of busy **Navarínou Square**, lined with *tavérnes*, snack bars and ice-cream parlours. The triumphal **Arch of Galerius** was built to commemorate the emperor's victory over the Persians: relief panels at its base depict scenes from the campaign.

Churches: Undoubtedly the most important building in the complex is the **Rotunda**, or **Church of Saint George** (**Ághios Yeórgios**), one of the few surviving examples of circular Roman architecture. Galerius intended it for his mausoleum, a function it never fulfilled as the emperor fell in battle and his enemy did not return the body to Thessaloniki. With the spread of Christianity, it was soon turned into a church and decorated with glorious wall mosaics which only partially survive around the upper part of the interior. The Rotunda is flanked by a half-standing minaret from the days when it served as a mosque. It dominates the views down to the sea from above and up to the **Chain Tower** from the seafront, marking the northeastern corner of the Byzantine fortifications.

Another early Christian building is the tiny **Church of Óssios Davíd**, tucked away in the old part of town up the hill. It was allegedly built by Galerius's daughter, Theodora. The unique 5th-century mosaic in the apse is one of the earliest samples of its kind. Its outstanding beauty derives from the *naif* depiction of Ezekiel's vision, the rare repre-

sentation of a youthful Christ, the fine colours and elaborate symbolism.

From Óssios Davíd one can continue a visit to the city's important Byzantine monuments by following one of two paths: one goes back down the hill to the major 5th to 8th-century basilicas while the other makes a long semi-circle across the old city past 14th-century churches.

The early Christian basilica was a plain rectangular building. In a sense, its plan derives from the classical Greek temple, replacing the exterior colonnade with walls. Both the 5th-century **Acheiropíitos Church** and the heavily restored **Church of St Demetrius (Ághios Dimítrios)** are such examples. Both have been badly damaged by fire and the surviving mosaics must be sought out: the first under the arches, the second above the pillars on the east and west sides of the church. The crypt in St Demetrius is supposed to mark the site of the Roman bath where the saint was martyred. The **Church of Aghía Sophía** (Holy Wisdom) shows a first attempt to convert the basilica into a domed struc-

ture. The inside of the dome, which represents the heavenly vault, is covered with a surprisingly well-preserved large-scale mosaic depicting the Ascension, illustrated by the corresponding scene of the 12 apostles, two angels and the Virgin Mary, separated by trees and gazing up at the "Pantocrator", the Almighty Christ.

The great controversies: During the Byzantine period, Thessaloniki lived through two major theological debates. The Iconoclast Controversy raged in the 8th and 9th centuries when excessive worship of icons led to an equally extreme reaction against them. The Óssios Davíd mosaic was covered with cowhides to save it from destruction, while the original mosaic of the Virgin in Aghía Sophía's apse was destroyed and restored after this storm had passed. The focal point of this controversy was Constantinople, while the 14th-century Hesychast Debate centred in Thessaloniki itself. Hesychasm (from *isychía*, meaning tranquillity) was propounded by the monks of Mount Athos, and **Church of St Demetrius.**

claimed that "by holding the breath, by making the spirit re-enter into the soul, and by gazing fixedly upon the navel they could attain to the vision of the uncreated light which shone on Tabor." This creed was ridiculed by the Calabrian monk Barlaam, leader of the Zealot opposition. A struggle ensued which was at least as social and political as it was theological. Hesychasm's major theorist, Gregory Palamas was Archbishop of Thessaloniki; his reliquary is kept in the city's cathedral.

If you take the second walk from Óssios Davíd, you cross the charming **Áno Póli**. A 20-minute walk from the town centre takes you to this part of town which still has the atmosphere of a village. Here and in the Acropolis, the highest part of town enclosed by fortifications, you can find good *tavérnes*. In the 14th century the hill was covered with small monasteries of which only some of the chapels survive. The **Church of St Nicholas Orphanos** has exquisite frescoes. The **churches of St Elias and St Catherine** represent interesting de-

velopments in the cross-in-dome architectural form, which culminates in the **Church of the Holy Apostles**. The latter's fine mosaics with scenes from the life of Christ are so high up that they can only be appreciated with a pair of binoculars.

Other influences: Thessaloniki was conquered by the Ottomans in 1430, just 23 years before the fall of Constantinople. Churches were conveniently turned into mosques by plastering over the interior decoration and building minarets up their sides. Fifteenth-century Ottoman monuments develop the style of elaborate dome constructions of late Byzantine churches. There are two mosques of particular interest: the graceful Ishak Pasha or **Alaja Imaret**, now turned into an exhibition hall, and the **Hamza-Bey**, now the Alcazar movie theatre. Drapers and goldsmiths sell their wares as they did long ago in the **Bezesten**, a six-domed covered market. The **Yahoudi**, once a Turkish *hammám* (public bath), now shelters an open-air flower market and a small fish *tavérna*

An exchange of goods in Thessaloniki's market.

which is recommended. Around it spreads today's central market area, displaying a colourful array of mounds of fresh fruit and vegetables, fish and meat, heaps of olives, sweets and spices, wooden utensils and straw baskets. A more contemporary Turkish monument is the house where Mustafa Kemal was born, today the Turkish consulate. Later known as Ataturk, he was a leader of the Young Turk Movement that overthrew the sultan and founded the Turkish Republic in 1928.

Contemporary things: Modern Thessaloniki spreads far beyond the old city walls. The university gives it a bustling student life which gathers at the bars near the seafront and White Tower at night. The International Fair held every October makes it an important trade centre for the Balkans. Along the eastern quay, modern apartment blocks stand beside grandiose old mansions. One of them, now the **Folk Art Museum,** offers an exhibition on ethnic differences in northern Greece.

Further along, the suburb of **Kalarn-**ana provides good seafood restaurants right on the sea. **Panorama**, an affluent suburb to the northeast, affords views which justify its name and features delicious triangular cream pastries called *trígona.* On a clear day, look out far to the south as you sip coffee by the waterfront or pause on the sinuous uphill pathways of the Áno Póli; you may see the massive form of Mount Olympus (Ólymbos) blocking the entrance to the bay, a link between modern Thessaloniki and ancient Greece.

Going east: Many roads lead east out of Thessaloniki. One of them first leads north to the town of Kilkís and the shore of the Greek half of Lake Doiran, then up the mountains to the Rupel Pass (the only access route to Bulgaria), and further east to Sérres. This route is also followed by the railway.

Sérres is best reached by the road branching off northeast of Thessaloniki. Both Sérres and Dráma, further east, were important in Byzantine and Ottoman days, and continue to be prosperous provincial towns. Both offer pleas-

Exhibits in the Archaeological Museum.

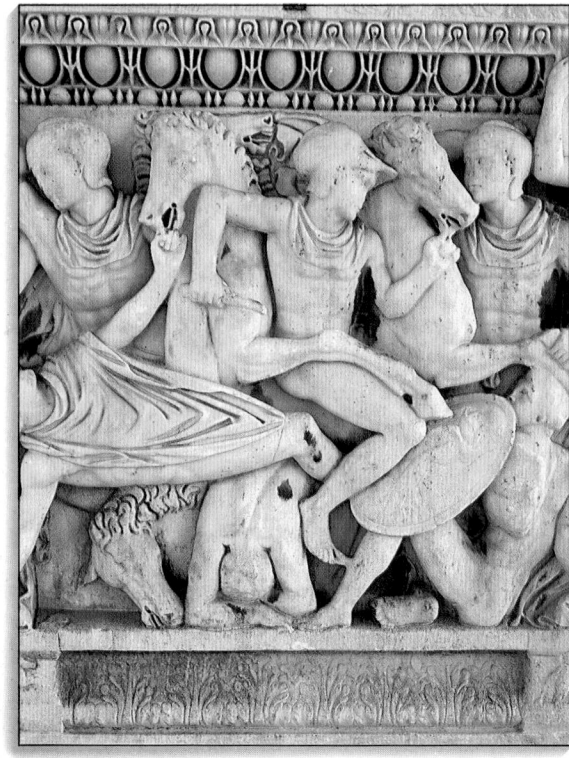

ant resting spots in shady central plazas and give access to hiking and skiing in the mountains behind them. Sérres was burnt down by the retreating Bulgarians in 1913 and was completely rebuilt, but two important Byzantine churches remain: the 11th-century **Church of the Holy Apostles** and the 14th-century **Church of St Nicholas (Nikólaos)**. A domed Ottoman building in the central square is a museum.

The land and villages lying between this area and the sea are mainly agricultural. Some come alive at specific times of the year. The Sarakatsánides, a nomadic Greek tribe of herdsmen, assemble in summer for their *paniyíri* (saint's day) near Sérres and Dráma. **Langadas** is the site of an old Thracian ritual of treading barefoot on red-hot coals, held on 21 May by the descendants of refugees from a Thracian village.

Chalkidikí: The main road east of Thessaloniki runs along the base of the Chalkidikí Peninsula, skirting lakes Koronía and Volví. The huge hand-like peninsula stretching three fingers out into the Aegean has now been overwhelmed by a tourist boom.

Little is left to show its important role in classical times when the colonies of various southern Greek cities served as the battlefield for the Peloponnesian War between Athens and Sparta (Sparti). **Potidea**, on the first finger, triggered off Sparta's declaration of war in 432 BC, while the Battle of Amphipolis put an end to the conflict in this area ten years later. Armies clashed across the land, and fleets fought offshore. Finds from the area are kept in a museum at **Políyiros**, the region's capital.

The peninsula also bears marks of other times. At the **cave of Petrálona**, fossils and a Neanderthal skull have revealed the existence of a prehistoric settlement. At **Stáyira**, a modern marble statue overlooking the Ierissós Gulf marks Aristotle's birthplace. **Xerxes's Canal**, now filled up, was built around 482 BC to help the Persians avoid the fate suffered in their previous campaign, when their fleet was wrecked sailing round Mount Athos. This and Xerxes's

The cave at Petrálona, where a Neanderthal skull was discovered.

bridge over the Hellespont were considered by the Greeks as products of Persian megalomania: "marching over the sea and sailing ships through the land." The medieval **Poteídaia Canal** still separates the Kassóudra peninsula from the mainland and serves as mooring ground for fishing boats.

Billowing hills and the beautiful forested slopes of Mount Cholomon cover the peninsula's palm. You may drive around the first two fingers, **Kassándra** and **Sithonía**, always finding an idyllic spot: charming inland villages alternate with seaside fishing hamlets, luxury hotels with camping sites, protected coves with sandy beaches, pine-clad slopes with bleak promontories. Sitting on the beach at **Sárti**, on the middle finger, you can make out the form of Mount Athos rising like a pyramid from the haze across the gulf. Here, women travellers should sign off, for the Holy Mountain is a male preserve.

Mount Athos: From the northern seaboard of Greece three long arms of land known as Chalcidice (Chalkidikí) reach into the Aegean. At the extreme end of the third and most easterly arm, the mountain which has given the peninsula its name, **Mount Athos**, rises in solitary magnificence. The fame of Athos rests on its large monastic community; these saints and humble monks have earned it the epithet "holy", now an intrinsic part of the name: Aghion Oros, the Holy Mountain.

The history of the monastic settlement begins with the advent of hermits in about the mid-9th century, roughly 100 years before the foundation of the first monastery. St Peter the Athonite, perhaps the most famous of the early monks, is supposed to have lived in a cave here for 50 years. The first monastery, the Great Lávra, was founded by St Athanásios in AD 963. He was a friend and councillor of the first historical benefactor of the Holy Mountain, the Byzantine emperor, Nikephóros Phokás. Thereafter, the foundations multiplied under the royal patronage of the Byzantine emperors who supported the build-

Xenofontos monastery, Mount Athos.

ing of the various settlements with imperial resources, in the form of money, land and treasures.

Thus all the monasteries share a rich heritage. The names of Byzantine emperors are still commemorated in their churches and imperial charters are zealously guarded in the library of each monastery.

The monasteries are now all coenobitic, in which all monks keep to strict regulations under the direction of an abbot or *ioúmenos*. Property is communal and meals are eaten in common in the *trápeza* or refectory. All monasteries are Greek except for the Russian Panteleímonos, the Serbian Chilandaríou and the Bulgarian Zográfou, and they all, with the exception of Vatopedíou keep the old Julian calendar, 13 days behind the rest of Europe, and Byzantine hours which begin at sunset and so vary every day.

The monasteries, however, form only one part of this holy community. A great number of monks prefer to live in smaller monastic establishments, the *skétes* and

kelliá dotted around the peninsula. The *kellí* or cell is a single building containing a little chapel inhabited by a smaller number of monks. The *skéte* is a small monastic village composed of a few cottages clustered round a central church. Both *skétes* and *kelliá* are dependent on one of the 20 monasteries. There are also monks who choose to live like hermits, following the traditions of St Peter the Athonite, in an *Isychastérion*, a rough unadorned hut or a cave, perched precipitously on a cliff's ledge. The hermits live in great poverty and are rarely seen.

If Athos continues to exercise a singular compulsion over the hearts and minds of outsiders, this is not because of the scenery, spectacular though it is, nor on account of its being one of the richest museums of Byzantine art and culture. Ultimately it is because it claims to represent the highest form of spiritual life known in the Orthodox, and indeed in the entire Christian tradition. Through the pursuit of a discipline demanding scrupulous attention to both outer ac-

The sun rises behind Mount Athos.

tion and inner prayer, the monk aspires to purify his body and soul from various alien attachments by which he is bound, and thus traverse the road that leads, via ascetic practice and the higher forms of contemplation, to his "deification."

All visitors to the Holy Mountain will recognise that they themselves have also traversed a road that leads to a very different realm, a realm which by ordinary human standards may even be conceived as divine. Thus the description of Athos by one of its poets as the "domain and garden of the Holy Virgin" echoes the feelings of most men who have had the luck to be born male, and so gain privileged entry to this holy place.

Visitors applying for "visas" to visit the Holy Mountain will be asked why they have come. Many have been turned away because they gave the "wrong" answer: to see the treasures, to hike in the woodland. The only acceptable reply, of course, is: "I have come on a pilgrimage to grow as a Christian, and to praise God." By the time you leave, it may well be the only *true* answer.

Back north: The main road leading east skirts the popular beaches at the head of the Strymonic Gulf on its way to **Amphípolis**. The city was founded by Athenian colonists in the 5th century BC on a Thracian site called "The Nine Ways" where, according to Herodotus, the passing Persians had seized nine boys and girls and buried them alive as a propitiatory sacrifice.

Its new name, meaning "the surrounded city," was derived from its position in a loop of the River Strymon, strategically commanding the inland flatlands, the mouth of the river, and the coveted gold mines of Mount Pangaion. Here was fought the battle that decided the first phase of the Peloponnesian War. Today the table-top plateau is strewn with limbs of broken statues, Hellenistic mosaics and the foundations of early Christian basilicas.

Crossing the Strymon over a bridge guarded by the **Lion of Amphípolis**, a colossal statue re-assembled from the 4th- and 3rd-century BC fragments, the road forks out to Kavála. The old road

The aqueduct at Kavála.

runs the length of the beautiful green valley between Mounts Pangaion and Symvolon, passing through slate-roofed villages with panoramic views. The new highway, faster but less scenic, follows the coastline.

Rising in the shape of an amphitheatre from the harbour up to the pine hills, **Kavála**'s magnificent location and manageable size make it one of the most pleasant towns in Greece. A colony of Thásos known as Neápolis in antiquity, it became an important port with access to Philippi during Roman and Christian times, while today it is the major export centre for tobacco from the surrounding plains. The local museum houses finds from Neápolis and Amphípolis.

The harbour has two parts: the modern part, and the old fishing harbour with small fish restaurants and a market backed by the arches of a 16th-century aqueduct. The old town surrounded by Byzantine walls rises on a promontory to the east. Walking up the narrow winding streets, you will notice a set of golden half-moons, the sultan's sym-

bol, shining above an outer wall. This was the Imaret, a Turkish almshouse, also known as *tembelhane*, the loungers' home, as the lazy had soon outnumbered the needy. You can push open the heavy wooden gate and ramble through its now desolate courtyards.

At the top of the hill, **Mohammed Ali's house** is a fine example of traditional Turkish architecture. Born in Kavála in 1769 of Albanian descent, Mohammed Ali became Pasha of Egypt and founder of the Egyptian royal dynasty which lasted until this century. In the square, his statue looks out to the south, the direction of the country he set out to rule.

Philippi, although named by Philip II of Macedonia, contains little that is Macedonian. From the Acropolis, where three medieval towers rise on the ruins of Macedonian walls, you get an extensive view of the battlefield which made this site famous. It was here that in 42 BC one of the decisive Roman battles was fought between the republican forces led by Brutus and Cassius, who had

taken part in the assassination of Julius Caesar in 44 BC, and the latter's avengers, Antony and Octavius.

Justice was meted out as both Cassius and Brutus committed suicide upon seeing their forces defeated. It was left to the Battle of Actium in 31 BC to decide the final struggle between the two victors of Philippi. The Roman ruins, which lie mainly to the south of the highway include the foundations of the **Forum** and the **Palaestra**, as well as the **Public Latrine** at the southwest corner of the grounds.

The beginning of Christianity: Philippi is reputed to be the first place in Europe where St Paul preached the gospel, nearly a century after the famous Roman battle. He arrived in AD 49, but was soon thrown into prison as the local religion was still a form of Thracian paganism. Six years later, however, he revisited the town to which he would later address his Epistle to the Philippians. By the 6th century, Christianity was thriving at Philippi, as the foundations of several early Christian churches of the basilica type testify.

Ferries for the island of **Thássos** leave regularly from Kavála or, if you are travelling by car, from Keramotí further east. Thássos is endowed with great natural beauty. On the east, pine trees slope down to golden beaches, pine-scent mingling with the salty sea breeze. The western shore is flatter, serene and spectacular at sunset when the sun's rays catch the silver-green of olive groves. Between the two main seaside towns, **Liménas** (also known as Thássos Town), the capital, and **Limenária** on the southern side of the island, small groups of houses along the shore alternate with large villages perched on the slopes. The slate roofs, running waters and shady plane trees of **Panaghía** and **Potamiá** could easily trick you into thinking you were deep in the mountains, were it not for glimpses of sand and sea far below. **Theológos**, reached from the southwest, is the site where the medieval capital moved for protection from pirates. In antiquity, Thássos was a Párian colony and, later, a colony of

Tourist fatigue on the ferry to Thássos.

the mainland shore opposite. In Liménas, traces of the ancient naval and commercial harbours can still be seen. You can also make a long walking tour of the ancient walls enclosing the modern town. The theatre has been informally restored with wooden benches placed amongst the pine trees. If you take the walk in late afternoon, be sure to carry a flashlight; it may be dark by the time you reach the crescent-shaped, rock-hewn **Sanctuary of Pan** at the top of the hill and if you are not prepared you might experience the "panic" known to have been induced by this mysterious half-man half-goat god! A detailed guide of the grounds can be obtained at the museum.

Back on the mainland east of Kavála, the **Nestos River** flows through the **Yellow Plain**, a vast expanse of corn and tobacco fields. The Nestos marks the boundary between Eastern Macedonia and Thrace. Its estuary is surrounded by poplar plantations used as a hideout by birds. It can be reached only by dirt roads leading to the fine beaches

facing Thássos. Some beautiful scenery along the Nestos Gorge can best be seen by train between Drama and Xánthi.

Muslim presence: Ancient Thrace stretched deep into present-day Bulgaria and European Turkey. Greek colonisation of the coast often led to conflict with the native Thracian tribes. The Roman Via Egnatia spanned the area, leaving scattered traces of Roman and, later, Byzantine fortifications. Thrace was overrun and settled by Slavs and Ottomans. It was eventually divided between Bulgaria, Turkey and Greece, as a result of 19th- and early 20th-century nationalist struggles. Although there was a population exchange between Turkey and Greece in 1923, the Turkish inhabitants of the Greek part of Thrace were allowed to remain in return for protection granted to Greeks living in Istanbul. (The Greeks In Istanbul have been reduced to a few thousand; the Turks in Greece have multiplied many fold. The Turkish minority is distributed between Xánthi, Komotiní and the tobacco-growing plains south of the

On the beach.

two cities. Gypsies who adopted Islam and the Turkish language are also settled here. Another Muslim minority, the Pomaks, live in the mountains of **Western** and **Eastern Rodopi**. They appear to be of Slavic descent as they tend to be fairer than Turks, and traditionally cultivate tobacco on the lush Rodopi terraces and valleys. Eastern Rodopi is a military zone which foreigners can visit only with permission from the Ministry of Defence in Athens. The process of obtaining permission can take a week.

The best place to see a motley crowd of Greek citizens belonging to different races is in the hubbub of **Xánthi's** Saturday **open-air market**. The Muslim women look very graceful in long black satin overcoats and white *yashmaks* (scarves), which are gradually being replaced by grey or brown shorter coats and printed scarves. The gypsy women stand out in their colourful wide trousers and their scarves tied behind the ears exposing their chins. Many of the men still wear burgundy-coloured velvet or felt fezzes, or white prayer caps.

Greek priests, their cassocks blowing in the wind and tall black hats sticking out of the crowd, also do their week's shopping. This market mainly caters to local needs, so you may find little to purchase, but it is worth spending a Saturday morning here to see a facet of Greece which you will not find in the rest of the country. In the evening, you can witness another aspect of Xánthi life; a street off the main square is closed off for the Saturday night *nifopázaro* (brides' fair). Traditionally this was the time for young men and women to exchange glances. Today it is more an opportunity for the whole town to meet and promenade.

Xánthi became a prosperous commercial and administrative centre in the 19th century. Renowned masons were brought from Epirus to build merchant homes, tobacco warehouses and *khans* (inns). The *khans*, large square buildings around a central courtyard, were resting-spots and trading-centres near the marketplace. South of the square, an intoxicating aroma of tobacco fills the air; this is the area of the tobacco ware-

Left, a priest stocks up. Below, Pomack women in the Xánthi market

houses, some still in use and featuring extraordinary facades. The whitewashed houses and slender minarets of the Turkish quarter rise up to the north.

In **Komotiní**, Muslims constitute more than 50 percent of the population. Two central mosques fill up with the faithful at prayer times. In the surrounding cobbled streets, small shops spread a colourful array of everyday items. Old men wearing fezzes sit solemnly outside coffee-houses, playing with their worry-beads. The museum houses archaeological finds from all over Thrace, two of the most important sites being Abdera, south of Xánthi, and Maróneia, south of Komotiní.

Both sites have little to show apart from the foundations of layers and layers of civilisation, but both are of historical significance. **Abdera**, especially affluent in the 5th century BC, was the birthplace of two major philosophers in antiquity: Democritus, who expounded an atomic theory of the constitution of the world, and the sophist Protagoras who incapsulated his relativism in the phrase, "Man is the measure of all things." Further east, **Maróneia** marks the site where Odysseus's ship is supposed to have strayed after leaving Troy for the return journey to Ithaca (Itháki). Although the natives were unfriendly, it was their sweet-smelling red wine which later saved Odysseus and his companions from the terrifying cyclops Polyphemus. Trapped in his cave, they managed to get Polyphemus drunk on the delicious wine and then while he slept they poked his single eye out with a huge red-hot pole and escaped by hiding under his sheep's bellies. A cave to the north of Maronia retains the name of Polyphemus's Cave.

The Evros valley and Samothrace (Samothráki): The road from Komotiní zigzags through barren limestone hills before coming down to the vast Evros plain and leading on to Alexandroúpolis. Formerly a charming seaside town, **Alexandroúpolis** has developed into an unruly urban conglomeration. About an hour's drive north of the city is the **Dadia forest reserve**, an extraordinary

A photo store window in Xánthi.

sanctuary for captors, many of them rare and endangered species and some of them huge, the Evros Aiver delta is also a major sanctuary, a wetland sanctuary for water fowl. Ferries leave the harbour for the island of Samothrace (Samothráki), while the road continues east towards Turkey and north along the Evros valley.

Unlike the other island of the Thracian Sea, the green and golden Thássos, **Samothrace** raises its forbidding granite heights above stony beaches and murky waters. The landscape was not always so inhospitable. Homer has the mighty Poseidon watching from here the action in the plains of Troy: he "sat and marvelled on the war and strife, high on the topmost crest of wooded Samothrace, for thence all Ida was plain to see, and plain to see was the city of Troy and the ships of the Achaians."

With time, the forest has receded, leaving the desolate lunar landscape of the aptly-named **Mount Fengári** (Mount Moon). Traces of the old luxuriant vegetation survive in the north-

east, where a variety of butterfly mingles with the spray of small waterfalls formed by creeks gurgling down the mountainsides. The ancient native cult of the Great Gods was retained after Greek colonisation of the island in the 7th century and flourished up to the 3rd century. This site and the **museum of Paleópolis** display evidence of the cult, its grounds and its mysteries.

The road from Alexandroúpolis leads northeast past the Roman staging-post of Trajanópolis to Féres, where the 12th-century **Church of the Virgin** has fine but faded frescoes. Corn and sunflower fields, which are spectacular in mid-summer, stretch as far as the eye can see.

Souflí was once famous for its silk production. The land sloping down to the Evros used to be planted with mulberry trees whose leaves nourished the silkworms. Today the trees have been replaced by corn fields and the single silk factory still in use imports cocoons from the East. A variety of silks are for sale at a shop near the central crossroads. **Didymóteicho** has a Byzantine fortress with a commanding view of the Evros valley, and an abandoned pyramidal-roofed mosque. A folklore museum offers an interesting overview of the region's traditional culture and handicrafts.

Cross countries: There are two ways to cross from here into Turkey. One is by train from the small railway station of **Pýthio**, a sleepy village below its once vigilant fortress. The other is farther north, from the border outpost of **Kastaniés**. The passage cannot be made on foot, so you must either have a car, take the one-day bus trip leaving twice a week from **Orestiáda**, or wait at the border for a lift. Just across the border, the four minarets of the 16th-century Selimiye Mosque, the architect Sinan's last masterpiece, rise above swaying poplar trees on the opposite bank of the Evros River.

From the Turkish town of Edirne, built on the site of Roman Hadrianople, you can look back to the once Byzantine city of Thessaloniki, and forward to the combined Byzantine and Ottoman grandeur of Istanbul.

Left, butterflies congregate. Right, looking across the Turkish border at the Selimiye Mosque.

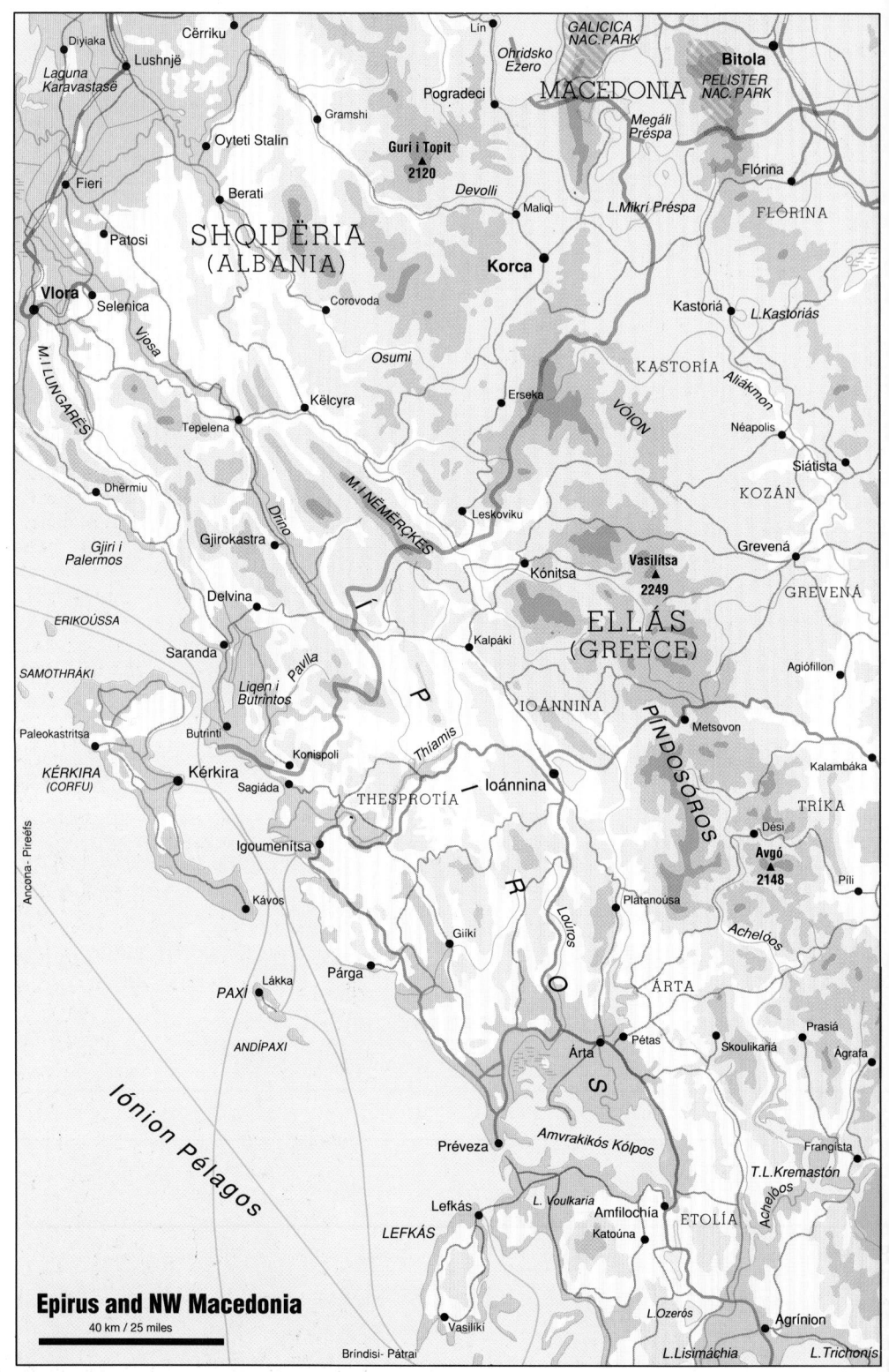

Epirus and NW Macedonia

40 km / 25 miles

EPIRUS AND NW MACEDONIA

Epirus and the northwest corner of Macedonia are worlds apart from the azure, sun-bleached Greece of Zorba. Here instead, you will find jagged limestone peaks and deep sunless gorges, mountains mantled by forests and rimmed with snow, villages cut from the same stone mountains and timber.

This tough, austere land sets the scene for a different way of life. You can feel the weight and sobriety of this existence when you walk down the stone streets of a village lined with stone houses or witness the slow, plodding steps of an Epirot dancing to the wailing clarinet. You can sense the social closure and restraint in the architecture of the Zagorochória houses set off far from the street by large gates, or when, at a village festival, you are not asked to join in the dance, but rather expected to stand apart, forever the foreigner.

More of the same: Even the rain which falls here more abundantly than anywhere else in Greece reminds that you are not in Nauplion or on Náxos. Still, the contrasts between this alpine Greece and that of the Mediterranean and Aegean are today beginning to blur in the increasing homogenisation of the modern Greek nation.

In their massive postwar migration to Athens, the Epirots have brought a bit of the mountains to the city, and, with each holiday vacation spent in their native villages, bring a bit of the city back to the mountains. These days a Sarakatsáni shepherd can finish milking his herd at noon in a highland pasture and, flying from Ioánnina, still make a doctor's appointment in Athens at 5pm.

How it started: While Epirus becomes more and more integrated into and unified with the Greek nation, it is crucial to appreciate how distinct its past history has been from the rest of Greece. It joined the modern Greek state only in 1913, some 80 years after most of the mainland had achieved sovereignty. At that time, moreover, it was hardly evident that this region was, in fact, Greece: the population of this wide strip of land was a melange of ethnicities, languages, religions and customs: Greeks, Turks, Albanians and Slavs, as well as the nomadic peoples – the Sarakatsanáoi and the Vlachs.

Following World War II and the Civil War, this region suffered a rapid loss of population to Greek and foreign cities. By the 1970s, many Epirot villages were in a state of physical and social decline. Houses were left to decay, and the few still inhabited sheltered an ever-diminishing population of old, economically inactive men and women.

But since 1980, things have changed. The government has worked to integrate the region into the national economy, emigration trends have been reversed and attitudes towards village life modified, the "traditional" now viewed less as a stumbling block to economic prosperity and more as a cultural heritage to be preserved.

The associated benefits and tensions of this new era for Epirus are most

visible in Zagóri. Stiff government regulations of building permits and low interest loans and subsidies have led to the restoration of many buildings, both public and private, so that whole villages have been preserved as traditional settlements in their pre-19th century architectural character. Simultaneously, new roads are being built, often right over the routes of old mule paths, giving access to the tiniest villages and most distant pasture lands.

Conflicting interests: Behind all these manifestations of modernisation, the astute observer will see a microcosm of Greek reality today – a stage for conflicting interests and world views. Conservationists who want to preserve the land as wilderness versus entrepreneurs who would like to develop skiing facilities and aerial tramways; farmers who rely on the constant flow of rivers versus the state-owned electricity utility which has embarked on a series of hydroelectric projects; mining versus land reclamation; and the big question: what sort of tourism to develop?

The new concept that is emerging here is that of "low-impact" tourism, or "ecotourism". It is being promoted by conservation organisations and most agencies of the central government but resisted, predictably, by some local interest groups. However, some villagers are beginning to recognise the benefits of an unspoiled environment and to side with the conservationists.

The territory covered here is vast by Greek standards, spanning some 375 km/233 miles from Igoumenítsa to Edessa, by the most direct route. A minimum of 10 days is suggested for this tour, but the more time you have the better. Note, too, that the coastal region of Párga, the Nekromanteíon of the Achéron, Kassópi, Préveza, Aktion and Arta (which is briefly treated in the Roúmeli chapter, pages 180–88) forms an historically important part of Epirus and that the Igoumenítsa-Arta-Ioánnina loop is an appropriate addition to the route indicated in this chapter.

Igoumenítsa: The modern port of **Igoumenítsa** which welcomes a great

A priest in Kónitsa, Epirus.

share of the travellers entering Greece from the west is the major port of Epirus and indeed of northern Greece. You may not even notice you are in Epirus until you walk by the man with his table of cassettes set up in the central square, blaring forth the plangent, bleating *klaríno* – the Epirot clarinet. Realise it or not, you have set foot in the land of the *klaríno*, whose sounds you will hear across the entire region in summer at the local village festivals or in winter in the town *tavérna*.

The road from Igoumenítsa to Ioánnina winds its way up through the valley of the **Kalamás River**, the ancient Thyamis, with every mile climbing further into the highlands of the **Píndos mountain range**. To the north lie the villages of the **Morgána**, one of which, **Liá**, was rendered famous in recent years with the book (and movie) *Eléni*, which recounts the tribulations suffered in this area during the Civil War. The Píndos is the most extensive Greek mountain formation and one of the largest in all of the Balkans, extend-

ing from Mount Morava in Albania to the Agrafa range in central Greece.

Ioánnina: On entering the upland plain near the Kónitsa road junction, the stark face of Mount Mitsikéli appears high above Lake Pamvótis and Ioánnina which lines its shores. Over the past 1,000 years, **Ioánnina** has perennially been one of Greece's great cities, a centre of Hellenic culture and education, an international crossroad of traders and in its last glorious epoch, the citadel of Ali Pasha, the "Lion of Ioánnina", the famed maverick-tyrant who broke away from the sultan to set up an autonomous kingdom. Today Ioánnina remains one of Greece's most lively provincial centres and a home to one of the country's seven universities. Apart from its own interest and the beauty of its setting, Ioánnina makes a convenient base from which to explore the surrounding area: the Zagorochória, Métsovo, Dodona (Dodóni).

Unlike most other large Greek cities, the history of Ioánnina does not extend back to ancient times. It has distinctly

Byzantine origins, supposedly taking its name from a local monastery of St John the Baptist. In 1204 it burgeoned in size and importance as a result of the Latin conquest of Constantinople and subsequent establishment of the Despotate of Epirus. Refugees from "The City" swelled its population and in the late 13th century it achieved the status of an archbishopric. It fell, with the rest of Greece, to the Turks in the 15th century, and in the late 18th century Ali Pasha designated this city of 35,000 inhabitants (large for that time) his headquarters.

Ioánnina today testifies ambivalently to Ali's legacy – for while he left behind the city's most distinctive monuments (its mosques and the redoubtable walls of the citadel), he also burned much of it to the ground during the siege by the sultan's troops in 1821. This, along with the postwar penchant for building large apartment blocks, has left Ioánnina with a decidedly modern face.

The people's square: The wide expanse of Ioánnina's central Plateía Pýrrou, joined with Plateía Dimokratías, lined by the regional army headquarters and various other public buildings, is the most obvious place to orient yourself for a tour of the city. This is where the people of Ioánnina meet: the students at noon at the bright sidewalk cafés, the old men in the traditional cafés lining Avérof Street playing *távli* and cards, families and old friends walking arm-in-arm for an evening *vólta*. Here too you can eat some of the *bougátsa* for which Ioánnina is famed – fine cheese or custard-filled pastry. In the summer the nocturnal hub is Plateía Mavíli, down by the lake, where roast corn and *halvá* vendors congregate around the packed outdoor tables of dozens of pubs, cafés, and *tavérnas*.

After a bit of nourishment, the **Archaeological Museum** at the north end of Plateía Dimokratías is a good place to visit. It has a fine array of Epirot archaeological artefacts spanning from Paleolithic to Byzantine times. Odós Avérof descends finally to the **Kástro**, the fortress of numerous Epirot despots

Even in Greece, it rains sometimes.

and, lastly, of Ali Pasha himself. In this tangle of buildings and alleyways set on the promontory jutting out into the lake are the most salient reminders of Ioánnina's past – the massive walls and its four gateways, the **Aslan Pasha** and **Fetiye** mosques. The first mosque now houses the Popular Museum with a diverse collection of Epirot costumes, jewellery and other relics.

The area around this mosque is the supposed scene of one of the famous stories linked to Ali Pasha in the popular imagination. Kyra Frosíni was the beautiful mistress of Ali's eldest son. In the most common variant of the story, the Pasha took a liking to her as well. But she resisted his advances and paid the price: a watery death. Ali had Kyra Frosíni and 17 of her female companions tied up in weighted sacks and dropped in the lake. To the east and below you can visit the derelict Fetiye ("Victory") Mosque and the abandoned, unmarked grave containing Ali Pasha's body (his head is buried in Istanbul).

Monasteries, paths winding among fragrant flowers and trees, and several *tavérnas* serving local freshwater specialities are on the small island of **Lake Pamvótis** a brief boat ride from the Plateía Mavíli. **The Monastery of Aghíou Nikoláou Filanthropínon** near the fishing village houses vivid frescoes, many depicting unusually gruesome martyrdoms, another by the entrance peopled by such ancient luminaries as Plato, Aristotle and Thucydides. At the **Monastery of Ághios Panteleímon** is one last piece of Ali Pasha memorabilia – the house into which he fled in 1822 when hunted by the sultan's troops. Stuck on the first floor, Ali was killed when the soldiers fired through the ceiling from below. The bullet holes are still there today.

Zeus's sanctuary: South of Ioánnina lies **Dodona (Dodóni)**, Epirus's main archaeological attraction. The road winds up towards **Mount Tomaron** to a small valley where the sanctuary is located. Homer calls it "wintry Dodona", emphasising again Epirus's alpine otherness and its distance from Odysseus's

Time for gossip at a bus stop in Métsovo.

"wine-dark sea." In antiquity the Dodona oracle was regarded as the oldest in Greece. Dodonian Zeus who was worshipped here was thought to reside in the trunk of the holy oak tree.

Herodotus tells us that the tree (the second oldest in Greece after the willow in the sanctuary of Hera at Sámos) became holy when a dove flying from Thebes in Egypt landed on it. Thereafter priests interpreted the rustlings of the holy oak tree in the wind. As at Delphi, their pronouncements were enigmatically worded. The importance of the sanctuary diminished by the 5th century BC as that of Delphi increased.

The beautifully restored amphitheatre dates from the 3rd century BC and the days of Pyrrhus, the great Epirot king who defeated the Romans in battle at the high price of most of his soldiers' lives. It has a capacity of 18,000 spectators and hosts a festival of classical drama and contemporary musical events during the summer.

Worthwhile diversions: The road north out of Ioánnina leads to the mountainous heart of Epirus – the Zagorochória. If you are unable to take this extraordinary trip and are instead heading east into **Thessaly**, you can partially console yourself with a visit to **Métsovo**, 58 km (36 miles) from Ioánnina. On this route you first pass **Pérama**, one of Greece's most spectacular caves. Then, after a long circuitous ascent towards the **Katára Pass** ("Curse Pass"), the only paved motor-crossing of the central Píndos, Métsovo appears to the southeast. It is a singular Greek village, justly famed for its stunning location, its Vlach culture and handicrafts, its cheeses and its traditional clothes still worn by some of the inhabitants.

A fine display of the baronial side of Métsovo's culture is at the reconstructed **Tosítsa Mansion**, an *archontikó*, or lord's manor, having much in common with the mansions of Siátista and Kastoriá. Inside are fine examples of Metsovite woodcarving, weaving and carpets. Another aspect of Métsovo will strike you: it is thriving. The people are industrious, and they are helped by long-

A bridge in Zagorochóri.

standing and substantial financial assistance from the many native sons who have earned fortunes abroad.

The Zagorochória: Zagoriá is a culturally and geographically distinct region of Epirus comprising 46 villages, the **Zagorochória**. Its physical boundaries are the imposing mountains and deep gorges that define the Ioánnina-Kónitsa-Métsovo triangle. The region enjoyed relative autonomy during the Ottoman occupation, since wealth from trading allowed local leaders to pay off the Turkish overlords and it was too inaccessible to administer directly. It became a centre of learning and the seat of a peripatetic professional class who emigrated to major commercial centres in the East and in Europe, subsequently returning to their homeland with considerable wealth. The west and east Zagóri villages are themselves somewhat distinct from one another in history and present appearance. The east is an area populated in large part by Vlachs, a people living in Greece since antiquity, speaking a language directly derived from Latin, and living as traushumant shepherds. The west bears the signs of more Slavic and Albanian influence. A more recent difference resulted from east Zagoriá's fierce resistance to the Germans during World War II. In retribution the Germans ravaged the area, so that today the west Zagoriá bears an architectural testimony to its past, while the eastern villages had to be almost entirely rebuilt after the war.

The Zagoriá landscape is dramatic and varied, embracing towering summits surrounded by sheer vertical rock faces, benign alpine meadows, deep forests, fertile plains and sinuous canyons. It is one of the few pockets of wilderness left in Greece and harbours some of the last remaining populations of wolves, bears, wild boars, lynx, the rare chamois and various types of eagles and hawks. Yet, even in the most remote corner the traveller will find signs of civilisation: a Byzantine church; a graceful, slender-arched bridge from the Ottoman period; a family of Sarakatsáni or Vlach shepherds grazing their flocks in the high plains.

That's life.

A Zagorochória itinerary: Here are two suggested circuits in the central and west Zagoriá region which can be done separately or linked together.

For the central route you leave the Ioánnina-Kónitsa road just past Kariés and follow signs for the Víkos Gorge. The village of **Vítsa** hosts some fine traditional houses and one of the oldest churches in the region, **Ághios Nikólaos**. To gain access to the church, ask at the local police station.

Just up the road, **Monodéndri** has a fine central square with the huge plane tree and the **basilica of Ághios Athanásios**, next to which a path descends to the floor of the **Víkos Gorge** (see page 177). The short walk to the **monastery of Aghía Paraskeví** and beyond, along the ledge above the Víkos Gorge is absolutely breathtaking.

Return to the crossroads below Vítsa and take the route to the villages of **Kípi**, **Negádes**, and on foot to half-deserted **Vradéto**. An extraordinary 19th-century three-arched bridge spans the torrent on the right just before enter-

ing Kípi, where, in the upper part of the village, there are well-preserved buildings, a church and school, in a *plateía* overlooking the village. Further up the road, Negádes is known for its three-churches in one basilica, dedicated to saints Demétrius, George and the Holy Trinity, containing good frescoes.

For the excursion to Vradéto, take the road to Tsepélovo. A few hundred yards past the fork to Kepésovo a footpath marked by a sign veers off the paved road to Vradéto. This one-hour hike includes the crossing of a small gorge, a unique climb on a sinuous medieval cobblestone path (these paths, known as *kalderímia*, and arched bridges are notable pre-modern engineering feats throughout the region), and a taste of the eerie stillness of this remote village (population seven during the winter). With another 40 minutes of walking you arrive at **Belói** from where you can see the entire Víkos Gorge. Finally, for a look at the last two undamaged villages before eastern Zagorá, continue up the road to

Tsepélovo and Skamnélli, each flanked by ancient rural monasteries.

Western Zagorochória: For the western Zagorochória continue further north on the Ioánnina-Kónitsa road. **Kalpáki** marks one of the most glorified battle sites in modern Greek history. Here in the early winter of 1940 the Greeks met the invading Italian army and rolled them back into the snowy Albanian mountains for a winter of hell.

Soon a sign indicates the road (on the right) to **Arísti** and **Pápingo**. This area, tucked among the high peaks of **Mount Gamíla**, comprises some of the best-preserved traditional settlements in Epirus. In recent years the two villages of Pápingo (**Megálo** and **Mikró**) have gradually become known as fashionable mountain retreats. And with good reasons: the *Pýrgoi* (sheer limestone towers) rise 610 metres (2,000 ft) at the villages' back door; some 20 well restored traditional houses are available for rent; good cheese *píta* and hearty stews are served at the various local *tavérnes*. And lastly, just off the road

Eating together *en famille*.

between the two villages there is an unusual swimming hole for a bit of alpine aquatics. From Pápingo too you can set out on various hikes in the mountains around Mount Gamíla.

Leave the valley of the ever ice-cold, spring-fed Voïdomátis River and enter that of the temperate Aoös by way of the Ioánnina-Kónitsa road. Just before entering Kónitsa, a late 19th-century arched bridge spans the river alongside the new one. A 90-minute walk along the southern bank leads through the thick forest of the National Park to **Moní Stomíou**, magnificently perched on a cliff inside the gorge.

Kónitsa is a regional centre with a distinct military presence. It is a good place to take on provisions and have a meal either before or after your mountain perambulations.

Northwest Macedonia: The road from Kónitsa to Neápolis (and Kastoriá beyond) is the single paved connecting route between Epirus and northwest Macedonia. Out of Kónitsa it climbs into the western foothills of **Mount Smólikas** (alt. 2,640 metres/8,650 ft), the tallest in the Píndos range and the second highest in Greece after Mt Olympus, and then descends into the valley of the **Sarandapóros River**. On this road just below Eptachorió is a 10-metre (32-ft) strip of bold blue letters emblazoned on the concrete embankment: FREEDOM FOR NORTHERN EPIRUS – a solemn reminder that, according to the reckoning of many Epirots, half of that region is out of reach in Albania .

On the other side of Mount Víon, having exited Epirus and entered Macedonia, you arrive in **Pendálofos**, which stands like a gateway between the two regions. Its fine, grey stone houses, still in the Épirot style, drape across the slopes which give the town its name – "Fivehills". During World War II some of these buildings formed the headquarters of the British Mission to the Greek Resistance. From Pendálofos the road continues east through remarkable limestone formations, waves of rock like layers of melted lead atop one another.

Siátista, a small town noted for its

fine, 18th-century mansions, is a brief detour from the road to Kastoriá. These mansions, called *archontiká* because they were the residences of the archons, or the town's leading men, offer a glimpse into the feudal society that flourished there during the middle centuries of Ottoman rule. It was a centre of fur trading, tanning, wine-making and a stopping point for caravans on the trade route to Vienna, but fell from prosperity when, after Greek independence, the commercial networks changed.

With some imagination, plus a bit of resourcefulness to gain entry into these houses (ask at the café in the main street), you can learn a good deal about the lifestyle and world view of the people who inhabited these dwellings. The most interesting are the Manoússi, Poúlikos and Nerantzópoulos houses. They are constructed in an architectural style which is widespread throughout northern Greece: a ground floor of solid stone walls whose few openings are often covered by iron gratings (as brigands abounded and security was uncer-

tain), storage cellars and workshops; a second floor also of stone – the main winter residence; and a third floor of painted plaster board which juts out over the rest of the building, supported by wooden brackets – a kind of summer parlour and reception room. The walls and ceilings of these are often finely painted. After Siátista you will be well-prepared to see the *archontiká* of Kastoriá, another town which grew wealthy from the fur trade.

Returning north, the road follows the upper valley of the **Aliákmon**, the longest river in Greece, whose 300 km (185 miles) flow in a great arc from high in the Píndos to the Thermaïc Gulf. Soon the road reaches **Kastoriá Lake**, which the town, built on a peninsula, seems nearly to divide in half. Before entering the town, on the left you pass a formidable military cemetery. Here are buried the Greek soldiers of the government forces killed during the Civil War in this area, the so-called Grammós-Vítsi where the last brutal stage of the Civil War was fought. The central **General James Van**

A cutter in Kastoriá.

Fleet Square reminds you that American equipment and advisers helped the Greek government defeat the communist insurgency.

A Byzantine centre: Kastoriá is one of northern Greece's most alluring cities. Its history as a Byzantine provincial centre and as a hub of the fur industry is well-reflected by its 54 surviving churches, many of which were commissioned by rich furriers. Kastoriá's churches embody the fine Byzantine art of a provincial centre, far from the grand imperial mosaics of Constantinople and Thessaloniki, although the work here often shows more folk and Slavic influence. If you have a morning you can see a few of these winding through the city and ending up in **Karyád**, the Old City, amidst the fine *archontiká*.

Ághioi Anárgyroi sits at the northeast edge of town, not far from the lake. It is the oldest church in Kastoriá, built in 1018 by Emperor Basil II to celebrate his victory over the Bulgars. Little of the original remains. Note the fine exterior brick walls decorated with geometric forms, the arched windows above the apse divided by a colonnette, and the frescoes on the west facade of Saints Peter and Paul flanked by Kosmás and Dámian on either side. The dark interior contains frescoes including St Basil and a scene of the Pentecost. This church is also well known as Greece's earliest example of groin-vaulting.

To the south, **Panaghía Koumbelidíki**, with its unusually tall, drum-shaped dome contrasts strikingly with Anárgyroi. Panaghía was built in the 11th century, and has frescoes on the facade, not just in niches but covering the whole wall. Further south it is the interior frescoes of **Ághios Nikólaostou Kasnítzi** that stand out in this simple single-aisled basilica. Further south again, the **Taxiárchis** of the metropolis has both external and internal frescoes. It also contains the tomb of the Macedonian liberation fighter, Pávlos Melás, who was killed by the Turks in 1904 just north of Kastoriá.

In the Old City above the city's south bank you find the many *archontiká* from

the 17th and 18th centuries, with their characteristic painted upper floors which project over the windowless lower ones. Most of these are quite dilapidated, save that of Nazim and Emmanuel, the latter now turned into a folk museum.

Kastoriá's fur industry: Strolling through these streets you'll also notice the most important aspect of Kastoriá's present social and economic life: the hundreds of small workshops belonging to tailors and fur-cutters and packed with rolls of sewn-together furs and patterns for coats-in-the-making, which form the network of Kastoriá's famous fur trade. The history of this trade goes back at least 500 years to when beavers made Kastoriá Lake their home (Kastoriá roughly means the beaver-place in Greek.) As these were hunted out of the lake, however, Kastoriá became the repository for the scraps of fur discarded by the fur industries of Europe and North America. Here in these workshops the scraps are cleaned and sewn together and then fashioned into fur coats which are re-exported to the same countries from which the scraps originally came.

Before leaving Kastoriá take the time for a promenade along its shores. On the south side you can walk to the **Monastery of the Panaghía Mavriótissas**.

To the Préspa Lakes and east: The road north out of Kastoriá continues along one of the upper branches of the Aliákmon River. We are now heading towards an unusual corner of the country, where Greece and all things Greek taper off into the cold blue waters of the **Préspa Lakes** and merge into the former Yugoslavia and Albania. These lakes are the nesting ground of two endangered species of pelicans (the Dalmatian pelican and the wild pelican) as well as numerous other birds, and are today protected as a national bird sanctuary.

The road to the east leads through Flórina and Edessa and finally to Pélla and Thessaloniki. We pass through **Flórina**, badly battered during the Civil War, and join the **Via Egnatia**, which connected the Roman Empire from Durazzo to Constantinople. To the north is **Mount Vóras**, the scene of many Balkan battles, and to the south, **Lake Vegorítis**. From Alexander the Great's campaigns to modern times, this has been a point where people converging from all directions have vied for turf.

At the turn of the century this was the land of the Macedonian Struggle, the conflict waged between the Greeks, the Bulgarians and the Turks to control Macedonia. Indeed, the area saw little peace in the first half of the 20th century – the Macedonian Struggle 1900–08, the Balkan Wars 1912–13, World War I and II, and the Civil War – a narrative of violence and contestation equalled by few corners of the globe.

Edessa is unlike any other town in Greece, thanks to the streams that wind through it and over its famous waterfall. A path takes you right down the cliffside and into the waterfall's mist. At the north end of town there is a Roman (or Byzantine) bridge which served the Via Egnatia. Edessa, perched on its high bluff, marks the edge of the Macedonian highlands, and from here you can gaze out to the well-cultured plains that spread towards Thessaloniki and the sea.

Left, fur trade in Kastoriá. Right, Ali Pasha, the famous despot of Ioánnina, on his lake.

HIKING IN THE PINDOS RANGE

Large tracts of unspoiled nature, a varied landscape with villages scattered at convenient intervals and a vast network of trails make this region of Greece a hiker's paradise – and one which is still not overcrowded. A great number of interesting walking routes can be found in the North Píndos, ranging from strenuous multi-day *haute route* traverses involving technical climbing, to a series of interconnected day hikes through wilderness and pasture lands between successive villages, to leisurely nature strolls.

Those relying entirely on the automobile for the exploration of this region will be rewarded by taking short walks around the villages, monasteries, and churches mentioned in the itineraries suggested below. Hikers in good physical condition can opt for a series of day hikes, designing their trip according to time constraints, car availability, bus schedules, and special interests.

Although the trail system is extensive, it is not always maintained and clearly marked (though improving constantly), and may confuse the first-time traveller in the Greek backcountry. Thus, a good map and compass, a specialist trekking guide, a keen sense of direction, an ability to get and double-check trail information from villagers and shepherds, and a good sense of humour are necessary for the enjoyment of foot travellers in North Píndos.

Both novices and seasoned hikers alike should be cautious as weather can change very rapidly with little warning. In recent years detailed maps and excellent trail guides have become available and should be used.

The hiking loop outlined here passes through a number of different ecological habitats, and connects some of the most beautiful villages of the region. It begins and ends in the Pápingo villages where there are ample accommodation facilities and reliable *tavérnes* and very basically stocked stores. It has the disadvantage of being the most popular route by far, though nowhere near as well-travelled as the footpaths of England and Central Europe. August is the peak month, worth avoiding if possible; June is best, with snow patches to lend interest.

● **Mikró Pápingo–Astráka Hut:** (Mountain

The mountain ridge above Pápingo.

Refuge visible from Pápingo: staffed by warden between June and September, on Mount Gamíla col: 3–3½ hours (water available at regular intervals), 900 metres (3,000 ft) ascent.

● **Side trip to Drakólimni** from Astráka (alpine lake at 2,100 metres [6,900 ft] altitude). Ideal site for views, meals, etc: 1 hour each way. Overnight at the Refuge or camp on dry bed of Ksyróloutsa pond (a 15-minute descent to the east of the refuge on the way to Drakólimni: spring water).

● **Astráka Hut/Ksyróloutsa–Tsepélovo:** a day-long hike through alpine meadows, high plains, head of a gorge (Mégas Lákkos), and, eventually, scree slopes, under the shadow of the sheer rock faces of Astráka. Water is scarce, so plan supplies accordingly: 5–7 hours depending on pace. Overnight at Tsepélovo (five inns and hotels – but it is necessary to make reservations in advance during August).

● **Tsepélovo–Vradéto–Kípi:** The first leg of the trip on foot (duration: about 2 hours), then another hour down the *kalderími* (skála) of Vradéto on to the main asphalt road. Walk an hour or hitchhike to Kípi. Overnight in Kípi, or catch the afternoon bus back to Tsepélovo. The old direct Kípi–Tsepélovo trail is overgrown but may be cleared soon – ask locally.

● **Kípi–Vítsa–Monodéndri–Víkos Gorge–Víko (Vitsikó) Hamlet:** From Monodéndri follow signs to the Gorge: a well renovated *kalderími* takes you to the usually dry bed of Víkos (45 minutes). A strenuous path (marked with red blazes and three diamonds) covers the length of the canyon, crisscrossing the river bed. At the intersection of Víkos Gorge and the side canyon of Mégas Lákkos (2–3 hours), a series of freshwater ponds are formed by nearby spring water (potable). Stop for lunch, but do not leave any garbage. This is bear country, as evidenced by scratch marks on trees. Continue through thick forest and pass a small meadow before reaching the source of the Voïdomátis River. The total hiking time to this point is 5–6 hours, depending on one's pace. You can camp here but, strictly speaking, it is forbidden and you should walk a couple of hours more to leave the canyon.

Take a left fork on the cobblestone path to the village of Víkos (1 hour) and hitchhike or take a bus to Arísti and then to Pápingo, or cross the Voïdomátis and follow the recently improved path there to either of the two Pápingos (2–2½ hours). ■

Drakólimni, the dragon lake.

ROUMELI AND THE IONIAN ISLANDS

The region usually known as Roúmeli is too often visited just for the sake of the classical site at Delphi. Roúmeli is not, it is true, as rich in classical monuments as the Peloponnese. But a taste for Roúmeli, a part of the country which lets you travel largely in peace, is not hard to acquire and is difficult to lose.

Roúmeli is properly "Western Roúmeli," its name originating in the Ottoman term for the Greek nation within the empire, *Rum Millet*. The word *Rum* is the one the Greeks themselves used: *Romaiói* or citizens of the eastern part of the Roman Empire. The notion of being, in today's Greek, a *Romaiós* is complex and persistent. *Romaiosíni* (the noun) is everything in Greek life and the Greek identity that is *not* classical, *not* Hellenic; everything, in short, that a one-sided view of the Greeks is liable to reject as "un-Greek".

Hellenism and *Romaiosíni* certainly do meet, merge and sometimes clash all over Roúmeli. At Delphi you will see shiny new shepherds' crooks being snapped up by pale Athenian school-children. Or, in the smallest out-of-the-way place, you may ask to see *t'archaía* (the ancient remains) and then, following a shepherd up a winding path to the tinkle of sheep's bells, find yourself at a little ancient fort (*acropolis*).

It is probably Roúmeli's natural setting that leaves the deepest impression. The hiker has the chance to see everyday marvellous sights such as a herd of goats tumbling down a slope much greener close up than it seemed from the road below. By contrast, the visitor who goes in search of traditional architecture is likely to be disappointed. The main reason is that much of Roúmeli suffered both in the War of Independence and later in 1940–49.

And the inhabitants of the region have long had a formidable reputation as guerrilla fighters. In the 5th century BC the Athenians found that with the "barbar- **Preceding pages: island transport.**

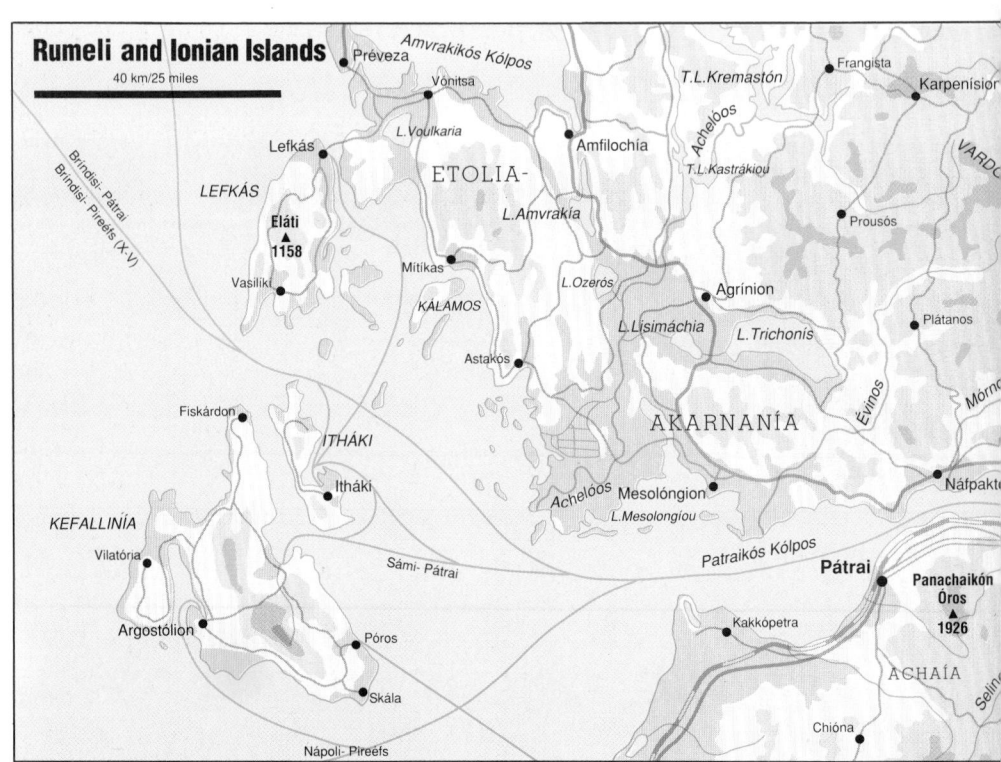

ian" Aetólians they had bitten off more than they could chew; in the middle of the 19th century the Athenian authorities were still having severe problems with banditry in Roúmeli. Some of the *kléphts* who had indeed helped to dislodge the Ottomans in 1821 were reluctant to give up the lawless, free and profitable life of rustling, kidnapping and roast mutton. More recently, it was from Mount Veloúch (Týmfristos) in Roúmeli that the communist guerrilla Áris Velouchiótis took his *nom de guerre*.

Banditry, the visitor will be relieved to know, has disappeared, and good roads with buses that go everywhere have put Roúmeli's main towns and villages within easy reach of the capital; but the rural communities continue to live a pretty dour pastoral life. And the Rouméliots' reputation in Greece is not for worldly sophistication. (One reason is their heavy accent: their speech is very short on vowels, which makes it laconic and often hard to understand.)

Towards Parnassus (Parnassós): The **monastery of Osios Lukás** (not Luke the Evangelist but an obscure Blessed Luke) is often visited in a hurry as a small Byzantine concession in the standard classical tour. But this 11th-century monastery with its two churches, an example of late Byzantine grandeur in scenic isolation, is well worth a longer visit. It is the nearest one may get to the experience of Mount Athos, and Osios Lukás deserves a day to itself before passing on to Delphi.

Crossing the edge of the mass of **Mount Parnassus** does something to prepare one for the experience of Delphi. Parnassus (Parnassós) dominates the centre of Greece from whichever direction one approaches it, whether it be from Lamía north, Livadiá east, Náfpaktos west or by ferry from the Peloponnese south.

It is the mountain's breadth and shape rather than its sheer height – Giónas is taller – that render it so impressive. In fact, the ascent can be performed on a clear day from late spring on – by the fit as well as the fanatical. Ask for details at **Aráchova**, a fresh and invigorating vil-

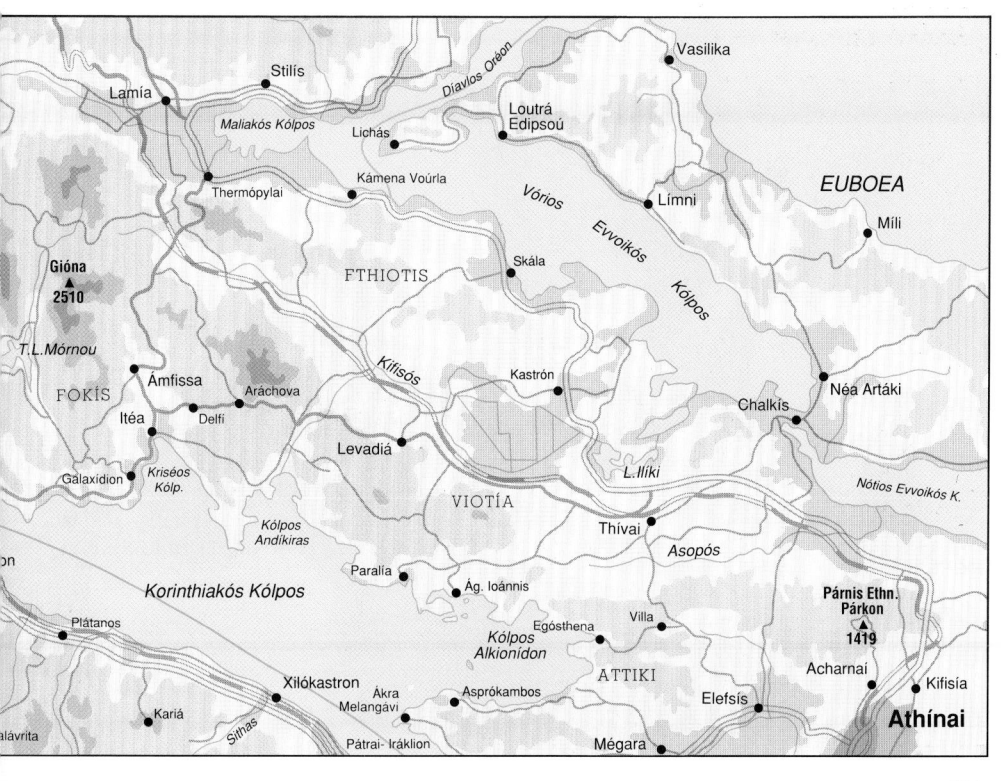

lage hung with expensive rural crafts.

Aráchova's skiing facilities are its main attraction; some years back ski-racks became obligatory wear for the Athenian station-wagon. In the upper square by one of the village's many tumbling streams there is an excellent *tavérna*. There is also a St George's Day festival (23 April) in which the air is heavy with the scent of lambs which the ancients offered to the gods above and which the moderns offer to their own senses, being roasted in the open air. Watch out for the old men's race; the old boys, some reputedly over 80, run to the top of a steep slope and then unwind with a cigarette.

Delphi: From here, it is only a few curving miles on to **Delphi**. This is the place which, of all others in Greece, visitors have found most memorable, ever since its excavation at the end of the 19th century. Mycenae (Mykínes) and Olympia fascinate; Delphi awes. Abrupt crags rise to the sky as hawks soar above them on winds that can suddenly turn to storms. The site involves

steep climbs with, as their reward, the continual glimpsing of new angles and further treasures.

Delphi's fascination is threefold: its stirring setting, the scale, beauty and diversity of its monuments; and, as a sub-text, its turbulent and often disreputable history. The site may be divided into three parts. (To appreciate Delphi to the full, stay the night in one of the many hotels.)

At the upper site, dedicated to the Apollo of the oracle, follow the Sacred Way, past the treasuries given to the oracle by Greek states. The Treasury of the Athenians is of particular interest, covered as it is with inscriptions of Athens's glories and the city's thanks to Apollo. It is easy to forget that the whole building has been put back together like a jigsaw puzzle in modern times.

From here the path winds up past the Temple of Apollo and the theatre to the stadium, the best preserved in Greece. The lower site, the preserve of Athena, contains the single most beautiful monument at Delphi, a columned rotunda. **Gypsies preparing for a siesta.**

Finally the museum near the site contains numerous marvels, including the famous Charioteer. The large quantity of Roman statuary – including a bust of the Emperor Hadrian's lover Antinous – is a reminder that Delphi had an enduring attraction.

Galaxídi and Náfpaktos: A few miles below Delphi is the port of **Itéa**, from where we look across the bay to **Galaxídi**, a strange little enclave, in a rugged pastoral setting, of the Greek maritime past before the days of steam. Once the third port of Greece, Galaxídi looks as if it is a bit of Sýros perhaps, transferred to Roúmeli. The island atmosphere used to be heightened by the fact that, before the main road was built, Galaxídi was most easily reached by ferry from Itéa. It has a virtually unspoilt core of grand bourgeois houses (*archontiká*), some of which rest on sturdy lengths of ancient wall.

Galaxídi is a very pretty harbour town, with impressive views outside it. Some of its old houses have painted ceilings, if you can get a look inside. The seafood

tavérnas along the harbour are well worth your time. Parnassus (Parnassós) is magnificently prominent above the villages that scale its slopes; from the hills above Galaxídi, Córinth can be seen on a clear day; and at night the lights of Aíghio in the Peloponnese twinkle across the water.

The coast road continues with innumerable windings to **Náfpaktos**. It was here that the Athenians defeated the Spartans in a naval battle in 429 BC and dedicated a ship to Poseidon, god of the sea, at **Río** opposite. And in 1571 a famous battle took place (in fact fought just outside the Corinthian Gulf off the west coast of Greece) through which Náfpaktos became famous as Lepanto. An Ottoman chronicler records, "The Imperial fleet encountered the fleet of the wretched infidels and the will of God turned another way." It is well worth the climb up from the toy-like Venetian harbour, past little gardens, to the almost impregnable castle above.

From Náfpaktos, one can return to Delphi by the old upland route, as

The Tholos (left) and the Temple of Apollo, both at Delphi.

beautiful as the coast road and more hazardous. On the way, the stone village of **Lidoríki** is near the birthplace of General Makriyánnis, a fighter in the War of Independence whose *Memoirs* are the best insight into the mind of old Roúmeli. Here is a chance to breathe the air and stretch your legs before going on past the shining waters of the **Mórnos reservoir**, which helps to supply Athens with water. Stark rocks are intermittently set off by green valleys with cattle; mountain fauna such as hawks (and occasionally eagles) and rock thrushes are noticeable.

Finally the road reaches **Ámfissa**, an old town in a crater-like setting. The old tanneries give you a good idea of an old neighbourhood without the old smells. **Sálona**, the castle above is a reminder of Ámfissa's medieval past.

Messolóngi and Agrínio: Continuing from Náfpaktos towards the west coast, the landscape becomes flatter. Messolóngi is the best known town here, one as rich in associations as Náfpaktos but with a less attractive present face. The lagoon with its feluccas is an unusual sight in Greece, but after a night in the company of Messolóngi's mosquitoes it is easy to see how it was that Byron died here and left his name – as *Výronas* – to a good many Greeks since.

Messolóngi's role in the War of Independence continued with a grim siege and the slaughter of its inhabitants, events commemorated in an unfinished poem by the national poet Solomós. Unfortunately, the poem, however fragmentary, is more evocative than the visible reality.

From Messolóngi there is a road up through the wild **Kleisoúra gorge**; further on, you will see tobacco leaves hanging outside almost every house. This is **Agrínio**, a prosperous commercial centre. From here one can take a rough road into the upland district of **Karpenísi** and then skirt **Mount Týmfristos** and continue along the oppressive **Sperchiós Valley** to **Lamía** (188 km/117 miles). Alternatively, we can deviate – and that's the word, for it's easy enough to get lost on the way – to **Galaxídi.**

the **monastery of Proúsos**. The faint-hearted may prefer the shores of **Lake Trichonís**.

The west coast: At first sight **Árta** is unspectacular, but it is of great interest to the historically minded. The town saw its heyday in the 13th century as the seat of the Despot of Epirus, whose realm stretched all the way up the west coast of Greece to what is now Dürres in present-day southern Albania. The extraordinary 13th-century church of the Parigorítissa, with its cantilevered columns on two levels, is unlike any other church in the country.

Arta is proverbial in Greece for its bridge, a fine Ottoman construction clearly visible on the northern edge of town. A well-known folk song relates that the bridge's builder, despite his "forty masons and sixty apprentices" could not get it to stay up until he had immured a living thing in the foundations whose spirit would guard it. By ill luck – or so the tale has it – this turned out to be his own wife.

The main road to the west continues to **Préveza**, a town which, like Árta, is known, if at all, through poetry but in a rather unfortunate way. In 1928 a young civil servant who had received a posting there, Kóstas Kariotákis by name, tried to drown himself, failing which, he shot himself in the head. Before accomplishing this he had avenged himself on Préveza by writing a poem entitled "Province" but which is universally known as "Préveza", in which the town is seen as the archetype of the boring, a place where hearing the band on Sunday is a major event. Even today teachers and civil servants quake at the thought of being sent to Préveza by central government; but the town's worthies revere the memory of their unwilling citizen.

A few miles to the north are the remains of **Nikópolis**, the city founded by the Roman emperor Augustus to celebrate his victory over Antony and Cleopatra off Actium in 31 BC. Impressive walls and a theatre survive as a reminder of the hated Roman domination. Foreign domination did bring tourism, however, and in the first two centuries,

The bridge of Árta.

Nikópolis was a real tourist trap. Visitors arriving there from Rome would either show off their Greek and perhaps pay a call on the philosopher Epictetus or buy Greek trinkets and drink too much Greek wine.

Some certainly visited the **Nekromanteíon** (the oracle of the dead) at Mesopótamos, before Párga. Here, under the watchful eye of Hades, Lord of the Underworld, visitors would believe or half-believe that they were communicating with the souls of the dead. Archaeology has revealed what appears to be special effects equipment.

Farther up the coast we reach **Igoumenítsa**, which is the port for Corfu (Kérkyra) or Italy. Roúmeli has been left behind.

The Ionian Islands: When people speak of "the Greek islands", it tends to be the Aegean that they have in mind. Very different in flavour, and largely free of the hubbub of the Aegean routes, are the Ionian Islands. In Greek they are called *Eftánisa* after the number (seven) of the principal islands; one of them, **Kýthera**, no longer administered with the rest and geographically an extension of the Peloponnese, will not be dealt with here. The visitor from any mainland country tends to relish the very insularity of the Aegean islands. The Ionian Islands by contrast are in two main respects far from insular.

In the first place, all of them are near the west coast of Greece, from Epirus north to Elis south of the Corinthian Gulf. Moreover, a formal and informal network of communications has always tied the main islands and numerous islets to small ports on the mainland, and such intercourse is the natural state of affairs. Cattle were taken across the straits in the world of Odysseus; today it is mainly smaller items – wine or those mysterious parcels that seem to fill every Greek mode of transportation.

The Ottoman rulers of mainland Greece did not want to break this chain, and an important consequence in the present is that the population of the Ionian Islands has remained relatively stable by comparison with that of the Dodecanese, where the loss of the main-

Párga, looking towards the Ionian islands.

land coast to Turkey has deprived islanders of their livelihood and led to large-scale emigration. In the Ionian Islands a large rural population still exists and the twang of Chicago or Melbourne Greek is rarely to be heard.

The other way in which the Ionian Islands are far from insular is that they are, in the high culture at least, an amalgam of East and West. Under Venetian rule – which on Corfu (Kérkyra), always the most important of the islands, lasted from 1386 until 1797 – the rich were bilingual in Greek and Italian, often educated in Venice or Padua and in some cases honoured with the noble titles of the *Libro d'Oro* in the manner of a European aristocracy.

Many were Roman Catholics, and the religious paintings of the 17th and 18th centuries clearly bear the mark of contemporary Western developments, as does the architecture of the churches to which they belong. It was native traditions as much as any interference, kindly or otherwise, by external powers, that made the Ionian Islands the first

home, in the lands that now make up Greece, of a university and of a form of representative government.

But the islands' geographical position has been a source of more than a distinctive culture. It has also meant turbulent times for a region of great commercial and strategic importance, ever since Corinth's colonisation of ancient Corcyra. Between 1797 and 1864 the islands were successively ruled, under a variety of constitutions, by Venice, France, the Ottoman Empire and Russia, then France again, Britain and finally Greece.

Corfu (Kérkyra) was famous in ancient times for a bloody civil war; more recently it came into vogue through the writings of the Durrell brothers. Much has changed since World War II, and the island is now an incomparable tourist asset. At the same time, however, it remains an island of great agricultural wealth, especially in olives – a blessing of Venetian rule. Its population is still overwhelmingly rural. So it is still easy to escape the "pubs" of the main tourist

Georgie Zárzas of "Georgie Loves the People" restaurant on Corfu.

centres and find a quiet spot, especially to the northwest.

Despite its crowds and considerable war damage, Corfu Town remains a unique conglomeration of public and domestic buildings in which one can detect all the influences that have affected the island: the emblem of the lion of Venice; a French-style colonnade; houses with a Neapolitan flavour; and a clear legacy of British rule, cricket on the esplanade (fox-hunting never caught on). Opposite loom the forbidding mountains of Albania.

Lefkáda is an increasingly popular island because of its clear water and long beaches. It is connected to the mainland by a floating drawbridge.

More often visited because of its name but still very peaceful for most of the year is **Ithaca (Itháki)**. The reason of course is its fame as the home of Odysseus (though envious Lefkáda has disputed the claim). Homer correctly describes the island as rugged; it is also beautifully green. **Vathý**, the capital, a deep port with white houses climbing

steep slopes on either side, is the best place to stay (the north of the island is within easy reach). Go to the little museum, test your connoisseurship on the supposed El Greco in the Cathedral, walk out of town a little way and you will understand why Byron once wished he owned it.

Cephaloniá, the largest and most rugged of the *Eftánisa*, is the island on which one most feels the loss of old ways and the passing of power and culture elsewhere. Lefkáda and Ithaca were always humble, but **Argostóli** was a charming town before the disastrous earthquake of 1953, and plays from **Liksoúri's** 18th-century days have been revived on the Athenian stage.

Zákynthos appears from the boat (from Kyllíni in the Peloponnese) like a little model town. The churches and other buildings restored or rebuilt after the great earthquake of 1953 look just a little too bright and new. But while the atmosphere of the old streets has been largely lost, the public buildings and churches remain charmingly decorous. Less overrun by tourists than Corfu, Zákynthos gives one some idea of what it was that the Ionian Islands brought to the Greece of today.

One of the greatest contributions, especially valued by the Greeks, is poetry. After the fall of Crete in 1669 many of the aristocrats who had produced the literature of the Renaissance in Crete left for the Ionian Islands and Zákynthos in particular. And the tradition was combined by the two great Romantic poets born on Zákynthos, Count Dionísios Solomós and Andréas Kálvos; a third poet, Ugo Foscolo, wrote in Italian, but the Greek government still claims him as Greek on his anniversary.

Off the main square by the harbour there are, in fact, two fascinating museums, one devoted largely to Solomós and the other to the paintings of the distinctive Ionian School.

These highbrow activities apart, it is only fair to mention that swimming on Zákynthos is as good as anywhere in Greece, and that a subsequent evening meal will sometimes be accompanied by serenades after the Italian fashion.

Left, Ayios Spiridon, Corfu Town. **Right**, an old Corfu woman.

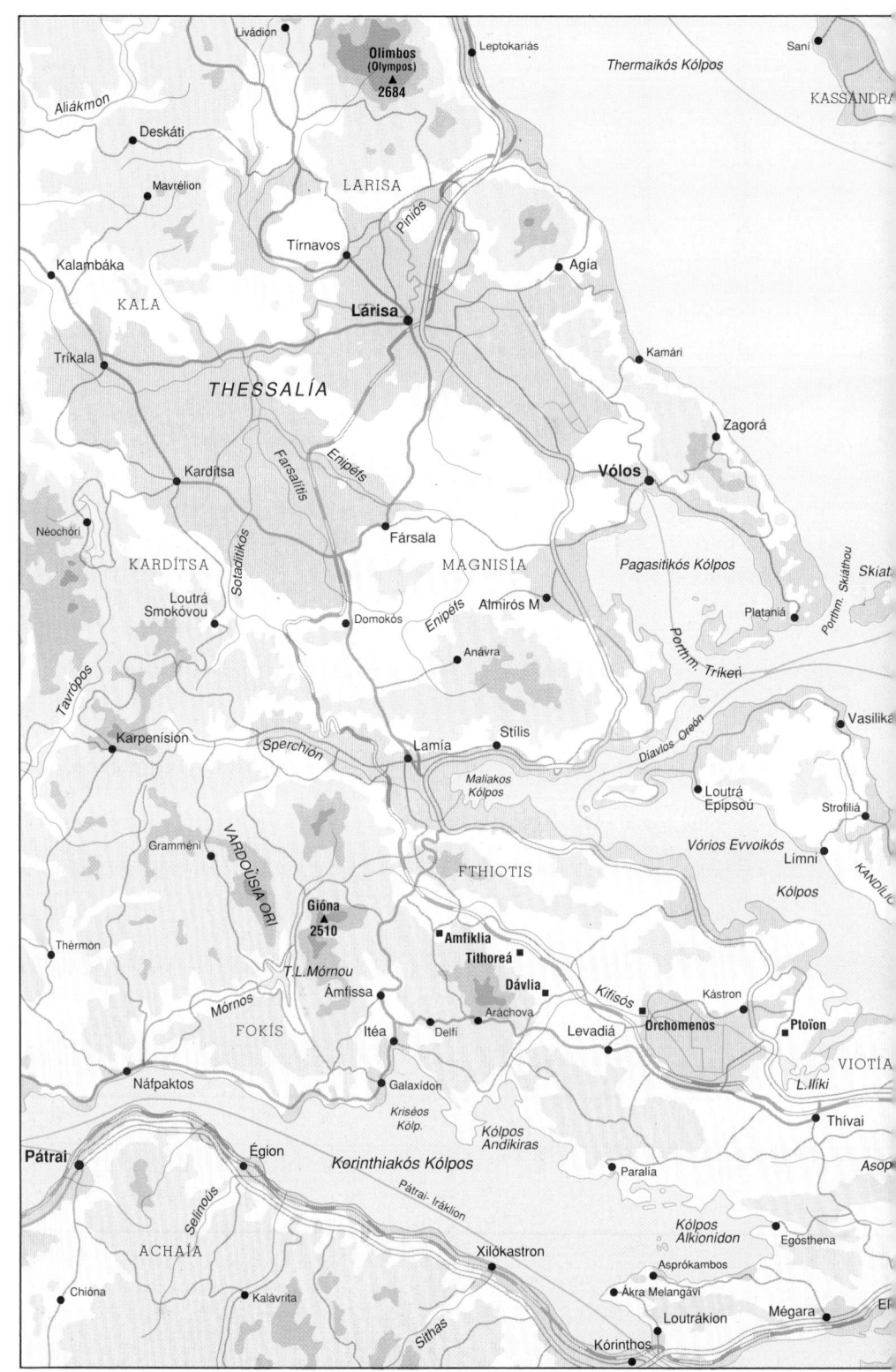

Central Greece

40 km/25 miles

Egéon Pélagos

Gioúra

Pipérion

Kirá Panagía

Alónnisos

Peristéra

Alónnisos

VÓRII SPORÁDES

Skópelos

SKIROS

Skiros

SKIROPOÚLA

Míli

Kími

Steni Dírfios

EUBOEA

Ólimbos
Évvias
1171

Kriezá

Nótios Evvoikós Kólpos

ATTIKI

Almiropótamos

Párnis
Ethn. Párkon
1419

Stira

Kalérgon

Kifisía

Óchi Ór.
1398

Athínai

Káristos

PETALLÍ

néos   SITHONIA   Sárti   Singitikós
Kólpos

Koufós

Kólpos

Ág. Konstantínos- Mírina   Thessaloníki- Mitilíni

Vólos- Limassól/Tartous

Porthmós Kafiréos

CENTRAL GREECE

What today we consider Central Greece was, until the end of the Balkan Wars in 1913, Northern Greece. At that point the northern boundary of Greece ran from Vólos through Lárissa, around the wide plain of Thessaly, through the southern part of the great Píndos range to Arta on the west coast. But whatever the name of this middle part of the country, the area comprises the best that Greece has to offer: mountains, trees, fertile land, sandy beaches, islands, running rivers, and excellent harbours. Vólos, situated about halfway between Thessaloniki and Athens, makes a convenient hub for our travels in Central Greece which can fan out in every direction.

One's first impression of **Vólos** is that some giant took an accordion made of Athens, Piraeus, Thessaloniki, and all their outlying suburbs, and compressed it. The city has a little bit of everything found in a huge metropolis.

Once there, the visitor senses immediately the unique charm of the small busy town. There is a lovely promenade along the quay. The harbour reminds one of island harbours more than big city ports. Running down to the sea are numerous narrow streets in whose arcades are hidden some great little *ouzeríes*.

Like most important port cities of Greece, Vólos has an incredibly long history, dating back to neolithic times (about 4600–2600 BC). The wonderful tale of the adventuresome Jason who set out from Iolkos, portions of which have been excavated on the outskirts of Vólos, in the famous ship *Argo,* to find the Golden Fleece long before the Trojan War, seems to come alive as you gaze out at the gulf named after the ancient port of **Pagasae**. Mythology is everywhere in Vólos.

The Sporádes: For those who choose the sea, Vólos is the boarding point for the tiny luscious group of islands known as the **Northern Sporádes**. What a mar-

Preceding pages: Ághios Stéfanos monastery.

vellous word! It means scattered, or sown, as the root of the word means seed. It is an accurate designation for these islands, which are strewn off the coast of Pélion.

Closest to Vólos is **Skiáthos**, which has lush greenery and sandy beaches. The most popular of these beaches, Koukounariés, has a sandy stretch more than half a mile long, shaded by pines and shrubs.

Skópelos is the next in the row of the Sporádes to the east. Its beaches are lovely. The one lying in the curve of the bay of the main town, **Skópelos**, is usually very crowded. Others, smaller and more intimate than those of Skiáthos, are accessible by car or bus.

The most lovely are **Stáfylos Cove**, and **Limonári** on the south coast near the main town and **Miliá** and **Loutráki** to the west and north. Rent a "put-put" and chug to your own isolated beach, of which there are many.

You should not miss the opportunity to visit this beautifully green island. It has two ferry boat stops, Glóssa, "the tongue," opposite Skiáthos, and on the east, the main harbour, which as you approach looks like a white-tiered wedding cake, decorated with brilliantly-coloured flowers. The harbour is intensely busy, what with the four-times-daily ferry service and the many private yachts.

For those interested in chapels and fascinating convents (some of these produce handwoven goods), or remote monasteries, Skópelos, for all its tiny size, has about 360 such – white dots on a variegated green landscape of almond, plum, fig, and olive trees and thousands of grape arbours. Skópelos even boasts some antiquities, including the remains of a Cretan colony, and, as everywhere in Greece, a ruined *kástro*.

Beyond Skópelos lies the oblong island of **Alónnissos**, with its steep, rocky coastline on the northwest, and undulating hills. On the dock you will witness a phenomenon, not unique to Alónnissos by any means, but surprisingly fervent here: that of soliciting rents for private rooms. Some locals hold out discreet **Skiáthos.**

cards; others wave large signs in the air.

If, by renting a moped, or hiring a "put-put", you can get beyond the harbour town, you will find Alónnissos one of the last bastions of unspoiled tourism in Greece. Here are deserted beaches; green pine groves without discarded film boxes and plastic bottles. The only paved road leads from the harbour to the old pre-1950 earthquake town of Alónnissos. To get anywhere else you must go by dirt road or skiff. Renting a small boat is worth it because you can make a round-the-island and across-to-Peristéra trip at your own pace.

Peristéra is the small island that hugs the shore of Alónnissos on the eastern side. For other areas on the island, such as the beach at **Marpoúnda** on the south, or **Kokinókastro** on the eastern peninsula, there are regular launches leaving from the main harbour during the summer.

Beyond Alónnissos and its small companion, Peristéra, are scattered three or four more islands: **Pélagos** (also called Kyrá Panaghía), **Yiaoúra**, which has a cave worth investigating and **Pipéri**. These can only be reached by *caïque*, or one's own yacht. It was off these rocky promontories that a Byzantine wreck was discovered in the summer of 1968 and subsequently explored by a team of archaeologists under the auspices of the Greek Archaeological Service. The brilliantly-coloured Byzantine plates, with their motifs of sailing vessels, fish and border designs, are now in the museum at Vólos.

The fourth major island of the Northern Spórades, **Skýros**, has the most history and legend of the group. It was the island where the two-timing Theseus was put to death by the king of the island, Lycomedes. It was here that Thetis hid her son Achilles, disguised as a woman, with Lycomedes' daughters so he would not be drafted for the Trojan War. The main town itself, also called **Skýros**, is built partly on a bluff overlooking the beach to the east, and then dips down to the beach

A statue of Rupert Brooke, the British poet who died off Skýros while on his

way to fight in the Dardanelles in 1915, dominates a tiny square at one edge of town. From there the view to the sea is out of this world.

Clearly the wealth of legend surrounding the island is an indication of its commercial importance. It was a centre of maritime commerce for thousands of years, and home to many of the Mediterranean pirates who defied law and order from the days of Pompey in 70 BC to the middle of the 19th century. All is calm there now, except during the hectic summer tourist season, when the few houses that have rooms are crammed.

Euboea (Évia): From Skýros's harbour of **Linariá** a ferry boat leaves regularly for the east coast port on **Euboea** of **Kími**. Up from the noisy broil of the dock, the hill village is charming. Stay there a night, if you can. Of course, Évia, as you must pronounce it or no one will know what you are talking about, is more usually reached via the road from Athens to the large sprawling city of **Chálkis** is the capital of Euboea. However, arriving on the island via the back

way gives you a chance to get a taste of the landscape.

After Crete, Euboea (about 180 km/ 115 miles long) is the second largest island in Greece. A thorough exploration of the island is most rewarding. It is a microcosm of Greece. Museums, restaurants, beaches, factories, refineries, discos, glamorous hotels, pollution, ancient, Byzantine, Frankish, Venetian, 1821 relics – all are there. Chálkis (perhaps named for the Greek word for bronze *halkós*) alone possesses all of these. The bustling city is located on the **Euripus (Evripos) Channel** whose irregular currents change direction as many as 14 times a day. Its maritime significance was as important in the 7th century BC as in the period of Venetian dominance (AD 1200–1400), when the island was known as Negropont.

All along the coast going north, and even further to the south, are the latest hotel development projects. Although the beaches are not very desirable for swimming, as they are mostly pebbly, the hotels are always full during the

Monument at Euboea.

summer. This is true of the whole Miami-like coastline facing the continent, as well as the southern ferry port of **Kárystos**, its cleaner, calmer beaches dominated by bare Mount Ochi.

The beautiful parts of Euboea are the central and northern portions. The road winds leisurely along, settles down in some valleys, and then goes up again. Most are green and wooded. A 19-km (12-mile) drive to the west from the main north–south road at **Strophyliá** leads to the resort of **Límni**, very much an enclave of the British, who maintain summer homes or even stay the year round. It is also a haven for yachtsmen.

If you get that far you should proceed southeast along the narrow coastal road to the very attractive convent at **Galatáki** with its frescoed church and peaceful rooms overlooking the sea between the island and the mainland.

In addition to the traces of Frankish and Venetian remains, most notably watchtowers at Alivér, Félla aand Avlonári, there are many ancient ruins. Most of these are in the northern part of the island near **Istiaía** and **Oreoí**, and are rather disappointing to the non-expert. It is more rewarding to visit the **sanctuary of Artemis** near **Vathý** on the mainland side of the Evripos Channel. There, close by the immense cement works of Chálkis, you can visit famous **Aulis**, where Agamemnon's youngest daughter, Iphigenia, was sacrificed on the altar of Ártemis, the virgin huntress goddess, so that the winds would be favourable for the Greek fleet to set sail for Troy.

A final place to visit in Euboea is **Edipsós**, with its renowned health springs. From there you can take off for the mainland. Sacred to the ancients for their healing powers, the springs were frequented by such famous Roman characters as Sulla, the conqueror of the east. Although the beach is hardly ideal, many large tourist hotels have been built around the small bay. Some of these nearest the springs boast mineral water piped directly into the rooms.

Thermopylae (Thermopýles): The monument dedicated to the men who died at

Fishing at Chálkis.

Thermopylae in July of 480 BC, defending the Greeks against the hordes of Persians, is on the National Road to Lamía, just beyond Kámena Voúrla (a mineral spring centre like Edipsós), mobbed in the summer in spite of mushy beaches and murky water. *Thermopýles* means "warm gates, or pass" because of the area's hot sulphur springs which bubble up today as they did in 480 BC.

The last part of Book VII of Herodotus has immortalised the romance of betrayal. How Leonidas and his 300 Spartan men were annihilated because of the treachery of a well-bribed local, Ephialtes (the word means nightmare in modern Greek) is a well-known tale. The Spartan flank was turned by the Persians climbing over a mountain path. Despite fierce resistance, Leonidas fell with all his Spartans and more than 1,000 other Greek troops. Their immortal epitaph rings sacred: "O stranger, announce to the Spartans that we lie here, obedient to their command."

Metéora: Suddenly, as you round a bend in the dull road that leads from Tríkala to Kalambáka, erectile, elemental rock formations piercing the sky confront you – the **Metéora**. Nothing you have ever seen in pictures can prepare you for this. On these projections are some of the most extraordinary monasteries in the world. The name is derived from the verb, *meteorízo*, which means to suspend in the air.

Few places in Greece are so intensely visual. The formations, which once supported 24 monasteries, defy description. Most geologists hold to the theory that the strange outcroppings of rock were created by millions of years of erosion by the **Pineíos River** as it split the Píndos range to the west of the Thessalian plain from that of Mount Olympus and Mount Ossa on the east.

Whoever was the first hermit to scale a pinnacle – Andronikos or Athanasios, depending upon which of the various histories you may read – you can only marvel at how long it took to get stone by stone, brick by brick, board by board up to those heights with a basket and a rope ladder.

Two landmarks of Metéora: St Nicholas…

The largest of the monasteries, the Megálo Metéoron, also known as Metamórphosis (Transfiguration) took three centuries to complete, having been founded around 1356. **Ághios Stéfanos** (now run by nuns) was completed at the end of the 1300s. Of the 24 monastic communities which flourished till the last part of the 17th century, their heyday being in the 14th and 15th centuries, 18 are in ruins, and only six are inhabited and open to visitors.

Clockwise, the visible monasteries are: **Ághios Nikólaos** built around 1388, with a small chapel containing frescoes by the monk Theophánes of the Cretan School (*circa* 1527); **Megálo Metéoron**, looked after by a few monks of the St Basil order with a valuable collection of manuscripts dating to the 9th century and ancient icons displayed in the old refectory; **Varlaám**, with 16th-century frescoes by Franco Catellano, partly restored in 1870 and an old windlass, now used only for lifting supplies but formerly used for elevating monks as well; **Aghía Triáda** (Holy Trinity)

which is approached by approximately 139 difficult steps chiselled out of the rock, and whose major claim to recent fame is being an on-sight location for the James Bond movie *For Your Eyes Only*; Ághios Stéfanos, where the renovated chapel is easy of access and whose small museum displays ecclesiastical robes, icons, manuscripts and similar treasures.

Olympus (Ólymbos): Today, as you drive through the beautiful **Vale of Témpi** along the gorge of the Pineíos River, you can hardly believe that until 1913, it was not even part of Greece. The vale, however, oblivious of time and armies, remains the same welcome lushness of cool and green as it has been for thousands of years. Even the encroachments of tourism have not changed the river, which forms the 10-km (6-mile) pass severing Mount Olympus from Mount Ossa. Along the way there are several touristy stops. One is the little church of **Aghía Paraskeví** across a narrow foot-bridge over the river. There you can light your

...and **Rousoúnou.**

candle and fill your canteen. Another is the **Spring of Aphrodite** at the end of the pass. In spite of these tourist traps, no one should travel the vale, celebrated by so many poets, without stopping somewhere – either to look down at the river and take a picture, or perhaps to wander down a path to its edge. Another possible diversion, just above Témpi, is the village of **Ambelákia**, which still preserves a few score rambling *archontiká* from the 18th century when it was a centre for the manufacture of botanical dyes. One *archontikó* is now a museum.

Leaving the cool vale you head north straight for the "home of the gods," Mount Olympus. There are several passages in Homer where he alludes to Zeus's habit of bringing down the clouds to cover the summit of Mount Olympus so that no one on earth could see what was going on. Well, that is just one way of stating an obvious fact. Very rarely can you get a good picture of the mountain from the narrow plain that lies between the mountain and the sea, the **Thermaïc Gulf** (from the word *thermós*, meaning warm because of all the warm springs) so continuously is the summit girdled with clouds.

The usual "base camp" for ascents of the gods' mountain is **Litóchoro**, a small town at the top of the coastal plain, where detailed information is available at both the youth hostel and a booth staffed by the alpine club on the central square. Ideally, you should set aside three full days for a U-shaped tour of Olympos, with overnights at each of two refuges bracketing the summit regions.

On the first day out from Litóchoro, you will follow the well marked E4 long distance trail up the Mavrólongos gorge carved by the swift Enipéus River. Some three to four hours along, picnic by the rapids below abandoned Ághios Dionýsios monastery, destroyed during World War II. Thereafter, a stiff climb through dense forest brings you to the **Spílios Agapitós refuge**, packed to the gills in summer; September or early October are better, usually cloud free months

Left, Mount Olympus. Below, two generations at Ambelákia.

anyway. With a dawn start – the warden will guarantee this – and a good head for heights as there are some frightening, on-all-fours scrambling near the end – you should be 2,917 metres (9,570 ft) up on the top, with the gods on Mítikas Peak, before lunch time.

The rest of the second day should be spent retrieving your full pack (the summit is no place for it) and traversing the base of the peaks to the **Apostolídi hut**, upon the evocatively named "Plateau of the Muses." Here you can contemplate fan-shaped **Stefáni**, reputedly the throne of Zeus, before the long half day of descent via a fire ridge trail, to Diakládosi, and hence a short hop down to the ruined monastery and another half-day along the river to Litóchoro.

Pílion: Having navigated the austere heights of Mount Olympus, let us now return to the "hub" of Central Greece, Vólos and **Mount Pílion**.

The mythological explanation for the mountains which circle the great Thessalian plain is wonderfully imaginative. Huge creatures called Titans or Giants (depending upon what version of the story you read – Homer, Hesiod, Ovid, Virgil) vied with each other to dominate the new gods, Zeus and Poseidon. What modern scientists call earthquakes, ice flows, tectonic shifts of plates, or whatever, were simply credited to the Titans. It was they who tried to pile Pílion on Ossa, and both mountains on top of Olympus to reach the heavenly realm of the gods.

The legend is often laughed at as being a tall tale until you have been there. Then the close juxtaposition of the three mountain massifs and the precipitous cleavage of the vale may make you wonder.

But let's leave such great endeavours to the gods and content ourselves with a trip around Mount Pílion, land of the centaurs. These famous beings had the legs and bodies of horses (indicating the importance of the horse in the development of civilisation) and the arms and heads of men. These creatures were the teachers of many of the major heroes, Achilles being the most famous. The

A Byzantine monastery.

intriguing historical fact is that the entire Pílion region was a principle centre of learning in Greece throughout the 17th and 18th centuries. Many of the important secretaries and governors of provinces in the Austro-Hungarian Empire, the sultan's inner circle and a few in the Russian court were educated on Mount Pílion.

There are few remains of this grandeur, but **Zagorá**, the largest village, still boasts an excellent library and **Makrinítsa**, about 19 km (12 miles) from Vólos, has preserved the highest concentration of 18th-century "Pílion-style" houses. Probably the original reason for the place becoming such a nursery of Greek erudition was its lush water supply, and its inaccessibility to the Turks, which meant no revenues for the overlords.

The northeast facing beaches, where Mount Pílion crashes into the sea, are beyond the power of words or pictures to describe. The sand is Carribean creamy – real sand. The sea is more turquoise and filtered purple than any photograph can convey. Sea-fashioned caves and hidden coves like Mylopótamos will lure you down the many steps at **Tsangaráda** or the twisty road that ends up at **Aghios Ioánnis**, a major resort with perhaps 30 places to stay.

You will need a number of days to see all the villages nestled on Pílion's slopes: **Miliés**, and **Vyzítsa**, one of Pílion's most beautiful villages with cobblestone streets and houses on a par with Makrinítsa's to the north; **Ághios Lavréndis**, dedicated to folk art, or **Trikéri**, an isolated fishing village, to the south.

However, it is worth the time. Indeed, time should be the password for the whole country. You cannot "do" Greece in two weeks. The ancients have left their relics, of which the museums are full. The Romans, Byzantines, Arabs, Slavs, Franks, Venetians, Turks have done the same. That encompasses about 6,000 years of high civilisation. Nowhere in Greece has this heavy mass of history, triumph and tragedy made itself more evident than in so-called Central Greece.

Along the coast of Pélion.

FESTIVE OCCASIONS

I t seemed as if the whole village had crushed into the tiny church. The air was heavy with the scent of basil framing the icon of the Virgin Mary. Hundreds of candles flickered, boosting the heat of the midsummer night, while the sweet voices of the choir – hired for the occasion – fought to be heard above the congregation.

The priest called for hush, largely ignored. Children shoved through the crowd for their chunks of holy bread, sliced with gusto by the local taverna owner. The greengrocer's wife, dressed in her best, handed out candles and guarded the brimming collection plate.

The Assumption of the Virgin Mary, the *Panaghía*, on 15 August is the most important festival in Greece (after Easter). People flock home from wherever they are currently living to take part in the celebrations, or *paniyíria*, with feasting and dancing, often lasting all night, which follow the religious ceremony.

The Greeks have a great knack of mixing piety with pleasure. Sombre, moving moments soon give way to rambunctious carousing. Grannies, toddlers, and teenagers all join in while the macho *pallikária*, brave young men, try to outdance each other.

The festival marks the reception of the Holy Mother into Heaven. Every island has its own celebrations for the national holiday, but at most *paniyíria* the icon of the Virgin, often framed in gold or silver, or encrusted in jewels, is paraded aloft during the feast. The faithful queue up to kiss the holy image – slipping money into the collection plate for the privilege, of course – or snatch sprigs of basil for good luck throughout the year. *Vasilikó*, the royal herb, isn't used for cooking here but to adorn the church. The Greeks believe it is sacred as it grew on the tomb of Christ.

Paniyíria, similar to *fêtes* or country fairs, stem from pagan times when ancient Greeks honoured the Gods with orgies, feasting and fertility rites, plus a bit of buying and selling. From the 4th century the *paniyíri fora* celebrated the Christian martyrs. The church frowned on the commercial aspect, although these days you'll find pedlars and market stalls selling everything from balloons to catapults, icons to amulets, crucifixes to tracts on the saints. Condoms have also been spotted among the fairground novelties. In olden times there was often a baby boom nine months after the festival.

The music is traditional, the electronics are recent.

The word stems from *pan* (all) and *agora* (marketplace), suggesting a public assembly. But the present Greek word to celebrate, *paniyirizo*, *pan* (all) and *yirizo* (return) seems nearer the mark when you see the exiles and expats pouring off the ferries to their islands for the big day.

On 15 August Greeks make pilgrimages to Tínos in the Cyclades where the icon of the Panaghía Evangelistría is said to work miracles. Pilgrims flock to Pátmos, too, where St John wrote the book of Revelation. But perhaps the most colourful celebrations of the *Panaghía* are at Olympos on Kárpathos. The village clings to the hillside, almost locked away in a time warp, and women wear their traditional costumes every day.

At festival time, musicians gather beneath the village church playing Karpathian music on the *tsambouna* (goatskin bagpipes). The village men lead the dancing and as they wend their way down the narrow streets young girls join in, the slow *mantinádes* giving way to the fleet-footed *soústa*. Old ladies hand out almonds in twists of net and the usual revelry ensues.

The festival attracts throngs of visitors, so beware. Transport and rooms are scarce, so plan to stay awhile. ∎

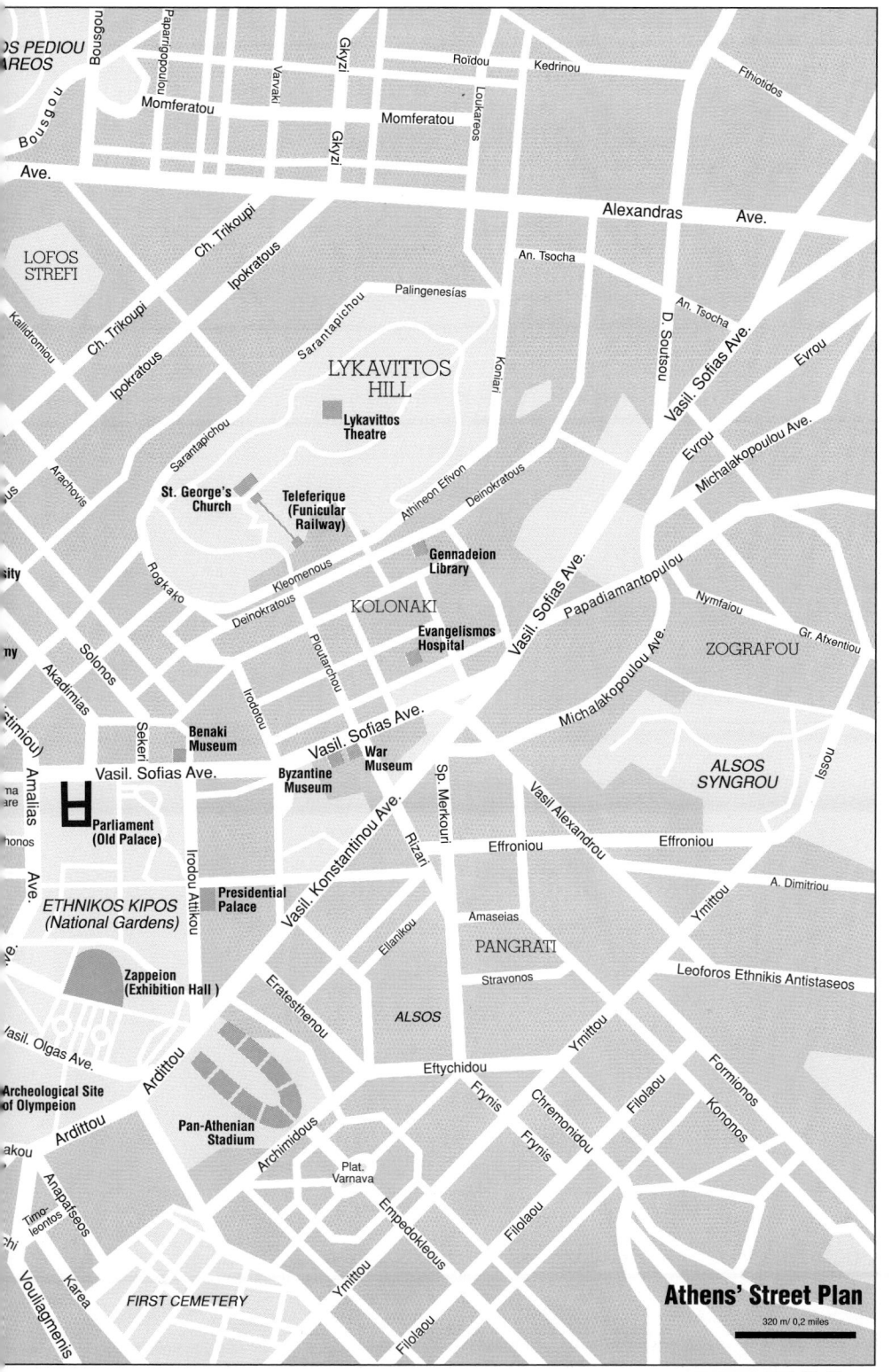

ΟS PEDIOU ΑREOS

Bousgou

Paparigopoulou

Gkyzi

Roïdou

Kedrinou

Fthiotidos

Varvaki

Momferatou

Momferatou

Gkyzi

Loukareos

Bousgou

Ave.

Alexandras Ave.

LOFOS STREFI

Ch. Trikoupi

Ipokratous

An. Tsocha

Palingenesías

An. Tsocha

D. Soutsou

Vasil. Sofias Ave.

Evrou

Kallidromiou

Ch. Trikoupi

Sarantapichou

Konari

Evrou

Ipokratous

LYKAVITTOS HILL

Lykavittos Theatre

Evrou

Michalakopoulou Ave.

Arachovis

Sarantapichou

Athineon Efivon

Deinokratous

sity

Rogkako

St. George's Church

Teleferique (Funicular Railway)

Gennadeion Library

Papadiamantopoulou

Nymfaiou

Gr. Afxentiou

ny

Solonos

Kleomenous

Deinokratous

KOLONAKI

Vasil. Sofias Ave.

ZOGRAFOU

Akadimias

Ploutarchou

Evangelismos Hospital

Michalakopoulou Ave.

nossi

timiou)

Sekeri

Benaki Museum

Irodotou

Vasil. Sofias Ave.

War Museum

ALSOS SYNGROU

Amalias

Vasil. Sofias Ave.

Byzantine Museum

Sp. Merkouri

Vasil Alexandrou

na are

Parliament (Old Palace)

Rizari

Effroniou

Effroniou

honos

Ave.

Irodou Attikou

Presidential Palace

Vasil. Konstantinou Ave.

Ellanikou

Amaseias

A. Dimitriou

Ymittou

ETHNIKOS KIPOS (National Gardens)

PANGRATI

Leoforos Ethnikis Antistaseos

e.

Zappeion (Exhibition Hall)

Eratesthenou

ALSOS

Stravonos

Ymittou

Formionos

Vasil. Olgas Ave.

Ardittou

Eftychidou

Frynis

Chremonidou

Filolaou

Kononos

Archeological Site of Olympeion

Archimidous

Frynis

Pan-Athenian Stadium

Plat. Varnava

Filolaou

akou

Ardittou

Timo-leomos

Anapafseos

Empedokleous

chi

Ymittou

Karea

FIRST CEMETERY

Athens' Street Plan

Voullagmenis

Filolaou

320 m/ 0,2 miles

ATHENS

If there is one quality which Athens should be credited with unreservedly, it is elasticity. It might be compared to an indestructible old sweater which has shrunk and stretched repeatedly through the centuries, changing its shape as circumstances required.

Athens is barely mentioned in Homer. It emerged as a growing power in the 6th century BC. Then came the Periclean high noon, when Athens became a great centre of art and literature, commerce and industry. With Macedonian expansion came the first shrinkage, though Athens remained a prestigious intellectual centre with particular emphasis on philosophy and oratory.

In the Hellenistic age, Athens was overshadowed by the great monarchies founded by Alexander's successors, but not obliterated. The rulers of Egypt, Syria, Pergamum courted the old city with gifts of buildings and works of art. Yet one can't help feeling it was perhaps already beginning to rest on its laurels, to turn into a museum-city, a "cultural commodity" rather than an active, living organism. Besieged and sacked by Sulla in 86 BC, restored and pampered under two philathenian Roman emperors, Augustus and Hadrian, sacked again by the Herulians in AD 267 and Alaric the Goth in AD 395, Athens entered the Byzantine era shorn of all its glory – a small provincial town, a mere backwater. The edict of the Byzantine emperor Justinian forbidding the study of philosophy there (529) dealt the deathblow to the ancient city.

Venetian incursion: Under Latin rule (1204–1456), invaded, occupied and fought over by the French, Catalans, Florentines and Venetians, Athens shrank even further. It was only after the Ottoman conquest in the 15th century that it began to expand again, but still falling far short of its ancient limits. There were more setbacks, including a devastating Venetian incursion in 1687. Athens finally rose from its ruins after the War of Independence, an "exhausted city", as Christopher Wordsworth noted in 1832, and was suddenly raised, unprepared, to the status of capital of the new Greek state.

Growing up fast: Athens is thus a city that has grown haphazardly, and too fast. It never had a chance to mellow into venerable old age. Old and new have not blended too well, you can still sense the small pre-war city pushing through the huge messy sprawl of today's modern capital, like the proverbial thin man struggling to get out of every fat man.

An unmellow city, then; a city in transition, it is said apologetically. But then one might say it has always been in transition; not the natural kind, but violent and irregular, leaving visible marks, glaring contrasts, untidy seams.

You occasionally come across what must have been a country villa, ensconced between tall office buildings, its owner still fighting against the tide, its windows hermetically closed against dust, pollution, the roar of the traffic. For traffic in Athens has to be seen (and heard) to be believed. For one thing, Athens must have the highest number of motorcycles of any city in Europe: cars are expensive and get stuck in the traffic, motorbikes wriggle through where everybody else fears to tread.

But branching off from these frenzied central arteries are the minor veins of the city, relatively free from congestion: narrow streets where the architecture may be shrilly modern, yet life retains in part some of the old patterns. Most apartment blocks have balconies and verandahs, and there you can see the Athenians in summer emerging from their afternoon siesta in underpants and nighties, reading the paper, watching the neighbours, watering their plants, eating their evening meal.

The hot weather makes life in the open air a necessity; this in turn means gregariousness, a kind of social exhibitionism – it is no accident that there is no word for "privacy" in Greek – though nowadays the pale blue flicker of television draws more and more people indoors. Yet even television sometimes turns into an excuse for gregariousness;

there are improvised World Cup parties, election-night parties; collective viewing while eating, drinking, talking, and playing cards.

Recently taxis have also turned into a sort of communal institution. Taxis are cheap in Athens and therefore in great demand. If you're lucky enough to get one, you soon find you have to share it with others. But what began as a necessity has evolved into one more occasion for social exchange, whether heated argument or comfortable chatting. Are the Athenians then such sociable and funloving creatures? Not really; they are simply easily bored and immensely restless. Byron called the Greeks "an intriguing cunning unquiet generation."

Another foreign traveller, the Frenchman Edmond About, observed in 1852 that the Greeks are vain, curious, furiously ambitious, set on a relentless quest for success and prosperity, as a result of the insecurity generated by decades of poverty; more than poverty, the sheer precariousness of life in Athens in those protracted dark ages. This is perhaps what gives the city its intent, bustling air, often mistaken, especially by disciplined northerners, for uninhibited Mediterranean exuberance. It's true that the incessant activity has nothing of the antlike industriousness engendered by the Protestant work ethic. Improvise, make do, contrive and combine, keep going, keep ahead, is more what it's all about. The feverishness is also due, no doubt, to the need for rapid adaptation to the modern world, to the crazy pace created by those abrupt, transitional pangs mentioned above.

It would be interesting to write a sociological study simply noting the kinds of shops that predominated in Athens with each successive transition: the 1960s saw an extraordinary eruption of "Scandinavian" furniture shops, in the 1970s it was fashion boutiques and art galleries; everybody became bathroom-conscious in the 1980s, and shop-windows displayed huge shell-shaped bathtubs, gold taps, an infinite variety of bathroom-tiles; then came the craze for Video Clubs – understandably, since **God and Mammon mingle.**

210

Greek TV is not all that exciting, and there were, until recently, only two channels, which seemed to copy each other with amazing fidelity. The 1990s have brought international designers like Armani to Athens, along with cowboy gear (saddles included) for the *nouveaux* urban cowboys.

There is a constant struggle to catch up with the West while clinging to the old traditional ways. *Tavérnes*, competing with pizza and fast-food shops, try to keep up a semblance of *couleur locale* (which is fast turning into *couleur internationale*: you find better *taramosaláta* in London supermarkets than in Athens). Arranged marriages are still going strong, but the matchmaker is now competing with a computer service. Doughnuts and *koulóuria*, popcorn and *passatémpo*; a priest, majestic in flowing black robes, licking an ice-cream cone or riding a motorbike – unthinkable 10 or 15 years ago. Coexistence – but the edges are still jagged.

City streets: One of the places where the meeting of old and new is most manifest is the commercial area between **Monastiráki** and **Omónoia Square**, at the heart of the city. It is a kind of huge chaotic bazaar, bringing to mind the market described in a comedy by Euboulos in the 2nd century BC, "Everything will be for sale together in the same place at Athens, figs, summoners, bunches of grapes, turnips, pears, apples, witnesses, roses, medlars, haggis, honeycombs, chickpeas, lawsuits, beestings-puddings, myrtle-berries, allotment machines, irises, lambs, waterclocks, laws, indictments."

Beestings-puddings and allotment machines sound mysterious enough, but the weird assortment of objects to be found in the market today is almost equally intriguing. Kitsch-collectors will find much to interest them; Greek kitsch is perhaps the most orgiastically hideous in the world. The modern age has brought mass production tourist trade on a grand scale. Even the shops around the **Mitrópolis**, specialising in ecclesiastical articles, have turned touristy; the manufacturers have perhaps caught on

to the fact that tourists often find bronze candle-stands just the thing for a garden-party; a priest's heavily-embroidered robes can be turned into a stunning evening dress, while pectoral crosses outshine the flashiest *faux bijoux*.

But if you move away from the robust vulgarity of **Pandróssou Street** to the narrow sidestreets off the **Flea Market**, you step into an almost pre-industrial era. This is the district of traditional crafts (crafts minus "arts"), wholesale shops selling refreshingly non-decorative, down-to-earth stuff like screws, all sizes and shapes, locks and keys, chains of varying thickness, boxes and crates, brushes and brooms, mysterious implements like futuristic sculptures, mousetrap shops, herb-shops (the mountains of Greece are reputed to be a botanist's paradise), shops selling incense, resin in big amber-coloured chunks, contrasting bright blue chunks of sulphate of copper used for plants (and fishing octopus) – a whole serendipitous accumulation of things no longer to be found in our brave new ready-made world.

Head for the hills: There's a peaceful busyness in these narrow streets. Only a few steps beyond, you are back in the great melting-pot, the high-rise buildings, the fumes, the heat. You panic, but not for long. The saving grace of Athens is that there are easy ways out; better still, visible ways out. Just when you're feeling buried alive in the asphalt jungle, you see at the end of a street a fragment of mountain, a slice of open country, trees, breathing outlets.

Athens is full of bumps, some big enough to deserve the name of hills, others mere excrescences. Eight of them have been counted (one up on Rome!) but there may be more. There's **Mount Lycabettus (Lykavitós)**, of course (you can't miss it); the equally conspicuous rock of the **Acropolis**, flanked by the **Pnyx** on one side, and the hill of **Philopáppus (Filopápou)** on the other, where it is the custom to fly kites on the first day of Lent; the hill of **Ardittos**, next to the marble horseshoe **Stadium**, built by Herod Atticus in AD 143 and totally reconstructed in 1896 (the first modern

Angelic dreams in the National Gardens.

Olympic Games were held there); the hill of the **Nymphs**, capped by the grey dome of the **Observatory**; the barren, windblown **Tourkovoúnia range**; and the hill of **Stréfi**, the poor man's Lycabettus, far less touristy, where the efforts of landscape-gardeners appear more strenuous than on the other hills.

There are small hidden cafés and a measure of coolness on some of these hills. Still, these small pockets of green don't really deserve the name of oases – you have to go further afield for that, up one of the three mountains that encircle Athens. **Mount Hymettus (Imitoú)**, beloved of honey-bees, glowing violet at sunset, provides a real oasis. Driving up the winding road past the monastery of **Kaisarianí** (30 minutes' drive) you reach a vantage-point of beauty and tranquillity from which to contemplate the whole of Attica (*also see page 219*.) The city is panoramically visible, yet totally, eerily inaudible. On **Mount Parnes (Párnitha)**, only two hours away, you can walk in a dark wilderness of fir trees, play roulette at the casino,

ski in winter. **Mount Pendéli** is crowded, lively, popular, with all the ensuing disadvantages: the air is thick with *souvláki*-smoke and the screams of overactive children.

But if you're not much of a climber, if you're simply "*las des musées, cimetières des arts*," as Lamartine said, you can escape to the **National Gardens**, within a stone's throw of the Byzantine, Benáki and War museums. You walk down **Herod Atticus Street**, watch – if you must – the changing of the Évzone Guard (whom Hemingway refers to as "those big tall babies in ballet skirts"), then turn right, into the park. Suddenly there is thick shade, tangled bowers, romantic arbours, and relative quiet.

Do not expect anything lush, the generous green expanses, the grassy carpets, the lakes and cascades of other European parks. Here are only modest fish-ponds, thin but constant trickles of water running along secret leafy troughs; a few forlorn deer, and a large population of cats, fed, and neutered, by Athens's few committed animal-lovers. Ci-

Below, classical kitsch. **Right**, sybaritic statue in Syntagma Square.

cadas whirr away, peacocks cry, mournful for all their spotted blue-green glory. Here you can observe the Athenians at rest; here students come to study, lovers meet, old men meditate, mothers brood, weary hitchhikers sleep on a bench, under a roof of wisteria, even the busy briefcase-men use it sometimes as a bridge, an interlude in between two hurried appointments.

There is a solitary, unexpected stretch of green lawn on **Vass. Sofías Avenue**; beautifully designed, it serves as the setting for the giant bronze statue of the eminent statesman Venizélos (1864–1936), who seems on the point of plunging into the traffic, and then thinks better of it. If you climb over the green slope to the back of the site, you come upon the **Park of Freedom**. It is not a park, by any stretch of the imagination; as for the word freedom, it has here a propitiatory (perhaps expiatory) function, for during the military dictatorship (1967–74) this was the HQ of the dreaded military police, where dissidents were detained and tortured.

There is a pleasant café, a lecture-hall, a tiny open-air theatre. The torture-chambers have been turned into a museum; posing again that difficult moral problem: what does one do with places like this? Cover them up, preserve them, embellish them? Remember or forget? Remembrance may breed hatred, oblivion begets apathy. Here the effort seems to have been to preserve and transform at the same time; to commemorate the horror while creating around it an atmosphere in which the ghosts may be laid to rest. An optimistic, perhaps utopian message: life goes on, the present takes over without disowning the past. The Greeks are good at carrying the burden of the past, they've been doing it for ages; but like all burdens, it sometimes interferes with their sense of balance.

Not particularly green, but certainly an oasis, **Pláka**, the old quarter clustering at the foot of the Acropolis, has now been refurbished, restored to its former condition, or rather to a fairly good reproduction of it. The garish nightclubs

Hemingway called *Evzones* "fighting men in ballet skirts".

and discos have been closed down, motor-vehicles prohibited, for the most part, houses repainted, streets tidied up. It has become a delightful, sheltered place to meander in; you almost think yourself in a village, miles from the urban monster below. You come upon small beauties: Byzantine churches, the Tower of the Winds, the Old University, fragmented arches and walls.

Night moves: The night is sure to provide some respite from the heat, as most nocturnal activities take place in the open air: restaurants, cafés, theatres, cinemas. (Even the clattering garbage collectors work at night.) Do not mistake the open-air cinemas for drive-ins; they have rows of seats like ordinary cinemas, and the only customers on wheels are the midnight babies brought there in their pushchairs by their harassed mothers and silenced with ice-cream. As for theatres, apart from the **Herod Atticus Theatre** which is the official venue of the Athens Festival, there is a large theatre on Mount Lycabettus, used mostly for concerts of modern music, and several abandoned quarries (Attica, land of stone…) converted into theatres, that put on some very good productions and provide a starkly dramatic setting.

The night is long in Athens; Athenians fiercely resist sleep, or make up for lost night-sleep with a long afternoon siesta (caution: *never* telephone an Athenian between 2pm and 6pm). Cafés and bars stay open until the small hours; bars and pubs here are unlike those of other European capital; they are larger, they have tables, provide music (usually loud) and serve food (usually expensive) as well as drinks.

Three o'clock in the morning, and the traffic still won't give up; groups of people linger on street-corners, good-nights take forever. The main streets are never entirely deserted; perhaps this is one of the reasons why Athens is a safe city to walk in at night, except for the occasional bag-snatcher, for real violence is rare. The "unquiet generation" finally goes to bed; verandahs and balconies go dark, cats prowl, climbing

Away from the centre, even the traffic eases.

jasmine smells stronger – and all the conflicting elements in the patchwork city seem momentarily resolved in the brief summer night.

Seeing the sites: Seen from the right angle driving up the Ierá Odós (the Sacred Way) or looking up at its rocky bulk from high in Pláka, the **Acropolis** still has a presence that makes the grimy concrete of modern Athens fade into insignificance. Climb up in early morning in summer or early afternoon in winter, when the crowds are thinnest and a strip of blue sea edged with grey hills marks the horizon. On a wet or windy day, walking across its uneven limestone surface feels like being on a ship's deck in a gale.

Until the year 2000 or so, the Acropolis will look like a stonemason's workshop, much as it must have done in the 440s BC when the **Parthenon** was under construction as the crowning glory of Pericles' giant public works programme. Some of his contemporaries thought it much too extravagant: Pericles was accused of dressing his city up like a harlot. In fact, the Parthenon celebrates Athena as a virgin goddess and the city's protector. Her statue, 12 metres (39 ft) tall and made of ivory and gold plate to Pheidias' design, used to gleam in its dim interior. (It was taken to Constantinople in late antiquity and disappeared.)

Conservators have installed a folding crane inside the Parthenon to lift down hundreds of blocks of marble masonry and replace the rusting iron clamps inserted in the 1920s with non-corrosive titanium. Rust made the clamps expand, cracking the stone. Acid rain turned carved marble surfaces into soft plaster.

The restorers also succeeded in identifying and collecting about 1,600 chunks of Parthenon marble scattered over the hilltop, many blown off in a 1687 explosion of an Ottoman munitions dump inside the temple. When they are replaced, about 15 percent more building will be on view. New blocks cut from near the ancient quarries on Mount Pendéli (14 km/9 miles north of Athens), which supplied the 5th-century BC constructors, will fill the gaps.

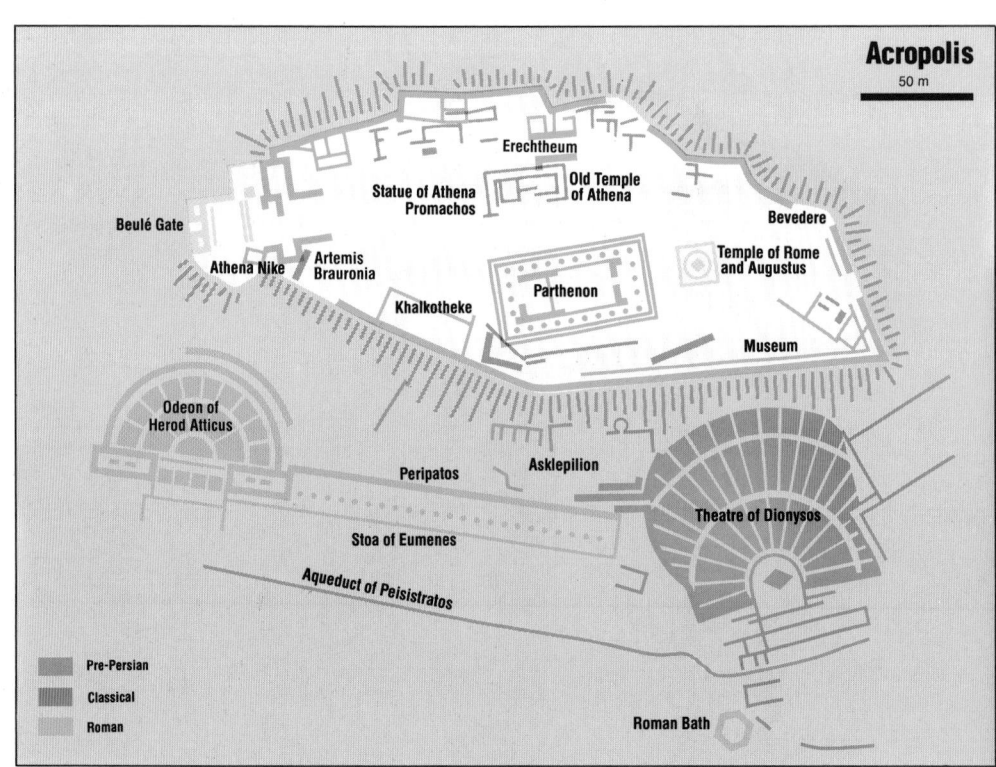

The **Erechtheion**, an elegant architecturally complex repository of ancient cults going back to the Bronze Age, is already restored. The original Caryatids who supported a porch over the tomb of King Kekrops, a mythical founder of the ancient Athenian royal family, have been replaced with copies to prevent further damage from the *néfos*, the ochre blanket of atmospheric pollution that hangs over Athens.

Completed in 395 BC, a generation later than the Parthenon, the Erechtheion also housed an early wooden statue of Athena, along with the legendary olive tree that she conjured out of the rock to defeat Poseidon the sea god in their contest for sovereignty over Attica. In Ottoman times, the building was used by the city's Turkish military commander as a billet for his harem.

The **Propylaia**, the battered official entrance to the Acropolis built by Mnesikles in the 430s BC, was cleverly designed with imposing outside columns to awe people coming up the hill. Parts of its coffered stone ceiling, once painted and gilded, are still visible as you walk through.

Roped off on what was once the citadel's southern bastion is the small, square temple of **Athena Nike**, finished in 421 BC. It supposedly stands on the spot where Theseus' father, King Aegeus, threw himself to his death on seeing a black-sailed ship approaching harbour. Theseus had promised to hoist a white sail for the return voyage if he succeeded in killing the Minotaur on Crete, but carelessly forgot.

The sculptures that Lord Elgin left behind are in the **Acropolis Museum**. Four Caryatids stare out from a nitrogen filled case, scarred but still impressively female. The coquettish *koraï* reveal a pre-classical ideal: looking closely, you can make out traces of make-up, earrings, and the patterns of their crinkled, close-fitting dresses (the spikes discouraged birds from sitting on their heads).

North of the Acropolis, the **Agora**, the ancient city's political centre, looks like a cluttered field of ruins. If archaeologists had their way, the whole of

A facelift for the Caryatids.

Pláka would have been levelled. But the reconstructed **Stoa** of Attalos, a 2nd-century BC shopping mall, is a cool place to linger among scents of ancient herbs replanted by the American excavators. The stolid **Thisseion Temple** opposite will help you appreciate that the Parthenon is truly a masterpiece.

Across from the Agora, on the far side of the Piraéus metro line, one corner of the **Painted Stoa** has been exposed in Adrianoú Street. This building gave its name to Stoicism, the stiff-upper-lip brand of philosophy that Zeno the Cypriot taught there in the 3rd century BC.

On the south side of the Acropolis lies the **Theatre of Dionysios**. The marble seating tiers that survive date from around 320 BC and later, but scholars are generally agreed that plays by Aeschylus, Sophocles, Euripides and Aristophanes were first staged here at 5th-century BC religious festivals. A state subsidy for theatre-goers meant that every Athenian citizen could take time off to attend.

Past Monastiráki, the **Kerameikos Cemetery** in the potters' district of the city was a burial place for prominent ancient Athenians. An extraordinary variety of sculptured monuments – tall stone urns, a prancing bull, winged sphinxes and melancholy scenes of farewell – overlooked the paved Sacred Way leading to the Dipylon Gate from Eleusis, where the mysteries were held.

Most of the original grave *stélai* are in the National Museum, but the replicas are still eloquent. Tortoises lumber through the undergrowth and frogs croak beside a slow-moving stream.

The museum's collection of grave goods is a magnificent guide to Greek vase-painting: from a squat geometric urn with a rusting iron sword twisted around its neck to the white *lekythoi* of classical Athens and self-consciously sophisticated Hellenistic pottery.

Hadrian's Arch: A few Roman monuments recall a time when Athens was a city to be revered, but stripped of its movable artworks. The 2nd-century Emperor Hadrian, a fervent admirer of classical Greece, erected an ornate arch **The Theatre of Dionysios.**

marking the spot where the classical city ended and the provincial Roman university town began. He also finished off the **Temple of Olympian Zeus**, a vast building abandoned when its original constructors ran out of funds around 520 BC, and dedicated it to himself.

Later in the century, Herod Atticus, a wealthy Roman administrator, built the steeply-raked theatre used now for Athens Festival performances, as a memorial to his wife.

And a 1st-century BC Syrian was responsible for the picturesque **Tower of the Winds**: a well-preserved marble octagon overlooking the scanty remains of the Roman Forum. It is decorated with eight relief figures, each depicting a different breeze, and once contained a water-clock.

Byzantine Athens is scantily represented: a dozen or so churches, many dating from the 11th century, can be tracked down in Pláka and others huddle below street level in the shadow of the city's tall, modern buildings. They are still in constant use: passers-by slip in to light a yellow beeswax candle, cross themselves and kiss an icon in near-darkness before returning to the noise and jostling outside.

One of the handsomest is **Ághioi Theódoroi**, just off Klafthmónos Square. It was built in the 11th century on the site of an earlier church in characteristic cruciform shape with a tiled dome. The masonry is picked out with slabs of brick and decorated with a terracotta frieze of animals and plants.

Ághios Nikodémos on Filellínon Street dates from the same time but was bought by the Tsar of Russia in 1845 and redecorated inside. It now serves the city's small Russian Orthodox community; the singing is renowned.

On Athens's eastern and western limits there lie two famous monasteries: Kaisarianí and Daphní.

Kaisarianí on Mount Hymettus, surrounded by high stone walls, is named after a spring which fed an aqueduct constructed on Hadrian's orders. Its waters, once sacred to Aphrodite, the goddess of love, are still credited with

Two's company on top of the Archaeological Museum.

healing powers (and encouraging child-bearing). The monastery church goes back to AD 1000 but the frescoed figures who gaze out of a blue-black ground date from the 17th century. Clustered around are stone-built cloisters, a kitchen and refectory and a former bath-house. The monks' wealth came from olive groves, beehives, vineyards and medicines made from mountain herbs.

Daphní, a curious architectural combination of Gothic and Byzantine, decorated inside with magnificent 11th-century mosaics, occupies the site of an ancient sanctuary of Apollo. A fierce-looking Christ Pantocrator, set in gold and surrounded by Old Testament prophets, stares down from the vault of the dome. The present building dates from 1080 and the Gothic porch was added in the 13th century when Daphní belonged to Cistercian monks from Burgundy and was used as the burial place of the Frankish Dukes of Athens.

Museum notes: Going back to 3000 BC, the **Goulandrís Museum** displays a unique collection of slim, stylised Cycladic idols in white marble, beautifully mounted and lit. They were scorned by 19th-century art critics as hopelessly primitive, but their smooth, simple lines attracted both Picasso and Modigliani. Mostly female and pregnant, the figures come from robbed graves in the Cyclades islands; scholars are still uncertain of their purpose.

Crammed with badly-labelled treasures from every period of antiquity, the **National Archaeological Museum** should be visited early in the morning before the guided tours turn the echoing marble halls into a deafening Babel. Not to be missed are the Mycenaean collection, the Thíra frescoes and the major bronze sculptures.

The **Mycenaean Gallery**, containing Schliemann's finds from the shaft graves at Mycenae, is stuffed with treasures from the 2nd millennium BC. Miniaturism was prized on coloured sealstones, daggers and signet rings. Gold gleams everywhere, barbaric and sometimes tawdry but a clear indicator of prehistoric Greek wealth.

Relics in the National Archaeological Museum: Mask of Agamemnon...

220

Upstairs, the Thíra Fresco Room reveals a lighter side of Bronze Age life: small rooms decorated with Aegean island scenes of dark-eyed boys boxing, blue monkeys swarming up a mountainside and statuesque, black-haired women with heavy make-up.

Few large-scale ancient bronzes have survived, but the statue of Zeus coolly poised to hurl a thunderbolt, which was netted by a fisherman off Cape Artemision in Central Greece, is one splendid exception. It dates from around 470 BC when classical naturalism in sculpture was just about to take off. By comparison, the bronze child jockey on his Hellenistic racehorse, cast two centuries later when heightened realism was the fashion, has a strained, almost frightened expression.

The bronzes in the **Piraeus Archaeological Museum** are more workmanlike but still fascinating. Both the graceful, rivetting archaic Apollo, one of the earliest full-sized bronze statues, and the soulful, helmeted, Hellenistic Athena were found in a sewer excavation in

...and a bronze rider.

1959, and perhaps belonged to a cargo of Rome-bound loot awaiting shipment.

The **Byzantine Museum**, a mock-Florentine mansion built by an eccentric 19th-century duchess, contains a brilliant array of icons and church relics from the 13th to the 18th centuries. The **Benáki Museum** houses a wonderfully eclectic collection of treasures – including jewellery, costumes and two icons attributed to El Greco in the days when he was a young Cretan painter called Domenico Theotocópoulos.

The **Canellópoulos Museum**, a 19th-century mansion, is also a treasure trove of objects from every period of Greek art, acquired by an erudite, obsessive collector. And the **City of Athens Museum**, an accumulation of 19th-century furnishings, pictures and fittings in a house where teenage King Otto lived while waiting for his palace to be completed, evokes upper-class life in newly independent Greece.

Outside Athens, a 69-km (43-mile) drive to **Cape Sounion** on the windy tip of the Attica peninsula takes you to Poseidon's temple. Completed in 440 BC, its slender, salt-white columns are still a landmark for ships headed toward Piraeus. Lord Byron carved his name on a column on the north side. The marble came from nearby Agríleza, where the Athenians also mined silver and lead. Following an impressive classical fortification wall down the hillside, you come to the remains of ancient shipsheds in the bay below: the Athenians once organised warship races off Sounion and it later became a pirates' lair.

More out of the way is the **Sanctuary of Artemis** at **Brauron** (now called Vravróna) on the east coast of Attica, 35 km (22 miles) from Athens through the wine-growing Mesógheio district. A 5th-century BC colonnade visited by owls at twilight is flanked by a 16th-century Byzantine chapel, built on the site of an altar to Artemis. In classical times, well-born girls aged from 5 to 10 ("little bears") performed a ritual dance at a festival honouring Artemis as goddess of childbirth. Their statues are in the site museum: plump with solemn expressions and dressed like miniature adults.

ISLANDS OF THE SARONIC GULF

Athens and the islands of the Saronic Gulf are often lumped together in guide books. There is sense to this since many Athenians frequent these islands on weekends, while during the summer the islands become veritable extensions of the more fashionable Athenian neighbourhoods. Yet this view of the Argosaronic islands doesn't take into account their separate identities. They are islands, not suburbs. Each has its own character and deserves more than a page of our attention.

Aegina: This is a privileged island, rich in natural beauty and prized for its healthy climate and clear air. About an hour and a half by ferry from Piraeus – or half an hour by the "flying dolphin" hydrofoil – Aegina has had little trouble attracting visitors. Although the island bears some of the scars inflicted by an expanding tourist industry it is large enough to allow refuge from the crowds. Long a favourite Athenian retreat, it remains more popular among weekend smog evaders than among foreign tourists or Greeks from elsewhere.

Shaped on the map like an upside-down triangle, Aegina's southern point is marked by the magnificent cone of **Mount Óros**, the highest peak in the Argosaronic islands, visible on a smog-free day from Athens's Acropolis. The centre and eastern side of the island is mountainous; a gently-sloping fertile plain runs down to the western extremity where Aegina Town overlays in part the ancient capital of the island.

When the world was small and a city or an island could aspire to be a Great Power, Aegina, strategically situated between the Peloponnese and Attica, looking out upon the Aegean and all the Mediterranean beyond, became a wealthy trading state with shipyards, fleets and a sophisticated banking system. In the 7th century BC Aegina produced the first Greek coins – the silver "tortoises" – and with these gained great financial leverage throughout the ancient world.

With the onset of the Persian Wars in 491 BC the people of Aegina first sided with the Persian army, to the chagrin of the besieged Athenians, but in 480 BC at Salamis, the greatest of all Greek sea battles, they returned to the Greek side and won the praise of the Delphic Oracle as the fleetest navy on the seas.

But Aegina (the "eyesore of Piraeus", as Pericles called it) posed a threat to Athens' expanding maritime empire. In 457 BC and again during the Peloponnesian War the Athenians defeated Aegina at sea, on the second occasion expelling the entire population and replacing it with Athenian colonialists.

After the defeat of Athens in the Peloponnesian War, the Spartan Lysander, in recognition of the help the people of Aegina had given Sparta during the war, returned them to their home. After this Aegina played a less conspicuous role until the 1820s when it became the temporary capital of liberated Greece from 1826 to 1828.

The Aegina Town one confronts today is typical of small Greek cities a

Preceding pages: the harbour at Hydra. **Left**, morning coffee.

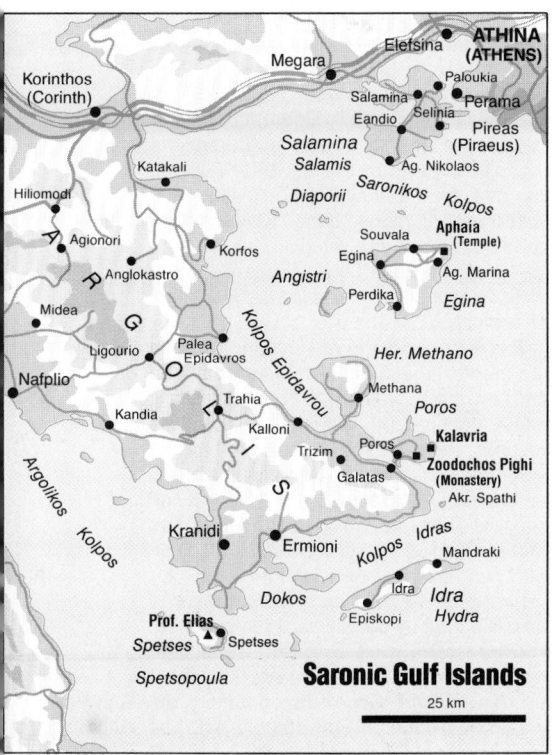

Saronic Gulf Islands

25 km

MEMORIES OF AEGINA

Katerína Angheláki-Rooke, the well-loved
poet, gives her impressions of Aegina

Aegina is a place of return. It is a place that
opens, receives, consoles and heals. Other
islands are points of departure; you leave
them behind and set off on expeditions,
exploits, conquests. Dry, arid islands like
Hydra, Ios, Mykonos and Santoríni inspire
action. Aegina, on the other hand, is a
feminine island; as the boat turns the
corner, the horse-shoe shaped harbour –
the church of the little Virgin on the one side
and the old yellow house on the other –
provides the perfect enclosure for an ach-
ing heart. When I was small I thought the
yellow house had become yellow from the
passing of time, like an old photograph.

The harbour is alive. It is as alive in the
winter as it is in the summer. Tourists
barely alter this island. They make a brief
appearance and then disappear mysteri-
ously, like the summer sirocco, the hot,
humid wind that sweeps in from the south,
the Sahara. In September the air smells of
resin from the pistachio nuts that are

harvested there and the freshly washed
barrels ready for new wine. The light is soft
and caressing, having lost the harshness
of August. Across the water the mountain
of Methana turns a dusted blue. I sit at
Skotádis's *oúzo* shop watching the *caïques*
unload fruit and vegetables, while Babouas,
the Down's Syndrome sufferer who owes
his name to the only sound he can produce,
smiles at the familiar faces. He is grateful
for this place which forgives human and
divine mistakes and accepts us all.

Inland, the landscape is reminiscent of
Attica. Perhaps the island retains something from its motherland, across the water,
in the same way we often keep the facial
characteristics of our parents. The curves
of the hills and the tops of the olive trees
follow and at times interrupt the sky. The
clouds add a touch of frivolous imagination
in the midst of so much blue seriousness.
These are the elements Aegina shares with
Attica. But Aegina is distinctly an island;
your nostrils quiver in the salty air which
reaches you wherever you go. There's a
sense of being cut-off, set apart; there's an
atmosphere of independence, of autonomy,
of solitude. A dual personality, then, is the
key to this island's charm. Aegina is both
the sweetness and the severeness of life,
all in one slight stretch of land.

Sometimes my godfather, the novelist
Kazantzákis, would leave his rock promontory and go to town to buy sweets from
Prokópis, the Greek from Asia Minor, a
master when it came to Oriental pastry, or
to chat with the village idiot – a different one
then, at the end of the 1930s. "Tell me,
Thomas, have you ever gone to school?"
"Couple of times, boss, I wasn't very
good at it, but then I got sick, I became an
idiot and now I don't have to worry about a
thing!" Kazantzákis marvelled at the wisdom
of Thomas.

The deaf and mute man cleaning fish in
the market, the baker with his eternal grin
and his apron covered with flour, the fishing
boats nonchalantly bobbing in the little
harbour, the dogs relentlessly sniffing the
butcher's doorstep, the whole island stops
as the sun sets across the sea. Ah! the
sunsets of Aegina, the gold and red glories
that envelop us for a short instant, filling us
with nostalgia and anticipation.

I leave Skotádis's and the harbour and
take the road up the hill back to my house.
The trees and walls fence off my private
history. What is here contains me and I
contain it. Its presence is my continuity, the
impersonal continuity of someone who has
lived and loved a place: Aegina. ■ **Katerína
Angheláki-
Rooke.**

century ago. A number of classical mansions stand at the edge of town. Several buildings constructed after the liberation of Greece in 1828, from the time of the island's first governor, Ioánnis Kapodístrias (1776–1831), are also preserved. The **Archaeological Museum** in the centre of the town displays a number of interesting artefacts from the island's history. The modern harbour, oval in shape and crowded with picturesque *caïques*, was the city's commercial wharf in antiquity; small additions were built in the Roman period and under Venetian rule.

To the left of the port as you enter is the hill of **Kolóna** with the remains of the **Temple of Apollo**. All that is left from this famous temple is a single *kolóna* (column). The temple (Doric, six columns by 12, built in 520–500 BC) was superseded by a late Roman fortress, fragments of which survive on the seaward side. Although from the sea the position of the temple looks unimpressive, the view from the hill in late summer is breathtaking. Apart from the usual

day trips to small resort towns (**Souvála, Pérdika, Aghía Marína**) or to the two neighbouring islands of **Angístri** and **Moní** you should, even if Greek ruins or Byzantine churches are not your cup of tea, visit the **Temple of Aphaía** and the **Monastery of Ághios Nektários**.

The Temple of Aphaía stands at the top of a hill above the cape of Aghía Marína in a pine grove commanding a splendid view of the Aegean. Built in celebration of the victory at Salamis, it has been called "the most perfectly developed of the late Archaic temples in European Hellas". It is the only surviving Hellenic temple with a second row of small superimposed columns in the interior of the sanctuary.

Ághios Nektários (Anastásios Kefalás: 1846–1920), Metropolitan of Pentapolis, is the most recent Orthodox saint, having been canonised in 1961. The monastery named after him stands on a hill across from another which is covered with ruins of more than 20 churches and monasteries, survivors from the 13th century and later, some

The Temple of Aphaía.

with remarkable stone iconostases (especially the **Monastery of Panaghía Chrysoleóntissa**). These churches were once part of the island's old *chora* (*Palaíeóchora*) where the islanders sought refuge from sudden attacks by pirates (the town was destroyed once by the famous pirate Barbarossa and once by the Venetians). After 1800 the people began to move down to the port, leaving their churches behind.

A final word of advice: avoid the town of Aghía Marína (a dreadful package holiday centre), though its beach is worth a visit. The beaches on the little islands of Angístri and Moní, admittedly not the most beautiful in the Aegean, are still a good bet. Aegina Town with its loud fishmarket, its picturesque port where *caïques* unload their fruits and vegetables, its lively *ouzeriés* and *tavérnes* and its traditional pistachio sellers make up for a possibly uneventful swimming trip.

Hydra (Ydra): The island of **Hydra**, once Ydrea, "the well watered", is now ironically a long, barren and waterless rock. The heart of the island is its harbour-town. All around the picturesque bay white houses climb the slope accented by massive gray *archontiká*, the houses of the gentry. Along the quay are the colourful shops of the marketplace, with the marble tower of the Holy Virgin Cloister in the centre. The harbour, girded by a little thread of a breakwater, forms a soft and perfect crescent, its two ends flanked by 19th-century cannons.

Hydra has aspired to be a fashionable artists' colony and retreat for intellectuals, and has also attracted a less orthodox fringe of idlers. The combination of Hydra's raw natural beauty and the wonderful harbour town continues to be quite irresistible.

The foundation of Hydra's greatness was laid in the 18th century, when reviving commerce provided the Hydriots with an outlet for their abilities. Hydra, once no more than a small port in the Venetian empire, gradually became the dominant maritime power in the Aegean. During the War of Independence the Hydriots threw themselves heart and **Hydra's fashionable port.**

soul into the fight with merchant families, notably that of Koundouriótis, converting at their own expense their trading vessels into war ships.

Some of these well-preserved and imposing houses are open to visitors. The Athens School of Fine Arts has established a branch in the huge **Mansion of Admiral Tombazis**, which hosts artists of international acclaim. A Merchant Navy Training School occupies the **House of Tsamádos** and across the way are the Hydriot Archives.

The higher reaches of the town and the hills beyond remain surprisingly untouched, charming and full of Greek colour. Narrow alleys and steep staircases lead from one quarter to the next. The uniformity of white walls is broken again and again by a century-old doorway, a bright blue window frame, a flight of striking scarlet steps, or a dark green garden fence.

With plenty of *tavérnes*, cafés, bars and nightlife, Hydra should also appeal to the tourist who may have no interest in the island's glorious past. For many, Hydra is just a point of departure, a base from which to organise a series of expeditions to the mainland and other islands. For others Hydra, this immaculate little town bathed in white and blue colours, is the Greece one is so eager to rediscover time and time again.

Póros: The island of **Póros** is separated from the Peloponnese by a small passage of water – the word *póros* in Greek means "strait". The island can be reached not only by ship and "flying dolphin" but also by driving along the Peloponnesian coast via the **Isthmus of Corinth** and **Epídauros** to the little town of **Galatás** which lies opposite the main harbour. As one sails in through the northern entrance, the harbour opens up. It is almost landlocked and one of the finest anchorages in the Aegean. Your first glimpse of the island will be of the white houses and bright orange rooftops of Póros Town.

Built on a hill with its highest point at the centre, the town resembles an inverted amphitheatre and the effect is disarming. On the mainland opposite,

The 19th-century bridge at Vlichos, Hydra.

the village of Galatás with its white steps and dark alleys and its *Lemonódassos* where lemon groves grow amidst water-mills, makes a wonderful sight. It is easy to understand Henry Miller's enthusiasm (in his book *The Colossus of Marousi*) as he sailed between Póros and Galatás. "I don't know which affected me more deeply – the story of the lemon groves just opposite us or the sight of Póros itself when suddenly I realised that we were sailing through the streets. If there is one dream which I like above all others it is that of sailing on land. Coming into Póros gives the illusion of the deep dream. Suddenly the land converges on all sides and the boat is squeezed into a narrow strait... To sail slowly through the streets of Póros is to recapture the joy of passing through the neck of the womb. It is a joy too deep almost to be remembered."

It is not an illusion that one is sailing between houses; friendly faces actually hang out of the windows just above your head while the scents of *retsína*, *oúzo*, lemon and grilled fish fill your nostrils.

Although a number of hotels have been built on Póros and prominent Athenians have owned vacation houses here for decades, the island has never been fashionable like Hydra or Spétses, but during summer it gets every bit as crowded as Aegina.

On the southwestern coast are the remains of the old military harbour that the Russians laid out. In 1830 the first naval arsenal was established here which survived until 1877 when it was closed in favour of Salamis. The building now houses the **Boys' Naval Training School**. This area contains several fine family mansions with well-tended gardens and can be a refreshing place to stroll on a hot summer afternoon.

The main sight on Póros is the **Monastery of Panaghía Zoodóchou Pighí** (Virgin of the Life-Giving Spring) beautifully situated on a wooded hillside (20 minutes from town by bus). Only a few monks still live there today. Noteworthy is a wooden, gold painted iconostasis dating from the 18th century and adorned with late Byzantine illustrations from

The Flying Dolphin hydrofoil calls at Poros.

the New Testament. It was presumably brought to Póros from Asia Minor.

In front of the monastery a new road encircling the heights to the east climbs through the pinewoods to the ruins of the **Sanctuary of Poseidon** in a saddle between the highest hills of the island. The temple was excavated at the turn of the century and little remains but its setting is rewarding.

The sanctuary was the headquarters of the Kalávrian League, an association of several towns that included Athens as well. The sanctuary served as an asylum for shipwrecked sailors, pirates and political refugees. It was here that the famous Athenian orator Demosthenes, in flight from Antipater's emissaries, took refuge, trusting that not even the Macedonians would dare to profane so ancient and famous a shrine. Demosthenes agreed to return to Athens but took poison instead, dying just outside the sanctuary.

The visitor to Póros must not leave without making a side trip to **Troizen** on the Peloponnese. To reach it you can take a boat from the harbour of Póros to the town of Galatás and then a bus to the ancient town. En route between Aegina and Póros, the boat stops at the town of **Méthana**. There is no need to stop in this tourist village. Póros is by far a more exciting choice.

Spétses (Spétsai): At the southern end of the Saronic Gulf is **Spétses**, the ancient *Pitiusa*, or "pine tree" island. Although only 22 sq. km (8 sq. miles) in area, it offers the most picturesque beaches and the most sophisticated nightlife of the nearby islands. On any given weekend, one is likely to find as many British tourists on Spétses as Athenians on Aegina. As a British writer observed: "Spétses lacks only titular recognition as a possession of the United Kingdom."

Although Spétses Town is full of noisy bars and cheap fast-food places, the *Palió Limáni* (**Old Harbour**) still radiates a gentle grace, its own particular magic that is apparent to even the short-term visitor.

The 18th-century *archontiká* one sees in this part of the town are now the

Town Hall, Spétses.

property of wealthy Athenian families who return to the island every summer.

Like Hydra, Spétses was one of the main centres of activity during the Greek War of Independence, using its fleet of over 50 ships for the Greek cause. The island is distinguished for being the first in the archipelago to revolt against Ottoman rule in 1821 and the fortified harbour, still bristling with cannons, now forms the town's *Platia*, the **Dápia**.

Bouboulína, Greece's national heroine, was a Spétsiot woman who took command of her husband's ship after he was killed by pirates off the North African coast. The fleet, under her command, blockaded Nauplion until the Turks surrendered in December 1822.

In September an Ottoman fleet attempted to lift the blockade by threatening Spétses. The fighting was indecisive but the Ottoman fleet eventually withdrew. They were encouraged to leave by fezzes being placed on the asphodel plants that grew in masses along the shore.

From a distance the fezzes swaying in the wind looked like warlike hordes. This victory of 8 September 1822 is celebrated annually by a *paniyíri* in the name of *Panaghía Armáta* (her little chapel stands on a hill close to the Old Harbour). A mock battle is staged, a Turkish flagship made out of cardboard is burned in the middle of the harbour and there follows a display of fireworks.

Although after the War of Independence Spétses's fleet declined with the emergence of Piraeus as the main seaport, the traditions of shipbuilding continue unabated. The small naval **museum** in the imposing 18th-century *archóntikó* of Hadziyiánnis Mexis, Spétses's first governor, contains coins, costumes, ship models, weapons and other memorabilia from the island's past including the bones of the famous Bouboulína. The house in which she lived is behind the Dápia.

Outside the town to the northwest is the **Anargýrios and Korgialénios College**, a Greek impression of an English public school. John Fowles taught here and memorialised both the institution and the island in his 1966 novel *The Magus*.

The town's beaches of **Ághios Mámas** and **Aghios Nikólaos** are unattractive in contrast to the beautiful beaches of **Zogeria**, **Ághía Paraskeví**, **Ághioi** and **Anaryhyro** which are appropriately situated on the pine-wooded part of the island. In addition one can go to the various beaches opposite Spétses on the Peloponnesian coast. The prettiest of these is probably **Chinítsa** and for those who enjoy water-skiing, **Pórto Héli** with its protected bay provides the perfect setting.

Spétses can also be used as a useful communication link. From here one can get to Nauplion, Argos, Epídauros, Mycenae or to the southern town of Monemvasia. During the summer months when the Ancient Drama Festival is held in Epídauros a trip to one of the performances is a pleasure.

An evening walk in the Old Harbour or in the woods of Ligonéri, a ride in a horsedrawn carriage to Aghía Marína, a fish cooked *à la Spetsióta* are a few of the pleasures that await the visitor.

Island life is mirrored on Spétses.

ISLAND HOPPING

Island-hopping may be the choice of the tourist, but ferryboats are for the convenience of the Greeks. This fact – conflicting, frustrating and under-publicised – has been the undoing of many a holiday.

The pleasures of travelling from one island to another using the country's series of inter-linking routes are numerous. There is the never ceasing view – a blue, bas relief pattern of low, mysterious mountains. A chance to mingle with the Greeks themselves who pile on board with food, children, and as often as not, a *bouzoúki* or two. Plus, a unique opportunity to visit other islands not on the itinerary – 15 minutes in a port closely observed from the top deck can reveal much about a place and its people. A bustle of activity takes place within view – reunions, farewells, and the redistribution of a virtual warehouse of goods, from chickens to blankets to food.

Without advanced research, however, it's all too easy to fall prey to the worst aspects of island-hopping in the form of missed connections, being stranded, or – a particularly Greek pastime – sailing straight past a chosen island, requiring a two-day journey to reach it again. In order to travel wisely, it helps to be in possession of a few basic facts.

First, ferry journeys can be long. The trip from Piraeus to Crete can take anywhere up to 22 hours, an unenthusiastic prospect for anyone on a two-week holiday. Ferry journeys can be frustrating. Should a trip to one of the smaller islands terminate in the middle of the night, no one will bother to wake you even if you've paid for sleeping accommodation. Seasoned travellers always pack an alarm clock, just in case. This haste to disembark in darkness has resulted in more than one traveller finding himself on the wrong island altogether.

There are ways to circumvent these problems, however. One is to travel in the high season, when Greek transport is relatively organised and hydrofoils, caiques and the little known inter-island sub-routes are fully operative. A trip from Paros to Sífnos in the Cyclades, for example, will take about four hours in August (when ferries sail direct); and up to 20 hours in late September, when the only way to travel the minor distance between them is to return to Piraeus and head out again.

Fortunately, there are some established ferry routes which provide satisfying island-hopping several months of the year. The best known are the central Cyclades route (Santoríni, Ios, Náxos, Paros and Mykonos) and the Saronic Gulf route (Aegina, Hydra and Poros). Another is by cruising the major Dodecanese; travelling between Rhodes, Kos, Kalimnos, Leros and Patmos should pose few problems.

Less well known are the western Cyclades (Kythnos, Serifos, Sífnos and Mílos) and three of the four Sporades islands (Skiáthos, Skópelos and Alónissos). These chains depend on domestic – rather than tourist – travel and operate all year, albeit at a reduced level. Both Rhodes and Kos in the Dodecanese act as hubs for a number of satellite islands. The connections are good, at least in the summer.

Bookshops in Athens sell a monthly guide called the *Greek Travel Pages* which gives details of most sailings. A map is useful when studying it, for some islands are listed under the name of the island; some under the name of the port.

There is one final, vital rule: always leave plenty of time at the end of your holiday to travel back to Piraeus. Greek ferries may be cheap and cheerful, but expensive international flights are another matter.

One for the alarm clock, perhaps. ∎

234

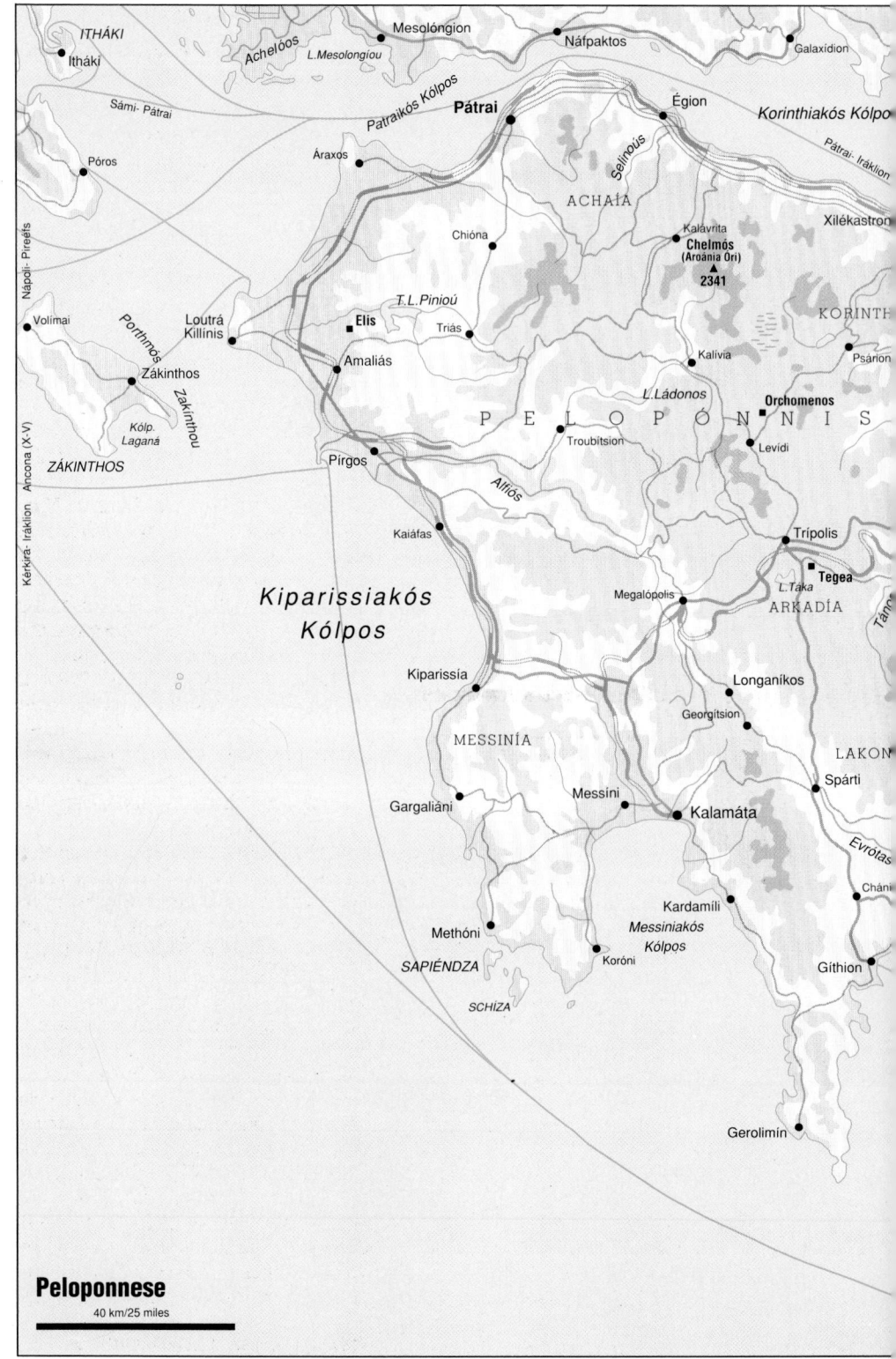

Peloponnese

40 km/25 miles

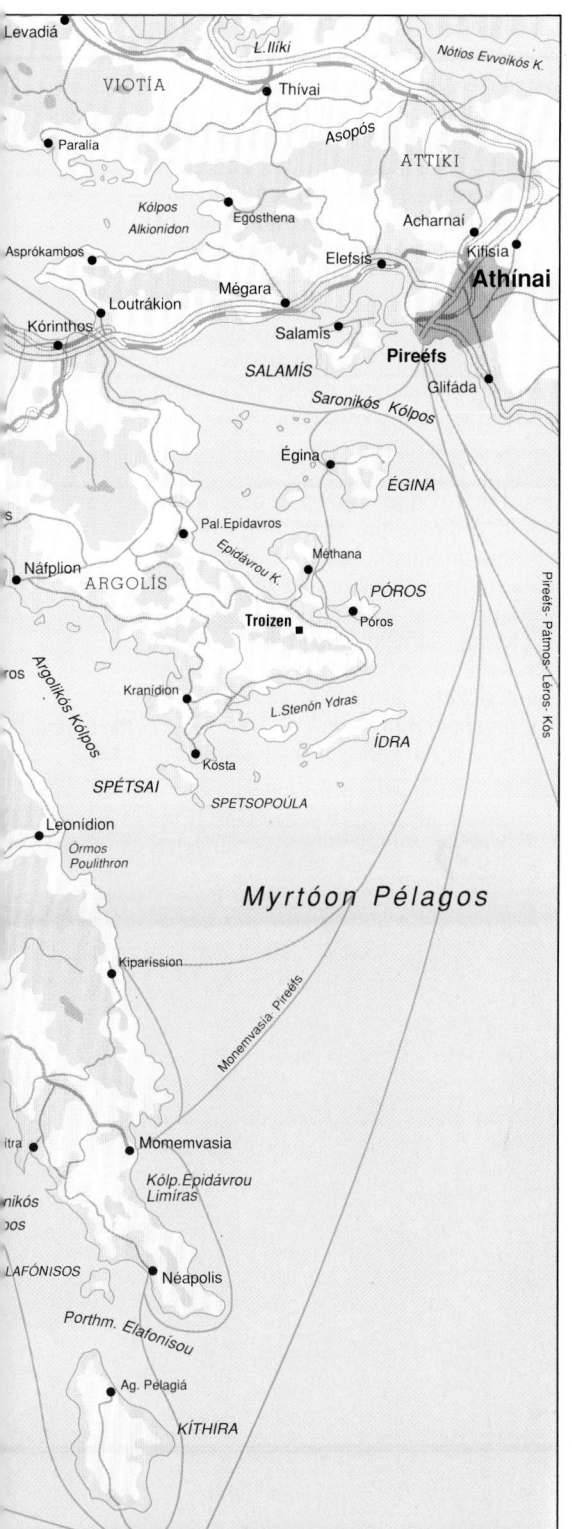

THE PELOPONNESE

The **Peloponnese** (Pelopónnissos) takes its name from the fabled hero *Pelops*, and the word for island, *nísos*. But it is scarcely thought of as an island. Should you blink, however, in passing over from Attica (Attikí) you might miss the slight isthmus that joins the Peloponnese to the mainland. The *Moréa* was the medieval name for the Peloponnese, now only rarely used. The name may come from the abundance of mulberry trees (*moriés*) or from the shape of the Peloponnese resembling a mulberry leaf.

The Peloponnese is divided into seven *nómoi* or provinces: Corinthia in the northeast; Argolis, the eastern peninsula, that juts into the Aegean; Elis, pushing west towards the Ionian Sea; Achaïa, to the north; Arcadia, in the central mountains with a brief shoreline along the Argolis Gulf; Lakonía, the two southern prongs; and Messenía, the last promontory to the southwest.

The Peloponnese stands a world apart. Not only is its landscape unsurpassed in archaeological importance and variety, its history mirrors every major shift, from the Mycenaean period to modern times. Even Athens has not been prone to so much upheaval.

Ancient ruins: The ruins of ancient **Corinth (Kórinthos)** convey a melancholy reality. The city was destroyed several times by earthquakes and what can be seen here, particularly in the walkways with marketplace stalls, is of Hellenistic-Roman vintage and comparatively late. The city was completely razed to the ground by the Romans in 146 BC, and well into the next century, by order of Julius Caesar, Corinth was "founded" once again by the Roman Empire. It moved quickly into prosperity and influence. When St Paul delivered his Epistle to the Corinthians, the Apostle had God say to the city, "I will destroy the wisdom of the wise, make void the intelligence of the intellectuals…" Apparently Paul thought that this

Preceding pages: a field of poppies.

self-confident and affluent centre of paganism needed instruction.

The ancient site is to the southwest of the modern town and built on rising plateaus with its acropolis at the top of the mount, the Acrocorinth (Akrocórinthos). What stands of the Greek city today is the great temple of Apollo, or rather seven of its columns.

The rest is the Roman city with many homely touches along the walkways. But what makes the whole trip here worthwhile is the climb up to Acrocorinth, the most complete 17th-century Venetian fortress. The view is spectacular: to the east, the expanse of the Saronic Gulf; ahead, near the shore, lies Isthmia where the second most important games of the Hellenic world were held every other spring. Next in the line of vision lies the old part on the Saronic side where St Paul had his head shaved; and nearby, the healing springs, called the Baths of Helen.

Nowadays a road runs along the shore which will get you to Epídauros in half the time you need by the inland route.

The modern road is well engineered with spectacular views: you travel high up above the sea, looking down at the white-sand beaches; on a clear day you can see the islands of Salamís and Aegina. Looking in the other direction, to the west of the Acrocorinth, the Corinthian Gulf, with the mountains of the Peloponnese, is on your left.

The road along the shore to the west is a modern highway that leads to Pátras the port city. The shore towns along the whole coast to Pátras are very lovely, as are the beaches; the landscape is tame and refined with a spattering of soft pine trees, particularly around Kiáto and Aígion. It is only with a glance southward that you are brought up against a harsh contrast, the sheer cliffs of the Cyllene mountain range – wild nature close to the tame shore – a motif of the Peloponnesian terrain.

Leaving Corinth: The road south to Argos is treacherous. It crisscrosses the same rickety railroad line several times for no apparent reason.

The **Argive valley** is most spectacu-

The Corinth Canal.

lar when approached from the other end, the descent along the coiling road of the Arcadian mountains. In early morning, as you take the last turn for Mount Parthenion, you find yourself before a breathtaking panorama. The salt air from the sea accents the smell of wild flowers that grow on the mountain; the deep shadows of the gorge to your left hang down into darkness; and the peak opposite the gorge is covered in early sun. The descent to the valley takes a short while. When you reach the straight road amid the citrus groves which are in bloom, you will be greeted by the sweet perfumes of lemon and orange blossoms.

There is an amusing tale in Theophrastus about the people of **Tiryns**, a place in mid-valley between Argos and Nauplion, where Herakles was born. It seems the people here were incapable of any serious accomplishment because they laughed too much. So they sent an embassy to the oracle at Delphi to find out how they might cure themselves of this weakness. Delphi's answer: they must sacrifice a bull to Poseidon; throw the offering into the sea without laughing once; and the god would cure their affliction. So they prepared for the sacrifice, taking care to keep the children far away, for their laughter could not be easily controlled. After the sacred ceremony, as they were taking the offering to the sea, a little boy who had escaped from the others and followed the procession, asked some ingenuously funny question and brought the entire population to their knees with fits of laughter.

Argos valley: Before you know it, you find yourself in modern **Argos**. It is a bustling capital, the busy market centre for the entire Argolis province. The people here live well by comparison with the rest of the Peloponnese. Their valley produces fruit and olives and their only complaint is they cannot find enough labourers at harvest-time: it isn't rare these days to see German or English students working in these groves. But modern Argos, apart from its exquisite climate, isn't much fun.

The true elegance of this valley is

reserved for **Nauplion (Náfplio)**, perhaps the most classy small city in the whole of Greece. It has a tradition and culture all its own. After the Greek Revolution, between 1829 and 1834, Nauplion served as the first capital of Greece. Some of its neoclassical houses, its carefully planned streets along the sea, and the large official looking buildings date from this period. This small city seems to have retained its dignity: anybody who is anybody in the Peloponnese seems to live in Nauplion.

The road to Neméa breaks off from the main pass at Dervenákia. Here, at the southern end of the Neméan fields the Ottoman army marching to relieve the siege at Nauplion was defeated by the Greeks in the summer of 1822.

The Neméan games: The Neméan plain beyond this road was the roaming ground of the famous lion that Herakles defeated. Here, too, is the place where the Neméan games were held, which rivalled those of Isthmia and Olympia. Part of the stadium can still be seen.

The whole of the Argive plain: Nauplion, Tíryns, Mycenae (Mikínes), Neméa and the full distance of the fertile valley, can be seen from the castle on the top of Lárissa hill that rises at the edge of Argos. The townscape below, undistinguished cement and brick buildings, dissolves into the primary shades of fields and groves in every direction.

On the other side of the gulf lies Nauplion, while a little more than half way there the solitary Cyclopean walls of Tiryns rise up. To your left, and a bit northeast, stand the majestic ruins of Mycenae, and a little further, straight north, beyond Dervenákia pass, lies Neméa. To the northwest and behind, you can always see Arcadian Cyllene and Artemision and their snow peaks, even in summer. You can even make out the white-stoned river-bed of Inachos, mostly streamless since ancient times, and on a clear day, far down along the cape, a very deep blue sea.

The Tiryns ruins: The ruins of **Tiryns**, though not a fine spectacle, have their own majesty. The ruins here are older than those at Mycenae, and, as legend **Climbing among Nauplion's ruins.**

240

would have it, this is where Perseus came to settle with Andromeda (though some say he was born here), bringing from Lydia the Cyclops who built the great walls. The blocks of the wall are 100 cubic feet each, making Pausanias marvel: "Why should we bother to visit the pyramids when we have something like them right here?" The tower and the gates, with a triangular gap, suggest a sophisticated knowledge of building.

Mycenae's buildings and walls are somewhat less impressive than those of Tíryns. The Cyclopean structures do not look as powerful or sturdy, but these are more tragic stones. Here Clytemnestra received her husband Agamemnon entering the Lion Gate, on his return from Troy. She decked the gate with purple carpets and insisted he step on them along with his slave-paramour Cassandra. Then, when he relaxed in a bath, she hacked him to death with an axe. Agamemnon's is one of the beehive tombs below the citadel. Here, in a shaft tomb, Schliemann excavated the famous golden death-masks and the

other exquisite gold ornaments displayed in the Mycenaean room of the National Museum at Athens.

Away from Mycenae we pass again through Tíryns and Nauplion to reach the sanctuary of Epidauros to the east. Nauplion is more impressive when compared with Mycenae. **Palamídi**, its citadel, has 1,000 steps to the top. Legend has it that the city was founded by Nauplius's son, Palamidis. On the promontory, there is a fortress which has a varied history. The dungeon was used during the late 1940s civil war as a prison for the whole Peloponnese.

The lower portion was built during the first years of the 18th century by the Venetians. The Greeks won their most decisive battle against the Ottoman armies on this hill in the 1820s. And while Nauplion was the first capital of a newly independent Greece, in 1829 trouble was not far away. Here, outside St Spyridon church, the first president, Kapodístrias, was assassinated. You can still see the bullet that struck a pillar.

Only a short distance from the first

Nauplion seen from the Palamídi fortress.

step of Palamídi lies the port, and in the centre of it the islet of Boúrtzí. This islet has a marvellous castle which covers nearly the whole area.

The theatre at Epídauros: Epídauros lies just beyond the short Arachneon mountain range to the east along the Argolid peninsula. Epídauros comprises three towns: Ligourió, which is about 2 km (1 mile) from the ancient sanctuary serves to receive the traveller; Old Epídauros, which is the port town as it was of old, and New Epídauros, above on the hillside, hidden behind the bend. Old Epídauros is now a resort town of exceptional charm; you are more likely to see a spattering of yachts coming and going than the arrival of pilgrims to the healing grounds.

New Epídauros, on the other hand, is virtually a mountain village; and in the old days most of its inhabitants were shepherds. Now they cultivate the small valley below which leads to a tiny gulf. The beach at the end of the fertile grove has grey-black sand and is clean, warm and secluded. Ligourió is an over-crowded village. Too small to accommodate the hordes who come during the theatre festivals, it has become a place where every home-owner rents rooms in summer. So during the tourist season this village changes character altogether. During normal times the inhabitants cultivate a rich olive grove that extends all the way to the sanctuary.

The sanctuary, less than a mile off the main road, is surrounded by pine trees. The grounds have that sacred aura about them, a kind of mystical quality. This place exudes good health: the air, the trees, the aesthetics of it transmit a healing quality. When you reach the theatre, the crowning glory of Epídauros even to this day, you feel sure this is a place of healing and celebration.

The annual festival, begun in the early 1950s, has hosted some of the great performers of our time, from Maria Callas to Katína Paxinoú. In any given summer you can see up to six or more tragedies, mostly by the National Theatre of Greece, though in more recent years other groups have been permitted

The renowned theatre of Epídauros.

to perform as well. The performances are geared for the tourist, but it wasn't long ago when the shepherds and local villagers came here on star-studded nights, and shed a tear or two over the plight of Agamemnon's daughter or Medea's children. This still happens on dress-rehearsal nights when the local townsfolk are admitted free of charge.

The theatre at Epídauros faces west and is the finest extant example of its kind. Its design and acoustical engineering have never been matched. In our own day, it stands as the sacred monument – a kind of patron saint – of every theatre artist the world over. It is every artist's dream to play at Epídauros. Britain's National Theatre has played there, and each year many companies ask to stage a performance.

The main road before the turn for the sanctuary continues in a southeast direction to end up at Galatás on the cape. The view of the *Lemonódassos* (forest of lemon trees) along the cape with the island of Póros in the distance, is an exquisite and refreshing experience. And

some of the finest beaches are around Hermióni and Pórto Héli.

Trípolis: Back now to the road towards Arcadia and the central Peloponnese. We climb the face of Parthenion and leave behind the grand view of Argolis, ending up at **Trípolis** (the name denoting the three ancient cities, Tegea, Mantinia and Palladian). **Tegea** was the site of a remarkable temple of Athena whose pediment Pausanias claimed contained some of the greatest art of his time. Tegea is well-known for its annual fair. Here is the largest animal trading ground in all of Greece. Gypsies come to buy and sell horses, mules and donkeys. **Mantinia** is now simply an elongated valley between two mountain ranges. Its ancient ruins contain a sanctuary. Of the three, **Palladian** is the only one with no ancient history. It was named by a fickle Roman emperor, who stopped there in the Antonine period. Trípolis was the capital of the Moréa during the Ottoman occupation. It still retains some of its gruff, trading character.

The people of Trípolis are intensely

The aberrant apostrophe reaches Greece.

political; you can observe them in the cafés, in the various squares, engaged in heated discussion. Aristotle's "man the political animal" (*zoön politikón*) is everywhere evident. Trípolis is too provincial to attract the traveller. But it has other charms: the best yoghurt anywhere can be found at *Kanatas*, on the side-street behind the Aghios Vassílis Church in the centre of town. The town is sprawling with the army at one end and the air force at the other. It serves as the "big city" of the central Peloponnese, where many young labourers from surrounding villages come for work. In contrast to the daytime rowdiness of the marketplace, the city's central square has a grace at night, when young couples take their stroll.

All roads that lead away from Trípolis take us into picturesque and important parts of the Peloponnese. Our first direction will be towards the Olympia mountains. A short side-trip northwest of Trípolis warrants attention. Here the traveller encounters a series of upland valleys which are narrowly linked from Tegea and Mantinia to Orchómenos, less than 25 km (15 miles) away. The irrigation of these valleys, lying as they do between mountain ranges, has always been a mystery. Pausanias, in AD 160, speaks of considerable controversy (and strife) when the Mantinians insisted on diverting the water from the Orchómenos valley to irrigate their own crops. By Pausanias's account this water came from subterranean springs, which is borne out by today's scientific accounts as well. It seems the entire Maínalon range converges its subterranean streams in this valley, forming in the winter season a virtual lake, just to the northwest of ancient Orchómenos.

Small villages: The road towards this valley away from Trípolis is an excellent one for travel. The mountain to the left is **Maínalon**. At its highest peak, Ághios Ilías, is a fine ski resort, limited in distances but very charming with a spectacular view of the valleys below. Along the main highway, at the foot of the mountain and just above ancient Orchómenos, is **Levídi**, a village of **Taking provisions to the monastery.**

great beauty. It is built on the hillocks that lead to the lowlands, and provides the centre for the villages which surround the valley. The people of Levídi, which is known for its excellent mountain climate, are the farmers of the Orchómenos valley, where the ancient water controversy has been raging.

This, too, is the birthplace of Alexandros Papanastasíou, who served as prime minister of the Republic in 1924, after the expulsion of the king. Orchómenos, on top of the hill that rises at mid-valley (and nearer to the Chelmos range on the opposite side), was, like Tegea and Mantinia, an ancient city; it had an acropolis overlooking the valley as its centre. Three temples: to Apollo, to Aphrodite and to Artemis Mesopolítis, as well as a fairly well-preserved theatre, stood here at one time. A certain loneliness and grace characterise this spot nowadays. Its water has not yet been taken away thanks to the clever arguments and civil disobedience of the populace.

Have rabbits, will travel. Further along on this main highway are two noteworthy places. One is the village of **Vytína** which is a well-known mountain resort, frequented mainly by Athenian Greeks. It has a rather damp climate, since it is surrounded by a pine forest. Summer and winter, this little village is always bustling with visitors. Further on, you will find the spectacular town of **Langádia**, built along a gorge.

What makes this town remarkable is not only the fact that it hangs on the edge of a mountain, but that it is so sturdy. The houses are built by the stone masons of Langádia, known throughout the whole of Greece for their skill.

For the remainder of the road to Olympía, the land is tamer. This is the country where the Great Mother, Demeter herself, searched high and low for her daughter Persephone. She changed herself into a mare, the better to travel through the mountains. At Phigalia, a bit south of here, on Mount Eleos, she was raped by Poseidon who had taken the shape of a stallion for the sacrilege. For a long time after that she hid in a cave on the mountain until Panos, the warm-hearted shepherd boy-

god, found her and begged her to revive fertility for the earth that had lain fallow in her absence. Nowadays the legend has been expanded to include the Christian mother, with a small chapel at Demeter's sanctuary. Still, the old legend persists in local memory.

When the sacred flame burned: The Olympic Games were the most renowned of all the festivals in Greece. They took place once every four years, at the time of the full moon in August or September. The sacred flame burned long before the eloquent sanctuaries to Hera and Zeus and the Praxiteles statues were created. These can be seen at Olympía's excellent museum today. All enmity and war ceased during the games. A heavy fine was exacted on whoever disobeyed the Olympic committee. Hard-headed Sparta paid up more than once; so did many other cities. But, for the most part, everyone made a solemn effort to cease all hostilities. So sacred and serious were these games that the Hellenic world, starting in 776 BC, based its chronology on the four-year Olympiads, measuring its history accordingly.

Today the site is peaceful and green, surrounded by pines, poplars and plane trees and bounded on two sides by the Alphios and Kladeos rivers. All the temples can be traced; so can the stadium and the gymnasium. The best preserved is the temple to Hera, inside whose sanctuary the masterful Hermes statue (now in the museum) was found.

The great athletes who came here to compete were not the only competitors, and the games were not the only feature. It seems that writers, historians and poets frequented the festivals, coming here to read their work. The historian Herodotus read part of his work at Olympia. And the ever-present poet-for-hire, Pindar himself, read his commissioned Odes.

Pátras city: If you leave the Alphios valley, the road north will bring you to the lush and fertile province of Achaïa and the city of Pátras. If you turn south along the coast, you will enter the province of Messenía and will come to some of the loveliest beaches along the Ionian

Left, Hermes at Olympia's New Museum. Below, Palastra, Olympia.

sea. **Pátras** is Greece's third largest city, after Athens-Piraeus and Thessaloniki. Its patron saint is St Andrew, and many people keep his namesake in the family. Greece's prime minister, Andreás Papandréou, came from here. Pátras is a sprawling city, both a bustling port and a university town. Being the centre of traffic for the Ionian Sea, Pátras is the first place travellers from Italy see. There is also a ferryboat service for the Ionian islands, Zákynthos, Kephaloniá and Ithaca. Although the various occupations by the Venetians have given the city some finesse, one's first impression is still of an unappealing port city.

Backtracking from the Alphios valley, once again through Arcadia, we reach Vásses (Bassai), where one of the most complete temples to Apollo (now covered by a protective tent), is located. Next is Megalópolis, and finally down the Aegean coast of Arcadia through Leonídion to Monemvasiá.

The oak trees of Megalópolis look as if they are dying from the pollution of the hydroelectric plant. Megalópolis was always an artificial city. It was built in haste around 300 BC as the new capital. People were brought here from all over the central Peloponnese in an ancient experiment in migrant labour and political relations. Today, the electrical plant also draws workers from other regions. But if the ancient experiment did not work, the modern one is doing no better. Political historians insist, however, that the original experiment was one of the noblest of all in representative democracy, and that had it succeeded, it would have surpassed the Athenian model.

The shore drive from Astros to Leonídion has a special charm, with a towering mountain range on the right, and brilliant blue sea on the left. After Leonídion, however, the road must veer inland up the mountain, for only eagles can travel near the water, as the mountain itself falls suddenly into the sea. The monastery of Elonis perches atop these cliffs. Terracotta red buildings hang from the highest rock. Then, within a short distance past the monastery the world changes again, as we are greeted

St Andrew's Church, Pátras.

by soft green almond trees and oaks at the border of Lakonía.

Monemvasiá, the most dramatic place in all of the Peloponnese, is a great rock in the sea, connected to the mainland by a man-made causeway, hence its name *móni embásis* (which means only one way in). Its fame across western Europe was for the excellent wine that went by the name of Malmsey or Malvoisie, the Western variations of its name. The dark, fruity wine was at first a product of Lakonía, but later it came from Crete and other islands. Monemvasiá served as the broker and merchant port for its transfer west.

As you walk along the causeway from the mainland town you see nothing ahead of you but a bulky, squarish hill of solid stone. The fortress town is well hidden from view. But from inside the gate, though the street is initially dark and narrow, you will suddenly catch sight of the blue Aegean. When you reach the small courtyard of *Elkoménos Christós* (Christ in chains), stop and take in the vista. Above you is the old town and further up the great castle. The architecture is of Byzantine origin, but with the many invasions, the rebuilding and re-modelling, it is difficult to date any of the structures.

This strategic place, which commanded the Aegean from the west, lies on the east side of the Malea promontory and only about 30 km (18 miles) north of its cape. Until 1246 when it fell into the hands of Guillaume de Ville-hardouin, only the Byzantine eagle flew here. But even under Villehardouin its inhabitants insisted on self-rule and self-taxation with feudal service to the conqueror. After that time it passed again to Constantinople, then later to the Ottomans, again to the Venetians (and even to the Pope for a brief period), and once more to the Greeks during their War of Independence.

Whether under the Byzantine eagle, the Venetian lion or the Turkish crescent, Monemvasiá remained a strangely independent and virtually impregnable community. Its two ports far below its retaining wall made it a great trading **In Monemvasiá, a cemetery...**

ΓΕΩΡΓΙΟΣ Κ. ΚΥΡΙΑΚΟΓΚΩΝΑΣ
ΑΠ. 19-7-1986 ΕΤΩΝ 54

centre, like a giant battleship setting up business in the middle of the sea.

Mistrá: The other great centre of the Byzantine Greeks, is only 5 km (3 miles) outside of Sparta toward the sea, on an imposing promontory, almost like a toy hill in the vicinity of the great Taïgetos range. Mistrá was the capital of a resurgent Byzantine culture just before the fall of Constantinople to the Ottomans in 1453. Many of its churches are still standing.

Among the most notable churches are the Pantánassas monastery, the metropolis (Ághios Dimítrios), the Evangelistría, and Aghíoi Theódoroi, built in 1396 with a central octagon.

In 1400 Mistrá produced the last of the Greek philosophers, Gemistos Plethon, a Platonist, who lectured extensively on the works of Plato. Some of his students taught subsequently at Oxford. But his views were not in accord with those of the Church, so he was often criticised in Greece.

Sparta (Spárti): Sparta, the ancient ruins and the modern town, are best approached from the north, on the Trípolis road. From the top of the pass, flanked as we are by the Parnon range, the view is splendid. Once again the landscape has shifted radically. The Eurotas valley, lush and fertile, extends as far as the eye can see. Alongside the valley, as if leading it by the hand all the way to the sea, Taïgetos rises with such grace that you are only intermittently aware of the optical trick it is about to play on you. When the light falls at a certain angle the mountain stands right next to you; at other times, crowned by mist, it lurks at a distance.

Sparta's ruins are not well preserved. You can make out a sanctuary and a theatre on the gentle rise, but no acropolis, no grand hillsides with citadels, and no walls to enclose it. The Spartans were warriors of such mettle they needed no walls to hide behind. Besides, they never set much stock by the aesthetic look of things. These monuments were never spectacular; only functional.

The Spartans embarked on the disastrous Peloponnesian War with some

...and the ruins of a Venetian house.

reluctance, goaded by their allies; but once in the war, their nature was not to relent. As late as the 2nd century Pausanias told of how the people of the mountains of the Máni would call themselves Lacedaemonians and look upon themselves as the direct descendants of the ancient Spartans.

In fact, these same Lacedaemonians were still not converted to Christianity as late as the 12th century. They remained self-governed in wilful isolation, and no conqueror, friend or foe, would traverse the terrain, fearing the wild Spartans. Their terrible disillusionment and decision to abandon the social world must have come after the Romans destroyed their city at the end of the Hellenistic era. Neither Augustus later nor the Turks succeeded in conquering them. Máni remained independent.

Gýtheio: Travelling south from Sparta toward Gýtheio, it's difficult to imagine its dark history. The fertile valley with its olive and citrus trees is peaceful. The road towards Gýtheio is excellent. We leave Mystrás behind to one side and travel with the mountain always to our right. Along the way signs point to villages deep in the mountains. One such village is **Arna**. This is the place which boasts that all its children make it to university. This is quite a claim considering how competitive entrance examinations are. The village is the schoolteacher's dream. You can see a certain austerity in the eyes of the children, an intensity and gentleness – boys and girls alike – and your thoughts return to the ancient youth and their austere training for success in the world.

Gýtheio is a port town, and the astounding fact about it is that it hasn't undergone what the tourist-minded businessmen call "development". It is still, on any weekday, an unspoilt bazaar. It doesn't put on airs or fancy clothes for the evening promenade, as opulent Sparta does nowadays. The sea, they say makes people different, more refined – it blunts the edges. If that is true, the people of Gýtheio have much of the sea in them. In ancient times this served as Sparta's port. It was from here that

Open-air photographer in Sparta's museum garden.

Helen sailed for Troy with Paris. The place where they embarked is marked on the long causeway connecting the islet of Marathonísi with the mainland.

The road that heads for the mountain, towards Cape Matapan (or Cape Tenaron, as it is often called) leads first to Areópolis, across Taïgetos and almost to the other side on the Messenían Gulf. It is best to travel down the cape on the west side and return by climbing the face of the mountain on the east. **Areópolis** is already deep in Máni, and here you begin to discern a wild nature in the people. Deep isolation, as a way of life, has brought all manner of contradiction to the surface. The church of Areópolis has a telling militant nature. It is the church of the martial saints, *ton Taksiárchon*, and is adorned by primitive reliefs of these warring figures. The war-god Ares would certainly approve of his modern Areópolis.

Here the people of Máni cultivate olive trees; but the trees are so puny, growing on such tiny patches of red earth, that you wonder how they manage to survive, either the trees or those tending them. The view down the coast is spectacular. After the stalagmite and stalactite Caverns of Diros the road to Cape Matapan becomes more forlorn. In the distance you can see the architecturally distinctive cubistic towers breaking the bareness of the landscape.

The windy vistas and the aura of the sea far below end as we ease down to the fishing village of **Yeroliménas**. The few boats of the fishermen lie aslant along the jetty.

The remainder of the drive to Matapan is treacherous along unpaved road, but well worth the spectacular view at the cape. You can see the island of Kythira to your left off the coast of Cape Malea, south of Monemvasiá; and you can see, too, Cape Akritas to your right south of Koróni. And here a shiver runs down your spine as you turn your head 180 degrees and take in these three prongs of the southern Peloponnese and remember the time-worn stories of the old seawolves who have sailed along these capes. Since ancient times this has been

Shepherd and his flock in the Máni.

the most dreaded sea for all Greek sailors. Here, at Matapan, the free Lacedaemonians had their headquarters; and, where the temple to Poseidon used to be, the small Church of the Asómaton has taken its place.

From Sparta, embarking on the last leg of the journey, you leave Lakonía behind and enter the province of Messenía. The drive is the most spectacular of all, for you scale the highest peak of Taïgetos and begin your descent from the western side high above Kalamáta.

The *Keadas*, just before the village of Trýpi, is the dark, bottomless pit, marked by a wire mesh in front of an opening between two rocks, where military-minded Spartans threw their "unformed" children, those unfit for battle. The hole is unmarked; from its depth rises a cold air, a true chill several degrees cooler than the warm atmosphere. The mountain beckons, yet it's hard to get that eerie hole out of your mind.

Messenía province: Leaving Lakonía the road travels up the great Lagada

gorge over Taïgetos, and already we are in Messenía. The people in this province are famous for always trying to sell you something. They are the butt of many jokes across the Peloponnese. The inn on the descent here is too opulent-looking to belong to any but Messenians, as are the trinkets that are sold along the road. These are fine handicrafts and make good mementos of a visit.

Kalamáta down the valley produces olives, the best export olives from all of Greece. You also see the cigarette factory in the distance. It is a city with an inexcusable amount of pollution and dull buildings, saved only by a fair stretch along its shoreline and port, which displays some old-fashioned charm: a tumble of docks, jetties and riggings looking in the direction of the sea, the port thumbing its nose at the tawny central plain and sprawling city of Messenía.

The best way to cope with Kalamáta is to leave it and head directly for the Ionian coast. After a brief detour to the Methóni and Koróni promontories, where splendid Venetian castles will remind you once more of medieval Greece, you can head for Pýlos the city of old Nestor from Homer's *Odyssey*.

You should stay at **Pýlos** as many days as you can for this is a quiet, restful place by the sea. The fish is inexpensive and plentiful. The walk along the beach, beyond the high school, under the pine trees, comes as a healing and celebratory experience, after one has braved all these many centuries of the Peloponnese. And you can contemplate, if you wish, the terrible battle that took place at the islet across the way, Sphacteria, between the Spartans and the Athenians, described in masterful detail by Thucydides.

You might prefer to contemplate the later battle at Navaríno Bay, the one you're looking at, for in the 1820s the Bay at Sphacteria was called Navaríno. Here, the three fleets, French, Russian, and English decided to help the Greek Revolution by engaging the navy of Ibrahim Pasha, and destroying all his ships. The people of Pýlos have erected bronze busts of three admirals in their town square to commemorate the event.

Left, uphill struggle in Monemvasiá. **Right**, tradition lives on at Olympía's stadium.

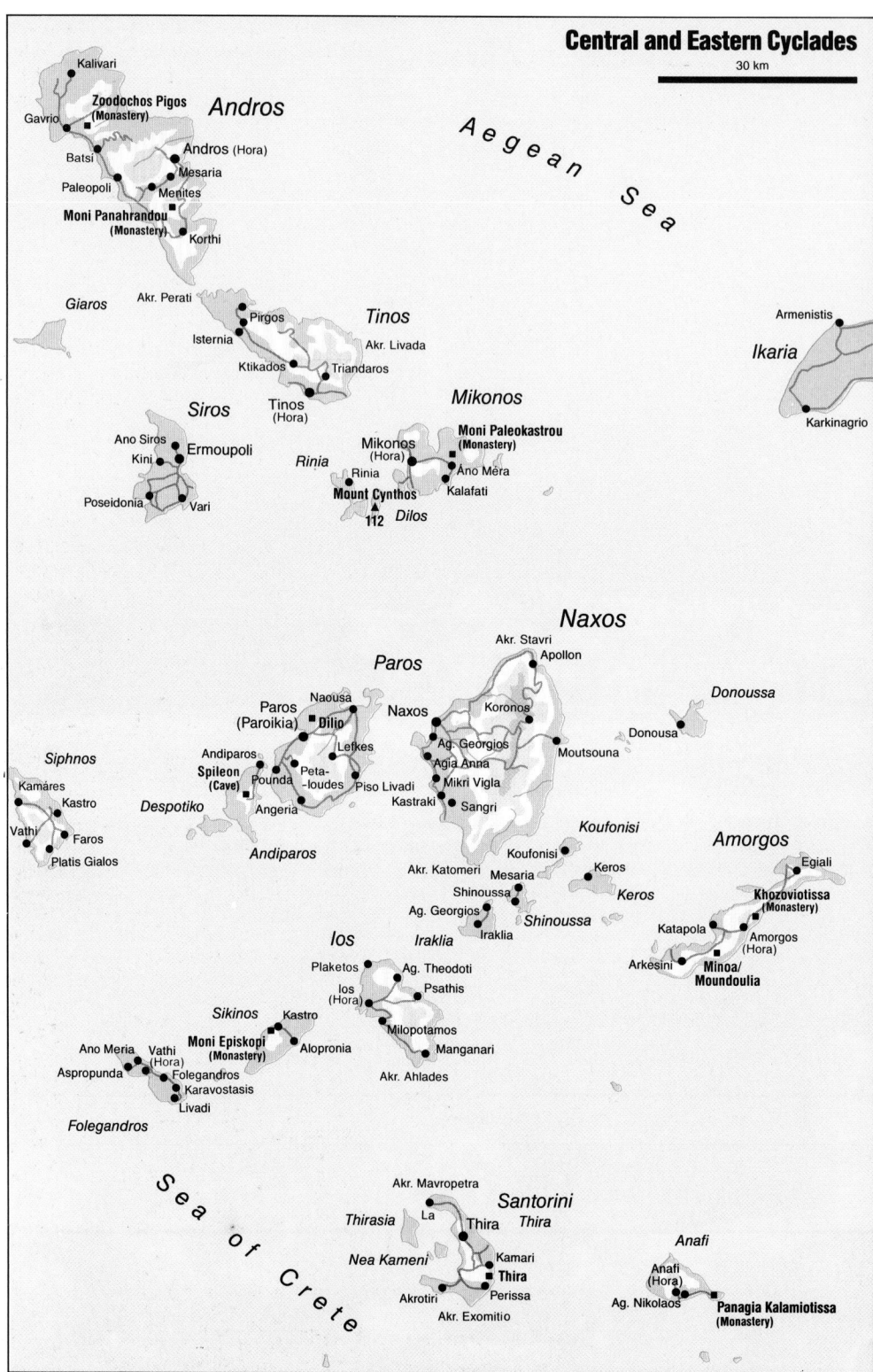

Central and Eastern Cyclades

30 km

Aegean Sea

Andros
- Kalivari
- **Zoodochos Pigos** (Monastery)
- Gavrio
- Batsi
- Andros (Hora)
- Mesaria
- Paleopoli
- Menites
- **Moni Panahrandou** (Monastery)
- Korthi

Giaros

Akr. Perati

Tinos
- Pirgos
- Isternia
- Akr. Livada
- Ktikados
- Triandaros
- Tinos (Hora)

Siros
- Ano Siros
- Kini
- Ermoupoli
- Poseidonia
- Vari

Mikonos
- Mikonos (Hora)
- **Moni Paleokastrou** (Monastery)
- Rinia
- Ano Mera
- **Mount Cynthos** ▲ 112
- Kalafati
- *Dilos*

Rinia

Ikaria
- Armenistis
- Karkinagrio

Naxos
- Akr. Stavri
- Apollon
- Koronos
- Ag. Georgios
- Agia Anna
- Mikri Vigla
- Kastraki
- Sangri
- Moutsouna

Paros
- Naousa
- Paros (Paroikia)
- **Dilio**
- Lefkes
- Andiparos
- **Spileon** (Cave)
- Pounda
- Peta-loudes
- Piso Livadi
- Angeria

Naxos

Despotiko

Andiparos

Siphnos
- Kamares
- Kastro
- Vathi
- Faros
- Platis Gialos

Donoussa
- Donousa

Koufonisi
- Koufonisi
- Akr. Katomeri
- Mesaria
- Shinoussa
- Ag. Georgios
- *Shinoussa*

Keros
- Keros

Amorgos
- Egiali
- **Khozoviotissa** (Monastery)
- Katapola
- Amorgos (Hora)
- Arkesini
- **Minoa/ Moundoulia**

Iraklia
- Iraklia

Ios
- Plaketos
- Ag. Theodoti
- Ios (Hora)
- Psathis
- Kastro
- Milopotamos
- Alopronia
- Manganari
- Akr. Ahlades

Sikinos
- **Moni Episkopi** (Monastery)

Folegandros
- Ano Meria
- Vathi (Hora)
- Aspropunda
- Folegandros
- Karavostasis
- Livadi

Sea of Crete

Santorini
- Akr. Mavropetra
- *Thirasia*
- La
- Thira
- *Thira*
- *Nea Kameni*
- Kamari
- **Thira**
- Akrotiri
- Perissa
- Akr. Exomitio

Anafi
- Anafi (Hora)
- Ag. Nikolaos
- **Panagia Kalamiotissa** (Monastery)

256

THE CYCLADES

The Cyclades are the quintessential Greek islands. They are what people think of when they think of Greece. Images of white and blue: whitewashed houses and domed churches surrounded in all directions by a shocking blue – the sea, the sky, even most doors and window frames are painted an electric blue.

Mýkonos, Santoríni, Folégandros… they are as magical as their names sound. But should you go in search of an unspoiled haven, beware; the Cyclades have been the focus of mass tourism for many years. It's best to avoid high season, and visit instead in June or September, when the coves and beaches are oddly empty, the people welcoming, the restaurants anxious for business.

The Cyclades islands – 39 in all, 24 inhabited – offer diversity, something for everyone. Mýkonos and Santoríni have more action than most large cities. In fact, single folk visiting any Cycladic island can expect not to remain single for long; here are better meeting places than any pub or club at home. Greek men look forward to the tourist season for *kamáki*, which translates roughly into "picking up" women (literally, it means "harpoon"). They've got it down to a science, staking out the discos in twos and threes, and using the basic English they know and think women want to hear.

Couples wanting a romantic holiday will find it in the narrow winding lanes of each island's *chóra* (main town), in the turquoise-green sea you dip into to escape the blaze of the Aegean sun, and at *tavérnes* where dining is alfresco and wine abounds. If money is no object, fine yachts can be chartered for personally designed island hopping tours, or villas rented for lengthy and decidedly non-touristy stays.

There is another version of island hopping: strap on a backpack and use the inexpensive network of Greek ferries to rough it at island campgrounds or cheap, uncomfortable rooms. It's a way of travelling much favoured by Europeans and young Americans, though islanders disdain it as it brings them little monetary profit. To their credit, backpackers discovered Greece's lesser-known islands. Greeks themselves followed the backpackers' example and started touring their own islands; Athenian youths can be seen, sleeping bag in hand, wearing jeans and writing postcards from tiny villages they would never have thought to explore 20 years ago.

No matter what mass tourism has done or will do to the Cyclades, they must be seen. Visually, nothing else in the world compares with them. Cycladic architecture is so original and impressive, it has influenced many modern architects, including Le Corbusier.

No nymphs: Some say the Cyclades are named after nymphs who were transformed into rocks when they refused to offer sacrifices to Poseídon. The truth is, the inner ring of the archipelago forms a circle, or *kýklos*, around the holy island of Délos.

The Cyclades were inhabited as early as 6000 BC. The heyday of Cycladic

civilisation came during the Bronze Age (2800–1100 BC) and parallelled the rise of Cretan and Helladic civilisations. The Cyclades islanders traded with Crete, mainland Greece, Cyprus, even Asia Minor and Africa. They had the world's best marble, the skill to carve it, and seamanship of unparalleled daring to offer. They enjoyed a high standard of living, judging from jewellery and household wares found mostly in tombs. Many modern artists, such as Picasso and Modigliani, have been influenced by their chaste female figurines. Towards 2000 BC, Cycladic maritime activity declined because of competition from Crete, and by 1500–1000 BC, the Cyclades fell under the domination of Mycenaean civilisation.

Later, in 487 BC, the islands came under the rule of Athens, but when Athens's power waned, a succession of foreign conquerors ensued: the Egyptian Ptolemies (3rd century BC), the Romans (2nd century), the Venetians (13th century), and finally the Turks (16th century). It wasn't until after the Greek War of Independence (1825) that the islands became Greek again.

Geographically, the Cyclades are flung like boulders in the Aegean Sea, south of the mainland between the Peloponnese and the Dodecanese islands. As you approach they look like huge, sterile rocks, greyish-brown in colour (but green and fragrant in early spring), jutting ungracefully from the sea; their only immediately inviting quality is a cove here and there, with turquoise water lapping onto a tiny bit of shore. Still, their aridity takes on a charm of its own; then there is the bustling harbour, and all the whitewashed houses you've read about.

When travelling to the Cyclades, the only difficult task is deciding which island to stop at. Asking friends or even Greeks won't help much. Each island has a distinct appearance and personality. But chances are you won't want to miss Mýkonos and Santoríni, the most trumpeted of all Greek isles.

The tourism trade on **Mýkonos** began 30 years ago, unlike other Cycladic

Little Venice, Mýkonos.

islands which only recently have drawn tourists' attention. In the 1950s, Mýkonos must have been surreal, otherworldly. Even today, under the trappings of souvenir shops, glitzy watering holes, Mýkonos's natural beauty is astounding – and evident at first sight of its semicircular harbour, sugarcube houses, and whitewashed windmills.

Every year from May to October, Mýkonos comes alive. Owners of bars, boutiques and hotels flock back to the island from their winter homes in Athens, Europe or New York to open for the season. The hordes descend; frenetic holidaying has begun. Though locals may frown at the intrusiveness of tourism, they prefer the new standard of living to their pre-tourism poverty. Land that was in their families for generations suddenly became an unimagined source of income. Fortunately, through zoning laws which dictate that buildings on Mýkonos may be only two storeys high, their island has maintained its human scale. In fact, Mýkonos has not allowed the physiognomy of its extraordinary

Mýkonos's Paradise Beach.

village to change a whit – so, paradoxically, it remains both the most touristy and most authentic of Aegean seaside towns. Outside the town limits, the usual chaos reigns.

Mýkonos has two scenes: beach and bar. At the beach you take off your clothes; at bars you put them on – your expensive, most fashionable clothes. It's a chic island where people come to see and be seen: Scandinavian models, Austrian doctors, Hollywood actors, Greek shipping types and the international yachting set. You may have heard Mýkonos is a gay haven. True, true. the island's first bar, Pierro's, opened in 1955 and is still operating.

A typical day on Mýkonos goes like this. You wake up late and go out for a large breakfast at around 11 or 12 (not a Greek custom at all but probably imported from America to ease hangovers). You swim and sun-worship at your choice of beach: Paradise (straight), Super Paradise (gay), Eliá (all nude), or Ághios Stéfanos, Platí Ialós, Psaroú and Ornós (at least topless). In the evening,

showered and carefully dressed, you stroll down streets lined with designer boutiques and galleries. You can shop or drop into an outdoor café for people-watching, a favourite pastime.

Dinner is late, around 10 or 11 p.m., at the waterfronts of Little Venice or the harbour, where you dine on grilled octopus and crab, fried kalamária, french fries, salad – all washed down with *retsína* or cold frosty beer.

Mýkonos has elegant restaurants as well, serving continental cuisine; it's best to take advantage of them here as this type of establishment is a rarity on the islands. At midnight, the nightlife really begins. Take your pick: Remezzo (celebrity-studded disco), Astra (new wave), the City Bar (with its drag show), Argo (a mix), Kastro (classical), the Mykonos Club (Greek dancing) and many others.

With all this club-hopping, it's good to know there isn't much of archaeological importance on Mýkonos. But nearby **Delos**, an uninhabited isle, should be seen. It's the holy island of the ancients where, as mythology holds, Artemis (just born on nearby Rheaeia) assisted her mother Leto in giving birth to Apollo, the most classical of the gods. The entire island is an archaeological site where you see floor mosaics, three marble temples to Apollo, sites of sacrifices, and the most impressive Street of the Lions – all bathed in a light and mystery that can't have changed much in 5,000 years.

Greece's answer to Lourdes, the island of **Tínos**, is just an hour from Mýkonos. Tínos is the site of a spectacular religious pilgrimage every 15 August. Thousands of faithful miracle-seekers flock to Tínos's shrine dedicated to the Virgin Mary, **Panaghía Evangelístria**, and pray to a sacred icon said to have healing powers. Tínos is more than this famous church; notable are its pretty interior villages and over 1,000 whitewashed dovecots – masterpieces of folk architecture.

If Mýkonos is cosy and like a storybook town, **Santoríni** is shocking, its topography an impossible triumph of

Pilgrims come from all over Greece to worship on Tínos.

nature and man. The island, also known as Thíra, has the misfortune of being located where two of the earth's plates meet. Brutal volcanic activity has destroyed the island again and again, yet people continue to live on the precipice, cultivating whatever is left of the land and building new homes.

It is eerie, chilling, exhilarating, to look from your white terrace at a volcano's crater floating in the sea. This dark, amoeba-like mass of land is surrounded by an ominous haze; though dormant, the volcano emits gas and steam at 80°C (175°F) even today. Again from the terrace you look down at the sheer drop of cliffs, actually walls of the caldera. Chunks of land have been blown away, exposing coloured layers of pumice and lavas – grey, brick, black, each stripe the trace of a different volcanic eruption. Once more from your terrace, you look right and left at the band of white cylindrical cottages surrounding yours, carved into the cliffside and fitting together like a jigsaw puzzle: your terrace is someone else's roof.

Santoríni.

This land is a ghost of what it once was, a crescent remnant of what used to be a perfectly round island, "Strongyle". The volcanic eruption *circa* 1500 BC which shattered Strongyle is said to have taken Crete's Minoan civilization with it. Santoríni's geological history is much too complex for us to do justice to it. Suffice it to say that what you see and learn supports the most spine-chilling theories: could Santoríni be Plato's lost Atlantis?

Today, approaching the island by boat, you see what seems to be a snow-capped mountain. Sailing closer, you realise the snow is actually whitewashed houses perched atop cliffs. Six hundred spiral stairs lead up from the harbour to **Firá**, the island capital, but you can hire a mule for what proves to be a rollicking adventure, or ride the modern funicular donated by one of Greece's shipping families. Firá is a disappointment though, drowned in a commercialism of "B" class *tavérnas* and pushy jewellery store salesmen who live for American cruise passengers, the proverbial "big

spenders". Santoríni's population swells from 9,000 to 70,000 in summer, and most of its visitors congregate in the capital. You should stop in at **Franco's Bar** or the **Kira Fira Jazz Bar** one night, a landmark on the island, and eat seafood at **Zorba's**, but it's best to stay elsewhere on the island.

From Firá, a 10-minute walk along the cliff path brings you to **Firostefáni**, the ideal spot to unpack your bags. Firostefáni offers the best view of the volcano on the island, and the most dramatic streaks of red and violet during sunset. It's almost exclusively residential, with fabulous villas tucked inconspicuously away, plus it affords easy access to the hub of Firá.

Oía, the village on Santoríni's northern tip, is billed as the most picturesque on the island. It is the old commercial centre where elegant mansions (damaged by a serious earthquake) testify to the wealth of the seafolk who lived here. Life is marginally quieter here than in Firá, with fewer bars and *tavérnes*, and earlier closing hours.

Renting a jeep is a good way to see the island. In the morning, set out for **Akrotíri**, one of the greatest archaeological finds in recent decades. Here, under a roof built to protect the excavation, is the 3,500-year-old city found buried under pumice and volcanic ash from the explosion which destroyed it around 1500 BC. A civilisation of great wealth thrived here, as revealed by paved streets (which you actually walk on), two- and three-storey homes complete with toilets, wood furniture, elaborate pottery and wall paintings. No bones were found, which means the inhabitants knew of the coming eruption.

The wall frescoes, similar to those of Minoan Crete, were found in surprisingly good condition and are on display in Athens's National Archaeological Museum. They depict monkeys, antelopes, and papyrus that never lived or grew on Santoríni, thus suggesting commercial ties with Egypt and Africa. Today, the dig is carried on by Athens University students during the summer, under the direction of Professor Christos

Shopkeeper, Santoríni.

Doumas; it may take 100 years to complete the Akrotíri excavation.

By midday on Santoríni, it's always time to swim. **Períssa Beach** is a favourite; lamentably, also with package tourists. The bay is packed with travellers who've arrived by bus from Firá, but the stretch of black sand is 8 km (5 miles) long and there are plenty of isolated spots. **Kamári Beach** is also popular, if crowded; often you won't find a place to lay your towel. It is separated from Períssa by a mountain which houses the site of ancient Thíra, a steep climb but well worth the hike. You can also ride to this site, which the Archaic Spartans settled in splendid isolation. **Monólithos Beach** is far from the madding crowd and features three of the island's best *tavérnes*.

To be perfectly fair, tourism has had positive side-effects. Previously, the whitewashed cylindrical houses so characteristic of the island were deserted, crumbled caves. When the island was "discovered", natives moved back and rebuilt Santoríni. The architects who came were committed to maintaining the traditional style in restorations and new constructions and they succeeded.

Today, Greeks and even foreigners will pay from 3 to 10 million drachmas (US$13,000–44,000/UK£8,000–27,000) for a cottage, and almost twice the buying price for restoration. It's hard to imagine paying hard-earned cash for so dilapidated a dwelling, but easier to fathom once you step into a would-be bedroom and witness the view.

If you can't find accommodations on Mýkonos, **Páros** is a good second choice; it rivals Mýkonos in its vibrant nightlife and cosmopolitan atmosphere although underneath, Páros is an uncomplicated, not especially distinctive fisherman's island with excellent beaches and whitewashed villages.

Paroikía, the harbour town, and tiny **Antíparos**, a nearby island known for its stalactite caves, are backpackers' meccas. The classier **Naoússa**, the snow-white fishing village on the northern coast, is overrun by "Rooms for Rent" signs and by droves of trendy youths

Below, Páros town. **Right**, fish for sale in Naoússa.

dressed up for drinks at the **Labyrinth Bar** on the waterfront.

Forty years ago, the Greek poet George Seféris called Páros the loveliest of all the Cyclades. From Naoússa, rent a jeep and head west to **Kolymbíthres**, a swimming beach with giant rock formations reminiscent of Greece's Metéora (*see page 198*).

A five-minute drive east from Naoússa in the direction of Santa María reveals splendid beaches which – for unknown reasons – are empty. The water is shallow here and deliciously transparent. But the best beaches on Páros are on the east coast just past Molos, in particular Kalogiros. This small bay is framed by cliffs that jut in and out, creating semi-private spaces for nude bathers. A swim here affords a fine view of Náxos. Continuing south, you arrive at the coastal towns of Písso Livádi, Logarás and Dryós, all commercial but with pleasant, sandy beaches.

Léfkes, an inland mountain village and the old capital of Páros, is off the beaten track and too often missed by

travellers. If there is time, visit **Márpissa village** and the ancient quarry at **Maráthi**, where the coveted Parian marble was mined.

Páros's central location in the Cyclades makes it a hub for boat connections to almost any place in the Aegean. The standard sea route brings you next to **Náxos**, the Cyclades's largest and most fertile isle, where in mythology Theseus abandoned Ariadne after she'd helped him kill the Minotaur. Náxos is still a fairly well-kept secret and offers a fine complement to Páros, with its orchards and vineyards, medieval fortresses, and giant archaic stone *kouroi*. From Náxos, boats leave two or three times weekly for Koufoníssia, a group of microscopic Robinson Crusoe islands (only six of 23 are inhabited) with names like Donoússa and Skinoússa, virgin beaches, and only a few rooms to let. **Íos**, next on the ferry route from Náxos, has an idyllic Cycladic harbour and spotless white town. But Íos – allegedly where Homer died, has been claimed by "party-ers" and counter-culture types, as you can see by the

On Náxos, the uncompleted 6th-century BC Temple of Delian Apollo (<u>left</u>) and the stone giant above Apollo on the north coast.

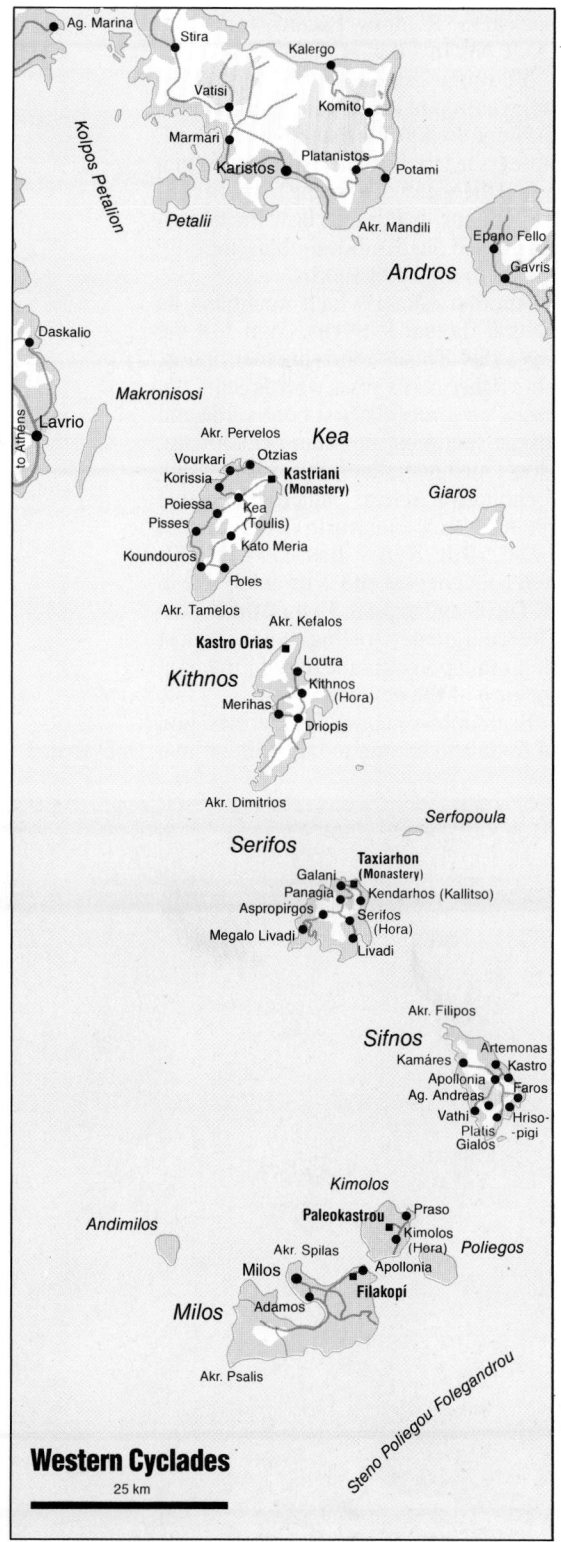

Western Cyclades

25 km

nudists sunning on cliffs as your ferry passes by.

Folégandros, the next stop, is worth getting excited about. Don't be fooled by what could be the blandest harbour in the Cyclades, save for nearby Síkinos. Folégandros gives you a sense that you are unearthing it; you are partaking in island life rarely glimpsed by tourists.

Visually, it's astonishing: rough, mean terrain, arrogant and forgotten. Its bald gray hills look like lunar landscape, while here and there efforts by the inhabitants to build terraces have succeeded, giving rise to olives and vineyards, though precious few.

Folégandros, named for a son of King Minos, has a population of 800. Since there is only one road and very few cars the islanders get around on foot and donkey. Public transportation consists of two minibuses, one running from Karavostássis harbour up the steep mountain to **Chóra**, and one from Chóra to Folégandros's only other village, tiny **Ano Meriá**.

There are inexpensive rooms to let and at least one second-class hotel in Chóra, a whitewashed village typical of the Cyclades but perhaps less self-consciously so. **Kástro**, the old quarter, is built on a huge cliff and has an entrance and exit which used to be sealed off each evening in case of pirate invasions.

You wake up early on Folégandros to a breathtaking view of whitewashed **Panaghía Church** towering over Chóra on a hillside. As you go in search of morning coffee, you soon discover island life revolves around three squares, situated back-to-back and framed by white churches. Breakfast, lunch and dinner are served here, and tourists can be seen at all hours of the day reading and underscoring book passages, writing postcards, holding hands, staring into space. You can easily adapt to the lazy island pace, and as you walk through Chóra to get ready for the beach, you take in the smells of onions cooking in olive oil.

Folégandros's **Angáli Beach** is also memorable. Yes, for its crystal-clear bay and two good *tavérnes*, but mostly for how one gets to and from Angáli.

The minibus lets you off on the paved road, high above sea level, and you climb down a steep mountain path for some 20 minutes, using whatever leg muscles you own for brakes. The return? Either you are wise enough to take the six o'clock *caïque* to Karavostássis, or you hike back up the mountain. There are donkeys to aid your trip, but there's something to be said for beating this forbidding terrain.

A Folégandros evening begins with coffee and the sunset, both readily available at the **Rainbow Pizzeria**, where you are served on a terrace overhanging the cliffs. Next, you'll want to compare dinner menus at **Kritikos's** and **Niko's**, Chóra's two main *tavérnés*. Don't expect to eat fresh fish on the island; your choice usually includes Greek salad with *sourotó* cheese instead of féta, stuffed tomatoes, meatballs, *souvláki*, *tzatzíki*, french fries, and delicious local bread. After a leisurely dinner, it's time to move on to one or another square for coffee, or better yet to Chóra's only pub, **Laoúmi**. Finally, just before bed, stop back at the Rainbow Pizzeria for homemade *baklavá* that is out of this world.

You may get stuck on Folégandros, not wanting to leave. It's a harmonious existence where tourism for once hasn't upset the traditional balance. When asked the secret of keeping tourism controlled, one waiter tells how the islanders chased out 50 undesirables, literally ran them off Folégandros.

Another island which maintains its natural flavour is **Sýros**, capital of the Cyclades. This is a thriving metropolis, not a fisherman's town, with an economy based on Greece's first boat yards and textile factories, not summer tourism. Don't misunderstand; Sýros is pleasant for holidays. Actress Catherine Deneuve spent her first-ever trip to Greece here in 1986. But Sýros has an opulent, independent past and is proud to live in it. The island capital, **Ermoúpolis**, was Greece's greatest trading centre, its most important port until the rise of Piraeus at the turn of the century.

Ermoúpolis (named for Hermes, god of trade and commerce) is built on two **Folégandros.**

peaks, one crowned with a Catholic church and the other by an Orthodox. It is full of Italian-designed neoclassical mansions, many open to the public today. Skylights, sweeping spiral staircases, painted ceilings and chandeliers are testimony to the fortunes made here, many in black market racketeering.

Ta Vapória (The Ships) is the city's most aristocratic corner, a line of neoclassical homes along a cliff over the sea, where waves crack against rocks in the style of Gothic thrillers. One of these mansions has been luxuriously transformed into the **Hotel Vourlís**, which in 1985 won an award as one of the seven best renovated buildings in Europe.

High above Ermoúpolis, on the Catholic peak, you can walk through 13th-century **Ano Sýros**, the typical Cycladic old town built up high for protection against pirates. **Lili's Taverna** offers a terrace view of the city and harbour below; on a clear night, you can even make out the lights of Mýkonos.

Sýros has lovely seaside towns, including Vári, Achládi, Mégas Ialós and Galissás, the latter featuring a popular campground. But the most impressive resorts are Delagrazia (or Posidonia), with its enormous Italian villas and castles, Agathopes and Finikiá. All are within a five-minute drive of each other and offer a good alternative to staying in Ermoúpolis.

While most Cycladic islands can be reached by ferry from Piraeus, there are several which require leaving from Rafína and Lávrion – Andros and Kea, for example. Being slightly out of the way has kept their beauties unsung, to the point of being omitted from guidebooks on the area, though not for long.

Andros, the northernmost of the Cyclades and home of many Greek shipowners, has two ports, **Gávrion** and **Batsí**, plus all-white villages with red-tile roofs. The island has much greenery, good beaches, and a noteworthy museum of modern art which opened in 1986. South of the Paleópoli–Andros road is the most spectacular of the island's 13 monasteries, **Panachrándou**, which is more than 1,000 years old.

Kea, also known as Tziá, heads the westernmost chain of Cyclades. It's just south of the mainland and has been popular for years with weekending Athenians who have summer homes there. What the island lacks in sandy beaches it more than makes up for in rocky coves and houses with red-tiled roof homes like those on Andros. Neighbouring **Sérifos** and **Sífnos** are particularly attractive islands and often pictured on Greek postcards. Today there are no traces of the gold mines for which Sífnos was celebrated in antiquity, but over the past few years it has become a favourite with tourists seeking the out of the way. There are ferry connections direct from Páros and other well-known islands.

Also part of this westernmost chain, **Kímolos's** chalk-white cliffs add to the already dazzling brilliance of its towns. Finally, you arrive at **Mílos**, where the famous *Venus de Milo*, now in the Louvre, was found. The island's 5,000-year-old civilisation was on a par with Crete's; today the main attractions are good swimming and eating.

Windmill interior.

A HARD NIGHT ON MÝKONOS

The inscription on a van waiting by the waterfront reads: "Follow me to Paradise". The bold lettering leads up to the figure of a female Pied Piper, a brown, lithe girl dancing under a huge yellow sun. Below, in small letters: *Paradise Camping, Mýkonos*. Even though this is simply an advertisement, the invitation retains its potency. During these summers, the small brown-and-white island seems to reiterate the promise: Follow me to Paradise. And the crowds raptly obey the summons.

The search begins the moment you set foot on the swarming landing stage, where the knapsack tribe with their huge Quasimodo humps mix with returning islanders (the jet-set tribe prefer to fly), gleaming motorbikes collide with primitive wheelbarrows, beach-buggies with heavily laden lorries. First, the search for accommodation. A frantic question rings in the air: "Room? Room?" In August, the cruellest month of tourism, a note of despair creeps in; the question changes to "Roof? Roof?" Even a roof will do (the white, cube-shaped houses all have flat roofs), a verandah, a balcony, anything. If you walk around late at night, you will see them: dark shapes, like Egyptian mummies, lying side by side in some sheltered corner, or on the beach. With the first rays of the sun, stray dogs will nudge them awake, or the steady slap of a fisherman beating an octopus on a nearby rock.

The provident or fortunate ones who have secured a roof over their heads sleep on till mid-morning. Most shops, geared to the needs of the late sleepers, don't open before 10.30. Serving breakfast is a thriving business; some places are famous for their gargantuan breakfasts, which are really brunches. Then there is the exodus to the beaches. Public transport is surprisingly good. Some people prefer to walk: brown leathery health-fiends in sensible shoes and straw hats. At Pláti Ialós the man who runs the boat-shuttle lures undecided bathers with the familiar summons: "Paradise!" he shouts. "This way to Paradise!" And if you think Paradise isn't good enough, there's Super-Paradise (Super for short) farther along the coast.

The choice of a beach requires subtle consideration. I've heard it said that there are 200 beaches on Mýkonos. Let us play safe and say there are at least a dozen easily accessible ones, with fine yellow sand, blue-green waters like great sea-chambers of flawless glass, tawny rocks all around, as smooth as giant pebbles. Nudism varies; choice ranges from fully-clothed "family-beaches" (rare) to those exhibiting pure, Edenic nakedness. But the nuances are finer than that. Innumerable small cliques subsist on mysterious distinctions: there are those who only bathe at Super and those who will consider no other beach than Eliá; both look down on those who go to Rolex Beach, so designated by the initiates to indicate it is frequented by the *nouveaux riches*. The same goes for bars and discos at night: on Mýkonos you *are* where you *go*.

In the late afternoon, after the return of the bathers, Mýkonos hoists its pennants, flies the banners of summer: huge mauve beach towels; flimsy, elementary swimsuits; *pareos*, *sarongs*, *loongies*; are hung up to dry in the wind, while their owners sink into a late, late siesta.

Around 11pm, the pleasure-seekers emerge, spangled, draped, tasselled, painted, scented, ready for the festivities of the night. They squeeze through the narrow, meandering streets – conflicting currents, this way, that way – wherever the **After dark, the fun begins.**

call of pleasure sounds stronger. Here and there small knots of people form, instantly attracting more people; the knot becomes a group, a crowd, what's going on, who is it, what are they doing, let us in.

Sometimes there is a real centre of attraction: a film star; a man impersonating a robot; a drag queen; a woman sporting a live snake like a long, undulating scarf. Actors and spectators, insiders and outsiders. Some people look exhilarated, almost surprised at themselves, at the ease with which they have slipped out of their city-bodies. Others are simply drunk, comfortably or miserably so. There are the over-eager, or the timid and the lonely, and those who look sullen, restless, having searched but not found. Pleasure is a hard and capricious taskmaster.

Here is a large blonde woman with burnt thighs tapering into extremely tight white cowboy-boots blowing thoughtfully into a pink balloon. Here is a hybrid figure in striped bermudas, top-hat, high-heeled lamé sandals, stranded with a loadful of wasted efforts, allurements unused and useless. And all through the night, you hear the steady beat of music, picked in relays by one disco after another.

The old lovers of Mýkonos, who "discovered" it in the 1950s, keep lamenting the desecration. Yet they still come back every summer, carrying around their bile and their scorn, putting on proprietary airs, betrayed but persistent lovers. Perhaps it is the invincible beauty of the place, the purity of the light, the linear perfection. Perhaps they are dimly aware that this island can never be totally spoilt.

Long before the "beautiful" people wake up, the Mýkoniots go about their business as if the invasion hadn't taken place. They gossip, discuss the coming municipal elections, cluster round the fishing-boats that have just come in with the night-catch. The sleepy idyllic island of the 1950s? Not quite. Many of the boats' names have changed: fewer *Aghíes Marínes* and *Thomadákia*; more fancy names like *Troubadour*, *Romantica*, *Super*. The ubiquitous whitewash that makes Mýkonos look like a snow-city in the middle of summer is often defaced by advertisements and graffiti, stained with the brown blood of melted chocolate ice-cream.

There are still donkeys carrying large baskets of melons, figs, tomatoes, bunches of flowers interspersed with fresh basil and verbena; but you suspect it's a deliberate touch of *couleur locale*; most other pedlars switched to three-wheelers long ago. You are never sure what is genuine and what is there for show. A boy rides bareback on a white horse along the beach. He gets off the horse, picks two white sea-lilies in the sand, sticks them behind the horse's ears. Two ladies in flowing djellabahs come up and talk to him; he offers them the lilies. Was it all stage-managed?

No matter how crowded, there is a peculiar sense of *lebensraum* on Mýkonos – dare one call it a capacity for freedom? It is a quality that can easily topple into destructive excess at one end, indifference at the other; yet somehow, most of the time, a delicate balance is maintained.

Consider this scene. A little, withered old woman, bundled in black clothes from top to toe, trudges every morning along one of the more dedicated nudist beaches selling fresh figs. She picks her way through the tangle of naked bodies; looking neither right nor left, she hands out figs, pockets money. When she reaches the far end of the beach, she sits down on a rock and puts away her basket. Very cautiously, she lifts the hem of her black skirt and dips one foot, then the other, in the shallow waters – untouched, in her small pool of privacy. ∎

NORTHEASTERN AEGEAN ISLANDS

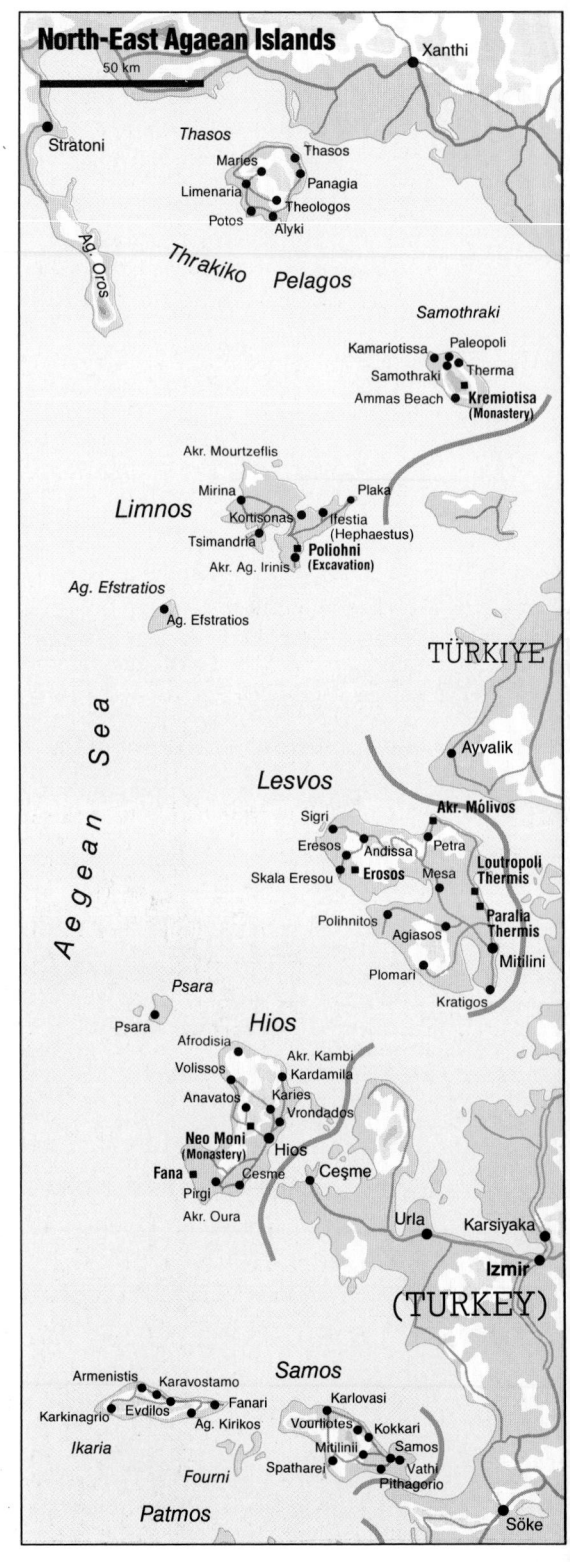

Lésvos (Mytilíni), **Chíos** (Híos) and **Sámos** form an extraordinary, if slightly arbitrary, trio. They are grand by Aegean standards and, marking the extreme north-eastern edge of Greek territory, are far from mainland Greece. They lie, more-over, at considerable distances from each other; geographically they are not a chain of islands but extensions of the Asia Minor mainland, to which they have been bound for millennia. Clearly they have distinct personalities, proud and resistant to being grouped together. They do, however, share a common East Aegean history, which merits a moment's reflection.

On Lésvos, Chíos and Sámos, Turkey is a constant presence. It manifests itself in everyday life in many ways: as a threat to the Greek soldier who mans the pill-boxes and camps that spot the coasts and hills, and who peers out across those narrowest straits that separate him from the Turk; as the lure of another world, Asia, for the tourist who wants to venture beyond; as a lost homeland to the elderly Greek refugee who, seeing it from her window, remembers what she left some 70 years before. For it was here, along this coast around Smyrna that the Greeks were driven into the sea in 1922 by Mustafa Kemal's troops. With this the hope of recreating the Byzantine Em-pire, the "Megáli Idéa", became an im-practicable dream and a millennial co-habitation was cut in two.

In the formidable depths of these is-lands' histories an interplay of shared and divergent fates can be traced. The early (3rd and 4th millennia BC) inhabi-tants of these islands appear to have been closely linked to the East – both Chíos and Sámos are said to derive from Phoenician words, and Lésvos is thought to be derived from a Hittite name. But it is in the west, in the dusk of the Bronze Age, that these islands' early destiny was forged. Around 1100 BC, shock waves of the Dorian invasion of the Greek main-land rippled across the Aegean to the coast of Asia Minor – whole peoples, Ionians mostly, transferring their homes to safer shores. Here too the first seed of difference between the three islands was sown – Iónian Greeks, apparently from Attica, settled on Chíos and Sámos; on Lésvos it was the Aeolians from northwest Asia Minor who differed in culture, language and customs from the Ionians.

Separate ways: These differences soon became clear in the civilisations that evolved on these islands between 900 and 500 BC – Lésvos developed as an independent island-state, achieving great economic and cultural prosperity in the 6th century under Pittacus, one of the Seven Sages. This was an era of innovation in music and poetry, the age of Alcaeus and Sappho. Meanwhile Chíos and Sámos were prospering as well, but as a part of a great economic and cultural network – the Ionian Confederacy, a league of 12 Ionian cities. Out of this matrix came Pythagoras of Sámos, Thales of Miletus and, it is said, Homer of Chíos.

This efflorescent moment was soon shaken, however, by the new political force in the east, the Persians. Just as the islands' history had been shaped by the shock waves of the Dórian Invasian moving east, they were the first to be hit by westward moving Persian tsunami which shortly struck, and, in so doing, galvanised the mainland Greek world. From around 550 to 480 BC, these three islands were overrun by the Persians. Their loyalties were somewhat divided in the Greco-Persian conflict – Sámos, for example, fought *against* the Greeks at Salamis, *with* the Greeks at Mycale, only to revolt against and be crushed by Pericles' forces decades later.

The middle of the 5th century belonged, of course, to Athens and consequently during this time the three islands belonged to the Athenian sphere of power. But by the turn of the century they began to sway this way and that with the successive arrival and departure of Spartans, Macedonians and Ptolemies, finally finding some stability and favour under the Romans.

Little is known about life on the islands in the centuries following Roman

decline. With the growing force of Christianity the Byzantines gained control of them, though not without devastating set-backs at the hands of Arab pirates in the 8th and 9th centuries. The year 1204 roughly marks the rise of Latin power – first the Venetians and then for two centuries the Genoese (1350–1550) who established important centres of trade and commerce on Lésvos and Chíos, but not Sámos. The Turks then arrived to rule for three and a half centuries; Greek independence was declared in 1821, and the Turks were defeated at Sámos, yet the islands did not join the Greek state until late in 1912.

During the Middle Ages it is the differences as much as the similarities which strike us. Sámos, for example, was nearly deserted for much of this time, while Lésvos and Chíos were dynamos of the Genoan trade machine. Their participation in the Greek independence struggle varied too. Chíos was the favoured island of the sultan and its wealthy traders, shippers and landowners enjoyed semi-independence. They were not eager to rock the boat that kept them afloat. The Samians, with less to lose, were fiercely opposed to the sultan and dealt him many defeats; "to go to Sámos" was a Turkish periphrasis for certain death.

Today, too, the islands are an admixture of the common and unique. Since union with Greece, Lésvos has been a somewhat cosmopolitan island with developed olive and spirit industries and a tradition of artists and poets. Its tourism is varied, from lesbians to meditators to beachcombers. Chíos, on the other hand was drastically depopulated in the 19th century by its two catastrophes, only to become the home of Greece's wealthiest shipowners. It is a rich island and does relatively little to solicit tourists who, at least until recently, have not visited there in great numbers. Tourism has probably changed Sámos the most. It has given a great boost to the formerly exiguous economy of wine producing, olive growing and lumbering.

Sámos, an island of dense forests and vineyard-clad hills, wild mountains and Byron-praised wines can, in its rich **A beach near Kokári, Sámos.**

diversity, accommodate nearly every type of traveller. The island tour proceeds in a circle around the island beginning from Pythagóreio (though you may arrive at Vathy or even Karlóvassi). One word of caution though: Pythagóreio is just the beginning and is the most commercialised part of the island.

Pythagóreio is on the site of the ancient city of Sámos whose three surviving monuments are the town's main attractions – the Temple of Hera, the Tunnel of Eupalinius and the harbour mole. They are all worth a visit, but perhaps the last of the trio is the most pleasant. Strolling down that immense arm originally constructed by slaves from Lésvos, you can watch the majesty of Cape Mykale, Turkey, fading into the golden evening.

By day Pythagóreio's neighbourhoods are alive with children playing hopscotch, vegetable vendors selling their wares from their pick-up trucks and an occasional baby gurgling under the shade of a cypress tree. These are the endlessly repeated rituals that go on just a block in from the loud touristic clamour of the

Painting boats in Pythagóreio harbour.

waterfront. This is the "frying-pan" (*Tigáni*) as the town used to be called for the harbour's shape, a name in keeping with the sound of motorcycles, the smell of suntan-lotion and the sizzling disco-beat that prevails here. Disco-cocktail bars lit with candles rim the frying-pan, booming out an aural smorgasbord to the corresponding Scandinavian clientele.

A change of names: The name "frying-pan" was perhaps too prophetic of what the town actually turned into. And so in 1955 the town fathers changed it to Pythagóreio, harking back to its most famous son, Pythagoras. This breeds a second irony for it seems that Pythagoras exiled himself from Sámos (for southern Italy) in disgust over King Polykrates' policies. But, under Polykrates, Sámos achieved its moment of glory between 550 and 500 BC, earning Herodotus' highest praise: "I have spoken at greater length of the Samians because of all the Greeks they have achieved the three greatest projects."

The ruins of the **Temple of Héra** lie outside of town past the airport. One re-

erected column and the temple foundations are all that remain to suggest the immensity of what was once one of the largest Greek temples ever built. The **Tunnel of Eupalinius** is perhaps even more notable (certainly better preserved) as it presents an under-emphasised aspect of the Greek civilisation – their technological expertise. The tunnel was built as an aqueduct to carry water through the mountain to the city and in later Byzantine times served as a refuge from pirate raids. Today you can walk through a good part of it. The less visited rear entrance in the hills also has been tidied up recently.

The minute **Archaeological Museum** has a number of beautiful *anthémia* (flora reliefs) from grave steles and some fine Roman busts. On the other side of town the **Logothétis Tower** and the **Church of the Transfiguration** with its graveyard is an interesting complex of buildings strewn with ancient fragments. On this site overlooking the sea the Samians, commanded by General Logothétis, defeated the Ottomans in 1824.

Vathý, the capital: Vathý, or Sámos Town lies facing a large bay on the north coast. It is the island's capital and, in contrast to Pythagóreio, its civic life is not dominated by tourism. In both size and population (8,000) it is a large town and has a bustling social and economic activity of its own. In the town centre there are some fine shop-lined streets, and a colourful garden across from the post office and Archaeological Museum.

Archaeological Museum: This museum is one of the best in the provinces, with a rich trove of finds from the sanctuary of Hera. The chief of these, given pride of place, is a 5-metres (16-ft) high *kouros*, the largest found and nearly intact.

The capital's most striking area is **Ano Vathy**, the "old city" a few miles up the hill from the town centre, the red-tile roofs of its old wood and plaster houses visible from afar. An hour's walk will take you through the winding streets (built for donkey and cart, but now used by cars), of a traditional Greek community which carries on a rather separate life from lower Vathý. The style of these 200-year-old houses with the over-hanging second floor is architecturally linked with those in northern Greece and the Sporades but worlds apart from the white-washed stone Cycladic houses.

The road to the western part of the island takes you along the harbour, winding through lush stands of pines at Malugúri and along the north coast to **Kokkári**. With its long, pebbly, but windy beach it is one of the island's favourite resort spots. A small fishing village cradled by twin spits of land forms the original centre of this town which now sprawls down the entire beach, and there at the edge of all the bars and *tavérnes*, the bare-chested fishermen string out their nets for mending. Kokkári lies in the craggy shadow of Mount Karvoúnis.

The road continues west from Kokkári and traverses the mountain's vineyard-clad foothills. **Tsamadoú** and **Avlákia** beaches are just two of several gravel or pebble beaches which appear at intervals. Just after Avlákia a road on the left leads towards **Vourliótes** and **Moní Vrondianí**, founded in 1566, the oldest town on the island. It is a pleasant 3-km

Card game in Vathý old town, Sámos.

(2-mile) walk from Vourliótes to get there. Vourliótes itself has some good *tavérnes* on its photogenic *plateía*. The main coast road continues to Karlóvassi and for one fine stretch passes right along the sea's edge.

Karlóvassi is a strange town. It may fascinate you, or disenchant you – but it probably won't bore you. First of all it is difficult to get your bearings here, for it is divided into at least four parts – **Ano Karlóvassi** at the far western edge perched on the mountain next to the Aghía Triáda church; Limín, where most tourist development is; the **waterfront**; **Meséo Karlovassi**, full of old mansions from the turn of the century when the town was set up as a tanning centre (which collapsed after the war when that industry was centralised in Athens); and **Karlóvassi**, which grew considerably after 1922 as a community for refugees from Asia Minor and as home to the cavernous, now empty leather warehouses. Like Ano Vathý, both Ano and Meséo Karlóvassi are filled with fine old houses, lovely winding lanes, the voices

Sámos old town.

of children arguing over who won the game, and even an occasional man's voice, a carpenter squaring a wall. Most of the men, though, are off in town, either working in the stores or sitting in the *kafeneía*.

Just beyond Karlóvassi on the coast lies an immense and usually deserted pebble beach, **Potámi**. The sea here is clean and outrageously blue, frolicked in by most of Karlóvassi's population on summer weekends. This too is the end of the line for most vehicles; to get to the island's rugged west end, you will have to walk (a fine walk at that), to take a boat or come around from the south side.

Karlóvassi roughly marks the halfway point in this circle around Sámos. From here the main paved loop road leads south, then east into the island's mountainous interior, dotted with small villages, few of which have any special sights to be seen.

Yet all of them have the simple attraction of being what they are: quiet, old settlements where the men drink coffee in plane-shaded squares; where the well

in the square bubbles cool spring water for the gold-chain Lothario washing his Mitsubishi, the contractor mixing cement or, more traditionally, the greengrocer and the laden donkey; where tiled, shuttered houses line the streets, with the typical Sámian churches of golden sandstone and a blue-and-white-striped cupola standing in the centre of town. These are villages for quiet exploring, for sipping a coffee in the *kafeneío* and for mustering all the Greek you've learned.

There are three possible routes through this territory. One takes you most directly back to Pythagóreio, by-passing the island's west side, through Kondeïka, Plátanos, Pýrgos and Chóra before reaching Pythagóreio. (**Pýrgos** is a fine old honey producing town worth visiting, and **Spatharuíoi** just to the south has one of the finest views on the island across to Foúrni and Pátmos.) The second takes you on the best road to the junction where you can head for Marathókampos or back to Pythagóreio. And the third leads up and around the slopes of **Mount Kérkis** (1,440 metres/4,725 feet) which

rises to the west, dead ending in the remote hamlets of Kallithéa and Drakáoi.

Mount Kérkis covers the west of Sámos and dominates the horizon of the eastern Aegean. From the summit you can take in Pátmos and other Dodecanese islands, Chíos and Turkey. Climbing it is a worthwhile challenge, requiring most of a day for both the ascent and descent. Start from Kosmadaíoi, from Drakaíoi or even from Kallithéa Beach, the trickiest route. In the days of pirate raids, Samians left their villages and took refuge on Mount Kérkis. More recently, Greek guerrilla fighters in World War II and during the Civil War made it their hideout. Some 400 guerrillas are said to have held out here between 1943 and 1948.

The Resistance links Mount Kérkis to the destiny of the village of Kastaniá, where 27 villagers were shot by an Italian firing squad in 1943. Every year on 30 August the villagers in the area walk to the site to commemorate the event.

A rough road leads from Kastanía south crossing the bizarre, burn-out landscape of a more recent local tragedy. In mid-

Left, groves of mastic trees on the slopes of Chíos. **Below,** scraping resin off the mastic trees.

summer 1986 a deliberately set fire ravaged much of this area, destroying not only precious forests but century-old olive groves as well. This was the first of nearly half-a-dozen fires on Sámos which to date have devastated nearly a third of its majestic Calabrian and black pines. The same sunny dry weather that attracts tourists also makes Greece extremely prone to forest fires in summer.

From Marathókampos you descend to Ormos Marathókampos, a small picturesque port. West extends **Votsalákia**, the newest burgeoning resort, favoured by families for its long beach of sand and little pebbles (*votsalákia* in Greek). The beautiful, untouristed west coast will reward you for the trouble of travelling its unpaved road, with the forested hillsides of Mount Kerkis, deserted coves reached only by foot, and a few quiet villages lying between here and Karlovassi.

Cultural centre: The history of **Chíos**, according to the French traveller Tournefort writing in 1701, is "too voluminous to be brought into the compass of a letter". Since then three history-filled centuries have gone by, rendering a survey of this island's past all the more formidable. Chíos, in contrast to Sámos, thrived during much of the Middle Ages and the modern era. The foundation of Néa Moní, Chíos's renowned Byzantine monastery, in 1049 marks the beginning of a millennium in which Chíos would play an important commercial and cultural role in the East Aegean. During the Genoan and Ottoman rule (1333–1556 and 1556–1912) Chíos became wealthy trading in silk, wines and, most important, mastic, the milky resin of the lentisk tree. Today Chíos prospers in the shipping trade, home to some of Greece's wealthiest shipping dynasties, as well as fish farming, with three giant offshore nurseries for sea bass and gilthead bream.

Between Chíos's former glory as a Genoan and Ottoman trade centre and its present modern shipping wealth stands its catastrophic 19th century. In the span of 60 years most of its people were either killed or driven away, its social and economic order devastated, and its cities

In the central factory in Chóra, the raw mastic is washed and drained.

destroyed. Chíos had enjoyed great privileges and favour from the sultan. In 1821, as movements for independence were stirring on the mainland and on neighbouring Psará and Sámos, the Chiots were disinclined to disturb the order that brought them such prosperity.

On the night of 22–23 March of 1822 General Logothétis and 1,500 men arrived from Sámos to instigate an uprising on Chíos. Word soon reached Istanbul and the sultan allegedly ordered: "Every Chiot must die." Within a week the Turkish troops landed and began a massacre which would last some two months. Some 30,000 Chiots were killed and another 45,000 enslaved, and all but the southern mastic producing villages were burnt. Life on Chíos as it had been known was over. Sixty years later, in 1881, the worst earthquake in modern Greek history destroyed much of what was left, killing 4,000 people.

Starting from scratch: It should be no surprise then that Chíos greets you upon arrival with a waterfront of concrete and steel buildings, not the quaint old houses

of a fishing village. It almost seems from the look of Chóra that, building on nothing, the Chíots have been so much the more enterprising. Chíos today is a bustling shipping centre of some 25,000 inhabitants and so preoccupied with that trade which provides over three-quarters of the island's annual revenues that it pays relatively little attention to tourism. To many this is a relief. Nonetheless, Chóra is not all shiny modern businesses. In at least three places it preserves a strong link with its past: in the old city inside the Kástro; in the Archaeological Museum and Koraïs Library; and in Kámbos, the southern suburb of old aristocratic gardens and mansions.

The **Kástro** with its towers and massive walls was the fortress built and modified by the Byzantines, Genoans and Ottomans. It formed the protected civic centre for the town – here were the state offices and churches and aristocrats' homes. Under the Ottomans it was the Ottoman quarter, the Greeks living in the settlement outside the wall. Today you can still walk through its alleys and by the old Turkish houses, visit the rather sumptuous church of **Ághios Yeórgios**, the "dark dungeon" where the Chiot nobles were imprisoned in 1822 and in the Ottoman cemetery the **tomb of Kara Ali** – the Ottoman admiral who supervised the massacres and was blown up in revenge by one of Admiral Kanáris's fireboats the same year.

The more archaeological and archival side of Chíos's past is preserved in the **Archaeological Museum** (currently shut because of earthquake damage) and in the **Koraïs Library**, which with 95,000 volumes is the fourth largest library in Greece. In the same building you will find the **Argénti Ethnographic and Folklore Museum**. Also, before leaving the centre of town walk through the bazaar of old shops ranged on either side of **Aplotarías Street**.

On the way out of Chóra heading south you pass through **Kámbos**, a "suburban" area of old mansions and country gardens and former residences of the Chiot aristocracy. Only a few remain from its former glory of 200 years ago, when European travellers described this place

Machines press the mastic leaves into "chicklet" shapes.

as a kind of paradise. Today you can see the high stone walls that enclosed these luxuriant abodes; the arched gateways, some etched with fine Turkish calligraphy and; peeking inside here and there, buildings in varying states of disrepair. One estate has been restored, that of the historian Phillip Argenti; it is now an ultra-exclusive hotel, the only Greek member of La Vie de Chateau group.

Beach, villages and the coast: Next, the road leads out of Kámbos towards the fascinating southern end of Chíos. First comes the turn-off for **Emborió**, a fine, volcanic pebble beach set on the side of some cliffs of unusually textured brown rock. Nearby was the site of different settlements starting in the early Bronze Age and ending in the early Middle Ages.

Returning to the interior we enter the mastic producing region around the villages of Pyrgí and Mestá.

Chíos is the unique source of mastic whose name is derived from *mastazo*. meaning "to chew" in Greek (like masticate in English). It was extremely popular in Istanbul as chewing gum and alleg-

edly freshened the breaths of the sultan's concubines. The Romans had their toothpicks made from mastic because it kept their teeth white and prevented tooth decay. Even the "father of medicine," Hippocrates, praised its therapeutic value for coughs and colds, and now some practitioners of alternative medicine are making even more ambitious claims on its behalf.

The first stages of the mastic production process are basically the same today as in ancient times. The villagers set off on late summer mornings for the mastic groves, some on donkey, some in a pick-up. They carefully scrape the resin "tears" from the bark of the lentisk tree and then bring them home to be separated from the leaves and twigs. In the last stage the material is sent to a central processing plant where the "tears" are washed, baked and formed into "chiclets". Some 150 tons of mastic are produced annually, most of it exported to France, Bulgaria and Saudi Arabia for up to 35 dollars a kilo.

Pyrgí, the first of the two fine mastic villages visited here, still showily dis-

Stringing tomatoes in Chíos.

plays the wealth it accumulated over the years in the mastic trade. The facades of many of its houses are incised with black and white geometric shapes called *ksisto*. In its fine central square you'll also find the **Church of Aghioi Apóstolo** colourfully frescoed and with an imposing *pantokrator* in the dome. A walk through the alleyways of Pyrgí will take you under the stone arches built to protect buildings from earthquakes, by cellars where a donkey eats hay next to the woman making coffee on a gas stove and, on certain midsummer days, around corners where the breeze blows thick with oregano, the men sifting truck-loads of it to send to New York.

Mestá, to the west, is a graver, more sombre village which lacks the colours of Pyrgí. Here one is left with the sensation of brute stone – of deep arched alleyways, walls, streets and homes. Some guesthouses have been set up in the old houses and tourism has begun to stir things up somewhat. For those with adventuresome spirits (and their own vehicle) the beautiful and quite deserted western coast awaits. Between **Limáni**, **Mestón** and **Sideroúnta** are some very fine coves and pebble beaches set among scenic promontories. The well-paved road eventually takes you to **Volissós** in the north. Otherwise you will pass through Chóra again in order to explore the island's middle region.

Néa Moní, almost at the exact centre of Chíos, is one of the finest surviving examples of mid-Byzantine architecture, founded in 1049 during the reign of Constantine Monomachus IX. It suffered along with the rest of Chíos the double disasters of 1822 and 1881, its monks first being killed and relics and manuscripts pillaged, and then the cupola being cracked in the earthquake. Its mosaics, despite the damage, are outstanding. The refectory and ruins of monks' cells evoke the days when a religious life thrived there. Ask the caretaker to see the charnel house where the skulls of deceased monks are kept. Those bones, stacked as they are, mark how differently the monks conceived of an individual life: not that of one man but of legions of

In Pyrgí, Chíos, the women work...

282

men passing their existence on earth under the knowing gaze of the Pantokrator depicted in the dome. Many bones supposedly date from the 1822 massacre.

The deserted villages of **Avgónima** and **Anávatos** are further along the road. Perhaps Anávatos gives the best idea of Chíos's 19th-century fall from prosperity. The village, set up on the hill for defensive purposes, was inhabited until the massacre. Today it crumbles away, its houses and churches slowly merging into the dry brown hillside. Meanwhile, an old man runs a makeshift *kafeneíon* at the bottom of the hill, and a woman tries to eke out a living selling figs, honey and spices to the few tourists who pass by.

The north of the island is a sparsely populated area of ruined towers and fortresses, semi-deserted villages and a few good beaches. Many parts were severely scarred in the forest fires of 1981 and 1987, when Chéos lost two-thirds of its tree cover. Perhaps in compensation for its relative poverty, the richest shipping families come from the north of Chíos, the town of **Vrontádos** in particular. Just

north of Vrontádos is the so-called **Stone of Homer**, where local tradition says that Homer sang his rhapsodies and taught his pupils. **Kardámyla**, where many sailors maintain residences, and Volissós, half empty, curled around a crumbled Byzantine castle, are the two most significant places.

The small island of **Psará** can be taken in as a side-trip, either by scheduled boat from Chóra or by regular caique from Volissos. It is a quiet island with a small fishing village. It became famous as one of the most active islands in the Greek Revolution and the home of Admiral Kanáris. For continuously harrying Ottoman troops it paid dearly; in 1824, 14,000 Janissaries landed in the north. Three thousand islanders escaped. The other 27,000 died.

Sappho's land: The island of **Lésvos** (also called **Mytilíni**, by extension from the name of the main town) has always been associated with poetry, culture, education and a democratic spirit. In antiquity one thought of the poetess Sappho, the Philosophical Academy where Aristotle

...while the men play backgammon.

and Epicurus taught, and the democratising rule of Pittacus, one of the Seven Sages. Today the Nobel prize-winning poet Odysseus Elytis; the folk painter Theophilos; the educated, cosmopolitan Lesvian upper class and a tradition of progressive government come to mind.

There may be few real continuities between the Lésvos of then and today, but something about its vast size, its fertile, olive-green expanses and its position on the margins of the Greek world seems to have favoured a Lesvian identity not wholly bound to the present. Lésvos is the opposite of the *nissáki*, the quaint little island; it is, in fact, Greece's third largest, measuring 70 by 39 km (44 by 24 miles) at its extremities, with a population of 90,000.

It has always set itself apart, culturally and politically, from the mainland. Its earliest inhabitants were probably related to the Trojans. At the time of the Trojan War both Achilles and Odysseus came with Achaean forces to punish and plunder Lésvos for siding with Troy. In the wake of the Dorian Invasion, Lésvos was settled, not by Ionian Greeks (who occupied the whole Asia Minor coast to the south), but by the Aeolians of Thessaly, a different ethnic group.

Through centuries of struggle between the island's five cities, Lésvos as a whole developed into a cultural dynamo, exporting to mainland Greece such poet-musicians as Terpander and Arion whose particular Aeolian styles and innovations helped to shape the new cultural movement from the Homeric epics and Hesiodic narratives to the lyric and later to classical tragedy. With Alcaeus and Sappho the lyric reaches unparalleled heights of refined thought and sentiment. At the same time the ruler Pittacus (who was no friend of the aristocrats Alcaeus and Sappho) was busy initiating democratic reforms.

But the Lesvian heyday soon ended as the Persians gained control of the East Aegean. Lésvos sided with Athens for some years, only to rebel against her in the early years of the Peloponnesian Wars, an incident made famous by Thucydides. Lésvos generally then shared the vicissi- **Lésvos harbour.**

tudes of Chíos and Sámos, dominated by Macedonians, Romans (for whom it was a favorite holiday spot), Byzantines, Venetians, Genoese and Turks.

During the early modern era a landowning aristocracy developed on Lésvos, along with a large population of labouring peasants. Peasant and working-class movements took hold here, and since then it has been a centre of progressive left government, earning the title of "the red island" among fellow Greeks.

Accompanying such economic and political activity, the arts and education have flourished since independence, producing numerous writers, thinkers and painters as well as an upper class noted for its high level of education. Since World War II, Lésvos's social and economic fabric has shrunk considerably with steady emigration to Athens, Australia and America. And yet the foundation in 1987 of the University of the Aegean constituted a hopeful sign for the continuation of Lésvos's cultural autonomy and strength.

Mytilíni is a bustling port town of around 25,000 inhabitants facing the Asia Minor coast. The Mytilíni waterfront is lined with some fine old *kafeneía* behind which runs Odós Ermoú, the main thoroughfare of the market. On the Fanári pier-arm which extends out into the harbour, opposite the ferry landing, there are a number of fine *tavérnes* which the Mytilineans frequent, dining late into the evening. Behind the ferry landing, you find the small, delightful **Archaeological Museum** housed in a villa, containing Roman mosaics depicting scenes from Menander's comedies, interesting grave *steles* and some other nice sculptural knick-knacks.

Just around the wooded hill stands the Genoan castle, a remnant from the 100-odd years of Gatteluci rule (1354–1462). If you have the inclination for folk culture, visit the **Popular Art Museum** behind the bus stand on the harbour. But even more noteworthy is the **Theophilos Museum** in Vareiá, 34km (21 miles) south of town. This has over 60 paintings by Theophilos, one of Greece's most noted primitive painters. The road to

Rooftops of Ayiássos, Lésvos.

Vareiá passes through the part of town where Lésvos's aristocracy built their mansions, living there until after the last war when most left for Athens and abroad.

The road running north from Mytilíni skirts the coast facing Turkey. To the west of **Mória** a few arches still stand from the Roman aqueduct that supplied water to Mytilíni. **Madamádos** is the site of the **Taxiárches Monastery**, famed for its black icon of the archangel Michael. Here, too, a strong ceramics tradition survives.

South of Madamádos, in the village of **Aghía Paraskeví**, an unusual festival takes place in the period after Easter. In this "festival of the bull" a procession of costumed men and women and cavaliers parade to the village chapel. After the church service a bull is sacrificed, a banquet held and horses raced.

At **Kápi** the road divides, the north fork descending to the seaside village of **Sikaminiá**, the west fork skirting around the edge of **Mount Lepétymnos** and eventually reaching the sea at **Pétra**. Pétra has a long sand and pebble beach below the **Church of Panaghía Gliko-filoússa** (Virgin of the Sweet Kiss) perched on a cliff. Pétra also has the **Vareltzidéna mansion**, one of Lésvos's few *archontiká* which can be visited.

Mólyvos, a hillside town of old stone and mortar houses with red tile roofs surmounted by a Genoan castle, is Lésvos's favorite tourist retreat. Package tour clients have gradually replaced the artists and meditation-retreat customers.

In pursuit of beaches: The west of Lésvos lies at an intimidating distance from Mytilíni and, if you are pressed for time, you will probably want to limit your travels to the east of Mólyvos. If you do have the time you'll find the west more barren and rugged than the east, consisting in large part of lunar volcanic terrain. Many of those who do venture out here do so in pursuit of some of Lésvos's finest beaches. **Skála Eressoú** probably wins the prize, and is turning into quite a little tourist resort. **Sígri**, the westernmost point, is a quieter, less touristy village with good beaches nearby.

The southeast of Lésvos is striking in its diversity. On the south coast **Plomári** combines a moderate orientation towards tourism with its indigenous industry – the production of *oúzo*. The **Varvayiánni distillery** is just east of town and produces a deluxe *oúzo* which is arguably the best in the world. Stop in to see the process and try a free sample. There are some decent beaches along the coast here, the best being at **Ághios Isidoros** just east of Plomari, and **Melínta** or Vaterá, both west of town and reached by a soon-to-be-paved, rough road.

The most remarkable place on Lésvos is the village of **Aghiássos** north of Plomári. Tucked away from the tourist thoroughfares on the shaded hillsides below Mount Olympos, Aghiássos seems to live by rhythms remote from the modern world. Its traditions of weaving, woodwork and pottery still continue, and the dialect spoken here is quite distinct from standard modern Greek. The Church has a renowned miracle-working icon and on Assumption Day (15 August) it is the site of pilgrimage for men and women from all over the island. Carnival is celebrated with gusto here as well.

Left, café in Ayiássos, Lésvos. **Right**, festival-goer in Lésvos.

THEODOR ELIAD
FRANKFURT A/M

PLAKAT-FABRIK
WUSTEN & HORNSAND, FRANKFURT A/M.

Die Schw

1. Ein Schwamm-Taucher, welcher von einem Haifisch verschlungen wird.
2. Ertrunkener Taucher, weil er Tau und Ballaststein verloren.
3. Schwämme-Sammler.
4. Taucher, das Zeichen zum Aufziehen gebend.
5. Taucher, die Wurzeln eines grossen Schwammes ausziehend.
6. Taucher, der die Besinnung verloren hat und ertrinken muss.
7. Zu Hilfe eilender Taucher.
8. Taucher, welcher sein Tau verloren hat und nach oben zu schwimmen versucht.
9. Zu Hilfe eilender Taucher mit Tau und Stein.
10. Taucher, im Moment des Aufziehens.
11. Taucher, welcher Tau und Stein verloren, mit Hilfe der Ankerkette heraufgezogen wird.
12. Tauche... Oberflä...
13. ...und 14.
15. Tauche... griff u...
16. Tauche...

288

Fischerei. ※

	17. Taucher, den Befehl zum Tauchen gebend.	21. Matrosen, das Taucherschiff leitend.	25. Schwamm, genannt Zimocca-Schwamm.
…nnoth an die	18. Zwei Männer, den Taucher aufziehend.	22. Matrose, den Sack mit Schwämmen in Empfang nehmend.	26. Felsen auf dem Meeresboden, mit Schwämmen bewachsen.
…nde Männer.	19. Matrose, das Hinablassen eines Tauchers vorbereitend.	23. Luft-Pumpe für den Taucher mit Taucher-Apparat.	27. Netz zum Abreissen der Schwämme vom Meeresboden.
…Stein, im Bo-	20. Taucher, welcher sich vor dem Ankleiden abtrocknet.	24. Fundort der Schwämme, 25—30 Meter tief.	28. Taucher mit Taucheranzug, Schwämme ins Sammelnetz werfend.
…um Tauchen.			

289

THE DODECANESE

Preceding pages: a 19th-century advertisement for Kalymnian sponges. **Left**, windmill on Kárpathos.

The names of places in Greece often tell much about their past history, and the **Dodecanese (Dodekánissos) Islands** are no exception. Dodecanese is a new name by Greek standards. For the 450 years of Ottoman rule they were called instead, the Southern Spórades. In this period the Turks granted these islands considerable privileges and tax-breaks by, generally, treating them with benign neglect. Thus, for the most part, these islands administered their own government, schools and medical care. But when the Ottomans hit on harder times they annulled the privileges, and 12 islands (*dódeka nissiá* in Greek) banded together in protest in 1908. Though the protest failed, the new name stuck: Dodecanese. This, despite the fact that today these islands number 14, not 12, but who's counting?

Today the Dodecanese form Greece's southeastern-most territory. Indeed, they were Greece's last territorial acquisition, making the Greek map we know today. In 1912 the islands passed from the Turks to the Italians, who promptly re-named them the "Italian Islands of the Aegean". The Italians were busy colonialists in their brief 20-year stay, building numerous odd edifices from Pátmos to Rhodes and imposing their language and culture in the schools. Today many middle-aged islanders can still utter bits of their scholastic Italian. In 1943 the Italians surrendered the islands to the Germans who in turn surrendered the islands to the British two years later. Finally, in 1947 these islands, spread in an arc across the Turkish coast, were united with Greece to be ruled by Greeks.

Today the people of the Dodecanese live largely, as they always have, off the sea. Recently the sea has brought them a novel catch and one of vital importance to the local economy: tourists.

Roses and butterflies: The best known of the Dodecanese islands is **Rhodes (Ródos)**. rich with natural beauty, architectural variety and bearing the signs of a colourful history. Hillsides greet the visitor with extravagant displays of rock roses – it is known as "The Island of Roses". Another name, "Butterfly Island", does not take much imagination to appreciate – butterflies are everywhere. And of course there is the sun and the exquisitely clean sea whose currents combined with summer winds, keep the air and water pure. Endless sandy beaches only a few miles from the hotels are so pristine that it is easy to imagine oneself the first to set foot there.

The City of Rhodes is one of the most architecturally varied cities in all of Europe. Within a few steps one can pass from the ancient splendours of Apollo's Temple, through the little Odeon Theatre, probably used for rhetoric lessons in Hellenistic times, to Byzantine churches some of which were turned into mosques by the Ottomans. A beautifully decorated Turkish bath is here, too. And still working. The best way to enjoy it? Go and take a bath!

Greek neoclassical examples are con-

Map: Rhodes (Ródos) — 20 km. Places shown include Rodos (Rhodes), Kremati, Ialissos (Trianda), Paradisi, Koskinou, Soroni, Faliraki, Kamiros, Kalithies, PETALOUDES, Psinthos, Afandou, Alimia, Kamiros Skála, 798, Appollona, Kolimbia, Profitis Ilias, Kritinia, Embonas, Archangelos, Mon. Tsambika (Monastery), Attaviros 1215, Laerma, Haraki, Siana, Monolithos, Lindos, Lardos, Rhodes Rodos, Profilia, Pefka, Apolakkia, Akr. Lardos, Skiadi, Gennadio, Steno, Kattavia, Plimiri, Karpathou, Akr. Prasonisi.

trasted with heavy state buildings, an ugly legacy of fascism, in this case the World War II Italian variety. Amidst this architectural variety travellers talk with animated gestures, catch each other's attention, and flirt in a babel of languages as they wander past ancient monuments, improvised record and souvenir stores and small *tavérnes*.

Far across the Aegean from the Greek mainland, separated from Asia Minor by only 11 km (7 miles), Rhodes in ancient times was renowned for its wealth and aggressive navy and was Athens' most feared enemy. In the 5th century BC, Athens attacked and pillaged what were then three independent villages, Líndos, Kámeiros and Iályssos. The elders consulted the Olympian gods and decided it was time to join forces and become one community, the City of Rhodes. Secretly and with great speed, fortifications and a city wall were completed in 408 BC. Well-defended, it prospered. Because its strong economy was built on trade, Rhodes tried to stay on good terms with its neighbours.

But twists of history brought trouble. Allied to Persia at the time when Alexander the Great laid siege to Tyre, Rhodes had to endure a Macedonian garrison. As soon as Alexander died, the garrison was thrown out and it was back to business. Wars followed, but Rhodes sided with Rome and prospered. Ptolemy I came to its aid when the city was besieged by Demetrios Poliorketes in 305 BC. Demetrios was defeated but was so impressed by the defenders' valour that he left them his artillery when his armies were forced to leave. The citizens sold this unneeded military hardware and used the proceeds to build a monument that became one of the Seven Wonders of the World, the Colossus.

The Colossus: The work of a local sculptor named Cháris of Líndos, the Colossus, by most accounts, stood 70 forearms high, about 31 metres (102 feet), and was a representation of Apollo. Impressive by any standards, rumour made it even more so by describing the figure standing with one foot on either side of the harbour entrance so that

Antelopes indicate the entrance to the Mandráki harbour on Rhodes.

ships passed between its legs. But to do so it would have had to have been 500 metres (1,650 feet) high, an impossible architectural feat. Nonetheless this beacon to passing ships and monument to peaceful prosperity stood for over a century before it fell to the ground during an earthquake in 226 BC.

Rhodes remained at peace and at the height of prosperity until, ironically, she tried to reconcile the warring Romans and Macedonians, only to have Rome take revenge in 168 BC by declaring Delos an open port and ceding it to Athens. Rhodes lost 15 percent of its trade. This punishment and the threat of more forced Rhodes to give up much of its independence and become subservient to Rome, which was not an easy course to take because the Romans were forever engaging in civil wars. Rhodes' trading partners took a dim view of her alliance with the trouble-making Romans. In one chapter of Roman intrigue, Rhodes sided with Julius Caesar only to have Cassius, after Caesar's murder, destroy its fleet, plunder the city and fill up Rome with its treasures.

Two years later, in 42 BC, Octavius triumphed over Cassius who committed suicide, and Rhodes regained much of its autonomy. However, its fleet was gone, as was much of its wealth. But Rhodes did regain its cultural influence and for three centuries was the place where many statesmen and literary leaders of the age were educated.

Changing tides swept Rhodes into obscurity after the 2nd century. It moved in and out of anarchy on the fringes of a waning Roman Empire, the Byzantine Empire and the Crusades. In the 14th century, the Knights of St John took control, ruling the island for two centuries until 1522. During this period the walls and fortresses that stand today were built around the medieval city. Even Suleiman the Great and his Ottoman armies found it formidable. A chain stretched across the harbour and the fortress Castle of St Nicholas at the end of the breakwater kept his ships at bay. Finally, hunger, disease and spent ammunition forced defeat. The wall was

Below, Líndos. Right, the Colossus of Rhodes.

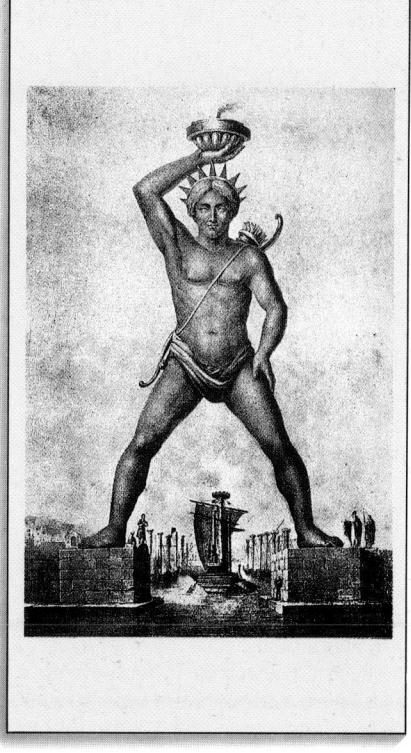

breached and the Ottomans marched in as the 180 surviving brethren of the Knights of St John capitulated on honourable terms, as a result of which they were given safe passage.

A Christian order, the Fathers of the Mission, was admitted to care for Christian slaves in 1660; French Franciscan Sisters came and built schools in 1873; the Brothers of Christian Doctrine founded the College of St John in 1889. The 20th century brought other visitors – once again armies. In 1912, the Turks, then the Italians and, during World War II, the Germans. British and Greek commandos liberated Rhodes in 1945 and with the other Dodecanese it became united with Greece in 1947. The **Castle of Ághios Nikólaos**, once an armed fortress, is now a lighthouse that welcomes today's visitors.

Island resorts: Rhodes is a big island, and it has more to offer than this marvellous city. Summer resorts are scattered across the northern part of the island; **Líndos**, a very old city, dating back to the Bronze Age, continues to thrive. It's the only natural harbour on Rhodes, except for the small **Mandráki**, the ancient harbour, now full of yachts. Its medieval city is extremely well preserved; an ancient acropolis also remains with two re-erected classical temples and a number of later Byzantine and Frankish elements.

Near the main square there is one of the most beautiful Byzantine churches on the island, with well-preserved frescoes. The water in the fountain still runs through the ancient water pipes. Lindos's large harbour with long sandy beaches adds the finishing touch. However, it's the light that has made Lindos so famous. The jagged barren mountains which surround Lindos reflect the light so that it almost blinds you. Italian and German painters were the first to rediscover Lindos; some moved there for good. Only later did the tourists catch on. The small city can't hold too many people so most come on day trips by bus or in small boats.

Ancient **Kámeiros** is well worth a visit. There's no new Kámeiros, so what has been uncovered of the acropolis has

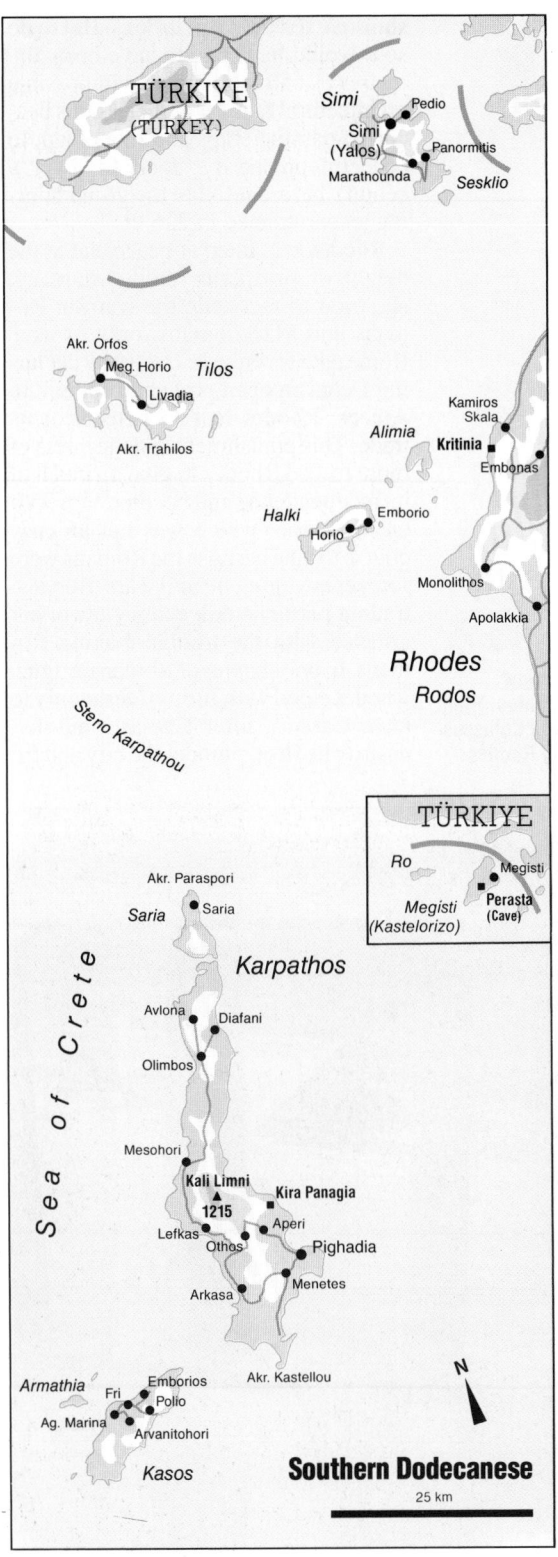

been beautifully laid out and gives the visitor an unadulterated picture of ancient life. This is partially true for **Filérimo** as well. At the top of the low hill the ancient acropolis of Iálysos is preserved. Over to the south we find the most beautiful Doric fountain with its water system amazingly still intact. The **Butterfly Valley** is also a must. Here a small stream meanders through the plane trees and creates little lakes. On the banks the vegetation grows thick as in a jungle. The plane trees are a particularly wonderful kind; the scent of their resin draws red-winged butterflies by the thousand. One abrupt movement or a cry and the butterflies rise up around you.

Archaeological centre: The second largest island in terms of population (20,000), **Kos** is also third largest in terms of size, after Rhodes and Kárpathos. It is a flat island with only one high mountain, **Mount Díktaio**, almost exactly in the middle. **Mandráki** is its only protected port. In 1933 a horrible earthquake destroyed the city but the damage was restricted to a very small area. So, although it flattened the city, it hardly touched the nearby towns. Italian archaeologists took advantage of this and excavated the area which they knew overlaid the ancient city. For this reason Kos's archaeological site offers more to the visitor than any other in the Dodecanese Islands. It is in the middle of the new city and constitutes a functional part of this urban centre which was rebuilt after the earthquake. The castle is the only part left from the medieval city. And, since it was only used for defence, it doesn't offer much information about the culture of its time.

In **Aspri Pétra** (which literally translates as "White Rock") in the western part of the island the finds from excavations go back even further, and it is obvious that there once existed a neolithic settlement there. Quite a few archaeological finds from the Mycenean period have been found in the city of Kos. Astypálaia, the second most important city of this period, is also referred to but it still hasn't been located. Other cities have been lost; for

example, it is written that Alkibíades in the 5th century BC defended Meropída, but no one is sure where it was.

Clinging on at the top of Díktaio is **Gía**, the most beautiful town on the island. The houses are built way up on the rocks and look like the monasteries of Metéora. Water rushes down in small streams and large walnut trees grow alongside.

Kos followed exactly the same course of fate as Rhodes. It reached its heights and declined during the same epochs; it suffered the same invasions and adventures. Its most famous ruin is the **Asklepeíon**, built in the 4th century BC, where Hippocrates, the father of medicine, conducted classes and cured the sick. The island from the time of the Romans has been used as a place for rest and rejuvenation; it has a long tourist tradition. But in tourist developments and economic achievements too it follows Rhodes. Hotels spring up like huge mushrooms on the sandy beaches that surround the island.

Kárpathos: The most dramatic way to arrive at Kárpathos is by ship from Rhodes. After seven hours of travelling on seas which are often rough in this part of the Mediterranean, Kárpathos comes into view with its imposing cloud-capped mountains.

The first port-of-call is Diafáni, a fishing village in the northeast, where passengers are ferried to shore on a small boat, as there is no pier for large ships to dock at. The passengers who continue have the time to get acquainted with Kárpathos. All down the 25-km (40-mile) coastline the slopes rise steeply, and the pine-forests which cover much of the island dip right into the sea. The massive forest fire which swept over much of the island in 1983 has left behind a charcoal scar on much of northern Kárpathos but even this somehow seems to lend an added mystery to the unworldly landscape. Occasionally, the slopes give way to large, white, empty beaches – proof that the island was a good choice.

After these magical first impressions, the main port of **Pigádia** is inevitably a

Kos Town.

disappointment, with very little to recommend it beyond the fact that it is well situated.

If you like warm seas, deep clear water with interesting underwater rock formations splashed with colour, and large beaches with white pebbles, then the southeast coast has some of the best (and least crowded) specimens in Greece. Try, for example, **Appella, Achatá** and **Kyrá Panaghía**. You can visit them by boat, but the land route will give you the chance to see some of the villages, as well as enjoy the breathtaking view of the beaches from the road above. If you hire a moped, though, be warned – the roads are very bumpy, the cliffs are high, and in places the wind is strong enough to blow you across the road.

The villages are mostly grafted high on the mountain slopes, primarily for historical reasons of security. Piracy was rampant in this region. The wealthiest villages are in the south (**Apéri, Othos** and **Menétes**), as is evident from the number of traditional and contemporary villas. What is less evident is the source of wealth, for there is hardly any flat farmland, industry is non-existent, and there is no mass tourism. In fact, most wealth is created outside the island, by Karpáthian seamen and emigrants (mostly in the United States), who send remittances to family members left behind, or to their native village in order to build churches and other public buildings, and who also boost the local economy when they return on holiday to see their homeland (and show off their fortune).

This economic structure has profound effects on local culture and attitudes, from their attitudes towards tourists (which range from indifferent to negative – you won't find cultivated smiles or servile behaviour on Kárpathos) to the position of women (who are both more dominant and more traditional than the men because they used to stay behind while their menfolk sought their fortunes abroad). One of the "cultural imports" has resulted in the establishment of a football tournament every

Traditional festival costume.

summer, through which the traditional rivalries between villages can be played out on the field rather than by the more violent means of former times. Another area where modernisation and emigration have left their mark is on the architecture and decoration of houses.

You can trace these changes easily as nearly all houses bear the date of construction (as well as the initials of the owner and very often a decorative emblem – such as a mermaid or an eagle) painted or sculpted above the entrance.

The traditional Karpáthian houses consist of one room which is split into two parts. In one corner is the *dórva* which is a wooden platform, bordered by an intricate railing at a higher level than the rest of the room, which generally has a mud floor. This platform houses the trunks where clothes and linen from the woman's dowry are kept, as well as straw mattresses which are rolled out every night for the family to sleep on; during the daytime, when the mattresses are rolled up to leave more living space, they are usually covered with embroidered cloths for decoration.

In the centre of the room stands a wooden pole which reaches to the ceiling, also covered with embroidered cloths and beads. This is the "pillar of the house", and to complete the symbolism a painting or photograph of the couple is pinned to the pole under their wedding wreath (*stéfana*) – perhaps this custom developed in order to acquaint children with their fathers, who were mostly absent. The walls are decked with rows of shelves with hundreds of decorative plates and other ornaments. Local handicraft products? Mostly not – they are plates from Hong Kong and France, dolls from Spain and Japan, and a myriad other seamen's trinkets from ports all over the world. The impression is of a splurge of silver, gold and bright colours which miraculously avoids being kitsch.

In modern villas, needless to say, the house is not limited to one room. However, although the external neighbourhood wood oven has been replaced by an electric stove, and although bath-

Ólymbos, Kárpathos.

rooms and washing machines have become a necessity, Karpáthians still model their living-room on the traditional style. And here Karpáthian women still display their embroideries and the presents they have received from abroad with the same pride as their foremothers.

In fact the most fascinating aspect of Kárpathos – beyond its natural beauty – is the way that foreign influences have been adopted and adapted to fit local needs and tastes. For example, in many villages, women still wear traditional clothes, whereas the well-travelled men have worn Western clothes for as long as anyone can remember.

The women's pantaloons, tunics and boots are all traditional local handicrafts, but the costume is completed by a woolen scarf which is imported from Ireland and modified to satisfy local tastes by adding a trimming of sequins and tassels.

At festivals, the tunics are replaced by magnificent dresses, in shades of silver and gold as well as fluorescent pinks and lime-greens on which families spend a small fortune. The ultimate decoration

is a collar of gold coins, the number of which indicates a girl's economic position. It is well worth attending one of the major festivals in order to see the young girls decked out in all their finery, on display for prospective suitors, patiently dancing to the monotonous *mantinádes*.

One of the main annual festivals takes place in **Ólymbos**, a village in the north. Perched on a mountain ridge, windswept and literally in the clouds, it is close to how one pictures the abode of the ancient gods at Olympus. The mountainside is cut into with endless terraces, giving the impression of a roughly chiselled sculpture. It is difficult to imagine that these terraces were cultivated as recently as World War II.

Ólymbos is very isolated and its inhabitants seem almost unaware of the 20th century. They marry among themselves and speak a dialect which retains many ancient Greek constructions. The women, dressed traditionally, bake their bread in neighbourhood ovens and even get their flour from a windmill which still functions. You are left with a bitter-

Waiting for the parade.

sweet taste: on the one hand feeling privileged to have seen the windmill's sails still turning, and on the other sensing that your very presence here, as a tourist, is speeding up the process by which these mills will inevitably grind to a halt.

It is this same taste that you carry with you as you leave Kárpathos, an *ex ante* nostalgia for a less frenzied way of life which you fear will not be there the next time you return.

Sými is is the closest island to Rhodes, 40 km (24 miles) from one port to the other. Wholly barren, it doesn't even have enough water for drinking, so people gather rainwater in cisterns.

This island was at its height at the end of the 19th century, mainly thanks to the sponge-divers and merchants. The **Panochorió** (literally upper city) was an important city, both for its large population, over 20,000, and its wealth, and even more for its extremely well-organised local government.

Interestingly enough, the economics of this local government didn't go under with the Italian occupation; sponge diving developed even more, even when the Italians occupied the Libyan coasts so rich in sponges. Somehow the Greeks managed to hold the monopoly on the trade in which they had always excelled.

It's worth a digression to talk about the way the local government organised itself at the time of the island's prosperity. Local elections were held every year on 25 January. The brief term of office implies that the voters were informed of common problems – otherwise their voting power made no sense. Voters had to be under 80, literate, energetic, impartial, capable of bearing witness, and with no penal sentence hanging over their head. The number of voters was unlimited. They called the local ruler a *Demoghérontas*, and his council was voted in for life by general assembly until 1902, and later by secret ballots. All men over the age of 21 who had paid their taxes had the right to vote.

The reason for the election of a first and second *Demoghérontas* is straightforward enough. The first presided over

Quiet times on Kálymnos.

the council and commanded the executive and judicial matters of the community, as well as relations with the High Gate and Turkish generals. The second took care of the community's revenues.

World War II interrupted this prosperity. The sponge fishing stopped, sea trade was destroyed; even the ferrying of food to the island became difficult and the islanders deserted their home. The end of the war didn't bring back many of the inhabitants, who were scattered in Rhodes, Athens and abroad, and the island never grew back to a population larger than 3,000. In the past few years it has become somewhat more lively because of the tourists who come on day trips from Rhodes, to see the distinctive city, and the famous **Monastery of Panormítis**.

Kálymnos is even more famous than Symi for its sponge-diving. Although the island on first acquaintance looks austere and dry, it is well worth further investigation. There are many lovely swimming coves and small out-of-the-way villages which offer simple pleasures – a plane tree for shade or a *kafeneíon* for a coffee or cold drink. But these you can easily discover on your own. The history of sponge diving is more difficult to come by. Signs of this dying trade are everywhere: Kalymnian mantelpieces laden with huge sponges and shell-encrusted amphoras, old men crippled from the bends, women in black, mourning the divers who never came back, but the visitor is often left with more questions than explanations.

Absorbing story: The sponge is a living organism, a colony of sea animals. Its size increases by a third each year. For this reason it is necessary to farm sponges selectively. Unfortunately this rule is rarely obeyed, with the result that the sponges of the Aegean are rapidly disappearing. The coasts of Libya and Cyrenaïca have also been exploited – although to a lesser degree since these countries impose prohibitive taxes.

The *ímero* (cultivated) sponge is different from most of the common black sponges you see at the bottom of the sea. But only a well-trained eye can tell

The colourful houses of Kálymnos.

which is which. The *ímero* is softer and can be cleaned and shaped with clippers while the wilder version is less pliable. There are various grades of *ímero* sponges. The heavier ones are for industry and the finer ones for cosmetic use.

The preparation of sponges for the market has two stages. First the divers beat them hard on the *caïque* deck "to get the milk out of them". Then they string them together and drop them back into the sea for two to three days of cleaning. The soft, fleshlike part dissolves and only the golden brown sponge skeleton remains. Then they compress them so that they fit in sacks for export.

Although artificial sponges have taken over the market some people will pay for the more resilient natural sponge. Be careful, though, that the natural sponge you buy has not been bleached; bleaching may make the sponge look more inviting to the uninformed tourist, but it weakens the fibres.

Over the years fishermen have developed various methods of gathering sponges: spearing them in shallow water, dragging a heavy blade and net behind the *caïque* along the bottom of the sea, so that everything – stones and seaweed as well as the odd sponge get pulled up together, and finally, diving. In the old days the divers used to sink themselves by tying heavy stones to their waists. Holding their breath, they scraped the sponges off the rocks which they had spotted from the surface; they could usually get two or three before they had to return to the surface for air. There were divers who could dive 40 fathoms deep long before the "machine" was introduced.

The "machine" is what islanders still call the diving apparatus. This consists of a rubber suit with a bronze helmet which connects to a long rubber hose and a handpowered air-pump. The diver is let out on a long wire and given enough hose for the distance he is diving. He can stay down for a long time because he has a constant air supply.

The sponge industry aided by the "machine" gained renown while the sponge-divers were less lucky: they got the bends. The air hose allowed the

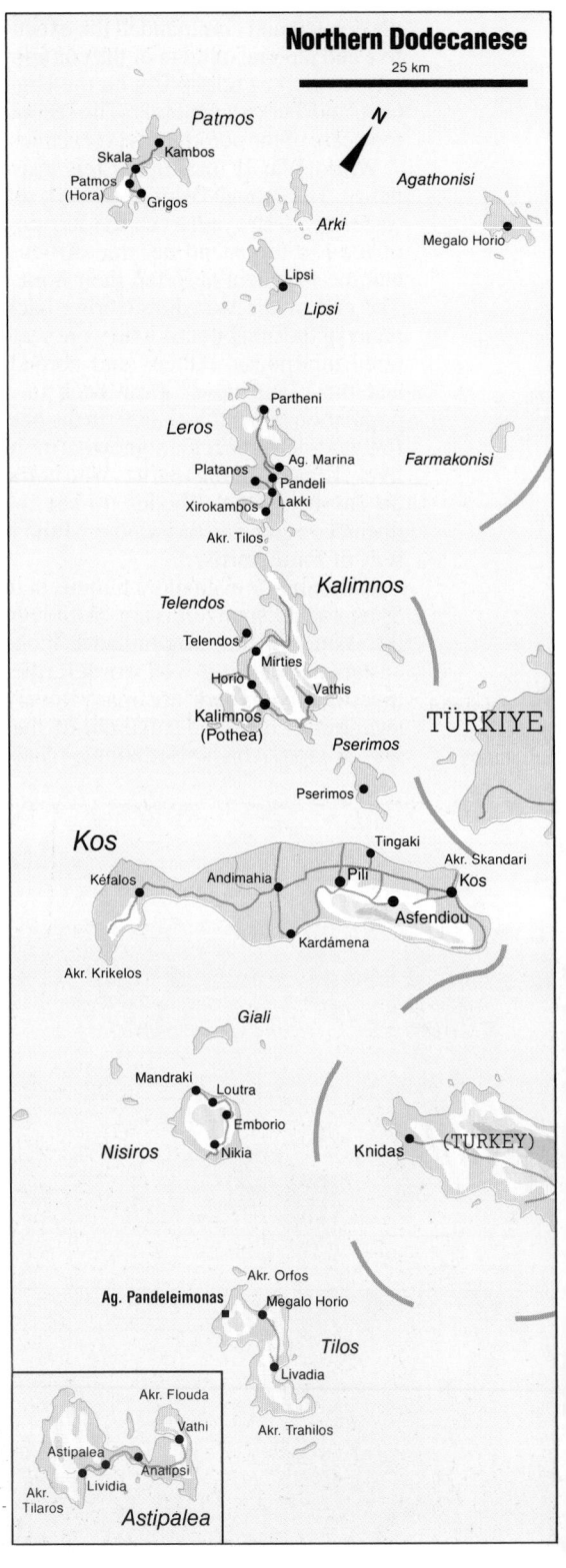

divers to go deeper, but they couldn't withstand the new depths; many were paralysed and many died.

Although this "machine" now appears quite outdated, you can imagine what an innovation it was when it was first introduced. It made both the captains and the sponge merchants rich but, ironically, the increased consumption of sponges also brought upon the downfall of the industry. The seabed was stripped bare to meet commercial demands. *Caïques* had to go farther and farther to find sponges. Today, sponge fishing is a dying art but there are many Greeks fishing for sponges in Tampa Springs, Florida and a fleet of *caïques* can still be seen setting out from the Kalymnian harbour for six months of sponge fishing on St Yeorgos's day.

Island of Revelations: If Délos, the holy island in the Cycládes, was the sacred place of worship for the ancients, its modern equivalent must surely be **Pátmos**. Pátmos has been a place of pilgrimage ever since the discovery that this small, rocky island is the place where St John the Divine is said to have dictated the text of Revelations to his pupil Prochoros in AD 95.

Greek Orthodox tradition identifies St John with the Apostle John although this has never been proven. Nevertheless, in AD 1088 the monk Christodoulos Latrenos founded a great, fortified monastery in honour of St John, and it has been a place of scholarship and religious enlightenment ever since. At Easter and on the saint's day, 21 May, the faithful flock to its shores to worship and give thanks. Pátmos is included on summer itineraries out of Piraeus, but a convenient approach is via Kos, which has an airport. Pátmos is less than two hours away by hydrofoil (*Flying Dolphin*) in season.

Although the island is no longer ruled by monks, their presence, along with the fortress which looms into view at almost every turning, tempers the rowdier elements found in most holiday resorts. There is no nudist beach on the island. Tourists are much in evidence, but those who elect to stay (as opposed

Skála port and the bay of Pátmos.

to those who arrive by hydrofoil from Kos or Rhodes) appreciate the unique, even spiritual, atmosphere which Pátmos exudes. Conversations in the cafés tend to be elevated, night sounds are muted, and many people return season after season to enjoy what one resident calls "the classical life".

Skála is the main harbour, best appreciated late at night when crickets serenade and the sailboats are illuminated against a dark sky. The lights of Chóra on the hill above are indistinguishable from the stars. A few paces from the sea lies a tiny cemetery. Its symmetrical tombstones, when lit by candles, provide a ghostly spectacle.

In the daytime Skála loses charm but gains in efficiency; all island commerce is here, from shops to banks to ferryboat agencies. Buses leave regularly from the main square for Chóra and the monastery. Bearded priests in long, hot cassocks vie for seats with sandalled and shorts-clad tourists; the priests, familiar with the tussle, usually win.

Halfway between Skála and Chóra is

the **Cave of the Apocalypse**. A silver band marks the spot in the wall where St John is supposed to have composed Revelations; just at the mouth of the grotto is a great cleft in the rock through which the voice of God spoke. This small, immaculate monastery is largely the province of one aged monk, who will gladly conduct you to the grotto. Light a candle here and make a small donation for the upkeep of the church.

The bus stops again at the monastery terrace where there is an unrivalled view of the Aegean. On a cloudless day it is possible to see, not only nearby Sámos, Ikaría, Kálymnos and Léros but also the far away Cycládic isles Amorgós, Páros, Náxos and Mýkonos.

Chóra, 40 minutes by foot uphill, is one of the most beautiful traditional towns. Bulky and well built, the town huddles around a medieval castle.

Inside the castle is the famous **Monastery of St John the Theologian**, built at Chóra's highest point. A brooding fortress surrounded by defensive walls, just inside is a stall where monks sell illustrated guides. These are well worth buying for a comprehensive interpretation. Within one of its five chapels is the body of the Blessed Christodoulos, the monastery's founder, which lies in a marble sarcophagus. The Treasury houses the most impressive monastic collection in Greece outside Mount Athos; priceless icons and jewellery can be viewed, even handled, but only by special appointment.

Of invaluable importance to scholars is the Library, which contains 2,000 printed volumes. It, too, requires special permission to enter but the greatest treasure, 33 leaves of the *Codex Porphyrius*, embellished with gold and silver, can be seen in the public part of the Treasury. Written in the early 6th century on purple vellum, the book contains most of St Mark's gospel.

The silent, shuttered windows in many of Chóra's villas highlight the fact that they are privately owned by Athenians. For this reason rooms are hard to come by, but Chóra's discreet restaurants and, at night, silent, echoing streets are worth savouring. Taxis can be found for the return trip to Skála.

Left, monk from the Monastery of St John. Right, sponges for export.

CRETE

The soul of **Crete** lies in its mountains: the Díkti peaks to the east, Psiloritis in the centre, and the White Mountains to the west, including Páchnes (2,450 metres/8,020 feet), the island's highest point. Dramatic, savage, awesome, they have for centuries provided the metaphors for the embattled *palikária*, the warriors of Crete. The mountains recede or come closer, sometimes a translucent shimmering white, other times, a burnt umber. But they are omnipresent, and dominate, exemplifying the history and psychology of the ferociously proud and independent people of this "Great Island". If you want to know the "real" Crete, head for the mountain villages you see from the main coastal road, nestling in the foothills of the mountains and looking almost as if they had sprouted there.

Access to Crete is easy from April until early October, and not difficult outside these periods. Domestic flights within Greece are both plentiful and cheap; in the summer months, there are six flights a day from Athens to Irákleion, and four from Athens to Chaniá. But the most romantic way to arrive on Crete is on one of the many overnight ferries from Piraeus.

One can visit Crete at any time of the year as the winter is mild by British and American standards, and the south coast is always warm – it is only 320 km (200 miles) from the coast of North Africa. But the best seasons for many are spring and autumn. From the end of March until the end of June, Crete is breathtaking. It is pleasantly warm without the relentless heat which can characterise July and August. September and October are also temperate months, although a sudden downpour is not unusual in October. But these autumnal harbingers of winter blow themselves out in a day or two, and the sun soon returns.

Inaccessible past: Crete has always been divided into mountain, plain and coast. In previous centuries invaders

Preceding pages: Loutró, the ancient port of Phoenix.

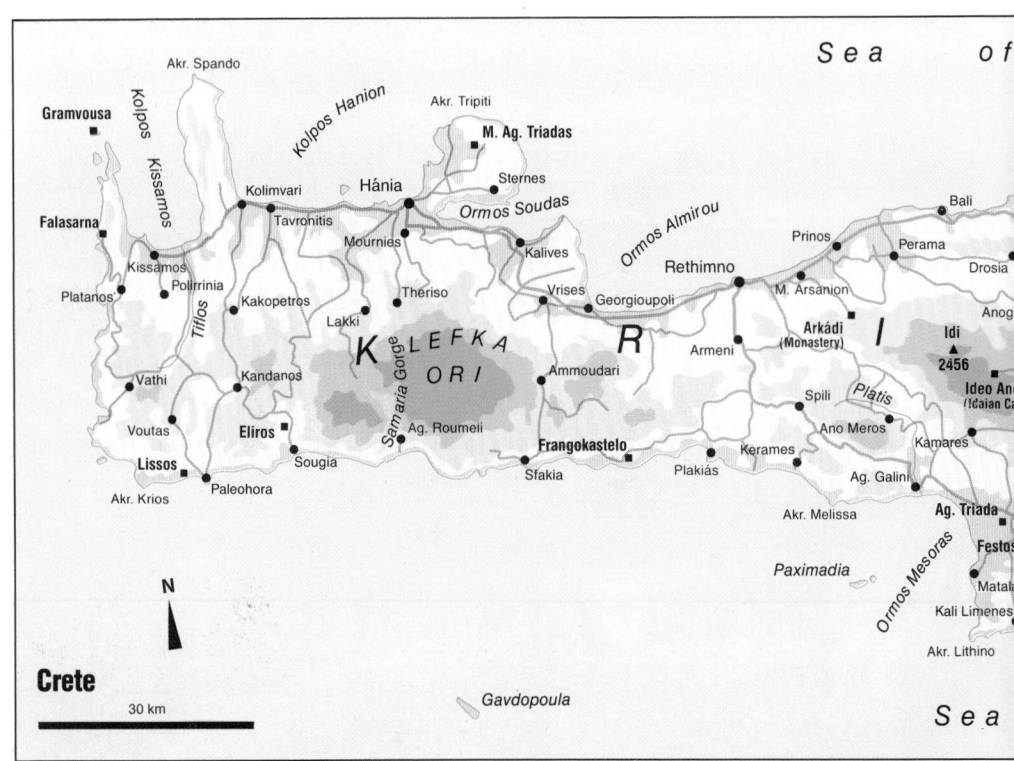

remained within the walls of their strategic coastal forts whilst the peasants in the outlying villages acknowledged a change of master. Less than 100 years ago, there were only 8 km (5 miles) of paved road on the entire island.

Tourism has changed many of the coastal villages throughout the island and encouraged people to move from more remote parts into the towns. Between a quarter and a third of the island's inhabitants now live in towns. But behind the statistics the old ties with the land linger on. In winter and summer the towns are more populous. Many people spend winter in the towns, and return to their upland villages in the spring. Some are attracted to the towns to work in the tourist industry during summer. During spring and autumn, people return to their villages for planting and harvesting, for most Cretans have some land, and all Cretans are emotionally close to the soil.

Once on Crete, the few major towns on the north coast, each the capital of its respective province, make good bases for exploring the island. Excellent networks of local bus routes fan out from each of these towns.

Irákleion is the largest town in Crete, and is noisy, bustling and dusty in the July heat. Until this century it was known as Cándia, the Venetian corruption of the Arabic *El Khandak*, "The Moat". It was given this name by the Arab marauders who seized it in 827. Its history is one of long and violent sieges. Byzantine admirals made repeated efforts to wrest it back from the Arabs before Nikephoros Fokas succeeded in 961, perhaps helped by his habit of catapulting the heads of Muslim prisoners over the city walls to break morale.

The Venetians had less trouble in capturing the town in the 13th century, but their rule was ended by one of the longest sieges in history. For 21 years the Turks besieged the town, kept out by the massive fortifications which had been erected in the previous century, before finally gaining control in 1669.

Today only isolated traces of their past remain. But there are two excellent

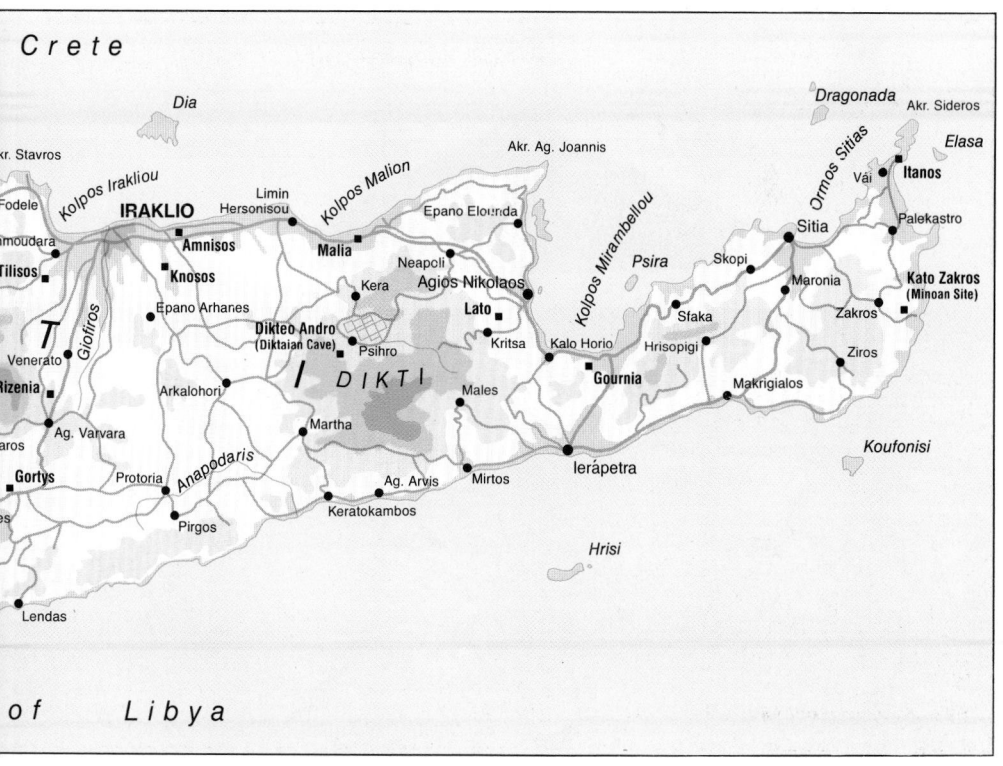

museums: the **Archaeological Museum**, whose vast collection from Knossós and elsewhere is the best introduction to Minoan Crete, and the **Historical and Folklore Museum**, filled with mementoes of the island's more recent past, as well as a well-displayed collection of textiles.

Just south of Irákleion (there are frequent buses) lies **Knossós**, the extensive late Minoan palace complex excavated and partially reconstructed by Sir Arthur Evans earlier this century. The site is well-known and usually crowded. For those who prefer their ruins untouched, there are several other Minoan settlements in this part of the island: **Festós** and **Górtyn**, to the south, and **Mállia**, to the east are all an hour's drive from Irákleion. Also in the vicinity is the **Church of Asómatos**, near **Acharnés**, with Byzantine frescoes, and the Byzantine church complex at Ardon.

Ághios Nikólaos is the most popular resort in Crete. It is a clean, well-organised tourist town, though bathing is surprisingly limited. Although it has become an international playground for the tour operators, it remains a good base for the adventurous visitor. The foothills of Mount Díkti are sprinkled with fine painted churches, including perhaps the best on the island – the **Church of the Panaghía Kéra**, with its superb Byzantine frescoes, at Kritsá. Nearby lie the deserted ruins of the Dorian city of Lató, just several hours' walk from Ághios Nikólaos.

A little further afield to the west is the windmill-studded Lassíthi plain, one of the most fertile areas of the island and worth visiting as an antidote to the tourist culture of the coastal towns. For a good day's swimming, leave Ághios Nikólaos and head south to the old port of Ierápetra from where you can catch a boat to one of the small coves that dot the south coast.

Frescoe road: From Irákleion there are two routes westwards to Réthymnon. You can follow the main road along the coast and through the foothills of **Mount Ída**. The bus does this regularly in just over two hours. Alternatively, if you

Beach in Irákleion.

have more time you can head south on the Dafní road. This brings you much closer to the overwhelming massif of Ida itself. Following the road which skirts the mountain, you come to the town of **Záros**, and just beyond that, two monasteries, **Vrondísi** and **Valsamónero**, which contain some of the most beautiful Byzantine frescoes in Crete. The road north to Réthymnon gives some idea of the rare beauty of the Cretan landscape. Below lie the lush orange groves of the Mérsara plain and high above on your right tower flanks of the mountain itself which remains capped with snow till well into May. From Plátanos the road winds through unspoilt country to emerge at Filákio at the head of a valley 24 km (15 miles) north of Réthymnon.

Réthymnon itself is an attractive, small port with an Oriental feel. When the Venetians took it over as a stopping-point for ships on the run between Chaniá and Irákleion its inhabitants were, largely, Greek Orthodox. Under Ottoman rule many people converted to Islam, as they did throughout Crete. These converts continued to speak Greek. By the 19th century the population was largely Muslim and even today the old town behind the Venetian harbour, with its narrow lanes and painted wooden houses with their over-hanging upper storeys, retains a Turkish air.

In 1923 most of Réthymnon's Muslim inhabitants were uprooted in the compulsory exchange between Greece and Turkey: their melancholy departure is described in the Cretan novelist Prevelákis's work *Chronicle of a City*. But the slender minarets which punctuate the Réthymnon skyline are a reminder of their presence. The Venetian harbour with its attractive waterfront restaurant, is a good place to eat, but it is worth exploring the back streets below the fortress where several less pretentious *tavérnes* are hidden away.

Chaniá is by far the most attractive of the provincial capitals. A bustling and vigorous town, Chaniá has a superb waterfront dominated by the Old Harbour, comprising a Venetian mole,

shipbuilding slip, lighthouse and fortifications. The town has an excellent range of hotels, pensions, *tavérnes*, and restaurants – and not all of them cluster round the Old Harbour, which tends to be more expensive. The **Kavoúriá Restaurant**, at the east end of the waterfront, is a good place to while away an evening, watching the lights reflected in the water, the local Greeks leisurely pursuing their evening *vólta*, or promenade, along with the tourists. The genial owner is an expert chef in both Greek and European cuisines, and can be patient in several European languages.

Chaniá has a superb market with small but seductive *tavérnes* where you can see the stall-owners and market-porters having an early lunch of fish soup or a roasted sheep's head. Chaniá is a town which infinitely repays a slow investigation on foot. The Kastéli quarter behind the Kavoúria is a maze of narrow, mysterious alleys, of starkly contrasted light and shade, of tiny artisans' shops and *ouzeriés*. Outside the houses, caged finches and linnets sing in the sun, while high above your head, housewives chat from their geranium-bedecked balconies only a few feet from each other.

Slightly farther out, in the **Chalépa** neighbourhood, there are many fine houses dating from the occupation of Crete by the Great Powers at the turn of the century. Here you can still find neoclassical villas which look for all the world as if they have been magically transplanted from Paris. Chaniá has – compared with Irákleion – a small but interesting archaeological museum, several art galleries, a surprisingly good public library, a municipal swimming pool and a beach. But an easy bus ride from the centre brings you to the more attractive beaches of **Kalamáta**, a few miles to the west of Chaniá, or to **Stavró**, to the east, on the Akrotíri Peninsula. The town also contains the central bus-station from Nomós Chaníon, the province of west Crete.

Mountain excursions: If you want to explore the mountain villages of this scenic province from Chaniá, you must first of all acquire a map and a bus

Chaniá port.

timetable. Here you encounter your first problem. The rural buses are quite properly scheduled to suit villagers, not tourists. Hence they tend to leave the outlying areas for Chaniá at about 6 or 7am, and return in the late afternoon. This is a nuisance. But remember that on Crete, taxis are plentiful and cheap, and cars can readily be hired. Take a taxi out early one morning to one of the villages – for example, **Thérisso**, about 18 km (11 miles) south of Chaniá. If you return the locals' greetings you may be asked to sit down for a glass of *tsighoudiá*, the local *rakí*. (*Rakí*, or *tsípouro*, is the Greeks' answer to "White Lightning". It is distilled from the skins of grapes after pressing.)

A word of advice: Cretans, even in the mountain villages, are inured to the sartorial eccentricities of tourists. But though they are used to women walking about in bikinis, or men in shorts, they do not approve, and at the very least, regard such people with amusement. Mountain villages are not the places for trendy and revealing beachwear. Dress-

ing with modesty will certainly make it easier to pass among the morally conservative people of the mountains.

From Thérisso a dirt road climbs up and contours along the mountains, heading initially south, then west. It passes through the tiny but impressively situated village of Zourvá, and drops down to the attractive village of Mesklá. Wear light sports shoes and always carry a sun hat, water and a picnic basket. This walk will take you no less than three or four hours at a slow pace but the views are splendid: the ramparts of the White Mountains tower above you to the south, split by dizzy ravines and small gorges as they tumble down precipitously to the foothills. To the north, there is extensive agricultural development among these hills, which are patterned like a patchwork quilt with small fields of wheat, olive-and orange-groves, vineyards and pasture.

On the outskirts of the villages you are likely to come across a curious bald circular patch, perhaps four to five yards in diameter, and rimmed by stones stuck

Cretan wildflowers.

vertically into the ground. This is an *alóni*, or threshing-ground, still used to this day in many of the villages. If you are about in the right season, you may be lucky enough to see a donkey being driven round and round the *alóni*, towing a heavy wooden sled over the grain. A couple of women sit on the sled with a pan and brush; their function is not immediately clear. Suddenly, however, amidst much laughter, they dart forward to catch the donkey's droppings before they get mixed up with the wheat!

Again, you may see a small group of women and children peering up into a tree and shouting encouragement and directions. As you approach, you may see the head of the household perched up the tree in his bare feet, knocking down walnuts with a long pole. The women below husk the green fruit with a knife, their hands stained dark brown from the natural dye of the husk which is also favoured by some women as the local substitute for henna. Inevitably, you will be offered a handful of walnuts.

In spring, Crete is garlanded with a seemingly limitless array of wild flowers, and the roadside meadows are ablaze with colour. You should easily be able to identify – by smell, if nothing else – the wild herbs such as mountain thyme, oregano and rosemary, which grow in clumps along the roadside. Birdlife, too, is rich; you will certainly see swooping flights of gold-finches, many kinds of warblers and buntings, and high up, planing on the thermals, you may see griffon vultures, or lammargeyer.

There are two areas which perhaps particularly repay exploration in west Crete. The first is the tangle of villages southeast of Chaniá and west of Vámos, west of the main road to Réthymnon: Frés, Tzitzifiés, Kiriakosélia, Mahéri. Secondly, there is the grouping south of Kastéli in northwest Crete: Vúlgaro, Kalathénes, Sfakopigádi, Horitianá. This area contains two interesting sites at **Poliriniá** and **Falasárna**. The small sleepy town of **Kastéli**, with its lovely beach, makes an ideal base for exploring this area. The monastery at Kolimbarión, with its impressive frescoes, and **Kastéli.**

Turkish cannonball embedded in its outer, seaward-facing wall, is easily accessible, and there is pleasant walking on both the Rodópou and Gramvoúsa peninsulas. A boat-trip to **Gramvoúsa Island** for swimming and a picnic makes an exciting and unusual excursion and, weather permitting, can be easily arranged in Kastéli. A longer trip, perhaps necessitating car hire for the day, is to the spectacular coral beach at **Lafóuissos** on the southwest tip of Crete. This is a truly beautiful spot, totally undeveloped, although there is a proposal to build a large hotel there. In the meantime, if going there, take a picnic and adequate water – there is no water supply in the neighbourhood.

No visit to west Crete would be complete without a visit to Omalós, and the Gorge of Samariá. The **Omalós** is an upland plateau characteristic of the limestone of the Cretan mountains. It is rimmed by mountains, and is perhaps 4 km (2½ miles) across, with the Gorge of Samariá starting from its southeast corner. This area was the very epicentre of

Worry-beads for the man; tree-pruning for the woman.

resistance against the Turks, celebrated in a famous Cretan ballad, roared out when mountain men are eating and drinking together:

When will the sun break out,
And when will February come,
That I can take my rifle,
My beautiful Patróna
And go down to the Ómalós...

Today, it is a tranquil place where potatoes are grown, and where the shepherds of villages like Lákki and Aghía Iríni bring their flocks for the summer grazing. Alas, a plethora of white concrete *tavérnes* is beginning to appear at the entrance to the plateau. The two or three modest *tavérnes* already in existence are more than capable of handling the current tourist traffic.

Most people hardly see the Omalós. They take a tourist or public bus up from Chaniá at about 6am to do the Gorge. Thus they miss the spectacular nature of the drive itself, which is undertaken in the dark. A better way is to take the day's last public service bus up to the Omalós, where you can spend the night

and enjoy its still beauty in the evening. The **Omalós Tavérna** is recommended – simple, clean rooms and good food; tel. 0821-93269. It is delightfully tranquil to sit outside the *tavérna* in the last hour of sunlight, looking south out over the Omalós, watching the face of the mountains glow in the evening sun, and being slowly mesmerised by the sound of sheep's and goats' bells.

The "Wooden Steps": In the morning, you can be up early to catch the first bus to Ksylóskalo the "wooden steps" – the abrupt start of the **Gorge of Samariá**. A word of warning: while there is a well-made path all the way down the gorge, and while there is plenty of water, and while first aid facilities are available at the deserted village of Samariá in the park ranger's house, wear something sensible on your feet. At the very least, sneakers are necessary. Avoid strapless slip-on sandals and stiletto heels.

The view from the top of the "wooden steps" is spectacular. Directly opposite you is the massive crenellated face of **Gíngilos** (2,083 metres/6,834 feet). Although it is hardly credible from this position, the summit is easily accessible along a well-marked path… to the experienced *and* properly-equipped mountain-walker only. (For information on this and other mountain-walking routes, contact the Greek Alpine Club hut at Kallérghi, above the Omalós, or the author of this piece via the travel agency given in the Travel Tips section.) The gorge is a National Park; the route through it is 18 km (11 miles) long, and the park authorities have done an efficient job of fencing the path, providing water- and rest-stops, and information boards. It is impossible to get lost. Start early to give yourself time.

Coastal visits: When you finally leave the gorge on the south coast, you may well be surprised at the intensity of the heat. As you head into the sea for that well-deserved swim, beware: the stony beach is red-hot. The village where you end up, **Ághía Roúmeli**, is an unlovely place designed only to hoover money from as many tourists as possible. But one can sympathise with the villagers'

Left, Chóra Sfakíon. **Below**, lunchtime blues.

need to make money while the sun shines – Aghía Roúmeli is a desolate and deserted spot in winter. Take the first ferry-boat out, and go to the idyllic coastal village of **Loutró**, along the coast to the east. Loutró, the ancient port of Phoenix, surrounded by interesting and picturesque ruins, used to be a fishing village; now it subsists totally on tourism. However, as it is very small, there is an absolute threshold to the number of tourists it can absorb. But it is still a lovely spot, ideal for lotus-eating, swimming and idle contemplating. The water around Loutró is crystal-clear, because there is a layer of fresh-water over the sea-water.

A short hour's walk to the west brings you to an attractive deserted pebble beach. A small *tavérna* not far away supplies cold drinks and basic food. You can leave Loutró by boat, or preferably, walk east along the coast on a clearly marked path until you come to Chóra Sfakíon.

Sunshade on a Cretan bus. **Chóra Sfakíon** serves principally as the boat/coach interchange point for tourists coming down the gorge. But there is an attractive walk from there, along the coast road to **Frankokástelo**, about 12 km (7 miles) away. Here, there is superb swimming in a lagoon under the ruined but still impressive ramparts of a Venetian castle. This road passes through several east Sfákiot villages which, although not particularly impressive in themselves, *are* working villages where many traditional agricultural and pastoral activities persist.

From Frankokástelo, it is easy to return to Chaniá by bus via Chóra Sfakíon, while, for the more adventurous, a walking trip can be made inland on clearly marked paths, either to the village of **Kalikratés**, or up the **Gorge of Imbrós**, on a smaller scale than that at Samariá, and much less known, but equally spectacular. A little elementary map-reading is necessary for either of these expeditions, plus some help from the locals. Exit from both places is possible by public bus.

While on the south coast, those who like boat-trips have the option of hop-

ping between Chóra Sfakíon, Loutró, Aghía Roúmeli, Soughiá and Paleochóra. Indeed, this route is strongly recommended for those who are not into walking. These trips afford unbeatable views of the southwest coast of Crete, where the mountains drop dramatically into the sea. It is a stunning, and at times – particularly in the evening – a slightly sinister coastscape; the sense of profound depth in the sea is inescapable.

Every now and then you will see a small white church nestling close to the sea, or perched upon a high promontory. It is a feature of rural Greek Orthodox churches that they are frequently constructed on sites with good views – and often, water.

If you are in one of these coastal villages and you see a church high above, it is well worth the effort to find the way there – there is bound to be a path. There is a chapel above the long beach at Paleochóra, for example, which gives a complete panorama out over the peninsula. Some of these chapels, for example the one at Anídri, an hour on foot northeast of Paleochóra, have fine Byzantine frescoes dating from the 14th or 15th centuries. Resist the temptation to take flash photographs; this exacerbates the process of deterioration.

"The Cretan bus": This is not the kind of big coach which makes the regular runs east–west along the main road in the north of the island, or to the popular tourist destinations such as Chóra Sfakíon, Ksylóskalo, or Paleochóra. Instead these are the much smaller sturdier, and more battered village buses which make the run into Chaniá in the early morning and out again in the afternoon. The driver and conductor are usually regulars, often residents of the village in question. The bus takes passengers, of course; but it also takes an amazing range of parcels and boxes, and the mail, and carries messages and gossip up and down the district.

Although there is a timetable, there are infinite minor variations in its operation, and the bus is more likely to go when full rather than exactly at the appointed hour. So the way to outwit the driver is to check the departure time on the big destination board in the main bus-station; then ask for the *number* of the bus at the information desk (displayed on a round sticker on the windscreen – never mind what is said on the bus's destination-indicator); then find that bus, and watch it like a hawk! These rural buses, however, are a safe and reliable way to travel, and afford a unique opportunity to meet locals.

Food: Restaurant fare is by and large very good. But one must distinguish between "tourist-Greek-food", and food which the Cretans eat in the villages. In the former case, dishes such as *moussaká*, stuffed tomatoes and aubergines, *stifádo*, *taramosaláta* and so on are common and excellent. But these are not daily foods in the villages. Villagers eat what is in season, so their food, while wholesome, often lacks variety. In winter and spring, snails and *hórta* are common; the latter means up to 35 different kinds of wild "greens".

Cretan snails are widely favoured outside Greece as well as by locals, and many are exported to France. They – and dishes such as chicken and braised meat – are often served with a *piláfi* of rice cooked in the fat and juices of the meat. It is delicious.

All meat, of course, is cooked in olive oil. Roasted sheep's heads are common, and are eaten down to the bone: flesh, brains, tongue, and eyes. Another popular dish is *kokorétsi*, a very tasty sausage-shaped dish made of roasted lambs' intestines and giblets.

All kinds of lamb are eaten: boiled, roasted, stewed; including the liver, of course. A common proverb in the mountains of Crete says that the best tasting mutton is that which is stolen. It is all cooked in plenty of oil, and always, always served with bread. Similarly, wine is drunk with all meals but never on its own. Bottled wine is distrusted intensely; locals drink their own draught red wine, which is of good quality, having a slight "afterburn" like sherry.

Off the south coast of Crete, many fishermen use dynamite. The sea is terribly overfished. Fishing with dynamite, although prohibited, continues with predictably tragic consequences.

Right, the Samariá Gorge. Overpage, an Athenian interior.

INSIGHT GUIDES
Travel Tips

FOR THOSE
WITH MORE THAN
A PASSING INTEREST
IN TIME...

Before you put your name down for a Patek Philippe watch *fig. 1*, there are a few basic things you might like to know, without knowing exactly whom to ask. In addressing such issues as accuracy, reliability and value for money, we would like to demonstrate why the watch we will make for you will be quite unlike any other watch currently produced.

"Punctuality", Louis XVIII was fond of saying, "is the politeness of kings."

We believe that in the matter of punctuality, we can rise to the occasion by making you a mechanical timepiece that will keep its rendezvous with the Gregorian calendar at the end of every century, omitting the leap-years in 2100, 2200 and 2300 and recording them in 2000 and 2400 *fig. 2*. Nevertheless, such a watch does need the occasional adjustment. Every 3333 years and 122 days you should remember to set it forward one day to the true time of the celestial clock. We suspect, however, that you are simply content to observe the politeness of kings. Be assured, therefore, that when you order your watch, we will be exploring for you the physical—if not the metaphysical—limits of precision.

Does everything have to depend on how much?

Consider, if you will, the motives of collectors who set record prices at auction to acquire a Patek Philippe. They may be paying for rarity, for looks or for micromechanical ingenuity. But we believe that behind each $500,000-plus

bid is the conviction that a Patek Philippe, even if 50 years old or older, can be expected to work perfectly for future generations.

In case your ambitions to own a Patek Philippe are somewhat discouraged by the scale of the sacrifice involved, may we hasten to point out that the watch we will make for you today will certainly be a technical improvement on the Pateks bought at auction? In keeping with our tradition of inventing new mechanical solutions for greater reliability and better time-keeping, we will bring to your watch innovations *fig. 3* inconceivable to our watchmakers who created the supreme wristwatches of 50 years ago *fig. 4*. At the same time, we will of course do our utmost to avoid placing undue strain on your financial resources.

Can it really be mine?

May we turn your thoughts to the day you take delivery of your watch? Sealed within its case is your watchmaker's tribute to the mysterious process of time. He has decorated each wheel with a chamfer carved into its hub and polished into a shining circle. Delicate ribbing flows over the plates and bridges of gold and rare alloys. Millimetric surfaces are bevelled and burnished to exactitudes measured in microns. Rubies are transformed into jewels that triumph over friction. And after many months—or even years—of work, your watchmaker stamps a small badge into the mainbridge of your watch. The Geneva Seal—the highest possible attestation of fine watchmaking *fig. 5*.

Looks that speak of inner grace *fig. 6*.

When you order your watch, you will no doubt like its outward appearance to reflect the harmony and elegance of the movement within. You may therefore find it helpful to know that we are uniquely able to cater for any special decorative needs you might like to express. For example, our engravers will delight in conjuring a subtle play of light and shadow on the gold case-back of one of our rare pocket-watches *fig. 7*. If you bring us your favourite picture, our enamellers will reproduce it in a brilliant miniature of hair-breadth detail *fig. 8*. The perfect execution of a double hob-nail pattern on the bezel of a wristwatch is the pride of our casemakers and the satisfaction of our designers, while our chainsmiths will weave for you a rich brocade in gold *figs. 9 & 10*. May we also recommend the artistry of our goldsmiths and the experience of our lapidaries in the selection and setting of the finest gemstones? *figs. 11 & 12*.

How to enjoy your watch before you own it.

As you will appreciate, the very nature of our watches imposes a limit on the number we can make available. (The four Calibre 89 time-pieces we are now making will take up to nine years to complete). We cannot therefore promise instant gratification, but while you look forward to the day on which you take delivery of your Patek Philippe *fig. 13*, you will have the pleasure of reflecting that time is a universal and everlasting commodity, freely available to be enjoyed by all.

Should you require information on any particular Patek Philippe watch, or even on watchmaking in general, we would be delighted to reply to your letter of enquiry. And if you send us

fig. 1: *The classic face of Patek Philippe.*

fig. 4: *Complicated wristwatches circa 1930 (left) and 1990. The golden age of watchmaking will always be with us.*

fig. 6: *Your pleasure in owning a Patek Philippe is the purpose of those who made it for you.*

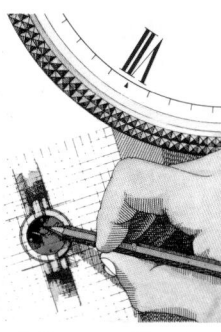

fig. 9: *Harmony of design is executed in a work of simplicity and perfection in a lady's Calatrava wristwatch.*

fig. 2: *One of the 33 complications of the Calibre 89 astronomical clock-watch is a satellite wheel that completes one revolution every 400 years.*

fig. 5: *The Geneva Seal is awarded only to watches which achieve the standards of horological purity laid down in the laws of Geneva. These rules define the supreme quality of watchmaking.*

fig. 7: *Arabesques come to life on a gold case-back.*

fig. 10: *The chainsmith's hands impart strength and delicacy to a tracery of gold.*

fig. 8: *An artist working six hours a day takes about four months to complete a miniature in enamel on the case of a pocket-watch.*

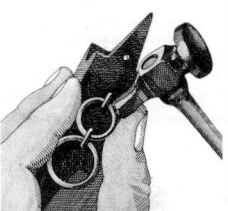

fig. 11: *Circles in gold: symbols of perfection in the making.*

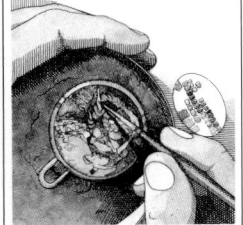

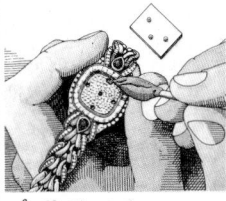

fig. 12: *The test of a master lapidary is his ability to express the splendour of precious gemstones.*

fig. 3: *Recognized as the most advanced mechanical regulating device to date, Patek Philippe's Gyromax balance wheel demonstrates the equivalence of simplicity and precision.*

PATEK PHILIPPE
GENEVE
fig. 13: *The discreet sign of those who value their time.*

Reality check. Call home.

—— *AT&T USADirect® and World Connect®. The fast, easy way to call most anywhere.* ——

Take out AT&T Calling Card or your local calling card.** Lift phone. Dial AT&T Access Number for country you're calling from. Connect to English-speaking operator or voice prompt. Reach the States or over 200 countries. Talk. Say goodbye. Hang up. Resume vacation.

Austria*†††......022-903-011	Luxembourg.........0-800-0111	**Turkey***..........00-800-12277
Belgium*..........0-800-100-10	**Netherlands***.........06-022-9111	**United Kingdom**..........0500-89-0011
Czech Republic*..........00-420-00101	**Norway**..........800-190-11	
Denmark..........8001-0010	**Poland**†◆¹..........0◊010-480-0111	
Finland..........9800-100-10	**Portugal**†..........05017-1-288	
France..........19-0011	**Romania***..........01-800-4288	
Germany..........0130-0010	**Russia***†(Moscow)..........155-5042	
Greece*..........00-800-1311	**Slovak Rep.***..........00-420-00101	
Hungary*..........00◊-800-01111	**Spain**●..........900-99-00-11	
Ireland..........1-800-550-000	**Sweden**..........020-795-611	
Italy*..........172-1011	**Switzerland***..........155-00-11	

AT&T
Your True Choice

For a free wallet sized card of all AT&T Access Numbers, call: 1-800-241-5555.

Getting Acquainted

Area: 131,950 sq. km (50,950 sq. miles), including 25,050 sq km (9,670 sq miles) of islands
Population: 10 million.
Capital: Athens.
International Dialling Code: 30 (Athens: 1)
Time Zones: Greek time is two hours ahead of Greenwich Mean Time. The clock is advanced one hour during summer to give extended daylight hours.
Geography: Mainland Greece is made up of Attica, the Peloponnese, Thessaly, Epirus, Macedonia and Thrace. Its backbone is the Pindos Range, and the highest mountain is Olympus, home of the ancient gods, at a height of 2,917 m (9,570 ft).

The coast is a series of so many coves and inlets that it runs to 15,000 km (9,320 miles), and the Mediterranean reaches its deepest point at the 4,850 m (15,912 ft) Oinousa Pit off the south coast of the Peloponnese.

The hundreds of islands that spill out into the Mediterranean are divided into groups: the Ionian islands to the west, the Sporades to the east and the Cyclades and Dodecanese running out southeast from Athens. The two largest islands are Rhodes and Crete, an island famous for its variety of flowers, though the flora of all Greece is remarkable.

Climate

The Greece seen in tourist posters is a forever warm and sunny place. And it is, by European standards, warm and sunny. But this picture does not do justice to the considerable climatic variety. The north and inland regions have a modified continental climate, so the winters are quite cold and summers very hot. In Ioánnina and Thessaloniki, for example, snow and freezing temperatures are not uncommon.

In the mountain regions, winters are even more inclement. The southern islands, most of the Peloponnese and the Attic Peninsula conform more to the traditional Mediterranean image: a long season of sun and warmth extending roughly from mid-April to mid-October. But here, too, the winters are cool and rainy.

In general, late spring (April–June) and fall (September–October) are the best times to visit. During these periods, you will find mild to warm temperatures, sunny days and fewer tourists. In July and August you will find Greece at its sultriest and most crowded. Still, millions of tourists seem to prefer the heat and the company, choosing this period for their holiday in Greece.

Seasonal averages (Min–Max):
January–March
6–16°C (43–61°F)
April–June
11–29°C (52–84°F)
July–September
19–32°C (66–90°F)
October–December
8–23°C (46–73°F)

People

Although nearly half the country's population lives in Athens, the city is often called a village. The Greek people do not seem to have moved far from their village roots, in spite of the depopulation in the countryside which has been a serious problem as young people move away. Thessaloníki, the second-largest city and a university town, has a population of 720,000.

The main religion is Greek Orthodox and the literacy rate 95 percent.

Economy

About 23 percent of the land is arable, and the country produces fruit, vegetables, olives, olive oil, grain, cotton and tobacco. Its natural resources include the minerals bauxite, lignitre and magnesite, and there is crude oil and marble. Some 20 percent of the 4 million labour force works in mining and manufacturing, producing textiles, chemicals and food products. Shipping is still an important source of revenue. The GDP is around $60 billion

In 1991 Greece became the 10th member of the European Union.

Government

Greece is a republic with a president, elected by parliament, who holds ceremonial executive power. The parliament has a single chamber made up of 300 elected members and led by the prime minister.

King Constantine went into exile following the dictatorship in December, 1967, and the monarchy was abolished after a referendum held after the collapse of the dictatorship in 1974. Since then three main parties have established themselves: New Democracy (ND, conservative), PASOK (socialist) and KKE (communist).

What To Pack

If you visit Greece during the summer months, you will want to bring lightweight, casual clothing. Add a sweater or jacket to this and you will be prepared for the occasional cool night breezes. Lightweight shoes and sandals are ideal for Greece in the summer, but you will also want to bring a pair of comfortable, already broken-in walking shoes. If you plan to do any hiking in the mountains or on the islands, bring lightweight hiking shoes. A hat or scarf is also highly recommended for protection from the intense midday sun.

In general, both Greeks and tourists dine in casual dress. You will only need formal dress if you plan to go to fancy establishments, casinos, formal affairs, etc. If you visit Greece during the winter months, bring the same kind of clothes you would wear during spring in the northern part of the United States or central Europe: that is, be ready for rainy, windy days and temperatures ranging between 3°C–16°C (40°F–60°F).

While in Greece be aware of the social significance of the way you dress, and of how the Greeks perceive it. Greece, like any other country, has a set of codes, both stated and implicit, which define the socially acceptable range of attire. The Greeks will not expect you as a tourist to dress as they do. In certain places and regions, however, you will encounter requirements or conventions concerning the way you dress. To enter a church, men must wear long trousers, and women, sleeved dresses. Often these will be provided for you at the church entrance if you do not have them. Not complying with this code will be taken as insulting irreverence on your part.

Nude bathing is another activity which merits discretion. Nude bathing is legally sanctioned on very few Greek beaches, though socially acceptable on many. The main rule-of-thumb is this: if it is a secluded beach and/or a beach that has become a commonly accepted locale for nude bathing, you probably wont be bothered by, nor offend, anyone.

Lastly, you may need to conform to the socially acceptable dress code depending on the region you are in. On Mykonos, for example, male and female tourists alike will shock no one by wearing shorts or a swim-suit in most public places. But this same apparel will be severely alienating if worn in a mountain village in Epirus or Crete or in any other area which is less accustomed to tourists. The best approach is to observe what people around you are wearing and to dress accordingly.

Entry Regulations
Passports and Visas

With a valid passport, citizens of the European Union, the United States, Canada, Australia and New Zealand can enter Greece and stay in the country for up to three months. No visa is necessary. To stay longer than three months, you must obtain a permit from the Aliens Bureau in Athens (9 Halkondili St, tel: 770-5711). Citizens of other countries should contact the nearest Greek embassy or consulate with regard to visa requirements.

Customs

According to Greek Customs you are allowed to bring into the country duty-free: all used personal belongings (clothes, camping gear, etc.); foodstuffs and beverages up to 10 kilos; 300 cigarettes or a comparable amount of tobacco; 1.5 litres of distilled spirits or 2 litres of still wine; and two packs of playing cards. Cards, like matches, are a Greek state monopoly.

You may also bring one of each of the following: a camera and film; a movie camera and film; a projector; a pair of binoculars; a portable musical instrument; a portable radio, phonograph or tape recorder; a bicycle; and sports gear (such as skis and tennis rackets).

You may bring $150 worth of new articles duty-free (excluding electronic devices), provided they are intended for your personal use or as gifts, but not for resale.

It is prohibited to import narcotics, medicine (except limited quantities prescribed by a licensed physician which is for your own use), explosives, weapons and (yes, that's right) windsurfers unless a Greek national residing in Greece guarantees they will be re-exported.

For other specific restrictions regarding the import and export of such things as animals, plants, shotguns, pleasure craft and antiquities, contact the nearest Greek embassy, consulate or Tourist Organisation.

Health

Greece has few serious diseases apart from those that you can contract in the United States or the rest of Europe. Citizens of the United States, Canada and United Kingdom do not need any health immunisations to enter the country.

Observe caution in rural areas, and thoroughly wash greens or vegetables: echinococcus is a hazard on unwashed lettuce. Also, in the islands, pit vipers are a problem in spring and summer. Be extra cautious, keep an eye out for snakes if you hike across country to distant beaches.

The drinking water in Greece is safe.

Currency

An unlimited amount of foreign currency and travellers cheques may be brought into Greece, as long as amounts over US$1,000 are declared. However, if you plan to leave the country with more than $500 (or an equivalent in other currency) in bank notes, you must declare that sum upon entry into Greece. Each traveller is permitted to import and export no more than 10,000 drachmas.

All banks and most hotels are authorised to buy foreign currency at the official rate of exchange fixed by the Bank of Greece. Though its safer to carry most of your currency in travellers cheques, it is also convenient to carry a limited sum in US dollars. On those occasions when you cant find a place to cash cheques, You will usually find a Greek who is interested in changing drachmas for dollars.

Credit cards: Many of the better established hotels, restaurants and shops accept major credit cards. The average pension or *tavérna* does not, however. Be sure to enquire before making your purchase.

Public Holidays

1 January: New Year's Day
6 January: Epiphany
Moveable: Feast of the Annunciation/Shrove Monday
25 March: Independence Day
1 May: Labour Day and Flower Festival **Moveable:** Good Friday
Moveable: (Orthodox Easter)
19 June: Pentecost
15 August: Assumption of the Holy Virgin
28 October: "Ohi" Day, National Holiday
25 December: Christmas Day
26 December: Boxing Day

Getting There
By Air

Greece has good air connections with all five continents and is serviced by numerous international airlines. Charter flights operate from mid-April to the end of October. There are ways of flying in at a much lower cost than the standard airline fares (apex, stand-by, last-minute seats or bucket shops, and you may want to familiarise yourself with the different possibilities, and their related advantages and disadvantages, before buying a ticket.

The great majority of airline passengers travelling to Greece make Athens Hellenikon Airport their point of entry. If you are flying with Olympic Airways you will arrive at the West Air Terminal. All other airlines service the East Air Terminal. Connecting the two terminals are taxi services and buses which depart every 20 minutes.

Between central Athens and Hellenikon there are various connecting services. A taxi ride from the West Terminal to Athens (Syntagma/Omonia) should cost approximately

550 drs. and will take roughly 30 minutes. From the East Airport, it should cost approximately 650 drs. and will take slightly longer. There's a fee of 40 drs. per bag as well.

The bus service is much cheaper and works well if you're not in a rush. Between the two terminals and Syntagma, Express Lines A and B bus run every 20 minutes for approximately 160 drs. (Every hour from midnight to 6 am, 200 drs.)

Between Piraeus and the East-West Terminals, Express Line No 19 runs to Akti Tzelepi, directly to the port centre for 160 drs. The same journey by taxi will cost up to around 1,000 drs.

By Sea

By far the majority of visitors entering Greece by sea do so from the west, that is from Italy. You can catch a boat to Greece from Venice, Ancona, Bari and Otranto, but the most regular service is from Brindisi. Daily ferry lines (somewhat less frequent in the low-season) connect Brindisi with the three main western Greek ports: Corfu, Igoumenítsa and Pátras. Corfu is a 9-hour trip; Igoumenítsa 11 hours; and Pátras 16 to 18 hours, depending on whether you take a direct boat or one that makes stops in Corfu and Igoumenítsa.

Igoumenítsa is the ideal port of call for those setting off to see central-western Greece. Pátras is best if you want to head directly to Athens or into the Peloponnese. Regular buses and trains connect Pátras and Athens (4 hours by bus). If you plan to take your car with you on the boat, you should definitely make reservations well in advance. Otherwise, arriving a few hours before the departure time should suffice, except during peak seasons when booking in advance is essential.

Italy and the west, however, are by no means the only provenance for Greece-bound sea travellers. Southward, boats connect Alexandria and Piraeus once every 10 to 15 days; eastward, boats run weekly between Haifa, Limassol and Piraeus, and once every five days between Vólos, Cyprus and Syria, not to mention the numerous crossing-points between the East Aegean Islands and the Turkish coast; northward, frequent boats connect Piraeus and Istanbul, and in the summer boats run twice a month between Odessa (Ukraine) and Piraeus.

By Land

From Europe: The overland route from northwestern Europe to Greece is a long one some 1,900 miles from London to Athens. It has always been a rather arduous and impractical travel option if you're just trying to get to Greece for a brief holiday, the fighting in former Yugoslavia has made it even less attractive, but it is still viable. Check with the your local Greek tourist office or motoring organisation for the latest information before leaving.

There is also the option of making use of the inexpensive bus services, like the famous Magic Bus, which connect Athens and Thessaloniki with many European cities a three and a half day trip from London. The various trains you can take from northwest Europe will take about as long as the bus, cost considerably more, but may get you to Greece feeling more intact. Hitching to Greece is also a possibility, though hitching through former Yugoslavia is inadvisible.

From Asia via Turkey: If you are travelling to Greece from Asia you will pass through Istanbul and cross into Greece at the Evros River. The recommended route is by car or bus. The road is good and the journey from Istanbul to Thessaloniki takes approximately 15 hours; various bus companies run the route.

The train has the mythic appeal of following the route of the old Orient Express, but unless you're a great train fan, the travel time may be prohibitive: some 25 hours. The Thessaloniki–Istanbul trip crosses the fascinating region of Thrace: a fine adventure if you have the time and the spirit to hitchhike through it.

Tourist Offices Abroad

Australia & New Zealand
Greek National Tourist Organisation, 51-57 Pitt St., Sydney N.S.W. 2000 (tel. 241-1663/4).
Canada
1233 Rue De La Montagne Montreal, Quebec H3G 1Z2, Canada (tel. 514-871-1535, tlx. 05560021).
80 Bloor Street, Suite 406 Toronto, Ontario M5S 2V1 Canada (tel. 416-968-2220, tlx. 06218845).
United Kingdom: Greek National Tourist Organisation, 195-197 Regent St., London WIR 8DR (tel. 0171 734-5997, tlx. 21122).
United States
Head Office, Olympic Tower, 645 Fifth Ave., 5th Floor, New York, New York 10022 (tel. 212-421-5777, tlx. 640125).
168 North Michigan Ave., Chicago, Illinois 60601 (tel. [312] 782-1084, tlx. 283468).
National Bank of Greece Building, 31 State Street, Boston, Massachusetts 02109 (tel. 617-227-7366, tlx. 940493).
611 West Sixth Street, Suite 1998 Los Angeles, California 90017 (tel. 213-626-6696, tlx. 686441).

The cable address of the tourist offices is GRECTOUR followed by the name of the city concerned.

Practical Tips

Emergencies

Pharmacies

In Greece there are certain pharmacies which are open outside normal shop hours and which work on a rotating basis.

If you need a pharmacy after hours or on weekends, you can find out which ones are open either by looking at the card posted in any pharmacy's window (which gives details on 24-hour pharmacies), or by consulting a local newspaper.

Hospitals

In case of a medical emergency requiring hospital treatment in Athens, call 166. If for some reason this fails, call the local Tourist Police (see listing below). They should speak English and will have information as to which hospitals have emergency facilities.

The Greek health system will be

bewildering to the foreign visitor who needs to make use of it, particularly in an emergency. Perhaps most important in emergencies is to find a competent speaker of both Greek and English who can make the necessary manoeuvrings for the patient's safety and inform you of what is going on.

If entirely helpless, call your embassy. US citizens can call the "emergency" number 721-2951 in Athens.

Greek Tourist Police:
Athens: Western Airport (01) 981-4093;
Eastern Airport (01) 969-9523
Aegina: (0297) 23-333
Agrínion: (0641) 23-381
Alexandroúpolis: (0551) 26-211
Argostóli (Cephaloniá): (0671) 22-200
Árta: (0681) 27-580
Aghios Nikólaos: (0840) 22-251
Chálki (Chalkidiki): (0221) 22-100
Chaniá: (0821) 24-477
Hios (Chíos): (0271) 23-211
Hydra: (0298) 52-205
Ikaria: (0275) 22-222
Ioánnina: (0651) 26-226
Irákleion: (081) 283-190
Itéa: (0265) 33-333
Kalamáta: (0721) 22-622
Kalambáka: (0432) 32-109
Kaména Voúrla: (0235) 22-425
Kassándra: (0374) 22-201
Kastoriá: (0467) 22-696
Kateríni: (0351) 23-440
Kavála: (051) 223-167
Kerkyra (Corfu): (0661) 39-503/30-265
Kimi: (0222) 22-200
Kíthnos: (0281) 31-201
Kórinthos (Corinth): (0741) 24-544
Kos: (0242) 22-444
Lamía: (0231) 22-431
Lárissa: (041) 227-900
Lefkas (Lefkáda): (0645) 92-696
Leros: (0247) 22-221
Loutra Edipsoú: (0226) 22-456
Loutra Kaiafa: (0625) 31-706
Loutra Kilínis: (0623) 41-213
Loutráki: (0741) 42-444
Missolóngi: (0631) 22-555
Methana: (0290) 92-463
Mytilíni: (0251) 22-776
Mykonos: (0289) 22-482
Namplion: (0752) 27-776
Náxos: (0285)22-100
Nea Moudania: (0373) 22-100
Olympía: (0624) 22-550
Párga: (0684) 31-222
Páros: (0284) 23-333

Pátras: (061) 220-902
Piraeus: (01) 4523-670
Pírgos: (0621) 23-333
Póros: (0298) 22-256
Préveza: (0682) 22-225
Réthymnon: (0831) 28-156
Ródos (Rhodes): (0241) 27-423
Samos (0273) 27-980
Sérres (0321) 64-033
Sitaía (Crete): (0843) 24-200
Skiathos: (0427) 21-111
Skyros: (0222) 91-274
Sparta: (0731) 26-239
Spétsai: (0298) 73-100
Spilaia Dirou (Máni): (0733) 522-000
Thássos: (0593) 22-500
Thessaloniki: (031) 522-589
Tínos (Andros): (0283) 22-255
Trípolis: (071) 222-265
Vólos: (0421) 27-094
Vouliagméni: (01) 8946-555
Xylókastro: (0743) 22-200
Zákynthos: (0695) 22-550

Electricity

220 AC is the standard household electric current throughout Greece. This means that appliances from the United States require converters, which are not available in Greece. Greek outlets and plugs are different from both American and most European types, so you'll probably need an adapter as well. It's best to purchase these items before your departure.

Business Hours

All banks are open to the public from 8am to at least 1pm Monday through Friday. Some banks close half an hour earlier on Fridays. In heavily visited areas, however, you may find banks open additional hours and on the weekends for currency exchange.

The schedule for business and shop hours is more complicated. Business hours vary according to the type of business and the day of the week. The main thing to remember is that businesses generally open at 8am and close on Mondays, Wednesdays and Saturdays at 2.30pm. On Tuesdays, Thursdays and Fridays most businesses close at 1.30pm and reopen in the afternoon from 5pm to 8.30pm.

You'll soon learn that schedules are flexible in Greece (both in business and personal affairs). To avoid disappointment, allow yourself ample time

when shopping and doing business. That way, you may also enter into the Greek spirit of doing business, in which a good chat can be as important as the matter of business itself.

Tipping

Most restaurants and *tavérnes* add a 15 percent service charge to the bill, so a tip is discretionary. When service has been particularly good, it is customary to leave around 100 drachmas at a *tavérna*, more at a restaurant, for the waiter.

Just as important as any such gratuity, however, is your appreciation of the food you eat. Greek waiters and restaurant owners are proud when you tell them you like a particular dish.

Media
Print

The many kiosks throughout the city generally receive British newspapers either late the same night (in Omonia Square) or, more usually, the next day. There are two home grown newspapers: the daily *Athens News* is of little use except for its classified ads and comic relief due to its fractured use of the English language; *Greek News Weekly* is published on Saturday night and is generally far more interesting and informative, with a regular What's On section, a more intelligible prose style and photographs.

The Athenian, Greece's English language monthly, is just that, with features covering Greek politics, topics of interest and the arts. Greece *Weekly* concentrates on business and finance and is sound in both areas. A mini-magazine, W*eek in Athens*, has been published for many years by the National Tourist Organisation of Greece, and is available at NTOG offices.

For those with more literary interests there is *The Southeastern Review: A Quarterly Review of the Humanities in the Southeastern Mediterranean*, available at Eleftheroudakis and Reymondos bookstores downtown and from *periptera* throughout the city.

Radio and TV Stations

ERT 1 and ERT 2 are the two Greek State radio channels. ERT 1 is divided into three different "programmes".

First (728 KHz) and Second (1385 KHz) both have a lot of Greek popular music and news, some foreign pop and occasional jazz and blues. Third Programme (665 KHz) plays a lot of classical music. ERT 2 (98 KHz) is much like the first two programmes.

News can be heard in English, French, German and Arabic on the First Programme at 7.40am every day of the week; in English twice a day on ERT 2 at 2pm and 9pm. The BBC World Service offers news on the hour (plus other interesting programmes and features). The best short wave (MHz) frequencies on which to pick up the BBC in Athens are: 3–7.30am GMT–9.41 (31 m), 6.05 (49 m), 15.07 (19 m); 7.30am–6pm GMT–15.07 (19 m); 6.30pm–11.15pm GMT–9.41 (31 m), 6.05 (49 m). United States Armed Forces Radio (AFRS) operates 24 hours a day on 1594 KHz and 1484 KHz with news on the hour.

There are two state-owned and operated television channels in Greece – ERT 1 and ERT 2. These channels often transmit American and English movies and programmes which, conveniently for the English-speaking viewer, are not dubbed, but rather carry Greek subtitles.

Postal Services

Greek post offices are officially open Monday to Friday from 7.30am to 7.30pm and on Saturday until 1pm. In practise, however, the hours are much more restricted. Certain sections within the post office, such as Registered Letters and Parcel Collection, may close as early as 1.30pm on weekdays. Some regional post offices are closed by mid-afternoon. So, if you want to get something done at the post office, it is advisable to do it in the morning.

Postal rates are subject to fairly frequent change, so you'll do best to inquire at the post office. Stamps are available at the post office, and from many kiosks (perptera) and hotels for a slight surcharge. If you want to send a parcel from Greece, remember not to wrap it until a post office clerk has inspected it. Some post offices will then provide you, for a fee, the necessary materials to wrap it up. Otherwise You will have to bring your own wrapping paper, string, scissors etc. If you're

sending home bought goods, get the store to do it for you. Sending a package from Greece can be an exasperating experience.

Letters can be sent Post Restante to any post office. Take your passport when you go to pick up mail.

Telecoms

Most kiosks have phones, and this is the most convenient way to make a local phone call. A call costs 10 drs. There are also coin phones, usually red, that may be found in coffee shops, hotels, restaurants and kiosks as well. And in certain places You will also find phone booths – the blue ones for local calls, the orange for long distance.

You can also make long distance calls from any one of the many kiosks which have metered phones. However, a call from a kiosk will cost somewhat more than from the state phone company, OTE. Still, sometimes getting to the local OTE is such a hassle that You will find the 15–20 percent additional charge worth it. Many hotels also have these metered phones.

Telegrams can be sent from the OTE. There are at least four different types of cables that you can send: the regular cable; the urgent cable which costs twice as much; the greetings telegram, again twice as much; and the letter telegram.

Most sizeable Greek towns and cities have an OTE office where you can make long distance calls and send telegrams. Some in the larger cities are open 24 hours, others from 7.30am to 11.30pm.

For a listing of the area codes of major Greek cities, see the Emergencies section, page 325.

Useful Addresses

If you would like tourist information about Greece before or during your trip, write, call or visit the nearest **Greek National Tourist Organisation** known as the **GNTO**, or **EOT** in Greece. There are 15 regional GNTO offices located across the country. The most complete GNTO is centrally located in Syntagma Square in Athens at this address:

EOT, Information Desk, National Bank of Greece, Syntagma Sq, 2

Karageorgis Servias St, (tel: [01] 322-2545, 323-4130).

The Greek Tourist Police, located in most large cities, can also be helpful in providing you with information about hotels and other services. They can also help you address a wide variety of travel-related questions and problems (see Emergencies section on the previous page).

For information and assistance related to motoring contact **ELPA**, the **Greek Automobile Association**, which grants the same help to members of home-country auto clubs as it does to its own members:

ELPA, 24 Messogeon St, Athens Tower B (tel. 799-1615) and 6 Ameriks St, near Syntagma (tel. 363-8632). It also offers tourist information on tel: 174.

Banks

GREEK
National Bank of Greece, 2 Karageorgi Servias St. (tel. 321-0411).
Commercial Bank of Greece, 11 Sophokleous St. (tel. 321-0911).
Ionian and Popular Bank, 45 Panepistimiou Ave. (tel. 322-5501).
Bank of Attica, 19 Panepistimiou Ave. (tel. 324-7415).
Bank of Greece, 21 Panepistimiou Ave. (tel. 320-1111).
Credit Bank, 40 Stadiou St. (tel. 324-5111).

OVERSEAS
American Express Bank, 31 Panepistimiou Ave. (tel. 323-5401).
Bank of America, 39 Panepistimiou Ave. (tel. 325-1901).
Bank of Novia Scotia, 37 Panepistimiou Ave. (tel. 324-3891).
Bankers Trust, 3 Stadiou St. (tel. 322-9835).
Barclays Bank, 15 Voukourestiou St. (tel. 364-4311).
Chase Manhattan, 3 Korai St. (tel. 323-7711).
Citibank, 8 Othonos St. (tel. 322-7471); Kolonaki Sq. (tel. 361-8619); 4749 Akti Miaouli Ave., Piraeus. (tel. 452-3511).
Grindlays Bank, 7 Merlin St. (tel. 362-4601); 15 Akti Miaouli Ave., Piraeus (tel. 411-1753).
Midland Bank, Kolonaki Square (British Council building) (tel. 364-7410); 93 Akti Miaouli Ave., Piraeus (tel. 413-6403).

Morgan Grenfell, 1920 Kolonaki Sq. (tel. 360-6456).

National Westminster Bank, 24 Stadiou St. (tel. 325-0924); 7 Merarhias St., Piraeus (tel. 411-7415).

Royal Bank of Scotland, 61 Akti Miaouli Ave., Piraeus (tel. 452-7483).

Airline Offices

Air Canada, 10d Othonos St. (tel. 322-3206).

Air France, 4 Karageorgi Servias St. (tel. 355-50957).

Air India, 15 Omirou St. (tel. 360-3584).

Alitalia, 10 Nikis St. (tel. 324-43838).

Austrian Airlines, 8 Othonos St. (tel. 323-08446).

British Airways, 10 Othonos St. (tel. 322-25215).

Canadian Pacific, 4 Karageorgi Servias St. (tel. 323-03447).

Cyprus Airways, 10 Filellinon St. (tel. 324-78013).

Egyptair, 10 Othonos St. (tel. 323-35757).

El Al, 8 Othonos St. (tel. 323-01168).

Finnair, 16 Nikis St. (tel. 325-52345).

Gulf Air, 23 Nikis St. (tel. 322-6684).

Iberia, 8 Xenofondos St. (tel. 324-55145).

KLM, 2 Karageorgi Servias St. (tel. 325-5041).

LOT, 4 Amalias Ave. (tel. 322-1121).

Lufthansa, 11 Vasilissis Sophias Ave. (tel. 369-2511).

Middle East Airlines, 10 Filellinon St. (tel. 322 69115).

Olympic Airways, 96 Syngrou Ave. (tel. 961-6161).

Sabena, 8 Othonos St. (tel. 323-6821).

SAS, 6 Sina St. (tel. 363-44479).

Singapore Airlines, 9 Xenofondos St. (tel. 323-91115).

South African Airways, 1214 Karageorgi Servias St. (tel. 322-9007).

Swissair, 4 Othonos St. (tel. 323-1871).

TAP, 3133 Voulis St. (tel. 325-1711).

Turkish Airlines, 19 Filellinon St. (tel. 322-0561).

TWA, 8 Xenofondos St. (tel. 324-4764).

UTA, 3133 Voulis St. (tel. 324-9300).

Varig, 10 Othonos St. (tel. 322-6743).

VIASA, 5 Mitropoleos St. (tel. 324-0233).

Virgin Atlantic Airways, 1214 Mitropoleos St. (tel. 323-0434).

Embassies

All embassies are open from Monday to Friday, usually from 8am until 2pm.

Australia: 37 Dimitris Soutsou St. (tel. 644-7303).

Canada: 4 Gennadiou St. (tel. 723-9511).

Cyprus: 16 Herodotou St. (tel. 723-7883).

Ireland: 7 Vasiliou Constantinou St. (tel. 723-2771).

New Zealand: 15 An. Tsoha St. (tel. 641-0311).

South Africa: 124 Kifissias Ave. (tel. 692-2125).

United Kingdom: 1 Ploutarchou St. (tel. 723-6211).

United States: 91 Vasilissis Sophias Ave. (tel. 721-2951).

Getting Around

Public Transport

By Air

Flying is considerably more expensive than travelling by boat, bus or train (two and a half times more on the average), though still cheap when compared to the price of domestic flights in other countries. The flight between Thessaloniki and Athens costs less than $50. You can book tickets at any Olympic office. Fare information and timetables are available at most NTOG offices and many hotels. For information and reservations by phone, call: 9616161.

By Road

A vast network of bus routes spreads across Greece, called KTEL. This is a privately-run syndicate of bus companies whose buses are cheap, generally punctual and will take you to almost any destination that can be reached on wheels. Among Greeks it's the most popular way of travelling, so you will have good company. KTEL buses often have a distinct personal touch. Many drivers also own the bus (or have some other familial stake in it), decorating and treating it with great care. They're proud of the bus and of the way they drive it.

The most important thing to note about KTEL is that in larger cities there will be different bus stations for different destinations. Travelling from Thessaloniki to Halkidiki, for example, you will leave from one station, and to Ioánnina, from another.

An additional bus service is that of OSE, the state railway organisation. This is a limited service and runs only the major routes.

City buses: Travelling by the regular Athens blue buses is a fairly miserable way of getting around the city. They are crowded and hot, and the routes are a mystery even to long-time residents. However, they are reasonable, at 50 drachmas per ticket. Tickets, good for trolleys as well, are sold in books of 10, from specific news kiosks and special booths at bus and metro stations, and at various non-strategic points around the city. Most bus services run until midnight.

Separate services run to air and sea ports, and these can be useful. The Express service of distinctive blue and yellow double-decker buses runs from Syntagma Square (on Amalias Avenue) to both airports at regular intervals: buy your tickets (100 drs) at the kiosk by the stop. The Green bus 040 runs from Filellinon Street (near Syntagma Square) to Piraeus 24 hours a day, every 20 minutes (every hour after 1am). The Orange bus runs from 14 Mavromateon St, Areos Park, and takes approximately 90 minutes.

Trolley buses: Though marginally more comfortable than the regular bus service, the yellow trolleys are not recommended for short-stay visitors as their routes are a mystery best left to the locals.

Taxis: On entry, ensure that the meter is switched on and registering 1 rather than 2, which is the rate between 1am and 5am. Don't be worried if you find yourself joined, en route, by a large cross-section of Athenian society going roughly your way. It is perfectly legal for drivers to pick up as many people as is comfortably possible, and charge them all individually.

During night hours, between 1am–5am, fares are roughly double the daytime rate.

There is a surcharge from airports, seaports, railway stations and bus terminals; passengers may also be charged a small fee for luggage.

By Rail

The best thing about rail travel in Greece is the price: it is even less expensive than taking the bus. Otherwise, the Greek rail service, known as **OSE**, is quite limited, both in the areas it reaches and frequency of departures. Greek trains are also quite slow and, unless you are doing the Athens–Thessaloniki run overnight in a couchette, you will probably find the bus more convenient.

You can speed things up by taking an express train for a small surcharge. If you're on a tight budget you can really cut costs by taking the train round-trip, in which case there is a 20 percent reduction.

Metro: Due to extensive relics buried beneath the modern city, Athens does not have a comprehensive underground rail service. However, the one that exists runs between Piraeus and Kifissiá, is clean, reliable, and connects Piraeus with Monastiráki and Omonia. City centre stops are at Thisseon, Monastiráki, and Omónia. Tickets are the same as those used on buses and trolleys, and are available at the stations.

By Sea

It is hard to imagine a trip to Greece without a boat trip. Nearly every island in the Greek seas can be reached by one kind of boat or another, be it a large car ferry, small passenger boat or fisherman's *caique*.

Ferries: Piraeus is the nerve centre of the Greek ferry network, and chances are you will pass through it at least once. In general, you can get information on ferries at the port police (in Piraeus and most other ports), known as the *limenarhío* in Greek, at most NTOG offices and at certain travel agents. The *limenarhío* has the most complete and up-to-date information. The NTOG bureau in Syntagma Square in Athens offers a weekly schedule which should be checked for accuracy.

And when you inquire at a travel agent, be aware that they sometimes will inform you only of the ferry lines with which they are affiliated. In the high season the routes are numerous and it is worthwhile looking around before purchasing your ticket. It is also advisable not to purchase your ticket too far in advance of the boat's scheduled departure: very rarely do tickets for the boat ride actually sell out; more frequently there will be changes in schedules and you are left trying to get a refund. It is also possible to buy tickets on board and though it is sometimes more expensive, it is a last-minute alternative.

When you board your vessel in Piraeus, be sure you are on the right boat. With the number of last-minute changes, delays etc., it is possible to get on a boat headed to some other destination, or one not stopping at your chosen island.

All the above invokes this suggestion: be flexible when travelling the Greek seas. Apart from schedule-changes, a bad stretch of weather can keep you island-bound for as long as the wind blows. Strikes, too, occasionally are called during the summer, usually lasting a few days. However, when they do occur, there is usually advance notice given in the news media.

If you are travelling by car, especially during the high season, you will have to plan somewhat further ahead because during the peak season, some lines are booked for many weeks in advance. Also, if you want to book a room for an overnight trip during the high-season, its wise to book ahead. Otherwise *gamma* class – also known as deck, tourist, or third – is the classic, cheap way to voyage the Greek seas. There is always a space of one sort or another – in community with an international multitude, singing with a guitar, passing a bottle around under the stars. And if the weather turns bad you can always go inside to the lounge, the snack bar or some quiet hallway corner.

Hyrdofoil: At the other end of the naval spectrum, you will find scheduled hydrofoil service to certain islands on the *Flying Dolphins*. These connect Piraeus with most of the Argo-Sarónic region (Aegina, Póros and many other ports, as far as Monemvasia), as well as Vólos with

the Northern Sporades (Alónissos, Skiáthos, Skópelos etc.).

This is the executive way to island hop. The hydrofoils are more than twice as fast as ferries and twice as expensive. You will get there quickly but unless you get one of the few available spaces aft, you will have to weather the bumpy ride in a seat inside. Flying Dolphins: 69 Akti-Miaouli. Tel: 453-6107/4; fax 453-5403.

Having a car in Greece enables you to get to a lot of otherwise inaccessible corners of the country. As a tourist you will be able to drive for up to four months without having to pay Greek road taxes. When you enter the country with your car it will be written into your passport. This entry will state that you are not allowed to leave the country without your car. If for some reason you want to leave without your car, you are obliged to have it sealed and withdrawn from circulation before your departure. *Warning*: this process can be very complicated and time-consuming, and a real problem if you have to leave in a rush.

It is recommended that visiting foreign motorists have an international driver's licence (available through the auto club in your home country, or in Greece from ELPA, the Greek Automobile Touring Club).

Greek traffic control and signals are basically the same as in the rest of continental Europe. However, the actual practice of Greek driving has little in common with driving in Frankfurt or Oslo. Translate Zorba on wheels, if you will. A red light is often considered not so much an obligation as a suggestion. Greece has the highest accident rate in Europe after Portugal, so – drive defensively. Also, Greece has a mandatory seat belt law. If you don't wear one, you risk getting tagged with a considerable fine.

Cars: Renting a car in Greece is relatively expensive in comparison with other European countries. Prices vary according to the type of car, season, and length of rental and do not include local taxes and duties which can add to about 18 percent of the bill. Payment can generally be made with major credit cards. An International Driver's Licence (see above) is required and you must be at least 21 years old.

A few recommended firms in Athens are: Hertz (tel. 922-0102/03/04); Avis (tel. 923-8822 or 922-3760); Hellascars (tel. 323-3487). You can also make reservations through the Association of Car Rental Enterprises in Athens, 314 Syngrou Av., Kéallithea (tel. 951-0921). If you are a member of your home country's automobile club, chances are you're automatically granted full services from ELPA. For information call: 779-1615 (in Athens).

Motorcycles, Bicycles, Scooters: On most Greek islands and in many mainland tourist areas, you'll find agencies that rent small motorcycles, bicycles and various types of scooters. On the islands these are certainly the way to go. For a reasonable price, they give you the freedom to wander where you will. For longer periods, rates are cheaper. Before you set off, make sure the bike of whichever sort works.

Ask to take it for a test spin down the street. Otherwise you may get stuck with a lemon or, worse, they may hold you responsible for its malfunctioning when you return it. Above all, be extremely careful. More than one holiday in Greece has been ruined by the bumps, scratches and bruises of a moped accident.

Private Taxi Transfer Service: Affable Athenian cabbies are few and far between, and the inconvenience and sheer aggravation of finding a taxi in the city have given rise to private taxi services. One of the best may be contacted through Julie Hardenberg and Sylvia Rill, at tel: 323-2870 or 325-1176. This fleet of roomy, air-conditioned Mercedes and Volvos is available 24 hours to transport visitors to the airports, Rafína, Pireaus... anywhere at all.

Private guided tours of Athens' sites, daytrips, *bouzoúki* evenings, and shopping jaunts may all be arranged by phoning in advance. Drivers will even carry your luggage in to the check-out counter at the airport.

Cruises

If you would like to leave the planning and sailing and cooking in someone else's hands, then a cruise may be just the thing you want. A score of different Aegean Sea cruises are available, some limited to Greek territory, other ranging as far as Venice and Port Said. Their length also varies considerably, from a one-day jaunt in the Argosaronic Gulf to a 14-day tour of the eastern Mediterranean. The names of cruise companies offering Mediterranean and Greek Island cruises are listed below. For more information see a travel agent.

Cruise Companies: Chandris Cruise; Cycladic Cruises; Epirotiki Lines; K Lines-Hellenic Cruises; Hellenic Mediterranean Lines; Intercruise LTD.; Mediterranean Sun Lines; Sun Line Cruises; Viking Yacht Cruises.

Yacht Charter

Chartering a yacht is one of the more exotic ways of island-hopping in Greece. It is by no means cheap, although renting a boat with a group of friends may not far exceed the price of renting rooms every night for the same number of people.

Depending on your nautical skills and your taste for autonomy, you can either take the helm yourself or let a hired crew do so for you. There are over 1,000 yachts available for charter in Greece, all of which are registered and inspected by the Ministry of the Merchant Marine. For more information about chartering contact:

The Greek Bareboat Yacht Owners' Association, 56 Vas. Pavlou St., Kéastlla-Piraeus (tel. 452-5465).

The Hellenic Professional Yacht Owners' Association, 43 Freattydos St., Za Marina, Piraeus (tel. 452-6335).

The Greek Yacht Brokers and Consultants' Association, 36 Alkyonis St., P. Phliron, Athens (tel. 981-6582).

Fishing Boats

Apart from the major network of ferries there is also a whole informal sub-network of fishing boats that can get you to smaller, more remote islands. Sometimes, these boats cater to tourists, advertising their services in the harbour. Other times, if your destination is especially obscure, you will have to ask around.

Where To Stay

How To Choose

The most widespread type of accommodation in Greece is the pension or cheap hotels, where you can still find a decent room at reasonable rates. Besides these, there is also a wide range of other possibilities, from the deluxe hotels to pension rooftops. Listed are a sampling of different categories of hotels in Athens and Thessaloniki. The abbreviations referred to are single bed (Sglb) double bed (Dblb) suites (Stes), and renovated (Ren).

On the islands and in many parts of the mainland, another kind of cheap lodging is renting private rooms (*domátia*). These are rented out by local residents at prices controlled by the tourist police.

In general, when looking for any kind of accommodation, the Tourist Police can be of considerable help. If you're in a fix, you can inquire at their office. If you'd like to make a reservation or arrangement in advance, call them and they'll often be able to help you out (see listing in the *Emergencies* section page 325).

Hotels

Athens

DELUXE

Acropole Palace, 51, Patission St., 104 33 Athens (tel. 5223851-7, tlx. 21-5909). Built 1930, Ren 1981. Number of rooms: Sglb 40, Dblb 47, Stes 18. Air-conditioned throughout, has 2 bars, restaurant, roof garden, night club, convention facilities, transfer service also available from several points in Athens.

Amalia, 10, Amalias Ave., 105 57 Athens (tel. 3237301-9, tlx. 21-5161). Built 1961. Number of rooms: Sglb 6, Dblb 92, Stes 1. Air-conditioned throughout, central heating, bar, restaurant.

Astir Palace, Vass. Sophias & El. Venizelou corner, 106 71 Athens, Syntagma Sq. (tel. 36443112 [8 lines], tlx. 22-2380, Cbl. Astirathen). Built 1983. Number of rooms: Sglb 10, Dblb 38, Stes 28, VIP Stes 2. Fully air-conditioned, 4 channel audio system in all rooms and public areas, Apokalypsis gourmet restaurant, Asteria coffee shop, Athos bar, all rooms with TV and video, news-stand, sauna, health care, beauty parlour, conference and banquet facilities.

Athenaeum Inter-Continental, 89-93, Syngrou Ave., 117 45 Athens (tel. 9023666, tlx. 22-1554). Built 1982. Number of rooms: Dblb 630. Air-conditioned throughout, central heating, 2 bars, 3 restaurants, swimming pool, convention facilities with simultaneous translation in 4 languages and closed circuit TV, automatic dialling, colour TV in all rooms with in-house movies, secretarial service, valets, health studio, bank facilities.

Athens Chandris Hotel. 385, Syngrou Ave., 175 64 P. Phaleron (tel. 941-4824-6, tlx. 21-8112, Cbl. Chandrotel-Athens). Built 1977. Number of rooms: Sglb 50, Dblb 300, Stes 22. Air-conditioned throughout, central heating, 2 bars, 2 restaurants, Four Seasons Restaurant, á-la-carte also for non-residents, coffee shop, room service, conference rooms, ballroom, swimming pool snack bar restaurant, parking facilities, free shuttle service between Hotel-Syntagma Sq.

Athens Hilton, 46, Vass. Sofias Ave., 106 76 Athens (tel. 7220201-9, tlx. 21-5808, Cbl. Hiltels). Built 1963, Ren 1974. Number of rooms: Dblb 480, Stes 24. Air-conditioned throughout, 3 bars, 5 restaurants, swimming pool, convention facilities, secretarial service, auto dress cleaning.

Athens Holiday Inn, 50, Michalakopoulou St., 115 28 Athens (tel. 7248322-29, tlx. 21-8870). Built 1979. Number of rooms: Dblb 200. Air-conditioned throughout, central heating, American bar, restaurant, coffee shop, discotheque, bowling, meeting and banqueting facilities up to 500 persons, parking, Bistro Greek.

Caravel, 2, Vass. Alexandrou Ave., 161 21 Kessariani (tel. 7290721-29, 7290731, tlx. 21-4401). Built 1975. Number of rooms: Sglb 100, Dblb 316, Stes 55. 3 bars, 3 restaurants, roof garden, indoor & outdoor swimming pools, room service, 24-hour coffee shop, all hotel operations fully computerised, conference facilities,

conventions and other professional group events, near business and sightseeing centre.

Grande Bretagne, Syntagma (Constitution) Sq., 105 63 Athens (tel. 3230251-9, 3250701-9 [72 lines], tlx. 21-9615, 21-5346, Cbl. Hotbritan). Built 1862, Ren 1962, Refurbished 1981. Number of rooms: 450 rooms, plus 25 suites from Junior to Presidential. Air-conditioned throughout, central heating, 2 bars, 3 restaurants, 24-hour room service, convention & function facilities.

Ledra Marriott Hotel-Athens, 115, Syngrou Ave., 117 45 Athens (tel. 9525211, tlx. 22-1833, Res. direct line 9324642). Built 1983. Number of rooms: 258, Stes 25. All rooms with individual climate control, air-conditioning, radio, colour TV, in-room movies, minibar, 24-hour room service, direct dial telephone with message light, rooftop swimming pool, hydrotherapy pool, bar, coffee shop, cocktail and lobby lounge, poolside bar, 3 restaurants, conference rooms, ballroom, pre-function space outside ballroom, audiovisual equipment.

Park, 10, Alexandras Ave., 106 82 Athens (tel. 8832711-19, tlx. 21-4748, Cbl. Parxente). Built 1976. Number of rooms: Sglb 15, Dblb 111, Stes 20. Air-conditioned thoughout, central heating, coffee shop, pizzaria, roof garden, swimming pool, congress hall, room service gift shop, beauty parlor, garage.

N.J.V. Meridien Athens, Vass, Georgiou A & Stadiou sts., 105 64 Athens, Syntagma Sq. (tel. 3255301 [9 lines], tlx. 21-0568, 21-0569). Built 1980. Number of rooms: Sglb 30, Dblb 124, Stes 28. Air-conditioned throughout, central heating, bar, restaurant, room service, all rooms with mini bar, colour TV & video.

Royal Olympic, 28, Diakou St., 117 43 Athens (tel. 9226411-13, 9220185, tlx. 21-5753, Cbl. Roytel). Built 1968. Number of rooms: Sglb 35, Dblb 262, Stes 8. Air-conditioned throughout, central heating, bar, restaurant, room service, convention facilities, transfer service is available.

St. Geroge Lycabettus 2, Kleomenous St., Dexameni, Kolonaki, 106 75 Athens (tel. 7290711-19, tlx. 21-4253, Cbl. Mantzotel). Built 1973. Number of rooms: Sglb 21, Dblb 128, Stes 5. Air-conditioned throughout, central heat-

ing, bar, restaurant, room service, swimming pool, bank and convention facilities, roof garden, hairdressing, grill room with panoramic view to Acropolis.

CATEGORY A

Astor, 16, Kéar. Servias St., 105 62 Athens (tel. 3255555, 3255111, tlx. 21-4018, Cbl Hotelastor). Built 1964, Ren 1983. Number of rooms: Sglb 32, Dblb 98, Stes 3. Air-conditioned throughout, central heating, bar, restaurant, room service.

Attica Palace, 6, Kéar. Servias St., 105 62 Athens (tel. 3223006-8, Res 3237905, tlx. 21-5909). Built 1962. Number of rooms: Sglb 9, Dblb 69. Air-conditioned throughout, central heating, bar, restaurant, room service, snack bar.

Divani-Zafolia Palace, 19-23, Parthenonos St., 117 42 Athens (tel. 9229650-9, 9229151-5, tlx. 21-8306, Cbl Dizafotel). Built 1977. Number of rooms: Sglb 27, Dblb 159, Stes 7. Air-conditioned throughout, central heating, bar, restaurant, *tavérna*, swimming pool, convention facilities.

Electra Palace, 18, Nikodimou St., 105 57 Athens (tel. 3241401-7, tlx. 21-6896). Built 1973. Number of rooms: Sglb 20, Dblb 100. Air-conditioned throughout, central heating, bar, restaurant, room service, swimming pool.

Golden Age, 57, Michalakopoulou St., 115 28 Athens (tel. 7240861 [9 lines], tlx. 21-9292, Cbl Goldenage). Built 1975. Number of rooms: Sglb 18, Dblb 96, Stes 8. Air-conditioned throughout, central heating, bar, restaurant, cafeteria, *tavérna* and room service.

King Minos, 1, Pireos St., 105 52 Athens (tel. 5231111-18, tlx. 21-5339). Built 1964, Ren 1980. Number of rooms: Sglb 56, Dblb 122. Fully air-conditioned, central heating, bar, restaurant, room service, convention facilities, transfer service available.

Olympic Palace, 16, Filellinon St., 105 57 Athens (tel. 3237611, tlx. 21-5178, Cbl Olpallas). Built 1960, Ren 1965. Number of rooms: Sglb 26, Dblb 70. Air-conditioned throughout, central heating, bar, restaurant, room service, convention facilities.

CATEGORY B

Acadimos, 58, Akademias St., 106 79

Athens (tel. 3629220-9). Built 1962, Ren 1975. Number of rooms: Sglb 19, Dblb 104. Central heating, bar, restaurant, room service.

Acropolis View, 10, Galli & Webster sts., 117 42 Athens (tel. 9217303-5, tlx. 21-9936). Built 1971. Number of rooms: Sglb 3, Dblb 20. Air-conditioned throughout, central heating, bar restaurant, roof garden.

Adrian, 74, Adrianou St., 105 56 Athens (tel. 3250454, 3221553, 3250461). Built 1962, Ren 1976. Number of rooms: Sglb 22. Air-conditioned throughout, central heating, bar, roof garden.

Alfa, 17, Chalkokondyli St., 104 32 Athens (tel. 5243584-7). Built 1960, Ren 1984. Number of rooms: Sglb 9, Dblb 79. Central heating, bar, restaurant, room service.

Arethusa, Metropoleos & Nikis sts., 105 63 Athens (tel. 3229431-9, tlx. 21-6882). Built 1971. Number of rooms: Sglb 16, Dblb 72. Air-conditioned throughout, central heating, bar, roof garden, restaurant, room service.

Athens Center Hotel, 26, Sofokleous & Klisthenous sts., 105 52 Athens (tel. 5226110-19, tlx. 21-4488, Cbl Centerotel). Built 1976. Number of rooms: Sglb 13, Dblb 123. Air-conditioned throughout, central heating, bar, restaurant, roof garden, room service, parking facilities.

Athens City, 232 Patission St., 112 56 Athens (tel. 8629115-6). Built. 1985. Number of rooms: Sglb 6, Dblb 31, Stes 3. 40 bedrooms & stes. with 2 channel music, also rooms with TV & video, bar, air-conditioned, snack bar, 24 hours room service.

Athinais, 99, Vass. Sophias Ave., 115 21 Athens (tel. 6431133, 6441815, 6461682, 6431240, tlx. 21-9336, Cbl Athinotel). Built 1976. Air-conditioned throughout, central heating, bar, snack bar, restaurant, roof garden, room service.

Atlantic, 60, Solomou St., 104 32 Athens (tel. 5235361-6, tlx. 21-5723). Built 1960, Ren 1972. Number of rooms: Sglb 41, Dblb 117. Air-conditioned only in double rooms, central heating, bar restaurant, room service.

Balascas, Liossion & Epirou sts., 104 39 Athens (tel. 8835211-5, tlx. 21-0618). Built 1978. Number of rooms: Sglb 14, Dblb 69. Air-conditioned throughout, bar, restaurant.

Christina, 15, Petmeza & Kéallirois

sts., 117 43 Athens (tel. 9215353-7, 9215342-4, tlx. 21-9304). Built 1975. Number of rooms: Sglb 13, Dblb 80. Air-conditioned throughout, has central heating, 2 bars, snack bar, restaurant.

Dorian Inn, 15-17, Pireos St., 105 52 Athens (tel. 5239782, 5231753-7, tlx. 21-4779, Cbl Hoteldorian). Built 1974. Number of rooms: Sglb 5, Dblb 112, Stes 29. Air-conditioned throughout, central heating, 2 bars, restaurant, room service, swimming pool, convention facilities, roof garden, direct dial telephone system.

El Greco 65, Athinas St., 105 52 Athens (tel. 3244553-7, tlx. 21-9682, Cbls Grecotel, Apriltd). Built 1958, Ren 1980. Number of rooms: Sglb 17, Dblb 75. Several rooms air-conditioned, central heating, bar, restaurant, room service, snack bar, cafeteria.

Eretria, 12, Chalkokondyli St., 106 77 Athens, Kéaningos Sq., (tel. 3635311 [10 lines], tlx. 21-5474). Built 1966 Ren 1980. Number of rooms: Sglb 7, Dblb 49, Stes 7. Air-conditioned throughout, central heating, bar, restaurant, room service, cafeteria.

Grand, 19, Patission St., 104 32 Athens (tel. 5243156-9). Built 1975. Number of rooms: Sglb 8, Dblb 91. Air-conditioned throughout, central heating, bar, restaurant, room service, convention facilities.

Ilissos, 72, Kéallirrois Ave., 117 41 Athens (tel. 9215371, 9223523-9, tlx. 21-0537). Built 1980. Number of rooms: Sglb 16, Dblb 80. Air-conditoned throughout, central heating, bar, restaurant, cafeteria, room service, convention facilities.

Ionis Hotel, 41, Chalkokondyli St., 104 32 Athens (tel. 5232311 [4 lines], 5230413 [4 lines], tlx. 21-8425, Cbl Ionishotel). Built 1977. Number of rooms: Sglb 10, Dblb 92. Air-conditioned throughout, central heating, 2 channel music in the rooms, bar, restaurant.

Palladion, 54, El. Venizelou Ave., 106 78 Athens (tel. 3623291-5). Built 1907, Renovated 1974. Number of rooms: Sglb 1, Dblb 57. Rooms air-conditioned, central heating, bar, room service.

Pan, 11, Metropoleos St., 105 57 Athens (tel. 3237817, tlx. 22-1911, Cbl Panhotel). Built 1960, Ren 1984. Number of rooms: Sglb 6, Dblb 46, Stes 8. Public rooms and most of

rooms air-conditioned, central heating, snack bar, room service.

Plaka, 7, Kéapnikareas St., 105 56 Athens (tel. 3222096-8, tlx. 22-1020. Cbl Plakotel Athens). Built 1960. Number of rooms: Sglb 11, Dblb 56. Air-conditioned throughout, has central heating, bar, restaurant, room service.

Titania, 52, El. Venizelou Ave., 106 78 Athens (tel. 3609611-9, tlx. 21-4673, Cbl Titanotel). Built 1976. Number of rooms: Sglb 42, Dblb 333, Stes 21. Rooms fully air-conditioned with private baths, radio music, TV sets on request, restaurant with Greek specialities and international dishes, snack bar, piano cocktail lounge Taboo in the roof garden, convention facilities, garage for 400 cars, shopping centre.

Xenophon, 340, Acharnon St. 111 45 Athens (tel. 2020310-24, tlx. 21-5294). Built 1970. Number of rooms: Sglb 22, Dblb 164. Air-conditioned throughout, central heating, bar restaurant, room service, convention facilities, garage, parking facilities, transfer service available.

CATEGORY C

Achilleus, 21, Lekka St., 105 62 Athens (tel. 3233197, 3225826).

Achillion, 32, Ag. Konstantinou St., 104 37 Athens (tel. 5225618).

Albyon, 20, Akominatou St., 104 37 Athens (tel. 5231137, 5223058).

Alma, 5, Dorou St., 104 31 Athens (tel. 5240858-9).

Ami, 10, Iras St., 117 43 Athens (tel. 9220820).

Apollon, 14, Deligiorgi St., 104 37 Athens (tel. 5245211, 5245214).

Arias, 20, Kéarolou St., 104 37 Athens (tel. 5228527-9).

Aristidis, 50, Sokratous St., 104 31 Athens (tel. 5223881, 5223923).

Artemission, 20, Veranzerou St., 104 32 Athens (tel. 5230524, 5230036, 5234959).

Astra, 46, Deligianni St., 104 39 Athens (tel. 8213772).

Athinea, 9, Vilara St., 104 37 Athens (tel. 5243884-5, 5245737).

Attalos, 20, Athinas St., 105 54 Athens (tel. 3212801-3).

Capri, 6, Psaromilingou St., 105 53 Athens Koumoundourou Sq. (tel. 3252085, 3252091).

Crystal, 68, Kolonou & Achilleos sts., 104 37 Athens (tel. 5231083).

Delph, 21, Ag. Konstantinou Sq., 104 37 Athens (tel. 5222751, 5226549).

Economy, 5, Klisthenous St., 105 52 Athens (tel. 5220520-2).

Elite, 23, Pireos St., 105 52 Athens (tel. 5221523, 5223610).

Epidavros, 14, Koumoundourou St., 104 37 Athens (tel. 5230421).

Evropa, 7, Satovriandou St., 104 31 Athens (tel. 5223081).

Fivos, 12, Petta St., 105 58 Athens (tel. 3220142-3).

Florida, 25, Menandrou St., 105 53 Athens (tel. 5223214, 5239712).

Helicon, 3, Dorou St., 104 31 Athens (tel. 5221695, 5228428).

Hera, 9, Falirou St., 117 42 Athens, Makriyanni area (tel. 9235618, 9236682).

Jason, 3, Nikiforou St., 104 37 Athens (tel. 5248031-3).

Imperial, 46, Metropoleos St., 105 63 Athens (tel. 3227617-8).

Kéalypso, 34, Epikourou St., 105 53 Athens (tel. 3251451-2).

Keramikos, 30, Keramikou & Iassonos Streets, 104 36 Athens (tel. 5247631, 5247443).

Kissos, 6, Mezonos St., 104 38 Athens (tel. 5243011-3).

Kronos, 18, Ag. Dimitriou St., 105 54 Athens(tel. 3211601-3).

Lido, 2, Nikiforou & Zinonos sts., 104 37 Athens (tel. 5248211-4).

Marina, 13, Voulgari St., 104 37, Athens (tel. 5224769, 5229109).

Medoussa, 4, Evripidou St., 176 74 Kéallithea (tel. 9426216).

Minion, 3, Mezonos St., 104 38 Athens (tel. 5234222-3).

Morfeus, 3, Aristotelous St., 104 32 Athens (tel. 5234601).

Museum, 16, Bouboulinas St., 106 82 Athens (tel. 3605611-3).

Nafsika, 21, Kéarolou St., 104 37 Athens (tel. 5239381-3).

Nefeli, 16, Hyperidou St., 105 58 Athens (tel. 3228044-5).

Neon Kronos, 12, Assomaton St., 105 53 Athens (tel. 3251106-8).

Nestorion, 8, Pentelis St., 174 64 Amphithea (tel. 9425010, 9420272, tlx. 22-1427).

Niki, 27, Nikis St., 105 57 Athens (tel. 3220913-5, 3220886).

Olympía, 25, Pireos St., 105 52 Athens (tel. 5222429).

Omega, 15, Aristogitonos St., 105 52 Athens (tel. 3212421-3).

Orpheus, 58, Chalkokondyli St., 104 32 Athens(tel. 5224996).

Parnon, Tritis Septemvriou & Chalkokondyli sts., 104 32 Athens

(tel. 5230013-14, 5235196).

Phedias, 39, Apostolou Pavlou St., 118 51 Athens (tel. 3459511-5).

Pringhipikon, 27, Veranzerou St., 104 32 Athens (tel. 5232376).

Rivoli, 10, Achilleos St., 104 36 Athens (tel. 5239714-6).

Roosevelt, 5, Favierou St., 104 38 Athens (tel. 5223413).

Sans Rival, 2, C. Paleologou & Liossion sts., 104 38 Athens (tel. 5248675, 5223431).

Stalis, 10, Akominatou St., 104 37 Athens (tel. 5241411-2).

Theoxenia, 6, Gladstonos St., 105 77 Athens (tel. 3600250).

Troikon, 20, Troias St., 112 57 Athens (tel. 8816695, 8217319).

Vienna, 20, Pireos St., 104 31 Athens (tel. 5225605-7).

Zinon, 3, Keramikou St., 104 37 Athens (tel. 5228811-13).

Thessaloniki

DELUXE

Makedonia Palace, Meg. Alexandrou St., 546 40 Thessaloniki (tel. 837520-9, 837620-9, tlx. 41-2162, 41-2164 Cbl Macepal). Built 1972. Number of rooms: Sglb 44, Dblb 228, Stes 15. Air-conditioned throughout, bar, restaurant, room service, congress facilities.

CATEGORY A

Capitol, 8, Monastiriou St., 546 29 Thessaloniki (tel. 516221, tlx. 41-2272). Built 1967. Number of rooms: Sglb 35, Dblb 152, Stes 7. Air-conditioned throughout, central heating, bar, restaurant, room service, convention facilities.

Electra Palace, 5a, Aristotelous Sq., 546 24 Thessaloniki (tel. 232221, tlx. 41-2590). Athens office: 5, Ermou St., (tel. 3232104). Built 1972. Number of rooms: Sglb 32, Dblb 93 Stes 6. Fully air-conditioned, central heating, bar, restaurant, grill room, room service, convention facilities.

Nepheli, 1, Komninon St., 552 36 Panorama (tel. 942002, 042024, 942068, 942080, tlx. 41-0357). Built 1967. Number of rooms: Sglb 10, Dblb 55, Stes 5. Partially air-conditioned, central heating, bar, restaurant, room service, roof garden, night club, convention facilities, parking.

Panorama, 14, Analipseos St., 552 36 Panorama (tel 941123, 941266, 941229). Built 1969. Number of

rooms: Sglb 12, Dblb 35 Stes 3. Central heating, bar, restaurant, room service, cafeteria.

CATEGORY B

Astor, 20, Tsimiski St., 546 24 Thessaloniki (tel. 527121-5, tlx. 41-2655). Built 1973. Number of rooms: Sglb 12 Dblb 72, Stes 6. Air-conditioned throughout, central heating, bar restaurant, parking facilities.

Capsis, 18, Monastiriou St., 546 29 Thessaloniki (tel. 521321-9, 521421-9, tlx. 41-2206, Cbl Capsotel). Built 1970. Number of rooms: Sglb 33, Dblb 395. Air-condition optional, central heating, bar, restaurant, room service, swimming pool, convention facilities, discotheque, hairdressing, sauna, dress cleaning.

City Hotel, 11, Komninon St., 546 29 Thessaloniki (tel. 269421-30, tlx. 41-2208). Built 1972. Number of rooms: 210 beds. Air-conditioned throughout, central heating, all rooms with telephone & verandah, bar, cafeteria, TV lounge.

El Greco, 23, Egnatias St., 546 30 Thessaloniki (tel. 520620-30). Built 1970. Number of rooms: Sglb 18, Dblb 72. Air-conditioned throughout, central heating, bar, restaurant, parking, automatic telephone service.

Metropolitan, Vass. Olgas & Fleming sts., 546 42 Thessaloniki (tel. 824221 [8 lines], tlx. 41-2380). Built 1979. Number of rooms: Sglb 12, Dblb 99, Stes 8. Stes air-conditioned, central heating, bar, restaurant, room service, olympic airways bus stop in front of the hotel, TV room, automatic outside telephone connection, parking facilities.

Olympía, Venizelou & 65, Olympou sts., 546 31 Thessaloniki, 12 km from the airport (tel. 235421 [5 lines], 263201 [5 lines], tlx. 41-8532, Cbl Olympotel). Ren 1980. Number of rooms: Sglb 15, Dblb 100. Air-conditioned throughout, central heating, bar, restaurant, cafeteria, fireplace, colour TV lounge, special halls for business or social events, car parking facilities.

Olympic, 25, Egnatias St., 546 30 Thessaloniki (tel. 522131-3). Built 1969, Ren 1975. Number of rooms: Sglb 13, Dblb 39. Central heating bar.

Palace, 12, Tsimiski St., 546 24 Thessaloniki (tel. 270505, 270855, 238838, 225368). Ren 1968. No. of rooms: Sglb 33, Dblb 25. Central heat-

ing, bar, restaurant, room service.
Philippion, Kedrinos Lofos, 5 km from the city centre (tel. 203320-22, tlx. 41-0210). Ren 1979. Number of rooms: Sglb 18, Dblb 70, Stes 2. Central heating, bar, restaurant, coffee-shop, mini golf, pizzearia, swimming pool, night club, disco.
Queen Olga, 44, Vass. Olgas Ave., 546 41 Thessaloniki (tel. 824621 [10 lines]). Built 1969. Number of rooms: Sglb 35, Dblb 113. Air-conditioned throughout, central heating, bar, restaurant, room service, parking facilities available.
Rotonda, 97, Monastiriou St., 546 27 Thessaloniki (tel. 517121-3, tlx. 41-2322, Cbl Hotel Rotonda). Built 1966. Number of rooms: Sglb 16, Dblb 63. Air-conditioned throughout, central heating, bar, restaurant, room service.
Victoria, 13, Lagada St., 546 29 Thessaloniki (tel. 522421-5, tlx. 41-2145). Built 1965. Number of rooms: Sglb 9, Dblb 58. Partially air-conditioned, central heating, bar, restaurant, room service.

CATEGORY C
ABC Hotel, 41, Agelaki St., Sidrivani Sq., 546 21 Thessaloniki (tel. 265421 [5 lines], 221761, 279765 tlx. 41-0056). Built 1968. Number of rooms: Sglb 15, Dblb 87, Stes 5. Partially air-conditioned, central heating, bar, cafeteria & breakfast room with fireplace and air-conditioning, suites with air-conditioning, colour TV, mini bar, balcony.
Aegeon, 19, Egnatias Ave., 546 30 Thessaloniki (tel. 522921-3).
Amalia, 33, Hermou St., 546 24 Thessaloniki (tel. 268321).
Anessis, 20, 26th October St., 546 27 Thessaloniki (tel. 515505-6).
Ariston, 5, Diikitiriou St., 546 30 Thessaloniki (tel. 519630).
Continental, 5, Komninon St., 546 24 Thessaloniki (tel. 516321-7).
Emborikon, 14, Syngrou St., 546 30 Thessaloniki (tel. 525560).
Park, 81, Ionos Dragoumi St., 546 30 Thessaloniki (tel. 524121-4).
Pefka, Panorama (tel. 941153, 941282).
Pella, 65, Ionos Dragoumi St., 546 30 Thessaloniki (tel. 524221).
Rea, 6, Komninon St., 546 24 Thessaloniki (tel. 278449).
Rex, 39, Monastiriou St., 546 27 Thessaloniki (tel. 517051, 517052).

Teleioni, 16, Ag. Dimitriou St., 546 30 Thessaloniki (tel. 527825-6).
Thessalikon, 60, Egnatias Ave., 546 27 Thessaloniki (tel. 277722, 223805).
Vergina, 19, Monastiriou, St., 546 27 Thessaloniki (tel. 527400-8).

Furnished Apartments
Athens
CATEGORY A
Ariane, 22, Tim. Vassou St., 115 21 Athens (tel. 6466361-2, 6437302-4).
Ava, 9, Lyssikratous St., 105 58 Athens (tel. 3236618).
Delice, 3, Vass. Alexandrou St., 115 28 Athens
Embassy, 15, Timoleontos Vassou St., 115 21 Athens (tel. 6421152-4).
Kolonaki, 7b, Kéapsali St., 106 74 Athens (tel. 7213759, 7228412).
Lion, 7, Evzonon St., 115 21 Athens (tel. 7248722-4).
Perli, 4, Arnis St., 115 28 Athens (tel. 7248794-8, tlx. 21-5444).

CATEGORY B
Egnatia, 64, Tritis Septemvriou St., 104 33 Athens (tel. 8227807).
Iokastis, House 65, Aristotelous St., 104 34 Athens (tel. 8226647).

Pensions
Athens
CATEGORY A
Blue House, 19, Voukourestiou St., 106 71 Athens (tel. 3620341).

CATEGORY B
Acropolis House, 6, Kodrou St., 105 58 Athens (tel. 3222344, 3244143).
Adams, 6, Herefontos & Thalou sts., 105 58 Athens (tel. 3246582, 3225381).
Adonis, Voulis & 3, Kodrou sts., 105 58 Athens (tel. 3249737, 3249738).
Akron, 16, Theras St., 112 57 Athens (tel. 8626220, 8626228).
Angela, 38, Stournara St., 104 33 Athens (tel. 5220216-7).
Antoniou, 232, Patission St., 112 56 Athens (tel. 8629841-2).
Apostolopoulos, 284, Patission & 5, Mistriotou sts., 112 55 Athens (tel. 2236375).
Aristofanis, 38, Aristophanous St., 105 54 Athens (tel. 3250872).
Athenian Inn, 22, Haritos St., 106 75 Athens (tel. 7238097, 7239552).

Athens House, 4, Aristotelous St., 104 32 Athens (tel. 5240539).
Byron, 9, Vironos St., 105 58, Athens (tel. 3230327).
Dryades, 4, Dryadon St., 114 73 Athens (tel. 3602961, 3622881).
Elisabeth, 46, Arkadias St., 115 27 Athens (tel. 7775448).
Elli, 29, Heyden St., 104 34 Athens (tel. 8823487).
Feron, 43, Feron St., 104 40 Athens (tel. 3632831-9, tlx. 21-5077).
George, 46, Nikis St., 105 58 Athens (tel. 3229569).
Heliki, 4, Enianos St., 104 34 Athens (tel. 8822560, 8810627).
Iokasti's House, 65, Aristotelous St., 104 34 Athens (tel. 8226647).
Iris, 8, Sorovits St., 112 52 Athens (tel. 8647442, 8653222, 8654229).
Kirki, 40, Kefalinias St., 112 57 Athens (tel. 8235733).
Kypseli, 7, Skyrou St., 113 61 Athens (tel. 8216232, 8213116, 8219898).
Lydia, 121, Liossion St., 104 45 Athens (tel. 8219980, 8237952, tlx. 21-9786).
Myrtc, 40, Nikis St., 105 58 Athens (tel. 3227237).
Nora, 38, Antiochias St., 112 51 Athens (tel. 8628876).
Odysseus, 39, Kimothois St., 172 36 Athens (tel. 9700571).
Oniro, 57, S. Trikoupi St., 106 83 Athens (tel. 8832731-3).
Patissia, 221, Patission St., 112 53 Athens (tel. 8627511, 8627512).
Pnyx, 51, Apostolou Pavlou St., 118 51 Athens (tel. 3468859).
Remvi, 284, Patission & 3, Mystriotou sts., 112 55 Athens (tel. 2024124, 2231405).
Roy, 15, Rodou St., 112 52 Athens (tel. 8615765, 8618763, 8610843).
Soudan, 47, Mavromichali St., 106 80 Athens (tel. 2605037).
Steyer, 123, Char. Trikoupi St., 114 73 Athens (tel. 3615731).
Volcan, 10a, Ithakis St., 113 61 Athens (tel. 8815385).
Zorba's, 10, Gylfordou St., 104 34 Athens (tel. 8232543).

CATEGORY C
Amazon, 7, Pendelis St., 105 57 Athens (tel. 3234002-6).
Annabel, 28, Koumoundourou & Satovriandou sts., 104 37 Athens (tel. 5243454).
Argo, 25, V. Hugo St., 104 37 Athens (tel. 5225939).

Art Galery, 5, Erechthiou St., 117 42 Athens (tel. 9238376).

Athens Connections, 20, Ioulianou St., 106 82 Athens (tel. 8213940).

Christ, 11, Apollonos St., 105 57 Athens (tel. 3220177, 3234581).

Diana, 3, Kotsika St., 104 34 Athens (tel. 8223179).

Dioskouros, 6, Pittakou St., 105 58 Athens (tel. 3248165).

Greca, 48, Syngrou Ave., 117 42 Athens (tel. 9215626).

Inn Student, 16, Kydathineon St., 105 58 Athens (tel. 3244808).

John's Place, 5, Patroou St., 105 57 Athens (tel. 3229719).

Kouros, 11, Kodrou St., 105 58 Athens (tel. 3227431).

Marble House, 35, An. Zini St., 117 41 Athens (tel. 9234058).

Milton, 4, Kotsika St., 104 34 Athens (tel. 8216806).

Paradise, 28, Mezonos St., 104 38 Athens (tel. 5220084).

Pella Inn, 104, Ermou St., 105 54 Athens (tel. 3250598).

Peters, 32, Nikis St., 105 57 Athens (tel. 3222697).

San Remo, 8, Nissirou St., 104 38 Athens (tel. 5243454).

Thesseus, 10, Thisseos St., 105 62 Athens (tel. 3245960).

Tonys, 26, Zacharitsa St., 117 41 Athens (tel. 9236370).

Thessaloniki

CATEGORY B

Athos, 20, Dagli St. (tel. 266990).

Elizabeth Motel, 293, Monastiriou St., 546 28 Thessaloniki (tel. 515712-3).

Haris Motel, Micra (tel. 417335).

Esperia, 58, Olympou St., 546 31 Thessaloniki (tel. 269321-5).

Haris, Oreokastron (tel. 696174, 696198).

Grande Bretagne, 46, Egnatias Ave., 546 25 Thessaloniki (tel. 530735).

Madrino, 2, Antigonidon St., 546 30 Thessaloniki (tel. 526321-5).

Minerva, 19, Syngrou Ave., 546 30 Thessaloniki (tel. 530844).

Oceanis, 35, Nik. Plastira St., Aretsou (tel. 418870).

Camping

Large numbers of tourists to Greece usually rough it in one form or another. Those who want to camp at organised camp-sites with facilities will find hundreds of them all over Greece, some run by the NTOG, some by the Greek Touring Club, and many privately.

The most beautiful camp-sites in Greece, however, are usually the ones you find on your own. While in most places it is officially illegal just to lay out your sleeping bag or pitch a tent, if you're discreet you will rarely be bothered. That means asking permission if you seem to be on private property, avoiding unofficial camp-sites set up in popular tourist areas, and always leaving the place looking better than when you came.

Youth Hostels

Greece has a number of youth hostels for which you need a youth hostel card. However, you can often buy one on the spot or just pay an additional charge. There are youth hostels in: Athens, Mycnae, Náfplion, Olympía, Pátras, Délphi, Litochoro, Thessaloniki, Corfu, Santoríni, and on Crete at Aghios Nikólaos, Chaniá, Irákleion, St. Basil (Réthymnon) and Sitía. There are also accommodations at the YMCA and YWCA in both Athens and Thessaloniki.

Monasteries

Monasteries and convents can often provide lodging as well for travellers. Mount Athos of course has a long tradition of this hospitality (for men). Certain other monasteries in Greece also welcome overnight visitors on a more informal basis. If you have found a monastery that does accept overnight guests, realise that you will have to dress (no shorts) and behave accordingly. The doors may close as early as sunset and some kind of donation may be expected.

Mountain Refuges

Mountain refuges are run by the various Greek mountaineering clubs and can range from a small 12-bed ski hut where you need to bring your own food and supplies to 100-bed lodges where all meals are provided.

Settlements

The traditional settlements are villages run by the NTOG and recognised by the Greek government as forming an important part of the national heritage. Buildings in these villages have been restored and set up by the NTOG for tourist use. At the moment, there are eight such villages with others to be restored and developed in the future. These houses and villages are, in their different ways, strikingly beautiful, and highly recommended for a week or month retreat in rural Greece. The NTOG traditional settlements are:

Kapetanákos Tower, Areópolis, Mán,. tel. (0733) 51233.

Papingo, Zagorohória, Epirus, tel. (0653) 25087/(0651) 25087.

Paradosiakós Ikismós Fiskárdou, Fiskárdo, Cephaloniá, Greece, tel. (0674) 51398.

Paradosiakós Ikismós Oías, Oía, Santoríni, Greece, tel. (0286) 71234.

Paradosiakós Ikismós, Mesta, Chíos, Greece.

Psará Island, tel. (0251) 27908.

Vizitsa (on Pélion Mountain), tel. (0423) 86373.

Xenia Hotel, Portaria Village, Makrinítsa (on Pélion Mountain),tel. (0421) 25922.

Reservations can be made either through the above addresses or by writing directly to: Greek National Tourist Organisation, EOT Dieftynisi Ekmetalefseos, 2 Amerikis Street, Athens 10564, Greece.

Eating Out

What To Eat

Eating out in Greece is above all a social affair. Whether it be with your family or your *paréä*, that sacred circle of friends, a meal out is an occasion to celebrate, a time for *kéfi*.

This may have something to do with the fact that eating out in Greece continues to be affordable and popular, not something restricted to those who have American Express cards. And the predominance of the *tavérna*, that bastion of Greek cuisine, reflects this popularity. These casual eating establishments have more or less the same style and set-up throughout Greece, and the menu is similar. Which is to say no frills, no packaging which tries to convince the consumer that this *tavérna* is different from the others, special, distinct. The place, and your being there, is somehow taken for granted: you eat the good food at Yanniss or Yorgos, you enjoy yourself, and you don't end up paying an arm and a leg for it.

This is the general background for eating out in Greece against which we find, of course, considerable variation. The *tavérna* is by no means the only kind of eating establishment. You will also encounter: the *stiatrio*, the restaurant as we usually think of it, fancier and more polished than the *tavérna*, with linen table-cloths and higher prices; the *psistari*, a barbecue-style restaurant which specialises in lamb, pork or chicken on a spit; the *psaro-tavérna* which specialises in fish; the *ouzerí* which is mainly an establishment for drinking, but which also serves *mezédes*, snacks of various types; the *gyros* stand with *gyro* sandwiches and the *souvlatzíthiko*, which is sometimes a sit-down place with salads.

There is also considerable regional variety in Greek cuisine and you should keep an eye out for those specialities of the house which you haven't seen before. Another thing you'll quickly learn in Greece is how strikingly different the same dish can be when it is prepared well or prepared badly, for example, a *Melitsanosaláta* or stuffed tomatoes. It is therefore worthwhile shopping around for your *tavérna* (especially in heavily visited areas), asking the locals what they suggest, walking into the kitchen to look at the food (a customary practice), instead of getting stuck with the tourist trap which spoils your appetite for *moussaká* for the rest of the trip.

Here are few notes about Greek eating habits. The main meal is eaten at midday, between 1.30pm and 2.30pm and is usually followed by a siesta break lasting until 6pm. The evening meal can either be another full meal, or an assortment of *mezéthes*. This is usually eaten between 9pm and 11pm. Breakfast in Greece is rather meagre, usually consisting of bread, butter, jam and coffee.

Some *tavérnes* you will find do not have menus, or have menus without prices. It is a good idea to inquire with the restaurateur how much things cost before you eat them. And, as mentioned above, you can always find out what dishes they serve by walking into the kitchen.

The list below is a partial listing of some of the more popular foods you will find on your travels.

Starter (Mezéthes)

Hors d'oeuvres and dips usually eaten as appetisers with *psomí* (bread):

Kolokithákia/deep-fried courgettes (zucchini)
Melitsánosálata/eggplant dip
rossikisaláta/cold potato salad with lots of mayonnaise
táramasaláta/fish roe pâté/dip
tzazíki/yoghurt/cucumber dip, heavily garlicked

Vegetables (Lahaniká)

angináres/artichokes
arakádes/peas
bámies/okra
dolmáthes/stuffed vine leaves
fasolákia/snap beans
horiátiki salta/olive, feta cheese, onion, cucumber and tomato salad
hórta/steamed wild greens
koukiá/horse beans
maróuli/lettuce
patzária/beets
yemistés/stuffed tomatoes or peppers
yígantes/large haricot beans

Various Meats (Kréata)

Note the following terms:
psitó/roasted
sti soúvla/barbecued on the spit
tiganitó/fried
sto forúno/baked
skáras/grilled
vrastó/boiled
kapnistó/smoked

arní/lamb
biftéki/beefsteak, ground beef patty
brizóla/chop (pork or beef) (*hirinó* or *mosxhári*)
keftédes/meatballs
kokorétsi/stuffed innards roasted on the spit

kotópoulo/chicken
loukániko/sausages
mialó/brain
padákia/lamb chops
sikóti/grilled liver
souvláki/chunks of pork or lamb roasted on the spit or fried

Dishes, Soups & Specialities

avgolémono/chicken stock thickened with egg and lemon
fasoláda/bean soup
moussaká/eggplant and ground lamb casserole with bechemel sauce
pastítsio/macaroni casserole
patsás/tripe stew, sold at *patsás* stands
salingária/snails in oil and herbs
stifádo/spicy stewed meat, often rabbit
souzoukákia/baked meat rolls
yiorvoulákia/meat-and-rice balls

Seafood

astakós/lobster
bakaliáros/cod
galéos/shark steak
garídes/shrimps
glóssa/sole, flounder
gópes/small, fried fish
kalamária/squid
ksifías/swordfish
ktapódi/octopus
péstrofa/trout
marídes/whitebait
sinagrída/red snapper
soupiés/cuttlefish

Desserts (Gliká)

Rarely will you find dessert served where you eat dinner. You'll find sweets instead at *zacharoplastía* and some *galaktopolía* (dairy stores). One sweet you will sometimes be served at *tavérnes* is *halvá*.

baklavá/strudel pastry, honey, nuts
bougátsa/sweet custard pie
galaktoboúriko/a heftier custard pie, less common
kataífi/chopped nuts wrapped in shredded wheat with honey
kréma/plain custard
loukoúmi/Turkish delight
moustalevriá/grape pudding, usually in autumn
rizógalo/rice pudding

Other snacks

kalambóki/roast corn on the cob, sold on the street

kástana/roast chestnuts, sold on the street

kouloúria/sesame-sprinkled pretzels

kreatópita/meat pie

spanakópita/spinach pie

tirópita/cheese pie

tost/toasted sandwiches sold at stands

Other useful words

aláti/salt

pipéri /pepper

bokáli/bottle

potíri/glass

piroúni/fork

koutáli/spoon

mahéri/knife

katálogo/*lista*/menu

to logariasmó/the bill

Where To Eat

Athens

COFFEE SHOPS

Metropol, 1 Pandrossou & Mitropoleos Square (tel. 321-1980, 324-3862). On the traffic-free square by the Cathedral, this is a pleasant oasis, summer and winter.

Zonars, 9 Panepistimiou St. (tel. 323-0336). A grand boulevard café. Breakfast, lunch and dinner are also available here, but Zonars is best for coffee and sweets like Black Venus.

CHIC LITTLE BARS & (NOT VERY GREEK) RESTAURANTS

Apenanti, 27 Haritos St., in Kolonaki (tel. 723-9400). A chic, Greek Yuppie watering hole whose name means "across the street". A good place to start the evening, or end it: this is less a place to dine than to see what young Kolonaki *aristos* are wearing, and drinking. Closed in summer.

Mets, 14 Markou Mousourou St., in Mets (tel. 922-9454). Another haunt of the young, trendy and thirsty, this lively little place is conveniently located on the same street as the excellent tavérnas, Manesis and Myrtia (see below under *Tavérnas*).

Montparnasse, or **Ratka**, 3032 Haritos St., in Kolonaki (tel. 729-0746). This split-level bar is one of the most fashionable district's most fash-ionable spots. (It is also the reason Apenanti is named as it is: it is across the street from Ratkas.) Reserve for a late dinner. The food is definitely not Greek. A hot spot, packed after 10pm. Closed in summer.

MEZODOPOLEIA

Apotsos, 10 Panepistimiou, in the arcade (tel. 363-7046). Since 1910, this has been a legendary nibbling and drinking spot for artists, politicians and important Athenians in general. Try *taramasalata* (fish roe spread), grilled liver, *ygandes* (giant broad beans) and *saganaki* (fried cheese) with your *oúzo*.

Kafeneio, 26 Loukianou St., in Kolonaki (tel. 722-9056). One of four places to book for dinner if you have only a day or so in the city. This 19th-century lookalike features 40 starters on the superb menu. Order four or five plates, and get a true feeling for the country's cuisine. The restaurant is refined, intimate, downright sexy, and the service a pleasant surprise. (The other three musts are **Gerofinikas**, **Vasilenas** and **Rodia**: see below.)

Kafeneio, 1 Epiharmou, in Plaka (tel. 324-6916). A less pricey version of the above, with a more limited menu, but warmhearted Plaka atmosphere. A cosy place till the wee hours, especially in winter. Try the *saganáki* and *keftethákia* meatballs.

O Kouklis, 14 Tripodon, in Plaka (tel. 324-7605). Another bargain-basement of *mezéthes*, including herring or Greek sausage flambé, this starters-only spot is best in summer, when the tables spill out on to the pavement.

Perix, 14 Glikonos St., across from Dexamini Sq. (tel. 723-6917). A pleasant, reasonable place for starters and Perix *oúzo*, as well as dinner, if you like. Perix spills out into the square in summer.

KOLONAKI TAVERNAS

Ongo, 20 Haritos St., next to the Athenian Inn (tel. 722-4731). Do reserve space at this small, swanky restaurant where fish and fillets are the order of the day. Open for lunch as well.

Rodia, 44 Aristipou St. (tel. 722-9883). One of the author's favourites, this is the haunt of foreign archaeologists. In summer or winter, the barrel wines good. Order veal in lemon or oregano sauce, *bourekákia* (cheese croquettes), *dolmáthes* (stuffed vine leaves), and a *horiatiki* (Greek salad).

Rouga, 7 Kéapsali St. (tel. 722-7934). A locals-only bistro, this *tavérna* has good *retsina* and grilled meats at reasonable prices.

To Kotopoulo, 3 Kolonaki Square. Between Citibank and Skoufa Street is a little hole in the wall with a few tables wobbling out front where, at lunch or dinner time, you can eat heavenly grilled chicken, *souvlakia* in *pítta* rolls, French fries, salad and beer. Too good to miss.

Vlassis, 16 Argiroupoleos St. (tel. 642-5337). This *tavérna*, down the street from Ileana Tountas art gallery/bar, is noted for fish. Reservations a must.

IN & NEAR METS

Karavitis, 4 Pafsaniou St., across from the statue of Truman (tel. 721-5155, 721-1610). An old friend of Athenians for 50 years, Mr. Linardos' garden is open May till October. Order grilled meats and *retsína*, all accompanied by guitar music.

Manesis, 3 Markou Mousourou St. (tel. 922-7684). Dry red barrel wine from Lefkada is featured here, along with a wide array of *mezéthes*, *stifádo* (sweet beef or rabbit stew with lots of spice), and *kokorétsi* (grilled lamb intestines and organs: please forget you read this, and try it).

Myrtia, 35 Markou Mousourou St. (tel. 701-2276, 751-1686). The garden makes this a lovely place to dine in summer. Order *gardoúmba* (lamb entrail roll), suckling pig, shrimp, mussels. And enjoy the live music.

PLAKA

Bakalarakia, also known as *O Damigos*, after the owner, 41 Kidathineon St. (tel. 322-5084, 322-0395). The author's favourite winter *tavérna*, this basement is supported by a truly ancient marble column and has a reputation for phenomenal *retsína*, fried cod with garlic sauce, radishes, herring and *loukaniko* (spicy Greek sausage). Closed late May through September.

Kalokerinos Tavern, 10 Kekropos St. (tel. 323-2054, 322-1679). This is an after-nine *tavérna* featuring traditional Greek fare, a *bouzouki* band (and Romanian violinist) plus a floor show of Greek dancing. Reservations required.

Platanos, 4 Diogenous St., near the

Tower of the Winds (tel. 322-0666). *Stifado* and grilled meats are the specialities here. (Avoid other *tavérnas* in this area. They don't hold a candle to Platanos.)

Socrates' Prison, 20 Mitseon St. (tel. 922-3434). After Athens Festival performances, have the grilled chicken or lamb with your Pikermi wine.

Xynos, 4 Aggelou Geronta St. (tel. 322-1065). Founded in 1936, this restaurant has a genuine old-Athens ambience, serves lamb fricassé and barrel wine, and has three strolling guitarists. Closed in July.

GREAT RESTAURANTS

Gerofinikas, 10 Pindarou St. (tel. 363-6710, 362-2719). Another favourite of the authors, this is the place to use your plastic. Reservations are a must. Order *Imam Baïldí* (Oriental eggplant starter), squab (baby chicken) with currant and pine nut pilaf, and finish with chocolate soufflé.

Kuyu-Kaplanis, 23 Nafarhou Votsi St., at Mikrolimano in Piraeus (tel. 411-1623). Choose from 25 *mezéthes* at your table by the harbour, and go on to shrimp and lobster.

Ta Nissia, at The Athens Hilton (tel. 722-0201). Try the dinner buffet here, a vast array of Greek and Turkish *mezéthes*. The wine list is impressive: try a hearty Nemean, red or white.

Vasilenas, 72 Etolikou St., in Piraeus (tel. 461-2457). Reserve a table, starve for at least a day, and then arrange for a taxi to pick you up afterwards: the table d'hôte consists of some 16 courses. Since Winston Churchill and Tyrone Power signed the guestbook, this unpretentious, underpriced beauty of a restaurant has been drawing gastronomes from the world over. Allow several hours to savour your meal, and try to go with a group of mellow friends.

NOT GREEK AT ALL

Kona Kai, the Ledra Marriott Hotel, 115 Syngrou Avenue (tel. 934-7711). Reserve ahead for authentic Polynesian cuisine.

Mitsiko, 27 Kidathineon St, in Plaka (tel. 322-0980). Sushi and saki in old Athens.

Pane E Vino, 8 Spefsippou St, in Kolonaki (tel. 722-5084). One of the two best, and most expensive, Italian restaurants in town.

Boschetto Ristorante-Bar, in the Evangelismos Park (tel. 721-0893, 722-7324). Alone in a green park, this is a pricey gem: Athens' other best Italian restaurant; reserve ahead.

Eden, 3 Flessa St, in Plaka (tel. 324-8858). Athens's first vegetarian restaurant. Peek in the kitchen before heading upstairs: the Spinach Special and lasagna are worthy choices.

BAKERIES & STREET FOOD

As you make your way around Athens on foot, you will pass a neighbourhood bakery about every 10 minutes. Stop in. This is where Athenians buy and eat breakfast, generally standing up.

An uptown bakery that features most of the goodies Greece has to offer is Mr Papayeorgious' shop at 14 Skoufa Street in Kolonaki. Try the *karidópitta* (walnut muffin) or grapemust flavoured biscuits, *moustoukoúloura*, or the old standbys, the *tirópita*, cheese pie, *spanakópitta*, spinach pie and the *milópitta*, the Greek version of apple pie.

Busy shoppers on Ermou Street should stop in at the Ariston, at 10 Voulis St, where morning queues trailing out the door advertise this shop's fine cheese pies.

On the street corners are other goodies: nuts and coconut sticks; *kouloúria*, the chewy, sesame-seed crusted bracelets commuters wear to work to eat with their coffee; roasted chestnuts, which scent the air downtown in autumn and winter; roast corn stop and nibble.

ZACHAROPLASTEIA OR PATISSERIES

Athens is a heaven for the visitor with an advanced case of sweet tooth. The place to indulge is the *zacharoplasteíon*, or confectioners shop. Downtown, the old fashioned **Zonars**, at 9 Panepistimiou Ave., is hard to beat. The elegant tables facing the street are a fine vantage point from which to watch the passing parade while consuming enormous numbers of calories. **Flocas**, at 118 Kifissias Ave. in Ambelokipi is another oasis for sugar addicts. For Greek pastries with a Middle Eastern flavour, **Farouk Hanbali**, at 4 Messinias St., also in Ambelokipi, has *baklavá* and other *fílo* (streudel leaves) and nut delicacies, for sale by the kilo. But the best confections in the city are probably

Evangelos Vlachakis versions of traditional Oriental sweets. The **Lalaggis** shop, at Spefsippou 23 in Kolonaki, features chocolate *baklavá*, among other things. Take a box home to make friends mouths water.

BREAKFAST

Kolonaki Square is a great place to have breakfast and people-watch. The **Ellinikon** café, at the corner of the square and Koumbari Street, has elegant tables, outdoors in season, great coffee, and Western breakfasts. Another nice place to start your day, especially if you are heading into the Flea Market, is the **Hermion Restaurant**, at 15 Pandrossou St. in Plaka.

For early risers and late-night owls, the **Bretania**, on Omonia Square, serves delicious yogurt, heavy cream topped with Attic honey, full breakfasts, hot milk — don't miss this place. You'll find yourself among deadbeats, theatre personalities, lawyers and other professionals, all with one thing in common: they know the best milk-bar in the city.

MILK BARS IN THE CITY

Elvetikon, 42 Ayios Sofias St. (tel. 275521).

Olympos-Naoussa, 5 Vas. Konstantinou St. (tel. 275715).

Stratis, 19 Vas. Konstantinou St. (tel. 234782).

Tiffanys, 3 Iktinou St. (tel. 274022).

Thessaloniki

LUXURY RESTAURANTS

Dionysius, Panorama (tel. 941813).

Teds House, 7 Mihalakopoulou St.Aretsou (tel. 427334).

TAVERNAS

I Folia Ton Filon Tou Falakra, 5 K. Melekinou (tel. 210905).

Iordanis, 1 Venizelou St.Panorama (tel. 941138).

Klimataria, .34 P. Mela St. (tel. 277854).

Liopesi, Platia Navarinou.

Ta Nisia, 13 Koromila St. (tel. 285991).

OUZERIES

Achileas, 17 Filikis Etairias St.

Anapiros, 20 P. Nikolaou St. (tel. 238269).

Corfu, 1 Stratigou Kéazari St. (tel. 269109).

Agapitos, 57 Tsimiski St. (tel. 279107).

Ellinikon, 209 Vas. Olgas St. (tel. 411133).

Hatzifotiou, 37 P. Mela St. (tel. 232166).

Drinking Notes

BEER AND WINE

Greeks never simply "go out drinking". Even if an evening involves heavy drinking of *retsína* or *oúzo*, these will always be accompanied by food, an inveterate habit which minimises the effects (and after-effects) of the alcohol.

When it comes to ordering your wine, check to see if they serve wine from the barrel (ask for *híma*). This is the inexpensive local stuff which varies from town to town. Otherwise you can choose among the various bottled wines, some of the better Greek labels being: Rotonda, Cambas, Boutari, Calliga. *Aspro* is white, *mávro* is red, and *kokkinélli* is rosé.

bíra/beer
kokkinélli/rosé wine
krasí/wine
mávro/red
me to kiló, or *hima*/wine by the kilo, local
neró/water
retsína/resin-flavoured wine
oúzo/aniseed-flavoured liqueur
rakí /rape-crush brandy
tsípouro/basically like rakí

COFFEE AND TEA

Greeks generally drink their coffee and tea with lots of sugar. An essential phrase for those who like their hot drinks without sugar is *horís záhari*, literally, "without sugar". Tag this phrase at the end of whatever drink you are ordering: for example, *nescafé horís záhari*. You can also ask for your drink *skétos* which means the same thing in a less emphatic way. If you like some sugar ask for *métrio*. If you love sugar say nothing and they'll probably dump a few teaspoons into whatever you're drinking. *Me gála* means "with milk".

Nescafé: freeze-dried coffee. In warmer weather, you may want *frapé*, cold nescafé mixed in a shaker.

Elenikó café: Greek coffee, boiled and served with the grounds in the cup. If you want a large cup of it ask for *diplós*. *Elenikó café* is also known as *turkikó café* but this sometimes provokes patriotic objections.

Tsaï: tea either with milk or with lemon, *me lemóni*

Kamomíli: camomile tea

Tsaï tou vounóu: mountain tea. Tea made with a mountain herbs such as sage. Not easy to find.

Attractions

Cultural

The main question here is surely which museums, sites and churches to visit. Greece has such an abundance of them that in any one trip you will just be able to see a fraction of what is available.

Below are listed most of the museums and archaeological sites and a few of the interesting churches and monasteries. Numerous aspects of Greece's cultural heritage have been necessarily excluded from this listing (fortresses, most churches, arches, mosques etc.). However, with patience and an inquisitive eye, you'll gradually discover them.

Museums and Sites

Guide to visiting hours: The archaeological sites and museums listed below are closed on 1st January, 25th March, Good Friday, Easter Sunday, 1st May and 25th December.

Museums will open from 8.30 am to 12.30pm on 2nd January, last Saturday of the Carnival, Good Thursday, Easter Tuesday, Christmas Eve and New Year's Eve.

ATHENS

Acropolis Archaeological Site, (tel. 3210219). Open: Daily 8.30am–4.30pm. Entrance fee (includes fee to the museum).

Acropolis Museum, on the Acropolis, (tel. 3236665). Open: as above. Closed: Tues. Entrance fee (including fee to the archaeological site).

Ancient Agora Museum in the Stoa Of Attalos, Entrance from Thisseon Sq., & 24, Andriano St. (tel. 3210185). Open: Daily 8.30am–3pm. Closed: Mon. Entrance fee (includes fee to the archaeological site).

Athens City Museum, 7, Paparigopoulou St. (tel. 3230168). Open: Mon., Wed. & Fri. 9am–1.30pm. Entrance fee. Free Wednesdays

Benaki Museum, 1 Koumbari Street and Vass. Sophias Av. (tel. 3611617). Open: Daily 8.30am–2pm. Closed: Tues. Entrance fee.

Byzantine Museum, 22, Vass. Sophias Av. (tel. 7211027). Open: Daily 8.30am–3pm. Closed on Mon. Entrance fee.

Cycladic Arts Museum, 4, Neofytou Douka St. (tel. 7249706). Open: Daily 10am–3.30pm. Closed: Tues. and Sun.

Daphni Monastery, (tel. 5811558). Open: Daily 8.30am–3pm. Closed: Mon. Entrance fee.

Epigraphical Collection, 1, Tossitsa St. (tel. 8217637). Open: Daily 8.30am–3pm. Closed: Mon. Admission free.

Greek Folk Art Museum, 17 Kydathineon St., Plaka (tel. 3213018). Open: Daily 10am–2pm. Closed: Mon. Entrance fee..

Historical And Ethnological Museum, Stadiou St. (tel. 3237617). Open: Tues. to Fri. 9am–2pm, Sat. & Sun. 9am–1pm. Closed: Mon. Entrance fee. Admission free on Thurs.

Jewish Museum of Greece, 36 Amalias Av. (tel. 3231577). Open: Daily 9am–1pm. Closed: Sat. Admission free.

Kéaissariani Monastery, (tel. 7236619). Open: Daily 8.45am–3pm, Closed: Mon. Entrance fee.

Kéanellopoulos Museum, Theorias & Panos Sts., Plaka (tel. 3212313). Open: Daily 8.30am–3pm. Closed: Mon. Entrance fee.

Keramikos Archaeological Site, Ermou & Pireos corner (tel. 3463552). Open: Daily 8.45am–3pm. Closed: Mon. Entrance fee (includes fee to the Museum).

Keramikos Museum, 148, Ermou St. (tel. 3463552). Open: Daily 8.45am–3pm, Sun. & Holidays 9.30am–2.30pm. Closed: Tues. Entrance fee (includes fee to the archaeological site).

National Archaeological Museum, 1, Tossitsa St. (tel. 8217717). Open: Daily 8am–5pm. Closed: Tues. Entrance fee (including fee to the exhibits from Thira & the Numismatic Museum).

National Gallery And Alexandros Soutsos Museum, 46, Vass. Sophias Av. (tel. 7211010). Open: Daily 9am–3pm. Closed: Mon. Admission fee.

Natural History, 13, Levidou St., Kifissia (tel. 8086405). Open: Daily 9am–2.30pm. Closed: Fri. Entrance fee.

Numismatic Collection, 1, Tossitsa St. (tel. 821779). Open: Daily 8.30am–3pm. Closed: Mon. Entrance fee.

Roman Agora, End of Eolou St. (tel. 3210185). Open: Daily 8.45am–3pm. Closed: Mon. Entrance fee.

Temple of Hephaistos And Ancient Agora, (tel. 3210185). Open: Daily 8.30am–5pm. Entrance fee.

Temple of Olympian Zeus, Olgas & Amalias Av. (tel. 9226330). Open: Daily 8.30am–3pm. Entrance fee.

Theatre of Dionysios, D. Areopagitou Av. (tel. 3236665). Open: Daily 8.30–3pm. Entrance fee.

War Museum of Greece, Vass. Sophias Av. (tel. 7290543-4). Open: Daily 9am–2pm. Closed: Mon. Library open: Tues. to Sat. 9am–2pm. Admission free.

AEGINA

Museum (tel. 0297-22637). Open: Daily 8.30am–3pm. Closed: Mon. Entrance fee (includes fee to the temple of Apollo).

Temple Of Aphaa (tel. 0297-32398). Open: Daily 8am–5pm, Sat, Sun. and holidays 8.30am–3pm. Entrance fee.

AMPHÍPOLIS

Archaeological Site (tel. 051-224717). Open: Daily 8.30am–3pm. Closed: Mon. Admission free.

ANDROS

Archaeological Museum (tel. 0282-23664). Open: Daily 8.30am–3pm. Closed: Mon. Entrance fee.

Basil & Elise Goulandris Museum, Modern Art (tel. 0282-22444). Open: Daily 10am–2pm, 6pm.–9pm. Closed: Tues. Admission free.

CHAIRONIA

Museum (tel. 0261-95270). Open: Daily 8.30am–3pm. Closed: Mon. Admission free.

CORFU

Archaeological Museum (tel. 0661-30680). Open: Daily 8.30am–3pm. Closed: Mon. Entrance fee.

Museum Of Asiatic Art (tel. 0661-23124). Open: Daily 8.30am–3pm. Closed Mon. Entrance fee.

CORINTH

Acrocorinth Archaeological Site (tel. 0741-31207). Open: Daily 8.30am–6pm. Closed: Mon. Entrance fee. (including fee to the Museum).

Museum (tel. 0741-31207). Open: Daily 8am–6pm. Entrance fee (including fee to archaeological site).

CRETE

Aghios Nikolaos Museum (tel. 0841-22462). Open: Daily 8.30am–3pm. Closed: Mon. Entrance fee.

Aghia Trias Archaeological Site (tel. 081-226092). Open: Daily 8.30am–3pm. Closed: Mon. Entrance fee.

Chania Museum (tel. 0821-20334, 24418). Open: Open: Daily 8.30am–3pm. Closed: Mon. Entrance fee.

Gortyn Archaeological Site (tel. 081-226092). Open: Daily 8.30am–3pm. Entrance fee.

Heraklion (Irákleion) Archaeological Museum (tel. 081-226092). Open: Daily 8am–5pm. Entrance fee.

Heraklion (Irákleion) Harbour Fortress (Koules) (tel. 081-286228). Open: Daily 8.30am–3pm. Closed: Mon. Entrance fee.

Knosss Archaeological Site (tel. 081-231940). Open: Daily 8.30am–5pm. Entrance fee.

Mallia Archaeological Site (tel. 081-226092). Open: Daily 8.30am–3pm. Closed: Mon. Entrance fee.

Other Archaeological Sites (tel. 081-226092). Saint Titus, Gournia. Open: Daily 8.45am–3pm, Sun. & Holidays 9.30am–2.30pm. Admission free.

Phaests Archaeological Site (tel. 0892-22615). Open: Daily 8.30am–3pm. Entrance fee.

Réthymnon Museum (tel. 0831-29975). Open: Daily 8.30am–3pm. Closed: Mon. Entrance fee.

Tylissos Archaeological Site (tel. 081-226092). Open: Daily 8.30am–3pm. Closed: Mon. Entrance fee.

DELOS

Archaeological Site (tel. 0289-22259). Open: Daily 8.30am–3pm. Closed: Mon. Entrance fee (includes fee to the museum).

DELPHI

Archaeological Site (tel. 0741-31207). Open: Daily 8.45am–3pm, Sun. & Holidays 9.30am–2.30pm. Entrance fee. (including fee to Museum).

Museum (tel. 0265-82313). Open: Daily 8am–5pm Mon, 11am–6pm. Entrance fee.

DÍON-PIERIA

Archaeological Site (tel. 0351-53206). Open: Daily 8.30am–3pm. Entrance fee (including fee to the museum).

Museum, (tel. 0351-53206). Open: Daily 8.30am–3pm, Mon. 11am–6pm. Entrance fee (includes fee to the archaeological site).

ELÉFIS

Museum (tel. 5546019). Open: Daily 8.30am–3pm. Closed: Mon. Entrance fee (includes fee to the archaeological site).

EPÍDAUROS

Archaeological Site & Museum (tel. 0753-22009). Open: Daily 8am–5pm Sat, Sun & Holidays 8.30am–3pm, Mon. 11am–5pm. Entrance fee.

ERETRIA (EUBOEA)

Archaeological Site & Museum (tel. 0221-62206). Open: Daily 8.30am–3pm. Closed: Mon. Entrance fee.

KOS

Asclepieion And Other Archaeological Sites (tel. 0242-28763). Open: Daily 8.30am–3pm. Closed Mon. Entrance fee.

Castle (tel. 0242-28326). Open: Daily 8.30am–3pm. Closed Mon. Entrance fee.

Museum (tel. 0242-28326). Open: Daily 8.30am–3pm. Closed: Mon. Entrance fee.

Restored Ancient Dwelling (tel. 0242-28326). Open: Daily 8.30am–3pm. Closed: Mon. Entrance fee.

LÉSVOS

Eresss Archaeological Museum (tel. 0251-22087). Open: Daily 8.30am–3pm. Closed: Mon. Admission free.

Mytilíni Archaeological Museum (tel. 0251-22087). Open: Daily 8.30am–3pm. Closed: Mon. Entrance fee.

MÍLOS
Archaeological Site & Museum (tel. 0287-21620). Open: Daily 8.30am–3pm. Closed: Mon. Entrance fee.
Catacombs (tel. 0287-21620). Open: Daily 9am–2.30pm. Closed: Wed, Sun. Entrance fee.

MISTRÁ
Archaeological Site & Museum (tel. 0731-93377). Open: Daily 8.30am–3pm. Entrance fee.

MYCENAE
Archaeological Site (tel. 0751-66585). Open: Daily 8am–5pm, Sat, Sun & holidays 8.30am–3pm. Entrance fee.

NAUPLION
Museum (tel. 0752-27502). Open: Daily 8.30am–3pm. Closed: Mon. Entrance fee.
Palamidi Fortress (tel, 0752-28036). Open: Daily 8am–5 pm; Sun. & Holidays 8.30am–3pm. Remains open on March 25. Entrance fee.
Popular Art Museum (tel. 0752-28379). Open: Daily 8.30am–3pm.. Closed: Mon. Admission free.

NEMÉA
Museum (tel. 0746-22739). Open: Daily 8.30am–3pm.Closed: Mon. Entrance fee.

OLYMPÍA
Archaeological Site (tel. 0624-22517). Open: Daily 8.30am–3pm. Closed: Mon Entrance fee.
Historical Museum of Olympic Games (tel. 0624-25572, 22596). Open: Daily 8.30am–3pm. Closed: Mon. Entrance fee.
Museum (tel. 0624-21529, 22742). Open: Daily 8.30am–3pm. Closed: Mon. Entrance fee.

OLYNTHOS (CHALKIDIKÍ)
Archaeological Site (tel. 0371-91280). Open: Daily 8.30am–3pm. Closed: Mon. Admission free.

OROPÓS
Amphiaraion Museum (tel. 0295-62144). Open: Daily 8.30am–3pm. Entrance fee (includes fee to the archaeological site).

ÓSIOS LUKÁS
Byzantine Monastery (tel. 3213571). Open: Daily 8.30am–3pm. Closed: Mon. Entrance fee.

PÁTMOS
Monastery Of St. John-Vestry-Library (tel. 0241-21954). Open: Daily 8.30am–3pm. Closed: Mon. Admission free.

PELLA
Archaeological Site (tel. 0382-31160, 31278). Open: Daily 8.30am–3pm. Closed: Mon. Entrance fee.
Museum (tel. 0382-31160, 31278). Open: Daily 8.30am–3pm. Closed: Mon. Entrance fee.

PIRAEUS
Maritime Museum of Piraeus, Akti Themistokleous (tel. 4516822). Open: Daily 8.30am–1pm. Closed: Sun, Mon. Entrance fee.
Piraeus Archaeological Museum, 31, Char. Trikoupi St. (tel. 4521598, 4518388). Open: Daily 8.30am–3pm. Closed: Mon. Entrance fee.

PHILIPPI
Archaeological Site (tel. 051-516470). Open: Daily 8.30am–3pm. Closed: Mon. Entrance fee.
Museum (tel. 05-516261). Open: Daily 8.30am–3pm. Closed: Mon. Entrance fee.

PYLOS
Museum (tel. 0723-22448). Open: Daily 8.30am–3pm. Closed: Mon. Entrance fee.
Nestors Palace, near Pylos (tel. 0723-31358). Open: Daily 8.30am–3pm. Closed: Mon. Entrance fee.

RHAMNOIS
Archaeological Site (tel. 0294-63477). Open: Daily 8.30am–3pm. Closed: Mon. Admission free.

RHODES
Acropolis of Ialyssos (tel. 0241-21954). Open: Daily 8.30am–3pm. Closed: Mon. Entrance fee.
Acropolis of Lndos (tel. 0241-21954). Open: Daily 8.30am–3pm. Closed: Mon. Entrance fee.
Acropolis-Theatre-Stadium (tel. 0241-21954). Open: Daily 8.30am–3pm. Closed: Mon. Admission free.
Camiros Archaeological Site (tel. 0241-21954). Open: Daily 8.30am–

3pm. Closed: Mon. Entrance fee.
Decorative Collections (tel. 0241-21954). Open: Daily 8.30am–3pm. Sat, Sun & holidays 8am–noon. Entrance fee.
Museum (tel. 0241-21954). Open: Daily 8.30am–3pm. Closed: Mon. Entrance fee.
Palace Of The Knights (tel. 0241-21954). Open: Daily 8.30am–3pm. Closed: Mon. Entrance fee.
Perimeter Of The Medieval Walls (tel. 0241-21954). Open to visitors accompanied by a guide on Mon and Sat. Visitors should gather in the courtyard of the Palace of the Knights. Open: 3pm–5pm. Admission free.

SAMOS
Efpalinion Orygma (tel. 0273-61400). Open: Mon, Thurs & Sat 10am–12pm. Admission free.
Hera Temple-Archaeological Site (tel. 0273-61177). Open: Daily 8.30am–3pm. Closed: Mon. Entrance fee.
Pythagorion Museum (tel. 0273-61400). Open: Daily 8.30am–3pm. Closed: Mon. Admission free.

SAMOTHRACE
Archaeological Site (tel. 0551-41474). Dorion: Doric marble temple dated 260 BC, Arsrnoeion circular construction dating 288281 BC. Open: Daily 8.30am–3pm. Closed: Mon. Entrance fee.
Museum (tel. 0551-41474). Open: Daily 8.30am–3pm. Closed: Mon. Entrance fee.

SANTORÍNI (THÍRA)
Akrotirion Thiras Archaeological Site (tel. 0286-81366). Open: Daily 8.30am–3pm. Closed: Mon. Entrance fee.
Archaeological Site (tel. 0286-22217). Well preserved ruins of the ancient town (theatre, agora, temple, site of athletics, government-house, fortifications, private house, tombs of archaic and classical periods, early Christian relics). Open: Daily 8.30am–3pm. Closed: Mon. Admission free.
Museum (tel. 0286-22217). Open: Daily 8.30am–3pm. Closed: Mon. Entrance fee.

SIKYON
Archaeological Site (tel. 0742-28900). Ruins of the towns walls, the Stadium, the Gymnasium, the Sacred

Spring, the Bouleuterion, the temple of Artemis and the theatre are well preserved. Open: Daily 8.30am–3pm. Closed: Mon. Admission free.

SOÍNION
Archaeological Site (tel. 0292-39363). Open: Daily from 9am–sunset; Sun & Holidays 10am–sunset. Entrance fee.
SPARTA
Museum (tel. 0731-25363). Open: Daily 8.30am–3pm. Closed: Mon. Entrance fee.

THESSALONIKI
Archaeological Museum and Treasures Of Ancient Macedonia: Vergina Findings, (tel. 031-830538). Open: Daily 8am–5pm; Mon 11am–5pm; Sat, Sun. & holidays 8.30am–3pm. Entrance fee (includes both museum & Vergina findings).
Crypt Of Saint Dimitrios (tel. 031-270008). Open: Daily 8.30am–3pm. Closed: Mon. Admission free.
Folklore Museum, 68, Vass. Olgas St. (tel. 031-830591). Open: Mon, Wed 9.30–5.30 pm; Tues, Fri, Sat, Sun 9.30am–2pm. Closed: Thurs. Admission free.
The White Tower-Byzantine Museum, Vass. Konstantinou St. Open: Daily 8.30am–3pm, Mon 11am–5pm. Entrance fee.

THEBES
Museum (tel. 0262-27913). Open: Daily 8.30am–3pm. Closed: Mon Entrance fee.

TIRYNS
Archaeological Site (tel. 0752-22657). Open: Daily 8am–5pm, Sun. & Holidays 8.30am–3pm. Entrance fee.

VERGINA
Archaeological Site (tel. 031-830538). Open: Daily 8.45am–3pm, Sun & Holidays 9.30am–2.30pm. Entrance fee.

VÓLOS (NEA ANCHIALOS)
Archaeological Site (tel. 0421-25285). Open: Daily 8.30am–3pm. Closed: Mon. Entrance fee.

VRAVRÓNA
Museum (tel. 0294-71020). Open: Daily 8.30am–3pm. Closed: Mon,

Thurs, Fri. Entrance fees includes archaeological site.

Dance and Music

A considerable part of the good music and dance performances takes place during the various festivals (see *Cultrtal Events* page 342). Besides these performances, however, there are numerous other events worth attending in both Athens and Thessaloniki.

In Athens, outstanding Greek and foreign musicians often perform at the Lykavittós Theatre on Mount Lykavittós, not to mention the larger concerts that take place in the soccer stadiums. Opera can be seen at the Olympía Theatre performed by the Lyriki Skini (the National Opera Company). In Thessaloniki, performances of music, opera, dance and theatre take place at the State Theatre of Northern Greece. In both Athens and Thessaloniki, the cultural institutes (Goethe, British Council, French) sometimes sponsor interesting events.

Athens has an active dance scene with ballet, folk, modern, jazz and experimental dance troupes. The various troupes are: The Athens Ballet; The Contemporary Dance Group of Haris Mandafounis; The Small Dance Theatre of Lia Meletopoulou; The Ilanga Dance Theatre; Bouri; The Hellenic Chorodrama; The Young Dancers and Choreographers of Katerina Rodiou; The Dance Theatre of Nafsika; The Hellenic Ballet of Rene Kabaladou; The Dora Stratou Group.

Greek Music

Greece has incredible music, or rather, musics, ranging from folk to light popular, *rembétika* to Byzantine chanting, Theodorakis and Hadzidakis to Dionisios Savopoulos. In the folk area, keep your ear tuned to the great regional variety which still exists today. Crete has one of the richest traditions, characterised by the *lyra* (fiddle), *laoto* (lute) and *santori* (hammer dulcimer).

Epirus is also notable, characterised by the extensive use of the *klarno* (clarinet) and an extraordinary, disappearing tradition of polyphonic singing. *Nisitika* is the general name for island music which has its own sound, style

and instruments, varying from island group to island group (the Ionian, Cycldic, Dodecanse etc.).

If you want to explore the world of *rembétika*, listen for these greats: Vassilis Tsitsanis, Markos Vamvakaris, Sotiria Bellou, Kéazantzides, Papazoglou, Papaioanou, and Tsaousakis. The best single introduction to *rembétika*, however, still remains the six-volume collection *The History of Rembetika* from EMI.

Little introduction is required for Mikis Theodorakis and Manolis Hadzidakis. You will hear their songs on every bus, boat and plane in Greece. In a very different vein is the folk-rock hero Dionisios Savopulos. Dipping into the Greek well of Byzantine and Asia Minor melodies, he draws out a unique style of contemporary folk-rock music. Another recent group which, working out of the Greek folk tradition, produces a distinctly contemporary music, is Himerin Kolimvits (with an album by the same name from Lyra Records in Greece).

Theatre

Athens has an active theatre life. As most productions are in Greek, however, options for the English-speakers are limited. Most productions in English take place during the various festivals (see *Cultural Events* opposite). You will do best to check the English-language publications for up-to-date information.

One recent cultural initiative has provided some excellent productions of both modern and ancient drama in English at one of Greece's most striking open-air theatres – the Stone Theatre (Ptra Theatre) in Petropolis in the suburbs of Athens. In summer, plays are produced under the auspices of the Stones and Rocks Festival.

Movies

Going to the cinema in Greece during the summertime is a special pleasure and not to be missed. Nearly all the movie theatres that run in the summer (the others shut down) are open-air, sometimes tucked among apartment buildings whose tenants watch the film from their balconies, while in other areas, perched on a seaside promontory under rustling palm trees, stars and the moon (on Aegina, for instance). The tickets are cheap and soundtracks are in the original language. It's also a great way to beat the dog-day heat of high-summer in Greece.

Cultural Hubs

In Athens there are two main cultural centres for those who speak English: the British Council and the Hellenic American Union.

The British Council in Kolonki Square (tel. 363-3211) has a library with a wide range of books, periodicals and newspapers. It also sponsors occasional lectures, exhibitions and performances. It is open Mon–Fri. 9.30am to 1.30pm. The Hellenic American Union, Massalias 22, 4th Floor (tel. 363-7740) similarly has a library and sponsors various cultural events. It also runs several courses in Greek dance, film, language, literature, etc. for foreign visitors. Open Mon–Fri. 9.30am to 2pm; Mon–Thurs. 5.30pm to 8.30pm.

In Thessaloniki there are also two main cultural centres for those who speak English, the British Council, on the corner of Egnatias and Vas. Sofias streets (tel. 235236) and the American Centre, in Mitropoleos St. just off Aristotelous Square (tel. 276347). Though somewhat more limited in scope, their activities are similar to those of the centres in Athens.

Bookshops

Athens has numerous bookstores which carry books in English:

Compendium, Nikis 33, located just behind Syntagma Sq. (tel. 322-6931). **Eleftheroudakis**, Nikis 4, Syntagma (tel. 322-9388). **Kakoulides – The Book Nest**, Panepistimiou 2529, Stoa Megarou Athinon (tel. 322-5209). **Lexis Bookshop**, Emm. Benaki and Academias Sts 72. **Pantelides**, Amerikis 11 (tel. 362-3673).

Festivals

January 1 Feast of St. Basil: celebrated all over Greece. **January 6** Epiphany–Blessing of the waters: all over Greece.

January 8 "Gynaecocracy"– men and women switch roles: villages in the areas around Komotiní, Xánthi, Kilkis and Sérres (village of Monoklissia). **February–March** The three weeks before Lent. Carnival season: all over Greece. Some villages with celebrations of special interest are: Náoùssa, Véria, Kozáni, Zánte, Skyros, Xánthi, Chíos (Mésta, Olimbi), Galaxídi, Thebes, Poligiros, Thimiana, Lamía, Cephaloniá, Messini, Sohos, Sérres, Agiassos (Lésvos), Kárpathos, Irákleion, Amfissa, Efxinoupolis (Vólos), Aghía Anna (Euboea), Réthymnon, Pátras. **Shrove Monday** Beginning of Lenten fast. Picnics in the countryside. Kite flying: all over Greece. **March 25** Independence Day anniversary of the day Bishop Germanos raised the standard of revolt against the Turks at Kalávrita in 1821: military parades in all main towns. **Easter Cycle** Good Friday, Holy Saturday and Easter Sunday are celebrated throughout the whole of Greece. **April 23** Feast of St. George: celebrated especially in Kaliopi (Lémnos), Aráhova, Assi Gonia (near Chaniá) and Pili (Kos) **May 1** Labour Day/Flower Festival picnics in the countryside: all over Greece. **Mid/late-May** Anastenárides: firewalking ritual at Aghía Eléni (near Sérres) and at Langada (near Thessaloniki). **August 15** Assumption of the Virgin: festivals all over Greece. Major pilgrimage to island of Tínos. **September** Cricket on Corfu. **October 28** "Okhi (No) Day" – anniversary of Greek defeat of Italian army in 1940 and Metaxás' response to Italy's ultimatum: "No". Military parades in major cities. **Christmas season** All over Greece. Little children sing carols door-to-door for a small gratuity. **December 31** New Year's Eve. More carols. Most of Greece plays cards on this occasion. Special celebration in the town of Chíos.

Cultural Events

April–October Sound and Light. Performances in Athens at the Pnyx; on Corfu at Old Venetian Castle; Rhodes, at Grand Master's.

May Folklore Festival at Eléfsis. Flower Festival at Gastouni in the Peloponnese. **May–September** Folk Dancing by the Dora Stratou Group at the Filopáppou Theatre. **May–October** Rhodes. Theatre, concerts, dance, etc. **June** Réthymnon Wine Festival. **June–August** Iráklion, concerts; theatre; opera etc. Lykavittós Festival. Theatre performances at the Lykavittós Hill Theatre. Pátras Festival at the ancient theatre in the Peloponnese. **June–September** Athens Festival. Ancient drama, opera, music and ballet at the Herod Atticus Odeon. **July–August** Alexandroúpolis Wine Festival. Crete International Festival. Performances organised by the Folk Art Museum on Crete. Philippi and Thássos Festival. Ancient drama performances in the ancient theatres at Philippi and on Thássos. Sun and Stone Festival. Greek folk dances at Nea Karvali in Kavála. **July–September** Epídaurus Festival. Performances of ancient drama in the open-air Epídaurus Theatre. Daphne Wine Festival (near Athens). **Mid-July** Daphni Wine Festival (near Iráklion). **Late-July** Music Festival. On the island of Ithaca. **August** Dodóna Festival. Ancient drama performances in ancient theatre at Dodóna. Epirotika Festival, Ioánnina. Epirot cultural and artistic events. Hippokrateia Festival, Kos. Various cultural events. Olympus Festival near Kateríni. Various cultural events in village of Litohoro and in the Platamona Castle. Raisin Festival Krestena, near Olympía. Colourful celebration. Réthymnon. Various cultural activities at the Venetian Fort. **Early-September** Thessaloniki Trade Fair. **October** Thessaloniki Dimitria Festival. Theatre, music, ballet, etc. Information and tickets for many of the above events can be obtained from the GNTO (EOT) Festival Office, 2 Spirou Miliou Arcade, (entrance from 4 Stadou St.), tel: 322-1459 or 322-3222, ext. 240.

Metropolitan nightlife in Greece (in fact in Athens and Thessaloniki) can be roughly divided into four categories: bars; live music clubs with jazz and rock; discotheques; and *boites*, *tavérnes* and clubs with live Greek music.

It should be noted first, however, that for most Greeks, the *tavérna* remains the most popular site for a night out; where you pass an evening eating, drinking and, sometimes, singing with your friends. In fact, locales with live Greek music are almost always *tavérnes* with music. In general, younger Greeks frequent the bars, music clubs and discotheques, while the locales for popular Greek music are more favourable among the older generations.

In Athens, the weekly *Athenrama* (in Greek) has an extensive listing of all the various locales and events. If you really want to find out what's going on in the city, ask a Greek friend to help you check out the listings. For information on the local music scene you can also inquire at the Pop 11 record shop, Skoufa 15, Kolonaki. However, do take note that during the late summer (July–August) many of these locales close down.

Sports

Greece offers a wide variety of possibilities for sports and recreation. The following is a partial listing of these activities.

Cave Exploration

Greece is honey-combed with caves. Usually the local tourist police has information on where local caves are and how you go about visiting them. The following caves have facilities for public visitation: Koutoúki, Peaneía, Attica; Pérama, Ioánnina; Drongorati, Cephaloniá; Melissani, Andíparos, the Cyclades; Glyfada and Aleopotripa at Diros, Laconía; Kokkines Petres, Halkidikí.

Diving

Greece is not the place to come to for scuba diving: submarine activity with divers' breathing apparatus is forbidden in all Greek waters (seas, lakes and rivers), with the aim of preserving the nation's cultural heritage of submerged antiquities. However, masks and snorkels are permitted and can add a whole other dimension to your swimming in Greek waters.

Fishing

Where can't you catch a fish in Greece? In the villages of most islands you will find boats and fishing tackle for hire. If you'd like some suggestions contact the **Amateur Anglers and Maritime Sports Club**, Akti Moutsopoulou, in Piraeus, (tel. 451-5731).

Golf

Greece is by no means a golfing country. Still, if you get the yen to tee-up try: The Glyfada Golf Course and Club, tel. 894-6820 (18 holes); The Afandou Golf Club, Rhodes, tel. (0214) 51225/6 (18 holes); The Corfu Golf Club, in the Ropa Valley, tel. (0661) 94220/1 (18 holes); The Pórto Carrás Golfcourse, near Neos Marmaras, Halkidikí, tel. (0375) 71381, 71221 (18 holes).

Health Spas

You'll find health spas with hydrotherapy in the following locations: Edipsós, Euboea; Eleftheron, Kavála; Kaiafa, Illia; Kaména Voúrla; Kyllini, Illia; Kíthnos, the Cyclades; Langada, Thessaloniki (also mud baths); Lefkáda, Ikaría; Loutráki, Corinth; Methana, Saronic Gulf; Platistomo, Smokovo, Kardítsa; Therma, Ikaría; Thermopylae; Vouliagméni, Attica; Ipati.

Hiking and Mountaineering

Greece is a paradise for hikers and mountain climbers, with extensive trails and trail systems, mountain refuges and expanses of mountains and forests untouched by the tourist masses. For information on trails, maps, refuges and excursions contact the Greek Alpine Club in Athens at Eolou 68-70, (tel. 321-2429), with offices in most major towns in mountain areas; Greek Skiing and Alpine Federation, 7 Kéarageorgis Street, Athens (tel. 323-4555); Greek Touring Club, 12 Politechnou St, Athens (tel. 524-8601); and the Federation of Excursion Clubs of Greece, 4 Dragatsaniou St., Athens (tel. 323-4107).

Sailing

Numerous locations in Greece have sailboats for rent. There are sailing schools, housed in the naval clubs of the following cities: Athens (Paleo Fáliro); Thessaloniki; Corfu; Vólos; Syros; Kalamáta; Alexandroúpolis. Further information can be obtained from the **Sailing Federation**, Akti Navarchou Kountouioti, Pireaus. Tel: 413 7531.

Skiing

Most Greek mountains have good snow cover for skiing from December to March with some of the higher mountains (Olympos, Parnássus and the Píndus) skiable until May. The following mountains have ski-lifts and are almost exclusively devoted to down-hill skiing, though there are also cross-country ski rentals: Mount Vermio, Náoüssa (chair-lift); Métsovo (chair-lift); Mount Pélion (chair-lift); Mount Parnássus (chair-lift); Mount Vitsi, Vigla Pissoderiou; Mount Vrondou, near Sérres; Mount Dirfis, Liri; Mount Lefka Ori; Kéallergi; Crete; Mount Mainalon, Ostrakina; Mount Olympus, Vrissopoules; Mount Pangeo, Kiladea Orfea; Mount Timfristos, Karpanísi; Mount Falakro.

For further information contact the Greek Skiing and Alpine Federation, 7 Kéarageorgis Street, Athens (tel. 323-4555).

Tennis

You will find tennis facilities at the tennis clubs in the following cities: numerous athletic clubs and centres in Athens; Glyfáda; Kalamáki; Thessaloniki; Pátras; Corfu; Irákleion; Chaniá; Lárissa; Ioánnina; Rhodes; Halkída; Vólos; Alexandroúpolis; Sérres; Agrínio; Kateríni; Véria; Kavála; Tríkala. Many hotels and resorts have tennis facilities as well.

Water Skiing

You will find facilities for water skiing at: Vouliagméni (on the coast southeast of Athens); Agrnio (Lake Trihonida); Vólos; Edessa (Lake Vegoritida); Ioánnina; Thessaloniki; numerous locations on Corfu; Chaniá, Crete; Elonda, Crete; Kthera; Mytilíni; Prto-Hli; Páros; Rhodes; Skiáthos; Gerakina, Halkidik; Kéalitha, Halkidik; Halkída; Chíos. For general information contact the **Water Skiing Association**, 32 Stournara Street, Athens. Tel 523 1875.

Windsurfing

You'll find windsurf boards for rental at many popular Greek beaches, and at all the beaches run by the GNTO. For information contact the **Hellenic Windsurfing Association**, 7 Filellinon Street, Athens (tel. 323-0068, 323-0330).

Spectator sports

Greece has a limited range of spectator sports. **Soccer** is the main one with matches played nearly every Sunday afternoon during the season. Check the local papers for information or contact the Soccer Federation, 137 Syngrou, Athens, (tel. 933-6410).

Basketball is becoming the second most popular sport in Greece after soccer and the national league competition is followed keenly. Check the local papers or call the Basketball Federation, 11 N. Saripolou Street, Athens, (tel. 824-5125, 822-4131).

Horse racing takes place at the Fliron Race-course at the seaward end of Syngrou Avenue in Athens. There are races every Monday, Wednesday and Saturday at 6.30pm. For information call: 941-7761.

Language

Instant Greek

It is possible to survive in Greece just knowing English. Greeks have seen so many English-speaking tourists and have such strong connections with the English-speaking world (through emigration, the media, education) that you are always bound to find Greeks that can understand your basic utterances.

This section is about beginning to bridge the gap between you the alien tourist and the native Greek, about being perceived as a *ksnos*, a foreigner or guest, instead of a *tourista*.

Greeks put great stock in their language and are highly responsive to the efforts of foreigners who try to learn it. Precisely because Greeks so effusively appreciate your efforts, Greek can be one of the most gratifying European languages to learn. With a little study and practice on your part, you too may soon be met with the stock praise: *Pos mathes tso kal ta elinik*? That is, How did you learn Greek so well?

The following crash course in Greek and listing of words and phrases will be useful to you. You will also want to carry a pocket-sized English-Greek/Greek-English dictionary. For those who actually want to study Greek, a few textbooks and dictionaries are listed in the Further Reading section.

Greek is a phonetic language. There are some combinations of vowels and consonants which customarily stand for certain sounds, and some slight pronunciation changes determined by what letter follows but, generally, sounds are pronounced as they are written, without additions or omissions. Thus, learning the phonetic values of the Greek alphabet, and then reading, say, street sounds out loud, is a good beginning to getting the feel of the language.

Most Athenians have some knowledge of English, and most Greeks are delighted to find a visitor making stabs at speaking Greek. (Unlike Parisians, the Greeks do not ridicule you for making mistakes: they themselves have a hard time with Greek spelling and the complicated Greek grammar.) Whatever you can accomplish guide book in hand will be rewarded.

In addition to pronouncing each letter, you should remember that stress plays an important role in modern Greek. When you learn a Greek word, learn where the stress falls at the same time. Each Greek word has a single stress (marked in the following list with an accent). Greek is an inflected language as well, and noun and adjective endings change according to gender, number and case. Case endings, the rules governing them, and the conjugation of Greek verbs, are beyond the scope of a guide. For visitors staying on for a long period, there are language classes at the Hellenic American Union and other teaching centres in metropolitan Athens.

The Greek Alphabet

Cap.	l.c.	Value	Name
A	α	a in father	alfa
B	β	v in visa	vita
Γ	γ		gama
		gh before consonants and a, o and oo; y before e, as in year	
Δ	δ	th in then	thelta
E	ε	e in let	epsilon
Z	ζ	z in zebra	zita
H	η	e in keep	ita
Θ	θ	th in theory	thita
I	ι	e in keep	yota
K	κ	k in king	kapa
Λ	λ	l in million	lamda
M	μ	m in mouse	mi
N	ν	n in no	ni
Ξ	ξ	ks in jacks	ksi
O	ο	o in oh	omikron
Π	π	p in pebble	pi
P	ρ	r in raisin	ro
Σ	σ	s in sun	sigma
T	τ	t in trireme	taf
E	ε	e in keep	ipsilon
Φ	φ	f in favour	fi
X	χ	h in help	hi
Ψ	ψ	ps in copse	psi
Ω	ω	o in oh	omega

Dipthongs

Type	Value
αι	e in let
αυ	av or af in avert or after
ει	e in keep
ευ	ev or ef
οι	e in keep
ου	oo in poor

Double consonants

Type	Value
μπ	b at beginnings of words; mb in the middle of words
ντ	d at beginnings of words; and in the middle of words
τζ	dz as in adze
γγ, γκ	gh at the beginnings of words; ng in the middle of words

Vocabulary

Note: This list is broken into syllables, the stressed syllable marked with an accent. Pronounce e as in pet; a as in father; i as in keep; o as in oh.

Numbers

one	é-na (neuter)/ é-nas (masc.)/mí-a(fem.)
two	thí-o
three	trí-a (neuter)/tris (masc. and fem.)
four	té-se-ra
five	pén-de
six	ék-si
seven	ep-tá
eight	ok-tó
nine	e-né-a
ten	thé-ka
eleven	én-the-ka
twelve	thó-the-ka
thirteen	the-ka-trí-a/the-ka-trís
fourteen	the-ka-té-se-ra etc. until twenty.
twenty	í-ko-si
twenty-one	í-ko-si é-na (neuter and masc.)/ í-ko-si mí-a (fem.)
thirty	tri-án-da
forty	sa-rán-da
fifty	pe-nín-da
sixty	ek-sín-da
seventy	ev-tho-mín-da
eighty	og-thón-da
ninety	e-ne-nín-da
one hundred	e-ka-tó
one hundred and fifty	e-ka-to-pe-nín-da
two hundred	thi-a-kó-si-a (neuter)
three hundred	tri-a-kó-si-a (neuter)
four hundred	te-tra-kó-si-a (neuter)
one thousand	hí-lia (neuter)

Note: Since the word for drachma, *thrak-mí)* is feminine, a number preceding this noun will also be in the feminine case. Thus, *hí-lies thrak-més,* for 1,000drs.

Days of the Week

Monday	Thef-té-ra
Tuesday	Trí-ti
Wednesday	Te-tár-ti
Thursday	Pém-pti
Friday	Pa-ras-ke-ví
Saturday	Sá-va-to
Sunday	Ki-ri-a-kí
yesterday	kthes
today	sí-me-ra
tomorrow	á-vri-o
day after tomorrow	meth-á-vri-o
next week	tin á-li ev-tho-má-tha

Greetings

Hello	yá sas (plural/polite) yá sou (sing./familiar) ya (abbreviated)
Good day	ká-li mé-ra
Good evening	ka-lí spe-ra
Good night	káli ník-ta
Bon voyage	ka-ló tak-si-thi
Welcome	ká-los il-tha-te
Good luck	ka-lí tí-hi
How are you?	Ti ká-ne-te? (plural/polite) Ti ká-nis? (singular/ familiar)
fine(in response)	ka-lá
so so (in response)	ét-si két-si
pleased to meet you	há-ri-ka

Getting Around

yes	ne
no	ó-hi
okay	en dák-si
thank you	ef-ha-ris-tó
very much	pá-ra po-lí
excuse me	sig-nó-mi
it doesn't matter	then bi-rá-zi
it's nothing	tí-po-ta
certainly/polite yes	má-li-sta
Can I..?	Bó-ro na..?
When?	Pó-te?
Where is..?	Pou í-n-e..?
Do you speak English?	mi-lá-te ta an-gli-ka
Do you understand?	Ka-ta-la-vé-ne-te?
What time is it?	Ti ó-ra i-ne?
What time will it leave?	Ti ó-ra tha fi-gi
I don't	then (plus verb)
I want	thé-lo
I have	é-ho
here/there	e-thó/e-kí
near/far	kon-dá/ma-kri-á
small/large	mi-kró/me-gá-lo
quickly	grí-go-ra
slowly	ar-gá
good/bad	ka-ló/ka-kó
warm/cold	zes-tó/krí-o
bus	le-o-for-í-on
tram	tró-li
boat	ka-rá-vi, va-pó-ri
bike/moped	po-thí-la-to/ mo-to-po-thí-la-to

ticket	i-si-tí-ri-o
road/street	thró-mos/o-thós
beach	pa-ra-lí-a
sea	thá-la-sa
church	e-kli-sí-a
ancient ruin	ar-hé-a
centre	kén-tro
square	pla-tí-a
East Air Terminal (for international connections)	A-no-to-li-kó Er-o-thró-mi-o
West Air Terminal (for domestic connections and Olympic Airways flights)	Thi-ti-kó Er-o-thró-mi-o

Hotels

hotel	kse-no-tho-hí-o
Do you have a room?	É-hie-te é-na tho-má-ti-o?
bed	kre-vá-ti
shower with hot water	douz me zes-tó ne-ró
key	kli-thí
entrance	i-so-thos
exit	ék-so-thos
toilet	toua-lé-ta
women's	yi-ne-kón
men's	án-dron

Shopping

store	ma-ga-zí
kiosk	pe-ríp-te-ro
open/shut	a-nik-tó/klis-tó
post office	ta-ki-thro-mí-o
stamp	gra-ma-tó-simo
letter	grá-ma
envelope	fá-ke-lo
telephone	ti-lé-fo-no
bank	trá-pe-za
marketplace	a-go-rá
Have you..?	É-hie-te..?
Is there..?	É-hi..?
How much does it cost?	Pó-so ká-ni?
It's (too) expensive	I-ne (po-lí) a-kri-vó
How much?	Pó-so?
How many?	Pó-sa?

Emergencies

doctor	ya-trós
hospital	no-so-ko-mí-o
pharmacy	far-ma-kí-o
police	as-ti-no-mí-a
station	stath-mós

Basic Expressions

yes	n
no	hi
okay	en dksi
please	parakal
thank you	efharist
(very much)	pra pol
excuse me	signmi
it doesnt matter	then pirzi
its nothing	tpota
certainly	mlista
good day	kli mra
good evening	kli spra
good night	kli nkta
goodbye	ado
Greetings/health	
	y sou, y sas
to you	plural or formal
Greetings/rejoice	
	hrete
bon voyage	kal taksthi
welcome	kals lthateh
good luck	kal thi
How are you?	ti knis, ti kneth
	plural or formal
fine, well (in response)	
	kal
so so (in response)	
	tsi ktsi
pleased to meet you	
	hrika (pol)
(very much)	
I also, me too	kai eg
Have you...?	heteh..?
Is there...?	hi...?
How much does it cost?	
	pso kni?
It's (too) expensive	
	neh (pol) akriv
How much?	pso?
How many?	psa?
Do you have	heteh na
a room?	domtio?
Can I...?	bor na...?
When?	pteh...?
Where is...?	pou neh..?
From where...?	po pu...?
Where are you from?	
	po pu steh?
	sing./formal
What is your name?	
	pos seh/sas lneh?
	sing./formal
Do you speak English?	
	mils/milteh anglik?
	(sing./plural-formal)
Do you understand?	
	katlaves?
What time is it?	
	t ra neh?

What time will it leave?	
	ti ra tha fgi?
I dont...	then + verb
I want	thlo
I have	ho
I am/we are	meh/masteh
I understand	katalavno, katalvo
I pay	plirno
I go	pigno, po
it must/I must	prpi na
I need a	krizomeh na/ma
today	smera
tomorrow	vrio
yesterday	kthes
now	tra
here/there	eth/ek
near/far	kond/makri
small/large	mikr/meglo
less/more	ligtero/peristero
quickly	grgora
slowly	arg, sig
good/bad	kal, oro/kak
warm/cold	zest/kro
shower with hot water	
	douz me zest ner
hotel	ksenothoho
bed	krevti
key	klith
room (with a window)	
	domtio (me parthiro)
entrance	sothos
exit	ksothos
toilet	toualta
women's	yinekn
men's	ndron
store	magaz
kiosk	perptero
open/shut	anikts/klists
What time does it open/close?	
	ti ra angi/klni?
post office	takithromo
stamp	grammatsima
letter	grmma
envelope	fkelos
postcard	krta
telephone	tilfono
bank	trpeza
bakery	fornos
embassy	presva
consulate	proksenon
marketplace	agor
pharmacy	farmako
doctor	yatrs
hospital	nosokomo
police	astinoma
station	stathms
stop (on a bus)	stsi
bus/train	leoforo/trno
automobile	aftoknito
boat	karvi, vapri

petrol station	venzinthiko
bike/moped	pothlato/mtopothlato
on foot	me ta pthia
ticket	isitrio
road/street	thrmos/oths
beach	parala
church	eklisa
ancient ruins	arha
centre	kntro
square	plata
sea	thlassa
village	hori
spring	pig

Further Reading

Ancient History and Culture

Bowra, Maurice. *The Greek Experience*. London: Weidenfeld and Nicolson, 1957.

Burn, A.R. *The Pelican History of Greece*. Harmondsworth: Penguin, 1966.

Dodds, E.R. *The Greeks and the Irrational*. Berkeley and Los Angeles: University. of California Press, 1951.

Finley, M.I. *The Ancient Greeks*. Harmondsworth: Penguin, 1963.

Finley, M.I. *The World of Odysseus*. New York: Viking Press, 1954.

Graves, Robert. *The Greek Myths*. Harmondsworth: Penguin Books, 1986.

Hammond, N.G.L. *A History of Greece to 322 BC*. Oxford University Press, 1965.

Kerenyi, K. *The Gods of the Greeks*. London: Thames and Hudson, 1951.

Kerenyi, K. *The Heroes of the Greeks*. London: Thames and Hudson, 1951.

Kitto, H.D.F. *The Greeks*. Harmondsworth: Penguin, 1951.

Pollitt, J.J. *Art and Experience in Classical Greece*. Cambridge: Cambridge University Press, 1972.

Renfrew, Colin. *The Emergence of Civilization: The Cyclades and the Aegean in the Third Millennium BC*. New York: Simon and Schuster, 1970.

Thompson, George. *Aeschylus and Athens*. London: Lawrence and Wishart, 1980.

Vernant, J.P. *Myth and Thought*. London: Routledge & Kegan Paul, 1983.

Byzantine History and Culture

The Alexiad of Anna Comnena. Trans. By E.R.A. Sewter Harmondsworth: Penguin, 1969.

Michael Psellu. *Fourteen Byzantine Rulers*. Harmondsworth: Penguin, 1966.

Norwich, John Julius, *Byzantium* (2 vols) Penguin, 1993.

Runciman, Steven. *Byzantine Style and Civilization*. Harmondsworth: Penguin, 1975.

Sherrard, Philip. *Byzantium*. New York: Time-Life Books, 1966.

Talbot Rice, David. *The Art of the Byzantine Era*. London: Thames and Hudson, 1963.

Talbot Rice, David. *The Byzantines* London: Thames and Hudson, 1962.

Modern History and Culture

Alexiou, Margaret. *The Ritual Lament in Greek Tradition*. Cambridge: Cambridge University. Press, 1974.

Beaton, Roderick. *Folk Poetry of Modern Greece*. Cambridge: Cambridge University. Press, 1980.

Campbell, John. *Honor, family and patronage: A study of institutions and moral values in a Greek mountain community*. Oxford: Oxford University Press, 1964.

Clogg, Richard. *A Short History of Greece*. Cambridge: Cambridge University Press, 1979.

Danforth, Loring H. and Tsiaras, Alexander. *The Death Rituals of Rural Greece*. Princeton: Princston University Press, 1982.

Du Boulay, Juliet. *Portrait of a Greek Mountain Village*. Oxford: Clarendon Press, 1974.

Eudes, Domenique. *The Kapetanios: Partisans and Civil War in Greece, 1943–1949*. NY and London: Monthly Review Press, 1972.

Fourtouni, Eleni. *Greek Women in Resistance*. New Haven: Thelphini Press, 1986.

Friedl, Ernestine. *Vasilika: A Village in Modern Greece*. New York: Holt, Rinehart and Winston, 1962.

Herzfeld, Michael. *Ours Once More: Folklore, Ideology and the Making of Modern Greece*. Austin: University of Texas Press, 1982.

Mackridge, Peter. *The Modern Greek Language*. Oxford: Oxford University. Press. 1985.

Marazower, Marc. *Inside Hilter's Greece*, Oxford University Press.

Matthews, Kevin. *Memoirs of a Mountain War, Greece: 1944–49*. London: Longman, 1972.

McNeill, William. *Metamorphisis of Greece Since World War II*. Oxford: Blackwell, 1982.

Mouzelis, Nicos P. *Modern Greece: Facets of Underdevelopment*. London: MacMillan Press, 1978.

Murtagh, Peter. *The Rape of Greece*, Simon & Schuster, 1994

Papandreou, Andreas. *Democracy at Gun-point*. Harmondsworth: Penguin, 1972.

Sarafis, Marion. Greece: *From Resistance to Civil War*. Nottingham: Spokesman, 1980.

Tsoucalas, Constantine. *The Greek Tragedy*. Harmondsworth: Penguin, 1969.

Woodhouse, C.M. *Modern Greece: A Short History*. London: Faber and Faber, 1984.

Ancient Greek Literature

Aeschylus. *The Oresteia*. Trans. by Robert Fagles. New York: Viking Press, 1975.

Aesop. *Fables of Aesop*. Trans. by S.A. Hanford. Harmondsworth: Penguin, 1954.

Aristophanes. *Lysistrata/The Acharnians/The Clouds*. Trans. by A.H. Sommerstein. Harmondsworth: Penguin, 1973.

Aristotle. *The Nicomachean Ethics*. Trans. by Martin Ostwald. Indianapolis: Bobbs-Merrill, 1962.

Grene, David and Lattimore. *Greek Tragedies*. (3 vols.). Chicago: University. of Chicago Press, 1968.

Hesiod. *Theogony*. Trans. by Norman Brown. Indianapolis: Bobbys-Merrill, 1955.

Herodotus. *The Histories*. Trans. by A.R. Burn. Harmondsworth: Penguin, 1972.

Homer. *The Iliad*. Trans. by Robert Fitzgerald. New York: Anchor Books, 1975.

Homer. *The Odyssey*. Trans. by Robert Fitzgerald. New York: Anchor Books, 1963.

Plato. *The Republic*. Trans. by H.D.P. Lee. Harmondsworth: Penguin, 1955.

Plato. *The Symposium*. Trans. by Walter Hamilton. Harmondsworth: Penguin, 1951.

Sappho. Trans. by Mary Barnard. Los Angeles: University. of California Press, 1958.

Thucydides. *The Peloponnesian Wars*. Trans by Crawley. New York: Modern Library, 1951.

Trypanis, Constantine. *The Penguin Book of Greek Verse*. Harmondsworth: Penguin Books, 1971.

Modern Literature by Greeks

Barnstone, Willis (ed.). *Eighteen Texts: writings by contemporary Greek authors*. Cambridge: Harvard University Press, 1972.

Cavafy, C.P. *Collected Poems*. Trans. by Edmund Keeley and Philip Sherrard. Princeton: Princeton University. Press, 1975.

Dalven, Rae (trans.). *Modern Greek Poetry*. (Anthology). New York: Russell and Russell, 1971.

Elytis, Odysseus. *The Axion Esti*. Pittsburgh: University. of Pittsburgh Press, 1974.

Elytis. *Selected Poems*. Trans. by Edmund Keeley and Philip Sherrard. London and NY: Viking Penguin, 1981.

Frair, Kimon (trans.). *Modern Greek Poetry*. (Anthology.) New York: Simon and Shuster, 1973.

Karapanou, Margarita. *Kassandra and the Wolf*. Trans. by N.C. Germanacos. New York: HBJ, 1976.

Kazantzakis, Nikos. *Zorba the Greek*. New York: Simon and Schuster/Touchstone, 1971.

Kazantzakis, Nikos. *Christ Recrucified (The Greek Passion)*. New York: Simon and Schuster/Touchstone, 1981.

Haviaris, Stratis. *When the Tree Sings*. New York: Simon and Schuster, 1979.

Haviaris, Stratis. *The Heroic Age*. New York: Penguin, 1985.

Makriyannis, Yannis. *The Memoirs of General Makriyannis*. London: Oxford University Press, 1966.

Myrivilis, Stratis. *The Schoolmistress with the Golden Eyes*. London: Hutchinson, 1964.

Ritsos, Yannis. *Ritsos in Parentheses*. Trans. by Edmund Keeley. Princeton: Princeton University. Press, 1979.

Ritsos, Yannis. *Yannis Ritsos: Selected Poems*. Trans. by Nikos Stangos: Penguin, 1974.

Papadiamantis, Alexandors. *The Murderess*. Trans. by Peter Levi, London: Writers and Readers, 1983.

Politis, Linos. *A History of Modern Greek Literature*. Oxford: Clarendon Press, 1973.

Seferis, George. *Collected Poems*. Trans. by Edmund Keeley. Princeton: Princeton University Press. 1981.

Sikelianos, Angelos. *Selected Poems*. Princeton: Princeton University Press, 1979.

Siotis, Dino (ed.). *Ten Women Poets of Greece*. San Francisco: Wire Press, 1982.

Taktsis, Costas. *The Third Wedding Wreath*. Trans. by John Choiles. Athens: Hermes Press, 1985.

Tsirkas, Stratis. *Drifting Cities*. Trans. by Kay Cicellis. New York: Alfred Knopf, 1974.

Vassilikos, Vassilis. *Z*. New York: Farrar, Strauss and Giroux, 1968.

Foreign Writers on Greece

Andrews, Kevin. *Athens Alive*. Athens: Hermes Press.

Andrews, Kevin. *The Flight of Ikaros*. Harmondsworth: Penguin, 1984.

Boleman-Herring, Elizabeth. *Greek Unorthodox*. Foundation Publishing, 1990.

Durrell, Lawrence. *Prospero's Cell*. London: Faber and Faber, 1945; *Reflections on a Marine Venus*. London: Faber and Faber, 1953.

Durrell, Lawrence. *Bitter Lemons*. London: Faber and Faber, 1978.

Fowles, John. *The Magus*. London: Cape, 1977.

Gage, Nicholas. *Eleni*. London: Collins, 1983.

Greenhalgh, Peter and Edward Eliopoulos. *Deep into Mani*. London: Faber and Faber, 1985.

Levi, Peter. *Hill of Kronos*. New York: Penguin, 1984.

Miller, Henry. *The Colossus of Maroussi*. New York: New Directions, 1958.

Renault, Mary. *The Last of the Wine*. London: Sceptre, 1986.

Travel

Constantine, David. *Early Greek Travellers and the Hellenic Idea*. Cambridge: Cambridge University Press, 1984.

Dubin, Marc. *Greece on Foot*. Leicester/London: Cordee, 1986.

Durrell, Lawrence. *The Greek Islands*. New York: Viking Press, 1978.

Harris, Andy. *A Taste of the Aegean*. Photographs by Terry Harris. London: Pavilion Books, 1992

Holst, Gail. *Road to Rembetika*. Athens: Denise Harvey, 1975.

Holst, Gail. Theodorakis: *Myth and Politics in Modern Greek Music*. Amsterdam: Adolf Hakkert, 1980.

Huxley and Taylor. *Flowers of Greece and the Aegean*. Chatto and Windus, 1971.

Leigh Fermor, Patrick. *Roumeli: Travels in Northern Greece* and *Mani*. Harmondsworth: Penguin, 1984.

Melas, Evi. *The Greek Islands*. Exeter: Webb and Bower, 1985.

Melas, Evi. *Temples and Sanctuaries of Ancient Greece: A Companion Guide*. London: Thames and Hudson.

Millard, Anne. *Usburne Pocket Guide to Ancient Greece: Everyday Life in Greek Times*. London: Usburne, 1981.

Pausanias. *Description of Greece*. 2 vols. Trans. by Peter Levi. Harmondsworth: Penguin, 1979.

Petrides, Ted. *Greek Dances*. Athens: Lycabettus Press, 1975.

Sfikas, George. *The Mountains of Greece*. Athens: Efstiadis, 1979.

Sfikas, George. *Trees and Shrubs of Greece*. Athens: Efstiadis, 1978.

Sfikas, George. *Wild Flowers of Greece*. Athens: Efstiadis, 1976.

Spencer, Terence. *Fair Greece Sad Relic*. London: 1974.

Stoneman, Richard (ed.). *A Literary Companion to Travel in Greece*. Harmondsworth: Penguin, 1984.

Stubbs, Joyce. *The Home Book of Greek Cookery*. London: Faber and Faber, 1963.

Stavroulakis. *Cookbook of the Jews of Greece*: Athens: Lycabettus, 1985.

Tsigakou, Fani-Maria. *The Rediscovery of Greece*. London: Thames and Hudson, 1981.

Other Insight Guides

Companion titles which highlight destinations in this region include: *Insight Guide: Greek Islands*, *Insight Guide: Athens*, *Insight Guide: Crete*, *Insight Guide: Cyprus* and *Insight Guide: Turkish Coast*.

The **Insight Pocket Guide** series, designed to guide short-stay visitors around their destinations by means of carefully timed itineraries, includes books on *Athens*, *Crete*, the *Aegean Islands*, and *Rhodes*.

Archiv Gerner 133
Ashmolean Museum 28L, 28R, 33, 52, 55, 56, 59, 60, 61, 64-65, 220
Gaetano Barone 173R, 217L, 221
David Beatty 10-11, 14-15, 16-17, 18, 32, 75, 76R, 80, 86, 88, 89, 115, 128, 131, 138-139, 198, 234-235, 251, 267, 273, 274, 275, 276, 278L, 281, 282, 283, 285, 286, 287, 290, 292, 295, 297, 298, 299, 300, 301, 303, 304, 305
Benaki Museum 23L, 23R, 45, 57, 62, 63, 195L
Marcus Brooke 49
Byzantine Museum 35, 54
Cyclades Museum 31
J. Allan Cash Ltd. 132R
Pierre Couteau 101, 208, 260, 320
Jane Cowan 119
Marc S. Dubin 129, 229, 258
Guglielmo Galvin 203, 233
Glyn Genin 306-307, 314, 316L, 316R, 319
Udo Gerner 132
Aliki Gourdomichalis 169
Margot Granitsas 76L, 96, 172, 241
Barbara Gundle 166, 187, 189, 315R
Terry Harris cover
Paul Herrmann 30, 184
Markos G. Hionos 2, 12-13, 227, 230
Irákleion Museum 50-51
Ann Jousiffe 111
Dieter Lotze 151, 199, 238, 242, 249, 253
Michele Macrakis 9, 68-69, 70, 81, 82, 83, 94-95, 99, 100, 102, 107, 113, 124, 130, 147, 164, 165, 167, 173L, 185, 226, 228, 284, 310
Spiros Meletzis 46
Emil Moriannidis 232
Susan Muhlauser 74, 77, 90, 182, 201, 202, 217R, 239L, 239R, 243, 250, 278R, 279, 280L
Ben Nakayama 259

P. Petrolpoulous 266
Gerd Pfeiffer 108
Ethiniki Pinakothiki 42, 43
G. P. Reichelt 29, 72, 78, 311, 315L
Jens Schumann 312, 313
Janos Stekovics 53, 104, 121, 127, 212L, 212R
Tony Stone Worldwide 26, 91, 134-135, 136-137, 150, 178-179, 183L, 186, 194, 195R, 204-205, 254-255, 293L
Topham Picturepoint 109
Princeton University Library 24-25, 54
Eileen Tweedy 22, 39
Karen Van Dyke 40-41, 44, 47L, 47R, 48, 58, 176, 177, 293R
Victoria & Albert Museum 175
Bill Wassman 123, 211, 214, 296
Amanda Eliza Weil 20, 21, 37, 66-67, 71, 73, 79, 84, 85, 114, 117, 120, 144, 153, 152, 154, 156L, 157, 210, 213L, 240, 244, 245, 248, 317
Marcus Wilson Smith 146
Phil Wood 87, 92, 93L, 93R, 116, 143, 145R, 146, 148L, 148R, 149, 155, 158, 160-161, 163, 174, 183R, 188, 190-191, 196, 197, 200L, 200R, 213R, 218, 219, 222-223, 224, 231, 246L, 246R, 247, 252, 257, 261, 262, 263L, 263R, 264L, 264R, 268-269, 270-271, 277
Xaritatos 288-289
Fay Zika 145L, 159, 168, 170, 171

Maps Berndtson & Berndtson

Visual Consultant V. Barl

Index

A
B
C
D
E
F
G
H
I
J
a
b
c
d
e
g
h
i
j
k
l